Across
the
Curriculum

**Longman Series in
College Composition and Communication**

Advisory Editor: Harvey Wiener
LaGuardia Community College
The City University of New York

Across the Curriculum

Thinking, Reading, Writing

Rose Zimbardo
*State University of New York
at Stony Brook*

Martin Stevens
*Baruch College
The City University of New York*

LONGMAN
New York & London

Across the Curriculum
Thinking, Reading, Writing

Longman Inc., 1560 Broadway, New York, N.Y. 10036
Associated companies, branches, and representatives
throughout the world.

Developmental Editor: Gordon T. R. Anderson
Editorial Supervisor: Jennifer C. Barber
Interior Designer: Eileen Beirne
Production Supervisor: Ferne Y. Kawahara
Composition: C. L. Hutson Co.
Printing and Binding: The Alpine Press

Library of Congress Cataloging in Publication Data
Main entry under title:

Across the curriculum.

   (Longman series in college composition and communication)
   Includes index.
   1. College readers.   2. English language—Rhetoric.
I. Zimbardo, Rose A.   II. Stevens, Martin.   III. Series.
PE1417.A28 1985   808'.0427   84-19462
ISBN 0-582-28515-1 (pbk.)

Manufactured in the United States of America
Printing: 9 8 7 6 5 4 3 2 1   Year: 93 92 91 90 89 88 87 86 85

This book is for our teachers—
James Hinchey, Honora Nolty,
Dennis Corrado, and Marion Defeis—
and for all our students—
past, present, and to come.

CONTENTS

CONTENTS BY DISCIPLINES

PREFACE

This book grew out of discoveries we made about teaching and learning in consequence of Rose Zimbardo's participation in the Federated Learning Communities, an interdisciplinary program, at the State University of New York at Stony Brook. The book was triggered when a student asked whether Zimbardo, whose English course was one of six federated courses, wanted the student to write "an English paper or a *real* paper." We learned from that incident, as we have been learning over the past thirty years, that the best way to master the craft of teaching is to take seriously what students have to say about learning. Our debt to the Federated Learning Communities, to Patrick Hill, its then director, and to all the students and colleagues who participated in it is most gratefully acknowledged. We are very grateful to Eric Neubacher, former Interlibrary loan librarian at Baruch College, whose help was invaluable, and to all the faculty members at Baruch College who responded so generously to Martin Stevens's request for materials from their disciplines. We owe special thanks to John L. Andreassi, Charles Bazerman, Selma Berrol, Lea Bleyman, Mitchell Cohen, Wayne Corcoran, Gerald De Maio, Douglas Muzzio, Susan Locke, Edward Pessen, Walter Reichman, Barbara Katz Rothman, Virginia Smith, Norman Storer, and Ann Swartz, all members of the faculty at Baruch College of the City University of New York.

We have been blessed with an enormously talented copy editor, Joan Matthews, whose suggestions were always on target and whose comments encouraged us. We acknowledge our debt to her, to Tren Anderson, our editor, to Harvey Wiener, our consultant, and to all those faceless but forceful critics who read the book in manuscript. To the known reader/critic, Edward G. Quinn, we have a greater debt; he is our friend, adviser, and literary consultant.

We are very grateful to our respective children for staying healthy, cheerful, and out of trouble long enough for us to write this book. We urge them to persist in this mode.

Our debt to Mrs. Connie Terrero is immeasurable. If we spent a year thanking her we should not begin to do justice. Mrs. Terrero patted our backs, held our hands, deciphered hand-written copy that would have daunted a paleographer, and, by her good-humored example, kept us from murdering one another. She prepared the manuscript at every stage of its evolution. Every writer should have such a paragon to help him or her.

We should like to thank particularly: Professor Marvin Levine, Department of Psychology at Stony Brook, Professor Max Dresden, Director of the Institute for Theoretical Physics at Stony Brook, and Professor Elof Carlson, Department of Biological Sciences at Stony Brook for their time and help. Although editorial cuts did not allow us to include the interview they gave us, we did use their ideas and suggestions throughout.

We are grateful to Professor Philip Zimbardo of Stanford University for taking time out from a manically busy schedule to grant us an interview, and for his always sustaining encouragement and support.

Last, but never least, we are most grateful to Adam Zimbardo, our music adviser, who brightens our lives and who has taught us everything we know about contemporary music.

Rose Zimbardo
Martin Stevens

ACKNOWLEDGMENTS

"The Nature of Love," Harry F. Harlow from *The American Psychologist*, (December, 1958). Copyright © 1958 by the American Psychological Association. pp. 673–685. Reprinted by permission of the publisher and author.

"Mother Love," Elisabeth Badinter pp. 58–72, 109–114 from "Maternal Indifference." Reprinted with permission of Macmillan Publishing Company from *Mother Love: Myth and Reality, Motherhood in Modern History* by Elisabeth Badinter. Translation Copyright © 1981 by Macmillan Publishing Co., Inc.

Preface to the 1950 edition, and abridgment of pages 279–289, 295–309 from *Sex and Temperament in Three Primitive Societies*, by Margaret Mead. Copyright © 1935, 1950 by Margaret Mead. By permission of William Morrow & Company, Inc.

"Biogenesis and Evolution," P. B. Medawar and J. S. Medawar from *The Life Science*, Copyright © 1977 by Peter and Jean Medawar. Pp. 22–28. Reprinted by permission of Harper & Row, Publishers, Inc. and authors.

"Sex Determination" from *Human Genetics* by Elof A. Carlson. Copyright © 1984 by D. C. Heath and Company. Reprinted by permission of the publisher. Figure on p. 83 reprinted by permission of Dr. R. J. Gorlin. Figure on p. 84 reprinted by permission of Dr. David Weaver. Figure on p. 88 courtesy of AP/World Wide Photos, Inc.

"Eros in Conflict with Sex," reprinted from *Love and Will* by Rollo May by permission of W. W. Norton & Company, Inc. Copyright © 1969 by W. W. Norton & Company, Inc.

"Liking and Loving," from *Liking, Loving and Relating*, by C. Hendrick and S. Hendrick. Copyright © 1983 by Wadsworth, Inc. Reprinted by permission of the publisher, Brooks/Cole Publishing Company, Monterey, California.

Mary L. Gottesfeld, from *Modern Sexuality*, special issue of *Clinical Social Work Journal*, articles "People vs. Mature Enterprises, Inc.," by Judge Joe Tyler, and "On Judge Tyler's Decision To Cut The Throat Of 'Deep Throat,' " by Albert Ellis, pp. 274–284.

Ellis, Albert. "On Judge Tyler's Decision. . . ." from *Clinical Social Work Journal*, Vol. 1, No. 4, 1973.

Work In America: Report of a Special Task Force to the Secretary of Health, Education, and Welfare. Prepared under the auspices of the W. E. Upjohn Institute for Employment Research (Cambridge, M.I.T. Press, 1973) pp. 1–17, pp. 23–28.

Frederick Herzberg, "Industry's Concepts of Man," from *Work and the Nature of Man* (Cleveland: World Publishing Inc.) 1966. Pp. 32–43.

"An Economy That No Longer Performs," from *The Zero Sum Society: Distribution and the Possibilities for Economic Change*, by Lester C. Thurow. © 1980 by Basic Books, Inc., Publishers. Reprinted by permission of the publisher.

Ronald C. Federico/Janet S. Schwartz, "Social Stratification and Social Class" from *Sociology*, 3rd Ed. Addison-Wesley Publishing Co., 1983, pp. 228–241, pp. 245–249. Table 1, pp. 194–195, Robert W. Hodge et al., "Occupational Prestige in the U.S., 1925–1963" *American Journal of Sociology* 70 (Nov. 1964) pp. 290–292. Table 3, pp. 201, "Poverty in the United States 1957–1980," July 27, 1982. Copyright © 1982 by the New York Times Company. Reprinted by permission.

"Working: Two Accounts," from *Working: People Talk About What They Do All Day and How They Feel About What They Do*, by Studs Terkel. Copyright © 1972, 1974 by Studs Terkel. Reprinted by permission of Pantheon Books, a Division of Random House, Inc.

Marc Leepson, "The Computer Age," from *Work Life in the 1980's* (New York: Congressional Quarterly Inc.), pp. 1, 4–23. Table on p. 228, "Glossary of Terms," Link Resources Corporation, 1980.

From *The Pursuit of Death* by Howard Congdon. Copyright © 1977 by Abingdon. Used by permission.

Ariès, Philippe, *Western Attitudes toward Death*, The Johns Hopkins University Press, Copyright © 1974.

Kübler-Ross, Elisabeth, "What Is It Like To Be Dying?", Copyright © 1971 The American Journal of Nursing Company. Reprinted with permission from *American Journal of Nursing*, January, Vol. 71, #1.

Report of the Ad Hoc Committee of the Havard Medical School to Examine the Definition of Brain Death, "A Definition of Irreversible Coma," *JAMA* 8/5/68, Vol. 205, No. 6, pp. 338–340.

Robert Veatch, "Death, Dying, and the Biological Revolution," permission granted by the Yale University Press.

Reprinted by permission of Dodd, Mead & Company, Inc. from *Whose Life Is It Anyway* by Brian Clark. Copyright © 1978 by Brian Clark.

"In Memory of W. B. Yeats." Copyright © 1940 and renewed 1968 by W. H. Auden. Reprinted from *W. H. Auden: Collected Poems*, Edited by Edward Mendelson, by permission of Random House, Inc.

Pp. 345–346, Martin Schongauer, *The Crucifixion*, National Gallery of Art, Washington, D.C., Rosenwald Collection.

Pp. 347 Michael Wolgemut, *The Crucifixion*, National Gallery of Art, Washington, D.C., Rosenwald Collection.

Philip G. Zimbardo, Interview: "Future Orientation," reprinted by permission of the author.

From "The New Atlantis." Copyright © 1975, 1982 by Ursula K. le Guin; reprinted by permission of the author and the author's agent, Virginia Kidd.

"The Future of Music: Credo," and "Experimental Music." Pp. 392–400 Copyright © 1958. Reprinted from *Silence* by permission of Wesleyan University Press.

Album cover notes for "Discreet Music" by Brian Eno. Copyright © 1975 Brian Eno/E.G. Records and album cover notes for "Ambient I: Music for Airports" by Brian Eno. Copyright © 1978 Brian Eno/E.G. Records. Reprinted by permission.

Article by John McDermott, "Do Not Bequeath a Shamble," from *The American Montessori Bulletin*, 1980, Vol. 18.

From *Future Shock*, by Alvin Toffler. Copyright © 1970 by Alvin Toffler. Reprinted by permission of Random House, Inc.

"I Have a Dream." Pp. 447–450, Reprinted by permission of Joan Daves. Copyright © 1963 by Martin Luther King, Jr.

Quentin Fiore "The Futures of the Book." From *The Future of Time* (New York: Doubleday & Co., Inc.), 1971.

ABOUT THIS BOOK

GLOSSARY

Before each reading, you will find a list of words which we have
extracted for definition and study. Most of the words are part of the
specialized vocabulary by which experts in the discipline under consideration communicate their knowledge to their readers. Reading
across the disciplines involves to a great extent learning new words,
many of which are defined for the reader in context. Hence, the
glossary lists are not meant to be simply a dictionary exercise, though
we advise you to keep a good collegiate dictionary handy when you
read. We suggest that, first of all, you try to define the words listed
by the context in which they occur. You will find that many of the
more specialized usages are actually defined in the selection itself and
that these contextual definitions will generally be more helpful than
the more abstract and less directly related definition you will find in
your dictionary. The paragraphs of each selection are numbered for
your reference, and each term in the glossary is followed by the
number of the paragraph in which it occurs. Also, all glossary terms
are underlined where they occur in the actual reading. In general,
we suggest you follow this procedure in focusing on the writer's
vocabulary:

1. Scan the terms in the glossary. Search for each term in the text,
   using the paragraph numbers as your guide.
2. Read the selection, and try to define each word as you read.
3. When you have finished the selection, record the words which
   you could not define in context and whose meanings you did not
   fully comprehend. Look those words up in a dictionary and write
   out a definition, preferably in context.

The lists we have compiled are not meant to be exhaustive; hence,
you may wish to add words to your own list of vocabulary that you
feel you must master to understand the experts in the various fields

included in this book. We encourage you to be very attentive to the specialized vocabularies; they are an important element in reading or writing successfully in disciplines that are unfamiliar to you. On occasion, we have included more general vocabulary items—i.e., words that are not part of a specialized discipline. Yet, a simple perusal of the list prior to the actual reading of the selection will give you some idea of the sort of language and ideas you will encounter.

QUESTIONS

You will find a series of questions after each reading. These questions are designed to highlight important points made in the essay, to promote close reading both for ideas and for methods of presentation, and to stimulate critical thought. By answering as many of these questions for yourself as you can, you will be better prepared to dicuss the reading selections in class and to write in response to the ideas that they raise. The main objective of the questions is to improve your skills in critical reading and thinking—skills that should help you master the kind of reading that you will be asked to do in many of your other classes as well. We suggest that you keep a section in your notebook in which to record those responses that you find particularly useful for a fuller understanding of the selection or that might lead to further exploration in writing. Make a point of noting page and paragraph numbers in your notes to facilitate future reference. We also recommend that you write notes in the margin of your book in answer to questions that seek interpretation or explanation. We believe that the more time you take in answering the questions, the more fully you will understand the selections and the more readily you will be able to think critically about them.

EXERCISES

The exercises that follow each selection are designed to provide you with a broad range of writing experiences. You will see as you proceed through the book that we have defined the act of writing very broadly. In our view, it consists of collecting ideas, note taking, evaluating, sorting out, putting down journal entries, assimilating ideas into sentences and paragraphs, rewriting, revising, correcting, discarding, and adding new material. It is an ongoing process that may or may not deliver, at some stage, the standard sort of essay, as for example an extended answer on a history exam. You will see that the exercises vary widely: some ask you to make surveys, others to write drafts of reports, others still to research an idea in the library, yet others to write a fictional account or to develop ideas that you have collected over some period of time. While your instructor may wish to assign specific exercises, we very much recommend that you read all of them and think about the approach you would take in responding to them. We suggest that you keep a notebook and dedicate a part of it to the collecting of data and to making a journal in which to record and develop ideas in response to the exercises.

THINKING, READING, WRITING

This book is intended to prepare you for the kinds of critical thinking and writing that your career in college will demand of you. The book consists of readings from experts in the fields in which you are, or will be, taking courses, such as philosophy, psychology, history, biology, literature, and art.

The readings focus on four timeless and universal human experiences: love and sexuality, work, death, and the future. These issues are fundamental to human life; they are, in fact, markers of the rhythm of human life.

Love and sexuality are the means by which we move out of our limited selves toward union with others. Just as we use work to define our place in human society, so we use love and sexuality to define ourselves in relation to other human beings within the human community. Moreover, love and sexuality can allow us to reach beyond the limited time of our individual lives through our children and grandchildren.

Work is one of the ways we define our lives and sometimes even our identities. The work I do defines how the time of my life is patterned and measured. As the historian E. P. Thompson has shown, the industrial revolution as it moved workers out of the home and into factories also changed the ways they (and our whole culture) measured time.

Death is the limit of the individual life of each of us.

Finally, we are the only living creatures who can conceive of the *future*. It is an exclusively human ability to be able to envision what has not yet happened and even to participate in creating the future. All cultures in all ages have thought about, written about, made rituals, songs, pictures, or literary images around those four human experiences.

However, it is not directly the purpose of this book to teach you about these basic human experiences. If you do learn something more about them we will be pleased, although that will be a fringe benefit. We chose these issues so that we could have stable, universal, and cross-cultural topics to illustrate how different academic disciplines think and write about particular issues. Keeping the topics constant will allow you to understand more fully the different approaches. What we want this book to give you is experience in confronting an issue critically—considering it from the point of view of a philosopher, a scientist, a computer specialist, a historian, etc. Our assumption is that the best way to prepare you to think and write in the various disciplines you will encounter in college is to show you by comparison what the differences among the disciplines are: how they define a problem; what methodologies they use; what their strengths and weaknesses are; and finally, what kinds of writing they demand of you. For example, in Unit I, "Love and Sexuality," you will learn how an experimental psychologist's way of measuring the effects of maternal love differ from the methods of a cultural historian. In Unit III, "Death," you will learn how the ways in which a philosopher defines death are different from the ways that physicians on the Ad Hoc Committee of the Harvard Medical School define it.

The reason we have designed the book in the way that we have is that we believe English classes in high school (and sometimes even in college) ignore the kind of writing that you will be asked to do in other classes throughout the curriculum. We expect this book to help prepare you for the paper on "the effects of the Industrial Revolution on cottage industries" that your history teacher might ask you to write, or the paper on "brain death versus heart death" that your health science teacher might assign you if you are a premed student.

WRITING IN COLLEGE

Writing can be the most useful tool you will acquire in your first year of college, or it can be the most difficult obstacle you will confront. Our aim is to help you to make it a useful, all-purpose tool.

There are many different kinds of writing. Each is shaped by several factors including (1) the discipline or approach of the writer, (2) the nature of what he or she is writing about, and (3) the reader at whom the piece of writing is aimed. All good writers, whatever their fields, know this. But most of them know it unconsciously. Consequently, when a history teacher asks you to write a paper on the effect of factory-based industry upon the structure of the family, or when a human biology teacher asks an essay question on the ethical issues involved in extending life by artificial means, neither the historian nor the biologist can really remember what it was like to be a beginner. They have forgotten that a beginner needs to know not just what the answer is but also how to formulate it. We assume that the first step in teaching you how to write "across the curriculum"—that is, in any class; on any subject; in response to any test, paper, or project as-signment—is to teach you to read critically and carefully the work of experts in a variety of academic fields and to become aware of their (probably unconscious) thinking and writing strategies. By reading critically, you will learn not only what to say but how to say it.

THE USES OF WRITING

TAKING NOTES

The chances are that you will not often be asked to write formal papers in introductory biochemistry, molecular biology, or astrophysics. Even if you decide to major in one of these fields, you probably will be asked to write lab reports and descriptions of your experiments rather than research papers. But when you have developed writing as far as we hope to help you to develop it—into another strong right arm—you will be able to use it in all kinds of ways, not just for formal paper writing.

The most basic and important use for writing is in studying. To be a fully effective student you must take good notes. You might respond, "I don't take notes; I underline important passages in my textbook." Well, underlining helps to highlight important points, but it is just not as effective a mnemonic device (or way of getting material to "stick" in your memory) as writing is, and besides you cannot underline the teacher in a large lecture section. "Come off it!" you reply. "I copy down everything in notes and all I have to show for it is a sore arm." Well, then let us consider the process of taking notes.

1. Taking notes is *not* copying your textbook into your notebook. It is, just as the word suggests, writing notes to remind yourself of what you have heard or read.

2. The process of taking notes is not the same for different courses. The notes you take in philosophy should not be the same as the notes you take in biology—largely because, their approaches to problems being different, philosophers and biologists do not deal with materials or solve problems in the same way, and therefore they do not express themselves in the same way. Let us think about taking notes on your reading for study purposes.

The Sciences

Typically the textbook in the natural sciences (physics, biology, chemistry, etc.) will lay out as clearly as possible the major generalizations and supporting facts on which a particular field of knowledge rests. It will in effect summarize what has been proved in the laboratories by experimentation and empirical tests. Thus, while a textbook itself may not replicate the scientific method per se, it will summarize the results of experiments that have employed the scientific method. The scientific method itself is likely to guide your work in laboratories where you will be asked, as a beginner, to gain practice in the method through testing the experiments as a way of confirming the evidence on which various generalizations rest. The sciences thus require you to observe and generalize, and the scientific method is a good guide to the systematic study of a phenomenon. It consists of four steps: (1) A problem is formulated or an inference made (e.g., Newton is awakened by an apple striking his head while he sits under the apple tree); (2) data are collected through observation and experiment (Newton notes that apples generally fall to the ground when ripe); (3) a hypothesis is formulated (gravity is postulated); and (4) the hypothesis is confirmed and becomes theory by means of experimental replication.

Almost any textbook in the sciences is written (1) to lay out basic principles as simply and as economically as possible (for example, "An electric current consists of a flow of electrons, and the quantity of current is measured in amperes, or 'amps.' "); (2) to note the kinds of data from which the principle is derived; and (3) to explain the nature of, or expand upon, those principles. Therefore, when you are taking notes for science courses you too should condense and outline. You do not want to think about the beauty of meiosis when studying for a biology exam, nor do you want to speculate about whether the moment of meiosis should or should not be considered the beginning of a new human life—as you might be asked to do in an essay for an ethics course. Instead you should write down and remember where in the process of reproduction meiosis occurs, and what the steps are in the process by which chromosomes align. In taking notes of science readings, then, you shall want to extract and list. You will probably find outlines much more useful than explanatory paragraphs. A rough guide is:

1. Extract essential principles.
2. Define them with particulars (e.g., *gamete* = sex cell). Be as economical as you can without leaving out any of the essential information.
3. Pay close attention to formulae, diagrams, charts, and tables. Where possible in your notes, draw charts and diagrams of your own. These will keep a picture of a process in your mind.

The sciences, as part of your general education, are particularly valuable in teaching you the nature of systematic study and observation. Mastery of the scientific method will teach you how to organize your ideas and to develop them in all fields of study.

Social Science

The social sciences (history, psychology, sociology, anthropology, etc.) employ the same scientific method as the hard sciences do, but while the textbook reading you do for the sciences is likely to be confined to "facts" (the verified truths that come *out* of experimentation) and general physical principles, textbooks in the social sciences are likely to stress hypotheses or theories concerning typical human or animal behavior. Usually the data—observations or evidence or examples offered in support of the hypothesis—form the bulk of a piece of writing in the social sciences. For example, in Unit III, "Death," you will find a selection by Philippe Ariès, who is a cultural historian. The hypothesis of the Ariès article is that people have thought about death in different ways at different times in history. The evidence (from paintings, songs, poetry, burial practices, religious beliefs) forms the bulk of Ariès's discussion. Therefore, when you are taking notes in studying one of the social sciences you should (1) locate and describe the hypothesis, (2) list the kinds of evidence given in support of the hypothesis, (3) under each kind give one or two examples, and (4) make notes to yourself about whether or not you believe each of the kinds of evidence that support the hypothesis.

The Humanities

Whereas the sciences offer the fruits of the scientific method or empirical observation as their truths, the humanities (literature, art, music, philosophy, etc.) give us the observation itself, either the experience of looking at, thinking about, or envisioning the truth, or methods of looking at and thinking about truths more sharply. For instance, while the scientists who write on the pathology of sudden coronary death "describe the pathogenetic sequence of events that lead to coronary heart disease and sudden death" (Ch. 18), the philosopher tries to define the phenomenon of death itself by various approaches that test how we know what we think we know about it (Ch. 15). The poet, in turn, flashes images at us that jar us into a variety of ways of envisioning death (Ch. 20). Critical writing in the humanities, then, offers arguments that are verifiable only by logic, truth, and feeling, or by an appeal to the imagination. In taking notes while you read in the humanities, or criticism of the humanities, you should, consequently, (1) summarize the central idea, argument, or concept in the piece, (2) extract and list the ways in which the writer makes this idea available to you (e.g., What images does Auden use to build up the idea that language and poetry outlive death?), (3) list the arguments the writer uses to persuade you to adopt his or her position, and test their validity (Ask yourself, does it really feel that way, or is that truly logical, or is this just some fancy intellectual footwork?), and (4) think of, and list in notes to yourself, counterarguments. Try to disprove, or challenge, the writer.

If you take notes this way, you will make several interesting discoveries. First, you will begin to realize that writing, when you are writing what only you need to see, can become a kind of thinking. It *sharpens* your thoughts. Second, you will find that you are really relating to a writer when you take these kinds of notes during your reading. It is almost like engaging in an intellectual argument with the author ("Hey, wait a second, there, Dr. Harlow, maybe you're right about monkeys, but does what you say hold for humans?" or "That's all very well, Dr. Kübler-Ross, but I couldn't tell my baby sister that she was dying!"). Writing notes is the best way of getting into an essay. Third, you will discover that you are studying while you are taking notes to study from. You will be, almost painlessly, committing the movements of those protons and electrons to memory when you start drawing their dance in little diagrams in your notes. Bear in mind that you needn't please anyone else with what you write when you take notes, and therefore you can write and annotate in any way that works for you. You are free to develop whatever methods are helpful to you. If, for example, you like to rely on memory devices, use them (e.g., the basic components of protoplasm are C,O,H,N,S,P, which our generation keyed for itself by an imaginary drugstore sign, "Cohn, Special Pharmacy").

WRITING FOR EXAMS

Exam writing, like all expository writing, varies with the subject of the examination. It is highly unlikely that exams in the hard sciences or the social sciences will require much writing; questions on them will probably be multiple choice. But the practice you have gotten in critical reading and in clear and appropriate note taking will serve you in good stead in answering multiple-choice questions. As you no doubt know from taking SATs, or qualifying exams, the possible answers to a multiple-choice question are purposely designed to be fairly similar to one another. The closeness with which you have been reading your science texts and the care with which you have been condensing and ordering information in your note taking will sharpen your perception of the design of the various possible answers, and help you to choose the right one. A science exam will also probably have at least one section of fill-in-the-blank questions or short definition questions. Once again, the practice you have had in condensing and in extracting essential principles will help you. The two centrally important ideas to keep in mind when you are giving a written short answer on a science exam are (1) get all the information down as economically expressed as possible, and (2) write in topic outline style wherever possible, because an outline will show that you have in mind a design of the whole process or method you have been asked to describe or define. An abstract outline of logical connections is better than a windy paragraph that leaves one or two essential steps out.

Exams in the social sciences and humanities will usually ask you to write essays that (1) present an argument; (2) compare or contrast two or more positions or approaches; (3) describe a line of development (e.g., "Discuss the economic crises that led to the French Revolution," or "Citing particular examples, discuss the development of the American novel between the two world wars"); or (4) evaluate or analyze a subject (e.g., "Discuss the use of space and color in Botticelli's *Primavera*"). When answering an essay question on an exam in one of the humanities, follow these steps:

1. Read the question carefully. Analyze the language of the question to discover key words such as "define," "trace," or "contrast," because these terms establish what the instructor wants you to do in the essay. Make sure to do what the question asks you to do. For example, do not respond by writing down all the events and characters in *Moby Dick* if the question has asked you to contrast different ways in which Melville and Conrad use the metaphor of the sea.

2. Before you set pencil to paper, take at least three minutes (that is a long time) to throw together a logically organized mental sketch of your *whole* answer. Then write out your main points, in outline form if possible. Once again, the practice you have had in note taking— of extracting the central idea of an argument, listing the pieces of evidence used to support the argument, and thinking of alternative arguments or other ways to use the evidence—will be a great help to you. Do not start writing until you have a rough outline of your whole answer in mind.

3. Make the first sentence of your answer a miniature of the whole answer; in other words, make the first sentence a general statement that summarizes all the points you will cover in your answer. Think of it as a hypothesis which the rest of your answer will explain and offer evidence to support (e.g., "The major causes of the Peasants' Revolt of 1381 were a weak king, Richard II; the high cost of living in relation to low wages for farm labor; and the scarcity of labor that resulted from the ravages of the Black Death").

4. Arrange the rest of your answer to develop step by step, or piece by piece, the first general statement.

5. Come to a conclusion that pulls together evidence or explanations you have offered.

As you can see, the shape of an essay exam answer is the same in general structure as that of our old acquaintance, the scientific method: hypothesis → evidence → conclusion. Remember: *The quality of an essay answer depends upon (1) the logic of its organization, and (2) the accuracy of its evidence.* For example, it would not be a good idea to offer space travel as one of the causes of the Industrial Revolution. A good answer is not made from lots and lots of words, but from carefully, logically arranged ideas.

WRITING PAPERS AND REPORTS

Since this book is largely composed of well-written essays and reports and since the questions we ask after each selection are designed to help you to read them critically and to imitate their writing techniques and strategies, we do not think it is useful to give instructions for paper writing here. In fact, in our opinion, giving a person abstract rules for how to write a paper is very much like teaching a person to drive a car by giving him or her a diagram of the motor. Academic writing is a skill—like playing the piano—that is mastered by practice and by close attention to what you are doing as you are doing it. The end toward which both you and we are working is to bring you to the level of mastery at which the process and the mechanics of writing will come more or less automatically. Here at the beginning you will have to take on trust our promise that if you pay very close critical attention to what we ask you to read, what we ask you to think about, and what we ask you to write, you will have the various skills needed to write "across the curriculum" when you are finished. However, the following are some tips on writing papers and reports:

1. Do not think of writing a paper as a different experience from the writing you have been doing in note taking and exam answering. Avoid "Oh-my-God,-I-have-to-write-a-paper!" thinking. There is nothing magical about papers. Instead think of a paper as an enlarged essay exam answer. The shape of a paper is the same as that we have been discussing:

Hypothesis. This is what I have observed to be true, or this is what my examination of the evidence convinces me is true, or this is the general concept I will be describing.

Evidence. These are some explanations of the significance of what I have observed, or these pieces of evidence are the bricks out of which I built my hypothesis, or these experts in these experiments have validated the parts from which I have derived my hypothesis.

Conclusion. You, the reader, having followed my proof and the logic of my argument, can now see that my hypothesis stands.

2. Try keeping a journal in this course and in other courses that you know will require papers. A journal stands roughly midway between note taking and paper writing and uses the thinking/writing skills of both. Jot down in your journal:

a. What you hear in class or discover when you review your reading notes that you think will point toward an exam question or a paper assignment.

b. What you think about what you have heard in class or what you have read in your textbook or in secondary reading for the course.

c. Questions you need answered either after a reading assignment or after a class session. If you can't answer the question perhaps you should ask the instructor or a classmate what the answer is. This is an invaluable function of keeping a journal—finding out what you don't know and how you can find an answer.

d. How you might argue, either in agreement or disagreement, with what you have read or heard. Something like this for example:

C. S. Lewis says,
(1) God is love.
(2) Human love is like God's love.
(3) We are near to God in resemblance when we love, but we can be distant from love for God at the same time.

I say,
(1) We have no proof that God is love. God may be supreme energy that cannot be differentiated into love/hate.
(2) Even if God, or a supreme power, loves us, how can we know what that love means or is like, since God is altogether other than we are?

This is just an example. The point is, make sketches of arguments that you hear or read. You may be able at some time to build an exam essay around such a sketch. One journal can, of course, cover many subjects (unlike notes, which summarize a given subject), and every journal will differ to some degree from every other. Unlike notes, which are an objective description of the material you are reading, a journal is the record of your particular intellectual response to what you are reading.

A journal is neither a diary nor a record of daily events though it can incorporate features of both. Whereas a record of events preserves what one does, and a diary preserves what one feels, a journal preserves one's thoughts about what what one has done, or read, or felt. The poet Louis Simpson has said that often a poem will grow out of an entry he has made in his journal five years before—one that recorded his response to a small item in the newspaper. A journal is a repository where we keep reactions to what we have done, read, or thought about until we can communicate them to others or until we are called upon to shape them into finished arguments, in papers or on exams. A journal is also a good place to think out loud in writing, and by that means to forge closer links between your writing and your thinking. Ultimately writing will become an extension of thinking and a method of clarifying your thoughts. And finally a journal is a place where your teacher may ask you to do prewriting exercises. You will find a good many of these following each of the readings in this book.

The exercises as well as the whole mode of instruction stressed in this book emphasize the point that writing is a *process*, not merely a *product*. The paper that you write is the outcome of much thought and revision, usually over a course of time. Even professional writers rarely regard a piece of writing as "finished"; it is left open for change, open for new thoughts and illuminations. Hence, we urge you to judge the success of your writing experience not by the neatly typed paper you turn in as your "finished" assignment but by the discoveries you have made through its creation.

UNIT I

LOVE AND SEXUALITY

This unit could have had several different titles: Love or Sexuality, for example. As the readings will confirm, in the twentieth century, thinkers are not quite sure whether there is a connection between love and sexuality. It strikes us rather funny that the one writer in this group who insists that there *is* a connection—that there is love, and that a creature who is deprived of love (not need satisfaction, but good old affectionate love) suffers in its sexuality— is not a poet, nor an artist but a very hard-nosed scientist.

We have chosen this thorny category for three reasons. First, because it is thorny. The first three selections will offer you three contradictory arguments: (1) there is mother love ("infant–maternal ties" are innate, part of our animal nature), (2) mother love is a myth invented in the late eighteenth century, and (3) temperament, loving or hostile, is culturally determined and is not sex-linked. Perhaps one of the most difficult conditions of the academic life to which students must adjust is that there is seldom one "right answer" to a complex problem. Three experts, each using the best scientific methods available, each exercising the most refined logic, can come to three different conclusions. That does not mean that academic research and reasoning are faulty. It means that *all* of us who devote ourselves to the life of study, from a great genius such as Einstein to the two middle-aged persons writing these words, are like the blind men trying to describe the elephant. The elephant is gigantic and each of us can describe only the small part of it which our method or our approach to discovery can see.

Our second reason is that no subject is more important in the beginning of a college education than our realization that we live in a world of interaction—one that is defined ethically and biologically by love and sexuality, respectively. No human being is an isolate. Scientific experiments have shown us that a creature isolated from its fellows for too long dies; other experiments in isolation tanks have shown that a human being deprived of human company hallucinates, or begins to go mad; and a great poet, John Donne, once told us that "no man is an Island, entire of itself; every man is a piece of the Continent, a part of the maine. . . . any man's death diminishes me, because I am involved in Mankind" (Meditation XVII). Love of any kind is reaching beyond one's self, a sure sign that each one of us is a *part* of the main body of our kind. So is sexuality, which in the Middle Ages was called the "law of kynd." From microscopic organisms to ourselves, and from ourselves to angels (if there are such beings), by the arithmetic of the law of kind, one plus one equals a great deal more than two. Sexuality is one of the ways we are involved in mankind.

Our third reason is that love and sexuality are the starting posts for the journey of humanity which this book maps. The pursuit and satisfaction of love and/or sexuality, like work (the subject of Unit II), is one of the primary ways we spend the time of our lives, and it is the instrument of humanity's march into the future (the subject of Unit IV). The seasons of our human nature are marked by the kinds of love we feel—filial, erotic, parental—and the sexuality of which we are capable. We might think of it this way. Our need to work drove us to create a certain measure of time (there was no such thing as 3 P.M. until human imagination invented it), and conversely, the seasons of our love and sexuality are nature's way of telling her cyclical time on us, as if we were her calendars.

To sum up, this unit presents you with readings that launch you into the cycle of time and the main forms of human response to it. We begin in Unit I with love and sexuality and progress in Unit II to an examination of work as the sustaining activity of our lifetime. We move on in Unit III to explore the mystifying issue of death and train our spotlight on the end or the limit of the individual life. Finally, in Unit IV, we enter the future, that visionary time which allows us to see death as part of cyclical time.

CHAPTER ONE

HARLOW: THE NATURE OF LOVE

Experimental Psychology

Harry F. Harlow, the late director of the Primate Laboratory at the University of Wisconsin, was president of the American Psychological Association when he presented this paper, the summation of a series of experiments he had conducted to determine whether there is an innate bond of affection between infants and mothers and how that bond is developed. Eight years later he and his wife, Margaret F. Harlow, presented the results of a second series of experiments with those monkeys that were experimental subjects in this experiment— monkeys who were raised with mechanical mother-surrogates made of cloth or wire. In the second series of experiments the Harlows found that these monkeys, deprived from birth of contact with their natural mothers, could neither establish normal social relations with their peers nor experience normal sexual behavior in adulthood. The Harlows' experiments are among the handful of scientific investigations of *love*. While scientists and social scientists have been very much involved in investigating sexuality in the last thirty years, they have not paid much attention to love, or "affect." Harlows' was a pioneer study and remains a classic in the field of experimental psychology.

As you read the selection, ask yourself first of all what problem Harlow is attempting to solve, and then observe how the experiments are designed to provide the answers for which he is searching. Why, for example, does he concentrate on the study of infant behavior rather than adult behavior? What does he say about "primary drives" and how does he define "love"? Does his definition differ from that of the poets? Why?

GLOSSARY

affectional [4]	manipulatory [22]
primary drives [5]	compulsive [23]
external stimulus [6]	retention [24]
innate [7]	deprivation [25]
neonate [7]	adjacent [34]
surrogate [14]	variables [36]
redundancy [14]	mammalian [41]
lactated [16]	

———— THE NATURE OF LOVE ————
Harry F. Harlow

[1]   Love is a wondrous state, deep, tender, and rewarding. Because of
its intimate and personal nature it is regarded by some as an improper
topic for experimental research. But, whatever our personal feelings
may be, our assigned mission as psychologists is to analyze all facets
of human and animal behavior into their component variables. So far
as love or affection is concerned, psychologists have failed in this
mission. The little we know about love does not transcend simple
observation, and the little we write about it has been written better
by poets and novelists. But of greater concern is the fact that psychologists tend to give progressively less attention to a motive which
pervades our entire lives. Psychologists, at least psychologists who
write textbooks, not only show no interest in the origin and development
of love or affection, but they seem to be unaware of its very existence.

[2]   The apparent repression of love by modern psychologists stands
in sharp contrast with the attitude taken by many famous and normal
people. The word "love" has the highest reference frequency of any
word cited in Bartlett's book of *Familiar Quotations*. It would appear
that this emotion has long had a vast interest and fascination for

SOURCE: Address of the President at the Sixty-Sixth Annual Convention of the American
Psychological Association, Washington, D.C., August 31, 1958. Reprinted from *The
American Psychologist*, vol. 13, no. 12, December 1958, pp. 673–685. Copyright 1958 by
the American Psychological Association. Reprinted by permission of the publisher and
author.

human beings, regardless of the attitude taken by psychologists; but the quotations cited, even by famous and normal people, have a mundane redundancy. These authors and authorities have stolen love from the child and infant and made it the exclusive property of the adolescent and adult.

Thoughtful men, and probably all women, have speculated on the [3] nature of love. From the developmental point of view, the general plan is quite clear: The initial love responses of the human being are those made by the infant to the mother or some mother surrogate. From this intimate attachment of the child to the mother, multiple learned and generalized affectional responses are formed.

Unfortunately, beyond these simple facts we know little about the [4] fundamental variables underlying the formation of affectional responses and little about the mechanisms through which the love of the infant for the mother develops into the multifaceted response patterns characterizing love or affection in the adult. Because of the dearth of experimentation, theories about the fundamental nature of affection have evolved at the level of observation, intuition, and discerning guesswork, whether these have been proposed by psychologists, sociologists, anthropologists, physicians, or psychoanalysts.

The position commonly held by psychologists and sociologists is [5] quite clear: The basic motives are, for the most part, the primary drives—particularly hunger, thirst, elimination, pain, and sex—and all other motives, including love or affection, are derived or secondary drives. The mother is associated with the reduction of the primary drives—particularly hunger, thirst, and pain—and through learning, affection or love is derived.

It is entirely reasonable to believe that the mother through association [6] with food may become a secondary-reinforcing agent, but this is an inadequate mechanism to account for the persistence of the infant-maternal ties. There is a spate of researches on the formation of secondary reinforcers to hunger and thirst reduction. There can be no question that almost any external stimulus can become a secondary reinforcer if properly associated with tissue-need reduction, but the fact remains that this redundant literature demonstrates unequivocally that such derived drives suffer relatively rapid experimental extinction. Contrariwise, human affection does not extinguish when the mother ceases to have intimate association with the drives in question. Instead, the affectional ties to the mother show a lifelong, unrelenting persistence and, even more surprising, widely expanding generality.

Oddly enough, one of the few psychologists who took a position [7] counter to modern psychological dogma was John B. Watson, who believed that love was an innate emotion elicited by cutaneous stimulation of the erogenous zones. But experimental psychologists, with their peculiar propensity to discover facts that are not true, brushed this theory aside by demonstrating that the human neonate had no differentiable emotions, and they established a fundamental psychological law that prophets are without honor in their own profession.

[8]   The psychoanalysts have concerned themselves with the problem of the nature of the development of love in the neonate and infant, using ill and aging human beings as subjects. They have discovered the overwhelming importance of the breast and related this to the oral erotic tendencies developed at an age preceding their subjects' memories. Their theories range from a belief that the infant has an innate need to achieve and suckle at the breast to beliefs not unlike commonly accepted psychological theories. There are exceptions, as seen in the recent writings of John Bowlby, who attributes importance not only to food and thirst satisfaction, but also to "primary object-clinging," a need for intimate physical contact, which is initially associated with the mother.

[9]   As far as I know, there exists no direct experimental analysis of the relative importance of the stimulus variables determining the affectional or love responses in the neonatal and infant primate. Unfortunately, the human neonate is a limited experimental subject for such researches because of his inadequate motor capabilities. By the time the human infant's motor responses can be precisely measured, the antecedent determining conditions cannot be defined, having been lost in a jumble and jungle of confounded variables.

[10]   Many of these difficulties can be resolved by the use of the neonatal and infant macaque monkey as the subject for the analysis of basic affectional variables. It is possible to make precise measurements in this primate beginning at two to ten days of age, depending upon the maturational status of the individual animal at birth. The macaque infant differs from the human infant in that the monkey is more mature at birth and grows more rapidly; but the basic responses relating to affection, including nursing, contact, clinging, and even visual and auditory exploration, exhibit no fundamental differences in the two species. Even the development of perception, fear, frustration, and learning capability follows very similar sequences in rhesus monkeys and human children.

[11]   Three years' experimentation before we started our studies on affection gave us experience with the neonatal monkey. We had separated more than 60 of these animals from their mothers 6 to 12 hours after birth and suckled them on tiny bottles. The infant mortality was only a small fraction of what would have obtained had we let the monkey mothers raise their infants. Our bottle-fed babies were healthier and heavier than monkey-mother-reared infants. We know that we are better monkey mothers than are real monkey mothers thanks to synthetic diets, vitamins, iron extracts, penicillin, chloromycetin, 5% glucose, and constant, tender, loving care.

Figure 1. Response to cloth pad by one-day-old monkey.

During the course of these studies we noticed that the laboratory- [12]
raised babies showed strong attachment to the cloth pads (folded
gauze diapers) which were used to cover the hardware-cloth floors
of their cages. The infants clung to these pads and engaged in violent
temper tantrums when the pads were removed and replaced for sanitary
reasons. Such contact-need or responsiveness had been reported previously by Gertrude van Wagenen for the monkey and by Thomas
McCulloch and George Haslerud for the chimpanzee and is reminiscent of the devotion often exhibited by human infants to their pillows,
blankets, and soft, cuddly stuffed toys. Responsiveness by the one-
day-old infant monkey to the cloth pad is shown in Figure 1, and an
unusual and strong attachment of a six-month-old infant to the cloth
pad is illustrated in Figure 2. The baby, human or monkey, if it is to
survive, must clutch at more than a straw.

We had also discovered during some allied observational studies [13]
that a baby monkey raised on a bare wire-mesh cage floor survives
with difficulty, if at all, during the first five days of life. If a wire-
mesh cone is introduced, the baby does better; and, if the cone is
covered with terry cloth, husky, healthy, happy babies evolve. It takes
more than a baby and a box to make a normal monkey. We were
impressed by the possibility that, above and beyond the bubbling
fountain of breast or bottle, contact comfort might be a very important
variable in the development of the infant's affection for the mother.

At this point we decided to study the development of affectional [14]
responses of neonatal and infant monkeys to an artificial, inanimate
mother, and so we built a surrogate mother which we hoped and
believed would be a good surrogate mother. In devising this surrogate

Figure 2.   Response to gauze pad by six-month-old monkey
used in earlier study.

mother we were dependent neither upon the capriciousness of evolutionary processes-nor upon mutations produced by chance radioactive
fallout. Instead, we designed the mother surrogate in terms of modern
human-engineering principles (Figure 3). We produced a perfectly
proportioned, streamlined body stripped of unnecessary bulges and
appendices. Redundancy in the surrogate mother's system was avoided
by reducing the number of breasts from two to one and placing this
unibreast in an upper-thoracic, sagittal position, thus maximizing the
natural and known perceptual-motor capabilities of the infant operator.
The surrogate was made from a block of wood, covered with sponge
rubber, and sheathed in tan cotton terry cloth. A light bulb behind
her radiated heat. The result was a mother, soft, warm, and tender,
a mother with infinite patience, a mother available twenty-four hours
a day, a mother that never scolded her infant and never struck or bit
her baby in anger. Furthermore, we designed a mother-machine with
maximal maintenance efficiency since failure of any system or function
could be resolved by the simple substitution of black boxes and new
component parts. It is our opinion that we engineered a very superior
monkey mother, although this position is not held universally by the
monkey fathers.

[15]   Before beginning our initial experiment we also designed and constructed a second mother surrogate, a surrogate in which we deliberately
built less than the maximal capability for contact comfort. This surrogate
mother is illustrated in Figure 4. She is made of wire-mesh, a substance

entirely adequate to provide postural support and nursing capability, and she is warmed by radiant heat. Her body differs in no essential way from that of the cloth mother surrogate other than in the quality of the contact comfort which she can supply.

In our initial experiment, the dual mother-surrogate condition, a [16] cloth mother and a wire mother were placed in different cubicles attached to the infant's living cage as shown in Figure 4. For four newborn monkeys the cloth mother <u>lactated</u> and the wire mother did not; and, for the other four, this condition was reversed. In either condition the infant received all its milk through the mother surrogate as soon as it was able to maintain itself in this way, a capability achieved within two or three days except in the case of very immature infants. Supplementary feedings were given until the milk intake from the mother surrogate was adequate. Thus, the experiment was designed as a test of the relative importance of the variables of contact comfort and nursing comfort. During the first 14 days of life the monkey's cage floor was covered with a heating pad wrapped in a folded gauze

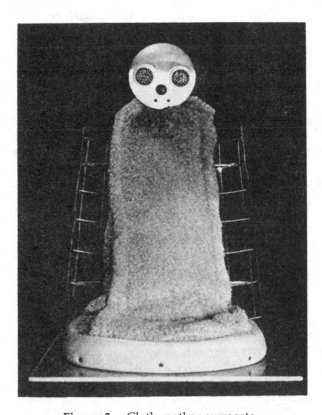

Figure 3. Cloth mother surrogate.

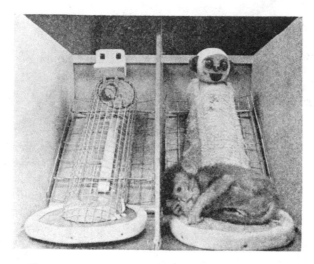

Figure 4.   Wire and cloth mother surrogates.

diaper, and thereafter the cage floor was bare. The infants were always free to leave the heating pad or cage floor to contact either mother, and the time spent on the surrogate mothers was automatically recorded. Figure 5 shows the total time spent on the cloth and wire mothers under the two conditions of feeding. These data make it obvious that contact comfort is a variable of overwhelming importance in the development of affectional responses, whereas lactation is a variable of negligible importance. With age and opportunity to learn, subjects with the lactating wire mother showed decreasing responsiveness to her and increasing responsiveness to the nonlactating cloth mother, a finding completely contrary to any interpretation of derived drive in which the mother-form becomes conditioned to hunger-thirst reduction. The persistence of these differential responses throughout 165 consecutive days of testing is evident in Figure 6.

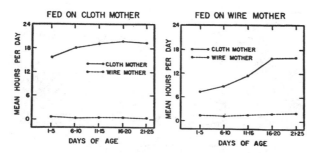

Figure 5.   Time spent on cloth and wire mother surrogates.

One control group of neonatal monkeys was raised on a single   [17]
wire mother, and a second control group was raised on a single cloth
mother. There were no differences between these two groups in amount
of milk ingested or in weight gain. The only difference between the
groups lay in the composition of the feces, the softer stools of the
wire-mother infants suggesting psychosomatic involvement. The wire
mother is biologically adequate but psychologically inept.

We were not surprised to discover that contact comfort was an   [18]
important basic affectional or love variable, but we did not expect it
to overshadow so completely the variable of nursing; indeed, the
disparity is so great as to suggest that the primary function of nursing
as an affectional variable is that of insuring frequent and intimate
body contact of the infant with the mother. Certainly, man cannot
live by milk alone. Love is an emotion that does not need to be bottle-
or spoon-fed, and we may be sure that there is nothing to be gained
by giving lip service to love.

A charming lady once heard me describe these experiments; and,   [19]
when I subsequently talked to her, her face brightened with sudden
insight: "Now I know what's wrong with me," she said, "I'm just a
wire mother." Perhaps she was lucky. She might have been a wire wife.

We believe that contact comfort has long served the animal kingdom   [20]
as a motivating agent for affectional responses. Since at the present
time we have no experimental data to substantiate this position, we
supply information which must be accepted, if at all, on the basis of
face validity.

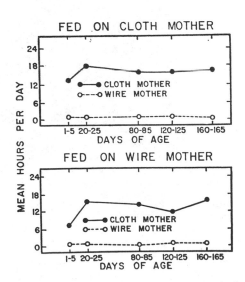

Figure 6.   Long-term contact time on cloth
and wire mother surrogates.

The Hippopotamus

This is the skin some
babies feel
Replete with hippo love
appeal.
Each contact, cuddle,
push, and shove
Elicits tons of baby love.

Figure 7. —From *Look*, August 19, 1958

The Rhinocerus

The rhino's skin is thick and tough,
And yet this skin is soft enough
That baby rhinos always sense,
A love enormous and intense.

Figure 8. —From *Zoo Guide*, Zoological Society of London

The Snake

To baby vipers, scaly skin
Engenders love 'twixt kith and kin.
Each animal by God is blessed
With kind of skin it loves the best.

Figure 9. —From *All About Snakes*, E. M. Hale & Co.

The Elephant

Though mother may be
    short on arms,
Her skin is full of warmth
    and charms.
And mother's touch
    on baby's skin
Endears the heart that
    beats within.

Figure 10. —Ylla

13

The Crocodile

Here is the skin they
love to touch.
It isn't soft and there
isn't much,
But its contact comfort
will beguile
Love from the infant
crocodile.

Figure 11. —Sponholz

Figure 12. You see, all God's chillun's got skin.

One function of the real mother, human or subhuman, and pre- [21]
sumably of a mother surrogate, is to provide a haven of safety for
the infant in times of fear and danger. The frightened or ailing child
clings to its mother, not its father; and this selective responsiveness
in times of distress, disturbance, or danger may be used as a measure
of the strength of affectional bonds. We have tested this kind of differential responsiveness by presenting to the infants in their cages,
in the presence of the two mothers, various fear-producing stimuli
such as the moving toy bear illustrated in Figure 13. A typical response
to a fear stimulus is shown in Figure 14, and the data on differential
responsiveness are presented in Figure 15. It is apparent that the cloth
mother is highly preferred over the wire one, and this differential
selectivity is enhanced by age and experience. In this situation, the
variable of nursing appears to be of absolutely no importance: the
infant consistently seeks the soft mother surrogate regardless of nursing
condition.

Similarly, the mother or mother surrogate provides its young with [22]
a source of security, and this role or function is seen with special

Figure 13. Typical fear stimulus.

Figure 14. Typical response to cloth mother surrogate in fear test.

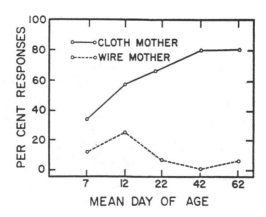

Figure 15. Differential responsiveness in fear tests.

clarity when mother and child are in a strange situation. At the present time we have completed tests for this relationship on four of our eight baby monkeys assigned to the dual mother-surrogate condition by introducing them for three minutes into the strange environment of a room measuring six feet by six feet by six feet (also called the "open-field test") and containing multiple stimuli known to elicit curiosity-manipulatory responses in baby monkeys. The subjects were placed in this situation twice a week for eight weeks with no mother surrogate present during alternate sessions and the cloth mother present during the others. A cloth diaper was always available as one of the stimuli throughout all sessions. After one or two adaptation sessions, the infants always rushed to the mother surrogate when she was present and clutched her, rubbed their bodies against her, and frequently manipulated her body and face. After a few additional sessions, the infants began to use the mother surrogate as a source of security, a base of operations. As is shown in Figures 16 and 17, they would explore and manipulate a stimulus and then return to the mother before adventuring again into the strange new world. The behavior of these infants was quite different when the mother was absent from the room. Frequently they would freeze in a crouched position, as is illustrated in Figures 18 and 19. Emotionality indices such as vocalization, crouching, rocking, and sucking increased sharply, as shown in Figure 20. Total emotionality score was cut in half when the mother was present. In the absence of the mother some of the experimental monkeys would rush to the center of the room where the mother was customarily

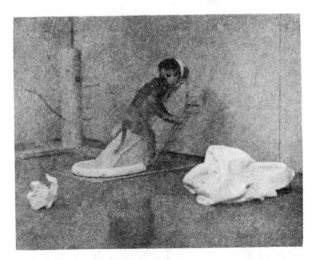

Figure 16. Response to cloth mother in the open-field test.

18

Figure 17. Object exploration in presence of cloth mother.

placed and then run rapidly from object to object, screaming and crying all the while. Continuous, frantic clutching of their bodies was very common, even when not in the crouching position. These monkeys frequently contacted and clutched the cloth diaper, but this action never pacified them. The same behavior occurred in the presence of the wire mother. No difference between the cloth-mother-fed and wire-mother-fed infants was demonstrated under either condition.

Figure 18. Response in the open-field test in the absence of the mother surrogate.

Figure 19.   Response in the open-field test in the absence
of the mother surrogate.

Four control infants never raised with a mother surrogate showed the
same emotionality scores when the mother was absent as the experimental infants showed in the absence of the mother, but the controls'
scores were slightly larger in the presence of the mother surrogate
than in her absence.

Some years ago Robert Butler demonstrated that mature monkeys   [23]
enclosed in a dimly lighted box would open and reopen a door hour
after hour for no other reward than that of looking outside the box.
We now have data indicating that neonatal monkeys show this same
compulsive visual curiosity on their first test day in an adaptation of
the Butler apparatus which we call the "love machine," an apparatus

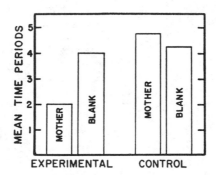

Figure 20.   Emotionality index with and without
the presence of the cloth mother.

designed to measure love. Usually these tests are begun when the monkey is 10 days of age, but this same persistent visual exploration has been obtained in a three-day-old monkey during the first half-hour of testing. Butler also demonstrated that rhesus monkeys show selectivity in rate and frequency of door-opening to stimuli of differential attractiveness in the visual field outside the box. We have utilized this principle of response selectivity by the monkey to measure strength of affectional responsiveness in our infants in the baby version of the Butler box. The test sequence involves four repetitions of a test battery in which four stimuli—cloth mother, wire mother, infant monkey, and empty box—are presented for a 30-minute period on successive days. The first four subjects in the dual mother-surrogate group were given a single test sequence at 40 to 50 days of age, depending upon the availability of the apparatus, and only their data are presented. The second set of four subjects is being given repetitive tests to obtain information relating to the development of visual exploration. The apparatus is illustrated in Figure 21. The data obtained from the first

Figure 21. Visual exploration apparatus.

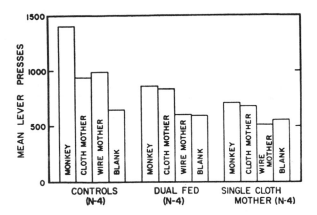

Figure 22. Differential responses to visual exploration.

four infants raised with the two mother surrogates are presented in the middle graph of Figure 22 and show approximately equal responding to the cloth mother and another infant monkey, and no greater responsiveness to the wire mother than to an empty box. Again, the results are independent of the kind of mother that lactated, cloth or wire. The same results are found for a control group raised, but not fed, on a single cloth mother; these data appear in the graph on the right. Contrariwise, the graph on the left shows no differential responsiveness to cloth and wire mothers by a second control group, which was not raised on any mother surrogate. We can be certain that not all love is blind.

The first four infant monkeys in the dual mother-surrogate group [24] were separated from their mothers between 165 and 170 days of age and tested for retention during the following 9 days and then at 30-day intervals for six successive months. Affectional retention as measured by the modified Butler box is given in Figure 23. In keeping with the data obtained on adult monkeys by Butler, we find a high rate of responding to any stimulus, even the empty box. But throughout the entire 185-day retention period there is a consistent and significant difference in response frequency to the cloth mother contrasted with either the wire mother or the empty box, and no consistent difference between wire mother and empty box.

Affectional retention was also tested in the open field during the [25] first 9 days after separation and then at 30-day intervals, and each test condition was run twice at each retention interval. The infant's behavior differed from that observed during the period preceding separation. When the cloth mother was present in the post-separation period, the babies rushed to her, climbed up, clung tightly to her,

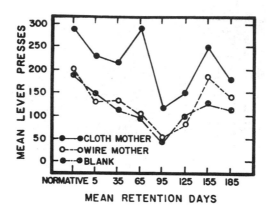

Figure 23. Retention of differential visual-exploration responses.

and rubbed their heads and faces against her body. After this initial embrace and reunion, they played on the mother, including biting and tearing at her cloth cover; but they rarely made any attempt to leave her during the test period, nor did they manipulate or play with the objects in the room, in contrast with their behavior before maternal separation. The only exception was the occasional monkey that left the mother surrogate momentarily, grasped the folded piece of paper (one of the standard stimuli in the field), and brought it quickly back to the mother. It appeared that <u>deprivation</u> had enhanced the tie to the mother and rendered the contact-comfort need so prepotent that need for the mother overwhelmed the exploratory motives during the brief, three-minute test sessions. No change in these behaviors was observed throughout the 185-day period. When the mother was absent from the open field, the behavior of the infants was similar in the initial retention test to that during the preseparation tests; but they tended to show gradual adaptation to the open-field situation with repeated testing and, consequently, a reduction in their emotionality scores.

[26]   In the last five retention test periods, an additional test was introduced in which the surrogate mother was placed in the center of the room and covered with a clear Plexiglas box. The monkeys were initially disturbed and frustrated when their explorations and manipulations of the box failed to provide contact with the mother. However, all animals adapted to the situation rather rapidly. Soon they used the box as a place of orientation for exploratory and play behavior, made frequent contacts with the objects in the field, and very often brought these objects to the Plexiglas box. The emotionality index was slightly higher than in the condition of the available cloth mothers, but it in no way approached the emotionality level displayed when the cloth

mother was absent. Obviously, the infant monkeys gained emotional security by the presence of the mother even though contact was denied.

Affectional retention has also been measured by tests in which the [27] monkey must unfasten a three-device mechanical puzzle to obtain entrance into a compartment containing the mother surrogate. All the trials are initiated by allowing the infant to go through an unlocked door, and in half the trials it finds the mother present and in half, an empty compartment. The door is then locked and a ten-minute test conducted. In tests given prior to separation from the surrogate mothers, some of the infants had solved this puzzle and others had failed. The data of Figure 24 show that on the last test before separation there were no differences in total manipulation under mother-present and mother-absent conditions, but striking differences exist between the two conditions throughout the post-separation test periods. Again, there is no interaction with conditions of feeding.

The over-all picture obtained from surveying the retention data is [28] unequivocal. There is little, if any, waning of responsiveness to the mother throughout this five-month period as indicated by any measure. It becomes perfectly obvious that this affectional bond is highly resistant to forgetting and that it can be retained for very long periods of time by relatively infrequent contact reinforcement. During the next year, retention tests will be conducted at 90-day intervals, and further plans are dependent upon the results obtained. It would appear that affectional responses may show as much resistance to extinction as has been previously demonstrated for learned fears and learned pain, and such data would be in keeping with those of common human observation.

The infant's responses to the mother surrogate in the fear tests, [29] the open-field situation, and the baby Butler box and the responses on the retention tests cannot be described adequately with words. For supplementary information we turn to the motion picture record.

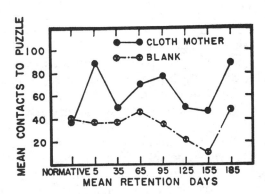

Figure 24. Retention of puzzle manipulation responsiveness.

(At this point a 20-minute film was presented illustrating and supplementing the behaviors described thus far in the address.)

[30]   We have already described the group of four control infants that had never lived in the presence of any mother surrogate and had demonstrated no sign of affection or security in the presence of the cloth mothers introduced in test sessions. When these infants reached the age of 250 days, cubicles containing both a cloth mother and a wire mother were attached to their cages. There was no lactation in these mothers, for the monkeys were on a solid-food diet. The initial reaction of the monkeys to the alterations was one of extreme disturbance. All the infants screamed violently and made repeated attempts to escape the cage whenever the door was opened. They kept a maximum distance from the mother surrogates and exhibited a considerable amount of rocking and crouching behavior, indicative of emotionality. Our first thought was that the critical period for the development of maternally directed affection had passed and that these macaque children were doomed to live as affectional orphans. Fortunately, these behaviors continued for only 12 to 48 hours and then gradually ebbed, changing from indifference to active contact on, and exploration of, the surrogates. The home-cage behavior of these control monkeys slowly became similar to that of the animals raised with the mother surrogates from birth. Their manipulation and play on the cloth mother became progressively more vigorous to the point of actual mutilation, particularly during the morning after the cloth mother had been given her daily change of terry covering. The control subjects were now actively running to the cloth mother when frightened and had to be coaxed from her to be taken from the cage for formal testing.

[31]   Objective evidence of these changing behaviors is given in Figure 25, which plots the amount of time these infants spent on the mother surrogates. Within 10 days mean contact time is approximately nine hours, and this measure remains relatively constant throughout the next 30 days. Consistent with the results on the subjects reared from birth with dual mothers, these late-adopted infants spent less than one and one-half hours per day in contact with the wire mothers, and this activity level was relatively constant throughout the test sessions. Although the maximum time that the control monkeys spent on the cloth mother was only about half that spent by the original dual mother-surrogate group, we cannot be sure that this discrepancy is a function of differential early experience. The control monkeys were about three months older when the mothers were attached to their cages than the experimental animals had been when their mothers were removed and the retention tests begun. Thus, we do not know what the amount of contact would be for a 250-day-old animal raised from birth with surrogate mothers. Nevertheless, the magnitude of

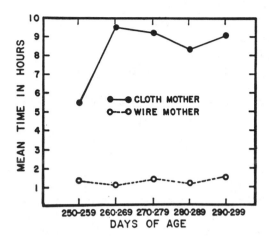

Figure 25. Differential time spent on cloth and wire mother surrogates by monkeys started at 250 days of age.

the differences and the fact that the contact-time curves for the mothered-from-birth infants had remained constant for almost 150 days suggest that early experience with the mother is a variable of measurable importance.

The control group has also been tested for differential visual exploration after the introduction of the cloth and wire mothers; these behaviors are plotted in Figure 26. By the second test session a high level of exploratory behavior had developed, and the responsiveness to the wire mother and the empty box is significantly greater than [32]

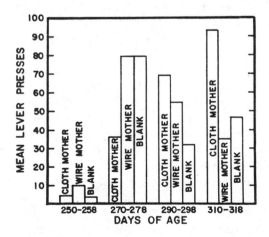

Figure 26. Differential visual exploration of monkeys started at 250 days of age.

that to the cloth mother. This is probably not an artifact since there is every reason to believe that the face of the cloth mother is a fear stimulus to most monkeys that have not had extensive experience with this object during the first 40 to 60 days of life. Within the third test session a sharp change in trend occurs, and the cloth mother is then more frequently viewed than the wire mother or the blank box; this trend continues during the fourth session, producing a significant preference for the cloth mother.

[33]   Before the introduction of the mother surrogate into the home-cage situation, only one of the four control monkeys had ever contacted the cloth mother in the open-field tests. In general, the surrogate mother not only gave the infants no security, but instead appeared to serve as a fear stimulus. The emotionality scores of these control subjects were slightly higher during the mother-present test sessions than during the mother-absent test sessions. These behaviors were changed radically by the fourth post-introduction test approximately 60 days later. In the absence of the cloth mothers the emotionality index in this fourth test remains near the earlier level, but the score is reduced by half when the mother is present, a result strikingly similar to that found for infants raised with the dual mother-surrogates from birth. The control infants now show increasing object exploration and play behavior, and they begin to use the mother as a base of operations, as did the infants raised from birth with the mother surrogates. However, there are still definite differences in the behavior of the two groups. The control infants do not rush directly to the mother and clutch her violently; but instead they go toward, and orient around, her, usually after an initial period during which they frequently show disturbed behavior, exploratory behavior, or both.

[34]   That the control monkeys develop affection or love for the cloth mother when she is introduced into the cage at 250 days of age cannot be questioned. There is every reason to believe, however, that this interval of delay depresses the intensity of the affectional response below that of the infant monkeys that were surrogate-mothered from birth onward. In interpreting these data it is well to remember that the control monkeys had had continuous opportunity to observe and hear other monkeys housed in adjacent cages and that they had had limited opportunity to view and contact surrogate mothers in the test situations, even though they did not exploit the opportunities.

[35]   During the last two years we have observed the behavior of two infants raised by their own mothers. Love for the real mother and love for the surrogate mother appear to be very similar. The baby macaque spends many hours a day clinging to its real mother. If away from the mother when frightened, it rushes to her and in her presence shows comfort and composure. As far as we can observe, the infant

monkey's affection for the real mother is strong, but no stronger than that of the experimental monkey for the surrogate cloth mother, and the security that the infant gains from the presence of the real mother is no greater than the security it gains from a cloth surrogate. Next year we hope to put this problem to final, definitive, experimental test. But, whether the mother is real or a cloth surrogate, there does develop a deep and abiding bond between mother and child. In one case it may be the call of the wild and in the other the McCall of civilization, but in both cases there is "togetherness."

In spite of the importance of contact comfort, there is reason to believe that other variables of measurable importance will be discovered. Postural support may be such a variable, and it has been suggested that, when we build arms into the mother surrogate, 10 is the minimal number required to provide adequate child care. Rocking motion may be such a variable, and we are comparing rocking and stationary mother surrogates and inclined planes. The differential responsiveness to cloth mother and cloth-covered inclined plane suggests that clinging as well as contact is an affectional variable of importance. Sounds, particularly natural, maternal sounds, may operate as either unlearned or learned affectional variables. Visual responsiveness may be such a variable, and it is possible that some semblance of visual imprinting may develop in the neonatal monkey. There are indications that this becomes a variable of importance during the course of infancy through some maturational process. [36]

John Bowlby has suggested that there is an affectional variable which he calls "primary object following," characterized by visual and oral search of the mother's face. Our surrogate-mother-raised baby monkeys are at first inattentive to her face, as are human neonates to human mother faces. But by 30 days of age ever-increasing responsiveness to the mother's face appears—whether through learning, maturation, or both—and we have reason to believe that the face becomes an object of special attention. [37]

Our first surrogate-mother-raised baby had a mother whose head was just a ball of wood since the baby was a month early and we had not had time to design a more esthetic head and face. This baby had contact with the blank-faced mother for 180 days and was then placed with two cloth mothers, one motionless and one rocking, both being endowed with painted, ornamented faces. To our surprise the animal would compulsively rotate both faces 180 degrees so that it viewed only a round, smooth face and never the painted, ornamented face. Furthermore, it would do this as long as the patience of the experimenter in reorienting the faces persisted. The monkey showed no sign of fear or anxiety, but it showed unlimited persistence. Subsequently it improved its technique, compulsively removing the heads and rolling [38] them into its cage as fast as they were returned. We are intrigued by this observation, and we plan to examine systematically the role of the mother face in the development of infant-monkey affections. Indeed, these observations suggest the need for a series of ethological-type researches on the two-faced female.

[39]   Although we have made no attempts thus far to study the generalization of infant-macaque affection or love, the techniques which we have developed offer promise in this uncharted field. Beyond this, there are few if any technical difficulties in studying the affection of the actual, living mother for the child, and the techniques developed can be utilized and expanded for the analysis and developmental study of father-infant and infant-infant affection.

[40]   Since we can measure neonatal and infant affectional responses to mother surrogates, and since we know they are strong and persisting, we are in a position to assess the effects of feeding and contactual schedules; consistency and inconsistency in the mother surrogates; and early, intermediate, and late maternal deprivation. Again, we have here a family of problems of fundamental interest and theoretical importance.

[41]   If the researches completed and proposed make a contribution, I shall be grateful; but I have also given full thought to possible practical applications. The socioeconomic demands of the present and the threatened socioeconomic demands of the future have led the American woman to displace, or threaten to displace, the American man in science and industry. If this process continues, the problem of proper child-rearing practices faces us with startling clarity. It is cheering in view of this trend to realize that the American male is physically endowed with all the really essential equipment to compete with the American female on equal terms in one essential activity: the rearing of infants. We now know that women in the working classes are not needed in the home because of their primary mammalian capabilities; and it is possible that in the foreseeable future neonatal nursing will not be regarded as a necessity, but as a luxury—to use Veblen's term— a form of conspicuous consumption limited perhaps to the upper classes. But whatever course history may take, it is comforting to know that we are now in contact with the nature of love.

QUESTIONS

Harlow says that the "assigned mission" of psychology is "to analyze all facets of human and animal behavior into their component variables."

1. What are the "component variables" of mother-love in monkeys, and what methods does Harlow use to test them?
2. What variables in the infant's attachment to the mother is Harlow getting at by constructing some mothers of cloth, some mothers of wire, and (for the control group) no mothers at all?
3. Why is the difference in amount of time spent in contact with the mother-surrogate crucial to Harlow's findings?
4. How did Harlow test for "affectional retention," i.e., the monkeys' "affection" for the cloth-mother after separation from it? List the kinds of behavior that were produced and the kinds of behavior that were inhibited by the cloth-mother's absence.
5. What is the significance of the infant monkeys' being able to play when the cloth-mother was present but enclosed in Plexiglas? What was Harlow testing by having the mother present but enclosed?
6. What is significant about what happens to the control monkeys (raised without either mothers or surrogates) (1) when they are *first* put in a cage with a cloth-mother, and (2) after they have been in the presence of the cloth-mother for 24 to 48 hours? What do the two levels of reaction prove about the tie between the infant and the cloth-mother?
7. Harlow says "thoughtful men, and probably all women, have speculated on the nature of love." Does his differentiation of *all* women and *some* men suggest that he has unconscious bias? If so, does that subjective bias interfere with the objectivity of his observation, experiment, or conclusion? What different interpretations could come from experimenters with other biases?

EXERCISES

1. When Harlow says, "It takes more than a baby and a box to make a healthy monkey," he is making an inside joke at the expense of B. F. Skinner, a major figure in the behavioral school of psychology and inventor of the Skinner Box. Do some research to find out who B. F. Skinner is and what has made him important. Write three note card summaries: one that extracts and lists the general principles of the Skinnerian idea of "reinforcement" of infant behavior; one that lists the general principles of the Harlow position, and one that lists in abstract outline form the essential differences between them.
2. In the sciences an *abstract* is a short summary, usually of an experiment. It attempts to highlight the main findings, and it usually

covers the steps that the experimenter took in completing the research. Write an abstract of Harlow's article. It should be no longer
than 300 words, and it should include the steps and conclusions
of the experiment in sequence. Abstracts are usually addressed to
persons who have some familiarity with the field of study; you
may therefore feel free to use the specialized vocabulary introduced
by Harlow.

3. In the follow-up studies Harlow also found that the motherless
monkeys could not mate:

> In several years of repeated trials no motherless male has ever
> achieved intromission, although these animals have shown sexual
> excitement. Often they have engaged in violent assault against
> the female forcing us to remove the male.

Write a short, 300-word exam answer on the truth or falsity of the
following proposition using Harlow's studies in making your answer.

> *Proposed:* Violence against women, including rape, is one long-
> range consequence of emotional deprivation in childhood.

4. Eight years after the series of experiments you read about, Harlow
discovered by accident that monkeys who had been used in the
experiments (raised with mother substitutes made of cloth or wire)
had severe difficulty in relating to other monkeys:

> Exposed, in test situations, to each other and to monkeys of their
> own age captured in the wild, these motherless monkeys have
> been consistently less responsive to other monkeys except for
> fighting. . . . Unlike normal animals, they avoid social contacts
> such as are customary among peers.

In your journal speculate about the fate of these monkeys. Using
this piece of data and your own experience and those of people
you know, try to decide whether the formula that Harlow's data
seems to suggest—i.e., deprivation of mother love in infancy leads
to antisocial behavior—is valid for human beings.

—— CHAPTER TWO ——

BADINTER: MOTHER LOVE

Social History

Elisabeth Badinter is one of a new academic breed in France. She is a philosopher who holds a second degree in sociology and who has worked closely with the cultural historian Philippe Ariès (see p. 269). Consequently, she takes a multivalent, interdisciplinary approach to questions and problems. This selection, from the book *Mother Love: Myth and Reality*, challenges the idea that mother love is universal, timeless, or innate. She dates maternal tenderness as a dominant cultural trend stemming from Romanticism, especially from the publication of Jean Jacques Rousseau's *Emile*, a book that introduced the idea that human beings are born innocent and benevolent and are morally deformed by bad child-rearing practices. Badinter says that in the two hundred years before Romanticism parents were cheerfully indifferent to the welfare of their children or, worse, were deliberately neglectful of them.

Badinter's study offers an interesting contrast to Harlow's. Although Harlow's study focuses upon how the infant monkey learns affection for its mother, it *presupposes* a mother monkey's love for her young as the *natural* condition. It assumes that what is learned from the mother by the infant and passed on to future generations is the mother monkey's *affection* for the infant, to which the infant learns to respond by body contact. Because Harlow's experimental subjects are animals, we tend to think that his findings are true to our built-in, or most fundamental, nature. Therefore, we think that mother-infant love is part of our programming—innate, invariable, and universal. Keep Harlow's study in mind as you read Badinter's, and try to determine which study offers better, stronger, or more reliable observations and evidence to support its position.

As you read the selection, pay particular attention to the sources available to the social historian for understanding the past. How does Badinter document her observation that well-to-do mothers were often indifferent to their children in eighteenth-century France? Do sources such as diaries or letters give us authentic information on such a subject?

GLOSSARY

documents [1]	implacable [28]
ex nihilo [3]	primogeniture [30]
chroniclers [4]	aesthetic [37]
viable [9]	antidote [42]
pathological [9]	conjugal life [44]
demographic [10]	mortality rate [52]
prerogative [14]	exogenous [59]
spontaneous [22]	endogenous [59]
variability [23]	foundlings [62]
narcissism [23]	artisans [64]
bequeath [24]	infanticide [67]
modicum [28]	

_____ MATERNAL INDIFFERENCE _____

Elisabeth Badinter

[1] In examining the nature of the relationship between mother and child in historical and literary <u>documents</u>, we have noticed either indifference

SOURCE: From Elisabeth Badinter, *Mother Love: Myth and Reality, Motherhood in Modern History*, Macmillan, New York, 1980, pp. 58–72, 109–114. Reprinted by permission of the publisher.

or injunctions to preserve a certain coldness, all betraying an apparent lack of interest in the newborn baby. This last point is often interpreted as follows: How could one take interest in a little being who had such a great chance of dying in his first year? This interpretation would have us believe that the coldness of the parents, and of the mother in particular, served unconsciously as emotional armor against the great risks of seeing the object of their affection die. To put it a different way: Better not to grow too attached or you'll suffer later on. Such an attitude would have been the perfectly normal expression of the parents' will to live. Given the high infant mortality rate that existed until the end of the eighteenth century, if the mother had developed an intense attachment to each of her newborn babies, she certainly would have died of sorrow.

Historians studying societal values have often supported this inter-   [2]
pretation.* We can understand their motivation, since without really justifying the actions of these mothers the explanation prevents us from condemning them. By emphasizing the terrible threats to life at that time and the various calamities (poverty, epidemics, and other inevitable misfortunes) that befell our ancestors, the twentieth-century reader is gently led to feel that, after all, in their place one might have felt and acted the same. Thus, we are led to a confirmation of our comfortable beliefs in the marvelous continuity of motherhood throughout the ages, reinforcing our conception of a unique feeling, mother love. Given this interpretation, some have drawn the conclusion that mother love may vary in intensity depending on the external difficulties, but that it always exists. Mother love thus becomes a constant throughout history.

Others will say that the written sources we possess indicating a   [3]
different view of history are generally concerned only with the well-to-do classes, for and about whom one wrote, and that a corrupt class does not a total condemnation of our vision of motherhood make. One can also cite the behavior of the peasant women of Montaillou, who at the dawn of the fourteenth century cradled and fondled their children and mourned their deaths.[1] But, in fact, this evidence merely shows that at all times there have been loving mothers and that mother love is not an *ex nihilo* creation of the eighteenth or nineteenth century. This example is not to be equated with a universal form of behavior.

We have already alluded to the importance of the economic factor   [4]
in mothers' behavior, as well as the force of social conventions. But what can we say about the women from the well-to-do classes who felt neither pressure, since their husbands did not need their help? What should we think of the women who had the financial means

---

* Flandrin, Lebrun, and Shorter are not among these.

necessary to raise their children themselves and who for several centuries chose not to do so? It seems they considered this an unworthy
occupation and chose to get rid of the burden. They did so, too,
without eliciting the slightest protest. Apart from a few strict theologians
and other intellectuals (all men), the chroniclers of the period seemed
to find such behavior normal.

[5]   These chroniclers were, in fact, so little interested in mothers, whether
loving or "warped," that one is led to conclude that mother love was
not at that time a social and moral value. These privileged women
did not have threats or guilt of any kind hanging over them. Stretching
a point, one might be tempted to view their behavior as a completely
exceptional case of a spontaneous and unexplainable behavior. For if
motherhood was not yet the "fashion"* women would play a large
part in spreading the fashion when it did come, even if at the end of
the eighteenth century they would see themselves as its victims.

[6]   An understanding of their behavior and their thoughts, which, in
accordance with the well-known law, spread from the top to the
bottom of the social ladder, are of importance, as are all efforts to
record faithfully the consequences of those attitudes for their children.

[7]   We shall, as a result, be forced to reverse the commonly held view
that their indifference was no more than a form of self-protection. It
was not so much because children died like flies that mothers showed
little interest in them, but rather because the mothers showed so little
interest that the children died in such great numbers.

SIGNS OF INDIFFERENCE

[8]   In our search for evidence of the existence of love, we must be prepared,
should we not find it, to conclude that love simply did not exist.

THE CHILD'S DEATH

[9]   We hold today the deep conviction that the death of a child leaves
an indelible mark in the mother's heart. Even the woman who loses
a barely viable fetus retains the memory of this death, if she wanted
the child. Without turning our attention to the pathological manifestations of mourning, there is little doubt that every mother remembers
the death of a child as an irreplaceable loss. The fact that she can give

---

* The word "fashion" is the term used by Talleyrand in his *Mémoires*, p. 8: "The
fashion of 'paternal' care had not yet arrived [he was born in 1754]; the fashion was
quite different during my childhood." Earlier he wrote: "Too much caring would have
seemed pedantic; affection too often expressed would have seemed something new
and consequently ridiculous." (In the eighteenth century "paternal" was often used
in the sense of "parental.")

birth to another child nine months later does not cancel the effect of the death. For the intangible worth we ascribe to each human being, including the viable fetus, no tangible substitute exists.

The reverse was held to be true in the past. In his thesis on sev- [10] enteenth- and eighteenth-century attitudes toward the death of a child, Lebrun writes: "On the human level, the death of a small child was perceived as an almost routine accident that a later birth would succeed in making good."[2] This attitude demonstrates a reduced intensity of love for each of a mother's children. Ariès, on the other hand, defended this insensitivity as "only natural given the demographic conditions of the period."[3] Whether natural or not, this insensitivity appears quite bluntly in family records of the eighteenth century. Where the head of the family recorded and commented on all events concerning the family, the death of children is most often entered without comment, or with a few pious phrases that seem more inspired by religious sentiment than by genuine grief.

Thus, a surgeon in Poligny recorded the deaths of his children and [11] added after each entry, as he had done for the deaths of his parents and his neighbors: "May God have mercy on his soul. Amen." The only regret he seemed to show was for his twenty-four-year-old son, whom he described as "a handsome young man."[4]

A middle-class lawyer in Vaux-le-Vicomte, married in 1759, lost all [12] six of his children, ranging in age from several months to six years, in as quick a succession as they had been born. He noted the loss of the first five without comment. With the sixth he could not refrain from drawing up a balance sheet: "And now I find myself childless after having had six boys. Blessed be the will of God!"

All this is in the tradition of Montaigne's famous comment: "I lost [13] two or three children during their stay with the wet nurse—not without regret, mind you, but without great vexation."[5]

The apparent absence of sorrow over the death of a child was not [14] the sole prerogative of the father. Mothers had identical reactions. Shorter cites the testimony of the founder of a foundling hospital in England, who was upset by mothers' abandoning their dying babies in the gutters or the garbage dumps of London, where they were left to rot. And elsewhere, the joyous indifference of a highly placed English woman who, "having lost two of her children, pointed out that she still had a baker's dozen in her."

Eighteenth-century French women did not lag behind the English [15] in this regard, as is evident from a passage from Mme. le Rebours's *Avis aux mères qui veulent nourrir leur enfants* (*Advice to Mothers Who Want to Nurse Their Children*): "There are mothers who on learning of their child's death at the nurse's, console themselves, without wondering about the cause, by saying, 'Ah well, another angel in heaven!'

I doubt that God makes allowance for their resignation in such matters. He sees to it that children are formed within them so that they may strive to make men of them. However, would they speak in such a manner if they gave any real thought to the cruel suffering that these children endured before passing away or to the idea that they themselves are often the cause of their children's deaths through their negligence?"[6]

[16]   And what better proof of indifference than the parents' absence at the child's burial! In certain parishes, such as those in Anjou, neither of the parents would make the effort to attend the interment of a child less than five years old. In other parishes, one of them would attend, sometimes the mother, sometimes the father.* Of course, in many cases, the parents learned of the death too late. But in any event they apparently did not make any great effort to keep themselves informed about the state of their child's health.

[17]   A last proof of this indifference is supplied by a reverse phenomenon: the degree to which expressed sorrow over the death of a child was always noticed by family, friends, and acquaintances. Apparently, grieving was considered a strange form of behavior.

[18]   Lebrun notes that the sorrow of Henri Campion upon the death of his four-year-old daughter in 1653 was so exceptional that Campion himself felt the need to explain it: " 'If it is said that these strong attachments may be considered excusable only toward mature persons and not for children, I answer that since my daughter had without doubt many more perfections than any ever had at her age, no one can with reason reproach me for believing that she would have progressed from good to better, and that therefore I did not only lose a loveable daughter of four years but also a friend, such as one could imagine her in her age of perfection.' "[7]

[19]   In a letter of August 19, 1671, Mme. de Sévigné makes a brief reference to Mme. Coetquen's sorrow over the death of her little girl: "She is very much upset and says that she will never have another as pretty." Mme. de Sévigné is not surprised by this sorrow because the object of the lamentations was unique. If the child had not had an exceptional characteristic (her beauty), would her death have been any more lamented than the others'?

[20]   One hundred years later Denis Diderot demonstrated the same sensibility as had Mme. de Sévigné and the unfortunate Campion. In a letter to Sophie Volland, dated August 9, 1762, he mentions the "mad" suffering of Mme. Damilaville upon the sudden death of one of her daughters, and cannot explain it except by referring to the

---

* Bideau pointed out that in the small town of Thoissey the majority of fathers did make the effort to attend their child's burial.

exceptional nature of the deceased girl: "I allow those to grieve who lose children such as this one."

All these statements suggest that sorrow was acceptable only in exceptional cases, depending on the special qualities of the dead child. For all others, it would have been out of place to mourn. Was it because the tears of sorrow would have appeared indecent? Because sorrow indicated a lapse in religious faith? Or simply because it would have been silly to lament a creature so incomplete and imperfect, a mere child, as today people often disapprove of those who mourn the death of their dog? [21]

SELECTIVE LOVE

A second attitude, shared by father and mother alike, will not fail to astonish the twentieth-century reader: the incredible inequality of treatment from one child to the next, according to sex and order of birth. How could it be that love, if it were indeed natural and spontaneous, would be directed toward one child more than toward another? Why, if these affinities were indeed matters of choice, would the boy be better loved than the girl, the eldest son more than the younger sons? [22]

Doesn't this variability only affirm that love was above all a response to the possible social gain a child might represent, as well as to the parents' narcissism? Each daughter would cost her father a dowry, and bring in nothing more than family alliances or the friendship of one's neighbor. These benefits did not amount to much, considering the fragile nature of alliances and friendships, which could be broken off when other interests were at stake. A girl whose dowry was too small for her to be married off successfully brought on the expense of entering a convent, being kept at home as a servant, or searching for employment as a servant in someone else's home. No, daughters were not profitable items for parents, and no special sympathy seems to have developed between the typical mother and daughter. The mother reserved her treasures of affection and pride for the eldest son, under French law the exclusive heir to the family fortune and, when the parents were noble, the family title. [23]

Throughout all segments of society the heir apparent benefited from highly privileged treatment by the family. If his parents had any goods at all to bequeath—a few modest acres or the crown of France— the eldest son became the object of an exemplary concern. In the countryside, daily practice brought the eldest son the sweet things of life that his sisters and younger brothers would not receive. He got the juicy morsels of salt pork or meat, whenever there was any. [24]

The younger sons were only rarely, and the daughters never, given such treats.

[25]   In his study of Languedoc, Yves Castan reveals the ambiguity inherent in the status of the eldest son.[8] He was all the more obedient due to his fear of being disinherited in favor of a more obliging younger son. On the other hand, according to numerous documents studied by Castan, the eldest son seems to have profited from his parents' emotional favor. The mother, instead of sharing her love among her children, or even attempting to make amends for the younger sons' future misfortunes by showing more affection toward them, believed it necessary to raise them as strictly as possible—in order to prepare them, it was said, for their cruel fate.

[26]   Thus, the mother would keep the eldest son with her during early infancy. She nursed him and took care of him herself. But she would readily agree to send the younger children away for many years. The eldest were without question nearly always more coddled and fussed over and better educated, insofar as the parents' means permitted.

[27]   In this context of highly selective feeling, where is the mother love that is said to exist in all places and at all times? The preference for the eldest son was not a pure emotion and probably not natural. Castan suggests that this maternal affection had its source in down-to-earth foresight: If the father passed away before the mother and if she became helpless, upon whom would her survival depend if not the heir? So it was necessary to maintain good relations with the person on whom her fate might depend.

[28]   As far as the younger son was concerned, she might dispense with such precautions. He would join the army or serve as a servant to his brother or to a neighbor. Should he possess a less robust constitution and a modicum of education, he could hope to take holy orders. In this light, the implacable hatreds that often grew up between brothers are easily explained. Even though the custom was observed at all levels of society and followed almost without exception,[9] it was nonetheless bitterly resented, from the lowest of peasants to the most titled of nobles.

[29]   In rich and noble families the younger sons could expect to marry more easily, but by and large only two careers were open to them: the military and the Church. Of two famous younger sons forced to enter the Church—Cardinal de Bernis and Bishop Talleyrand—the latter left revealing memoirs.

[30]   Talleyrand had an older brother and two younger brothers. He was baptized the very day of his birth in 1754 at St.-Sulpice in Paris and handed over to a wet nurse as soon as the ceremony was over. She took him immediately to her home in the St.-Jacques suburb of Paris. During more than four years his mother did not visit him a

single time and never asked about him. She was therefore unaware of a crippling accident that left him with a club foot. She learned of his misfortune only after she had lost her first son. Although he was now the eldest son, Talleyrand was barred from entering the military and upholding the glory of the family name. It was decided, against his will, that he would instead enter the Church. Even worse, he was forced to renounce his right of primogeniture in favor of his younger brother. In his *Memoirs* he relates how, at about the age of thirteen, he was dispossessed by a family council in favor of his brother Archambaud, aged five.[10] But Mme. de Talleyrand had learned a very useful lesson. Concerned with preserving the family line, she kept the new heir and his little brother with her at home.

Talleyrand's story is particularly hateful because we can so clearly   [31]
visualize the disability resulting from his parents' indifference. But his case was not unique; many children returned from their nurses crippled, sickly, or dying—not to mention those who did not return at all, lost in a mass of statistics. Economic and demographic necessity are insufficient explanations for such treatment. Many parents had to choose between their own interests and those of the child, and it was often the child's death that they chose out of negligence or selfishness. These mothers, let us not forget, cannot be glossed over in the history of motherhood. They are not its most glorious representatives, but they serve to reveal a harsh picture that cannot be ignored. This is certainly not the only picture, but it is one that must be accorded equal weight with the others.

THE REFUSAL TO NURSE

Women like Mme. de Talleyrand or the granddaughters of the counselor   [32]
Frossard were not inclined to give up their place and duties at court, or even their everyday social lives, to raise their children. The first step in this rejection was their refusal to nurse their children. To explain this unnatural action, women of comfortable means invoked several arguments not so much to justify their action as to excuse their inaction. Some, however, would not mince words: "It bores me, and I have better things to do."

WOMEN'S EXPLANATIONS

Among the arguments most frequently invoked, two excuses domi-   [33]
nated. Nursing was physically bad for the mother, and was rather unseemly besides. Arguments based on physical necessity concentrated on the question of the mother's own survival. If they nursed their babies, they would deprive themselves of "a precious chyle, absolutely

necessary to their own preservation."[11] Such reasoning, although without the slightest medical foundation, never failed to impress family and friends. Then there was the excuse of too great a nervous sensibility, which would be shaken by the child's cries.

[34]   But the same women who would have been shaken by a baby's cries were described by the eighteenth-century poet Nicolas Gilbert in his "Satyre" as follows: "But when Lalli [Tollendall], condemned to death, is dragged as a spectacle to the gallows, she will be the first to run to this horrible celebration, for the pleasure of seeing his head fall."

[35]   We know from other sources as well that women of the world showed no great reluctance to attend executions. During the torture of Damiens, which was especially barbarous, some women showed an enthusiasm verging on delirium. The cries of the condemned must have troubled them less than those of an innocent child.

[36]   Equally specious was the frequently advanced excuse of a frail constitution. Late eighteenth-century writers would mock this pretext. The same women, they would say, invoke their fragility and their poor health and then go off to sumptuous banquets with indigestible dishes, or dance at a ball until they drop from weariness, or run off to the theater to suffocate in the crowd.[12]

[37]   Sometimes, instead of moving others to pity with their claims of poor health, women resorted to an aesthetic argument, swearing that if they breast-fed they would lose their beauty, their principal asset. Nursing was believed (and still is believed) to make breasts misshapen and to soften the nipples. Many women did not want to risk such a violation of their bodies and preferred to make use of a wet nurse.

[38]   But if the risk to their health and their beauty did not arouse sufficient sympathy, women could always appeal to the moral and social order, which would leave no one indifferent.

[39]   First, women (and therefore their families) who believed themselves better than the common herd thought that it was injurious to their prestige to nurse their children themselves. Since noble ladies had for a long time set the example, such neglect rapidly became a sign of distinction. Breast-feeding one's child was the same as acknowledging omission from the best society. On this point an eighteenth-century doctor, Pierre Dionis, pointed out: "Women of the middle class, including the wives of the most insignificant artisans, shift the responsibility of motherhood onto others."

[40]   Intellectuals like Jean-Jacques Burlamaqui and the Count de Buffon showed the same contempt for the notion of a mother's nursing. Speaking of the small child, Buffon wrote: "Let us pass over in silence the disgust that might be aroused by the details of the care that this state requires."[13] A man's words, in no way disavowed by women.

Apparently, "the details of the care" children required brought them no satisfaction.

In the name of decency, nursing was declared ridiculous and dis- [41] gusting. The word "ridiculous" turns up often in letters and memoirs. Mothers, mothers-in-law, and midwives all did their best to dissuade the young mother from nursing, a task not sufficiently noble for a lady of quality. It was not seemly to expose the breasts. Beyond the fact that it would encourage an animalistic image of the woman as milk-cow, it was considered immodest. This was not to be taken lightly in the eighteenth century. Modesty was a real feeling that must be taken into consideration if we are to understand the refusal to breast-feed. If the mother nursed, she had to hide from the world and that in turn interrupted for a long time both her social life and her husband's.

Husbands in turn were not without responsibility for their wives' [42] refusal to nurse. Some complained of their wives' nursing as a threat to sexuality and a restriction on pleasure. Clearly, some men found nursing women repulsive, with their strong smell of milk and their continually sweating breasts.[14] For them nursing was synonymous with filth—a real antidote to love.

Even if the father was not disgusted, nursing was a considerable [43] annoyance. Doctors and writers of the era agreed in prohibiting sexual relations not only during pregnancy but for as long as the mother was nursing. The sperm, they said, would spoil the milk and turn it sour. The father would thus be endangering the child's life. Medicine perpetuated this false notion throughout the eighteenth century, leaving the father to anticipate a long period of pleasureless continence. When the taboo was defied, the nursing woman's reduced fertility did not escape notice, and the father found himself with a disagreeable choice on his hands. He could either take his pleasure without having to worry too much about a new pregnancy (a very agreeable temptation) and put the baby's life in danger, or deprive himself in order to preserve the infant's life. The most obvious solution was to flee the conjugal bed for adulterous affairs, a solution that evidently displeased many wives. In either case, family unity was threatened.

The young infant, an annoyance to his parents, was placed in the [44] hands of a hired nurse until his weaning. But the mother did not stop there, for she rejected children of all ages. Children interfered not only with mother's conjugal life but also with her amusements. To busy oneself with a child was neither enjoyable nor chic.

The women who put their peace and their pleasure first agreed [45] with the sentiments of a little poem by Coulanges:

> Was there ever anything less charming
> Than a heap of wailing babies?

> One says papa, the other mama,
> And the other cries for his darling.
> And if you take this on
> You're treated like a dog.

[46]   The pleasures of the woman of the world were to be found principally in social life: receiving guests and paying visits, showing off a new dress, running to the opera and the theater. Out until the wee hours of the morning, she preferred "to enjoy a peaceful sleep, or one interrupted only by pleasure."[15] "And noon finds her in her bed."[16]

[47]   All these women had clear consciences; social life was considered a necessity for women of a certain rank. Doctors themselves acknowledged that these social obligations were valid reasons not to play the mother's part. In the middle of the eighteenth century Dr. Moreau de St. Elier asserted that the care of children "is an embarrassing burden . . . in society."

[48]   According to the worldly idea of the period nothing was less fashionable than to "seem to love one's children too much"[17]* and to give up one's precious time for them. Women of the petty bourgeoisie, wives of merchants or of local judges, were hardly subject to the values espoused by high society but strove nonetheless to copy their more favored sisters. Lacking a brilliant social life, they could acquire the first mark of distinction by sending their children away. It was better to do nothing than to busy oneself with such insignificant matters.

[49]   But all of this is not sufficient to explain this type of behavior. We must not forget the warnings of the theologians of the sixteenth century, who reproached mothers for their blameworthy affection for their children. At the end of the eighteenth century, however, the entire intelligentsia would reproach them for the opposite reason and criticize their harshness. What was it that changed during those two centuries?

[50]   Certainly childhood's special joys had been unappreciated for some time before this period. Even so, women nursed their children almost without exception and kept them home until at least the age of eight or ten years. Oddly enough, it was at the very time when this new appreciation of childhood was emerging that women stepped away

* Montesquieu thought likewise (as cited by Father Dainville): "Everything concerned with the education of children, with natural feeling, seems something low to the common people." The same was apparently true for the well-to-do classes: "Our customs are that a father and a mother do not raise their children, do not see them anymore, do not nourish them. We have not yet reached the point of being moved at the sight of them; they are objects that one conceals from the eyes of all, and a woman would not be keeping up appearances if she seemed to concern herself with them." In the same spirit, Turgot confided in a letter to Mme. de Grafigny in 1751: "One blushes for one's children."

from the duties of motherhood. The facts are contradictory only if we try to restrict the definition of woman to her role as mother.

The seventeenth and eighteenth centuries form a period when the [51] woman who had the means attempted to define herself as a woman. Her attempt was facilitated by the fact that society had not yet accorded the child the place we assign to him today. In order to gain a clearer sense of her own abilities, the woman of this period strove to get beyond the two roles that formerly defined her in her entirety. The roles of wife and mother, which granted her existence only in relation to another person, were not enough. . . .

INFANT MORTALITY

In seventeenth- and eighteenth-century France the death of a child [52] was a commonplace occurrence. According to the figures presented by François Lebrun, the mortality rate of children under one year of age was consistently well above 25 percent.[18] In France as a whole the infant mortality rate was, for example, 27.5 percent from 1740 to 1749 and 26.5 from 1780 to 1789.[19]

In his study of nurslings in the Beauvaisis region during the second [53] half of the eighteenth century, Jean Ganiage found approximately the same average, one child in four not living more than a year. After the first, fateful year of life the mortality rate diminished noticeably. According to Lebrun the average number of survivors per thousand at different ages was as follows: 720 survived the first year; 574 made it past their fifth year; and 525 lived to celebrate their tenth birthday.* It is evident that the toll was heaviest in the first year.

These averages are somewhat misleading, since infant mortality [54] rates varied widely from one region to another—a function of the local health conditions, the climate, and the environment.†

A second factor that should be taken into account, and the most [55] important one for our study, is the difference in infant mortality depending on who nursed the child. The eighteenth-century child was more or less well cared for in direct relation to whether he was nursed

---

* The figures given by Ganiage in *Trois villages de l'Ile-de-France au XVIIIᵉ siècle* are substantially the same: 767 at one year of age; 583 at five; 551 at ten.

† In Crulai, in Normandy, the usual treatment seems to have been more favorable to the survival of children, since 698 out of 1,000 made it past their fifth birthday. In contrast, in Frontignan, a small town on the Languedoc coast, only 399 out of 1,000 survived. Between these two extremes, a great number of shocking estimates abound. In Lyon, during the eighteenth century, one child in two died—during good years. On the average, two-thirds of the children of Lyon did not live to see their twentieth year.

by his mother, sent away to a nurse by his parents, or sent to a nurse as a foundling through a hospital.

[56]   As a general rule, the mortality rate of children kept at home and nursed by their mothers was half what it was for those the mothers themselves sent to a nurse.

[57]   Thus, Jean-Pierre Bardet points out that in the city of Rouen the infant mortality rate for babies who stayed with their mothers did not exceed 18.7 percent for the years between 1777 and 1789.[20] These mothers were subsidized by the General Hospital and, therefore, not exactly rich. During the same period, the mortality rate for children sent to nurses by their parents, again with the assistance of the General Hospital, was 38.1 percent.

[58]   In Tamerville, a small village in Normandy, Pierre Wiel concluded that only 10.9 percent of the children nursed by their mothers died.[21]

[59]   In the southern suburbs of Paris, Paul Galliano noted with optimism that only 17.7 percent of the nurslings died during their first year.[22] But it must be borne in mind that the clientele of these nurses was relatively well-to-do and that the distances separating them were quite short, making the initial trip less dangerous: "The little Parisians who were not well-to-do and were placed by the nurses' bureau died at a rate of one out of four." But even under these optimal conditions, Galliano found that the exogenous mortality rate was double the endogenous mortality rate.

[60]   Finally, the figures for the city of Lyon and the surrounding area reveal even more of the dimension of the tragedy. Mothers who nursed their babies and were aided by the charitable board between 1785 and 1788[23] lost, as a group, only 16 percent during the first year. In contrast, according to Dr. Gilibert, the mortality rate for children entrusted to nurses was devastating: "We have found that the inhabitants of Lyon, both bourgeois and artisan, lost about two-thirds of their children under the care of hired nurses."[24]

[61]   The comment by Gilibert is interesting in that it shows, among other things, death was not reserved for the children of the poor. This is confirmed by Alain Bideau's study of the small town of Thoissey, where children from well-to-do families died in great numbers.[25] Here, as elsewhere, children nursed by their mothers were the fortunate ones. "The mortality rate of newborns is double if the newborn is not nursed by his mother."[26]

[62]   The fate of foundlings, the number of which rose constantly during the eighteenth century, was even worse. Lebrun notes that between 1773 and 1790 the average number of abandoned children each year was around 5,800[27]—an enormous number, when one considers that the annual number of births in Paris averaged somewhere between 20,000 and 25,000. Even when we take into account the fact that

nonresident mothers came to Paris to abandon their children, the figure is still impressive.

Bardet has shown that among Rouen's abandoned children, some [63] legitimate and others illegitimate, illegitimate children died more frequently and at an earlier age than did legitimate. Antoinette Chamoux confirms this phenomenon for Reims.[28] The reason is simple: the illegitimate were more severely mistreated.

Lebrun believes that, even in the absence of precise figures, roughly [64] one-third of all abandoned children were legitimate and two-thirds illegitimate. If in Reims the almost universal reason for the abandonment of children was the terrible poverty of the parents, the situation in Paris was somewhat different. A study of 1,531 parents who abandoned children at La Couche in 1778 revealed that social status and profession were not always significant determinants. One-third of these cases were from the Parisian middle class, a quarter from the class of master artisans and merchants, and another quarter from among journeymen and day laborers.[29]

The main causes for abandonment were economic and social. A [65] fair number of lower-middle-class citizens abandoned their children with the intention of taking them back several years later, believing that the children would get better care at the hospital than they themselves could provide. But only a minuscule number actually returned to claim their children—in part due to diminished attachment, and in part due to inferior hospital standards. In the last third of the eighteenth century the percentage of children who died after being left at a hospital was more than 90 percent at Rouen, 84 percent in Paris, and 50 percent in Marseilles.[30]

These figures demonstrate how greatly chances of survival increased [66] for children nursed by their mothers or, failing that, by good nurses, decently paid and carefully chosen by the parents. Generally speaking, the mortality rate doubled for children not nursed by their mothers and increased from six to ten times if the child was abandoned.

Thus, the wet-nurse system was "objectively" a disguised form of [67] infanticide—the greatest toll visited upon infants in their first year, and especially the first month.* Beyond the first month, the figures decreased, and after a year the infant mortality rate for children sent to nurses hardly exceeded that of those nursed by their own mothers.

If all such unfortunate children had been kept by their mothers, [68] even if only for a month or two, before being abandoned or sent to a nurse, nearly a third of them would have survived. Explanations

---

* Studies of Rouen and Reims support this. In Rouen 69.8 percent of all abandoned children died during their first month of life; in Reims it was a little less than 50 percent. In Paris, at the Hôtel-Dieu, it was 82 percent.

of this unconsciously murderous behavior have always relied upon allusions to poverty and ignorance: How, after all, could poor, uneducated people have known what awaited their children at the nurse's or in the hospital?

[69]   The argument is indisputable with regard to a large portion of the population—but not for everyone. Even if people generally did not know what became of abandoned babies, the growing number of accidents and deaths should have alerted and disquieted concerned parents. People obviously did not try very hard to find out what happened to all those children. The excuse that parents were ignorant of the dangers is even more open to question for parents who themselves sent their babies to nurses. By the end of the eighteenth century, in fact, many mothers of modest means were lodging complaints against bad nurses who returned their child in poor condition.

[70]   Prost de Royer cited cases of several mothers in Lyon who cried bitter tears when they saw their children return home close to death. One of them, who had lost seven children due to the inadequate care of wet nurses, asked the police lieutenant "if there is no way for poor women of the common folk who cannot nurse to save their children."[31] Other women brought proceedings against bad nurses. But all of this did not prevent the majority of mothers from continuing the practice when the necessity of their own work prohibited them themselves from nursing.

[71]   But what about the behavior of well-to-do artisan and merchant families? And what about Rousseau, who attempted to justify the abandonment of his own five children by insisting: "Everything taken into consideration, I chose for my children the best, or what I believed to be the best. I would have wanted, I would still want, to have been raised and cared for as they were"?[32]

[72]   Rousseau's selfishness is astonishing!

[73]   And what of the behavior of well-established middle-class families— such as the parents of Mme. Roland—who despite the killing off, one by one, of their children continued, seemingly unperturbed, to send them to wet nurses? Neither poverty nor ignorance explains such infanticides—only indifference, which until almost the end of the eighteenth century was not really frowned upon as a violation of the moral or social code. This last point is essential, for it seems to indicate that in the absence of any outside pressure of this kind the mother was left to act according to her own nature—a self-centered nature excluding the remotest hint of self-sacrifice for the good of the child she had just brought into the world.

[74]   Some have advanced the hypothesis that husbands pressured their wives to adopt such behavior. It was Rousseau's fault if Thérèse abandoned her children, the butcher's if his wife sent their children

to a nurse, the society gentleman's if the society woman did likewise. There certainly were cases where such things happened, but it is an unsatisfactory explanation which attempts to justify women only by making them the victims of men. Not all women lived under the control of unfeeling brutes demanding that they sacrifice their instinct and their love. On the contrary, many traditional fathers, like Chrysale, complained bitterly that their wives refused to care for the children.

Closer to the truth, there was no doubt a complicity between father [75] and mother, husband and wife, to adopt the forms of behavior that prevailed. Simply stated, we are less shocked by the male's behavior because no one has ever, even up to the present day, claimed that a father's love constitutes a universal law of nature. The wisest and most necessary course would be to resign ourselves to the varying qualities of mother love as well, recognizing that the so-called laws of nature often defy easy categorization.

We shall see that it became necessary, at the end of the eighteenth [76] century, to enlist many arguments to urge mothers back to their "instinctive" activities—appealing to their sense of duty, making them feel guilty, and even threatening them in order to convince them to resume their so-called natural and spontaneous functions of mother and nurse.

NOTES

1. F. Le Roy Ladurie, *Montaillou, village occitan,* pp. 305–17.
2. François Lebrun, *Les Hommes et la mort en Anjou aux XVIIe et XVIIIe siècles* (Paris: Mouton, 1971), p. 423.
3. Philippe Ariès, *L'Enfant et la vie familiale sous l'Ancien Régime,* p. 30.
4. Antoine Babeau, *Bourgeois d'autrefois* (1886), pp. 268–69.
5. Montaigne, *Essays,* Book II, chapter 8.
6. Mme. le Rebours, *Avis aux Mères* (1767), pp. 67–68.
7. François Lebrun, *La Vie conjugale sous l'Ancien Régime,* no. 51 (Paris: A. Colin, 1975), pp. 144–45.
8. Y. Castan, "Honnêteté et relations sociales dans le Languedoc." Dissertation (Paris: Plon, 1974).
9. See Castan on the murder of the eldest son by a younger son: "Pères et fils en Languedoc à l'époque classique," *La Revue du dix-septième siècle,* nos. 102–103 (1974).
10. Charles Maurice de Talleyrand, *Mémoires,* Note 1, Part One, chapter 1 (Paris: Plon, 1957).
11. Linnaeus, *La Nourrice marâtre* (1770), p. 228.
12. Verdier-Heurtin, *Discours sur l'allaitement,* p. 25.
13. Cited in Roger Mercier, *L'Enfant dans la société au XVIIIe siècle (avant "Emile")* (University of Dakar, Senegal, 1961), p. 55.
14. Louis Joubert. Cited in *Entrer dans la vie,* p. 160.
15. Toussaint, *Les Moeurs* (1748).
16. Mme. Le Prince de Baumont, *Avis aux parents et aux maîtres sur l'éducation des enfants* (1750), p. 77.
17. Alexandre Vandermonde, *Essai sur la manière de perfectionner l'espèce humaine* (1750).
18. François Lebrun, "Vingt-cinq ans d'études démographiques sur la France d'Ancien Régime: Bilans et perspectives," *Historiens et géographes,* October 1976, p. 79.

19. Jacques Dupaquier, "Caractères originaux de l'histoire démographique française au 18e siècle," *Revue d'histoire moderne et contemporaine*, April–June 1976.
20. Bardet, "Enfants abandonnés et enfants assistés à Rouen," p. 28–29.
21. Pierre Wiel, "Tamerville," *Annales de démographie historique*, 1969.
22. Galliano, "Mortalité infantile dans la banlieue sud de Paris," pp. 150–51.
23. Garden, *Lyon et les Lyonnais au XVIIIe siècle*.
24. Gilibert, *Dissertation*, p. 326.
25. Bideau, *L'Envoi des jeunes enfants en nourrice*, p. 54.
26. Chamoux, "L'Enfance abandonnée à Reims à la fin du XVIIIe siècle," p. 277.
27. Lebrun, "Vingt-cinq ans d'études démographiques," pp. 154–55.
28. Chamoux, "L'Enfance abandonnée à Reims à la fin du XVIIIe siècle," p. 156.
29. Lebrun, "Vingt-cinq ans d'études démographiques," p. 156.
30. Bardet, "Enfants abandonnés et enfants assistés à Rouen," p. 27; Tenon, *Mémoire sur les hôpitaux de Paris*, p. 280.
31. Prost de Royer, *Mémoire*, p. 21.
32. Rousseau, *Les Confessions*, volume 1, Book VIII, pp. 357–58.

QUESTIONS

1. How does Badinter structure her argument? Does the *way* that it is arranged make her argument more or less forceful? More or less persuasive?

2. Is the evidence of the social historian wider or more limited in scope than that of the laboratory experimentalist? Cite examples from the selection and explain why they would not be helpful to laboratory experimentalists.

3. One could argue that in constructing mother surrogates, providing careful diet, and introducing unusual stimuli, experimentalists create *artificial* conditions that slant their data. Is the social historian observing a natural or an artificial (i.e. man-made) environment? List some of the sources from which Badinter derives her evidence. Does the nature of her sources suggest any bias?

4. The social historian of necessity depends upon records, literary works, diaries, and letters to determine dominant attitudes in a particular culture at a particular time. What are the limits of historical veracity in such documents? Consider the attitudes toward children or childrearing illustrated by the following:

   a. the TV show *Happy Days*
   b. the TV show *Dallas*
   c. child-abuse statistics provided by the Bureau of Child Welfare
   d. teenage runaway statistics
   e. teenage runaway pregnancy statistics
   f. abortion statistics

g. Joan Crawford's adopted daughter's book *Mommie Dearest*

h. depictions of parents and children in toothpaste commercials, McDonald's commercials, Skippy peanut butter commercials, and detergent commercials

How do these sources confirm or contradict your experiences and attitudes? Which ones most closely resemble what you consider to be the predominant attitudes in America?

5. Badinter says that the evidence she offers disproves an earlier-held theory that parental indifference to children in the seventeenth century was "emotional armor against the great risks of seeing the object of their affections die." *Does* her evidence force us to conclude that this explanation is wrong? What would Badinter have to show about the relation of maternal abandonment of infants to infant mortality to refute the "emotional armor" explanation?

6. Badinter suggests that economic realities prevented the working classes from loving their children while social standards and customs interfered with the love of upper-class persons toward their children. In addition she claims of middle-class women:

> Women of the petty bourgeoisie (shopkeepers), wives of merchants or of local judges, were hardly subject to the values espoused by high society but strove nevertheless to copy their more favored sisters.

Why should we consider Badinter's claim valid? Could we question her assumptions? Consider the following:

a. How widespread do you think literacy was among seventeenth-century shopkeepers? Why would such a statement assume wide literacy?

b. How widely known do you think the values of "high society" were to shopkeepers before the invention of mass media of communication?

c. Do you think that the sources upon which a social historian draws to find out what merchants or shopkeepers felt or thought are likely to be reliably accurate accounts? For comparison, how reliable an image of policemen does *Kojak* give? How reliable is the image of a doctor derived from *General Hospital*?

7. If we were to accept all of Badinter's evidence as completely reliable, would it be possible for us to come to a conclusion different from hers, or are we bound to accept hers as the only logical conclusion that can be drawn from this particular evidence?

EXERCISES

1. Imagine that Elisabeth Badinter has written her essay as an answer to the question: What was the seventeenth- or eighteenth-century attitude of parents toward children?

    a. Extract the essence of her argument: hypothesis → evidence → conclusion.
    b. Make a detailed outline of it. Show exactly what evidence fits under which parts of her hypothesis. Indicate by the arrangement of the steps in your outline what her line of logic is and how it reaches her conclusion.

2. Try to imagine how an experimentalist might deal with Badinter's hypothesis. For instance, if you were Harlow, how would you try to find out whether mothers love infants? Consider:

    To what experimental conditions would you subject the mothers?

    Would you separate them from the infants?

    Would you inflict punishment in the presence of the infant or infant surrogate and stop it when the infant is withdrawn?

    What behavior would you be looking for?

    Could you morally excuse such an experiment using human beings?

3. Choose *one* major mass medium—newspaper, television, film, popular magazine, novel—and collect data for two weeks to support one of these two hypotheses:

    Mother love is *not* a value in America in 1985.

    Mother love *is* a value in America in 1985.

    Make notes about your observations in your journal and be sure to list the source of each notation. Then write a draft of a textbook section on the subject *as if* you were a historian in the twenty-second century.

CHAPTER THREE

MEAD: SEX AND TEMPERAMENT

Anthropology

Anthropology, as its name implies, is the study of humankind. Often anthropologists will investigate cultures that have not been influenced by modern technological values and attitudes. Studying "primitive" societies can help us discover the fundamentals of the human species. Even when a study or group of studies focuses on one culture or society, the anthropologist is seeking information about humans in all times and places.

There are three basic ways in which anthropology attempts to do this. First, it gathers and compiles information about as many cultures as possible and thereby adds to a composite picture of all the people in the world at this time. Second, it collects information about universal human activities rather than particular processes or products. Third, it does cross-cultural study and indexing; it compares the patterns of *x* culture with the patterns of *y* to discover what it can about pattern making in humankind.

Margaret Mead was a great anthropologist, one of the two or three seminal thinkers who were the makers of the discipline. She was among the first to recognize that an anthropologist must be extremely careful in studying cultures very different from her own to keep from ascribing the values, prejudices, and judgments of her own culture to the people being observed. Unlike many of the anthropologists who came before her, Mead did not usually restrict her fieldwork to the study of one culture. She always attempted to make the studies cross-cultural. While earlier anthropologists might have said, "Tchambuli men are not manly," measuring the Tchambuli culture against their own culture's definition of "manliness," Mead would say,

"Tchambuli, Arapesh, and Mundugumor people define humanness, maleness, and femaleness in different ways." Mead's approach was comparative because, in her judgment, comparison helps observers avoid ethnocentrism and subjective bias.

In reading the chapter from Margaret Mead's *Sex and Temperament in Three Primitive Societies*, note her use of the method of anthropology. Her study is based upon close observation of several cultures acting as they normally do. From these observations she makes generalizations true of one group, and by comparison, generalizations true of all people. Try to compare Mead's method and approach to Badinter's. Does Badinter make the same assumptions about sex-linking of temperaments that Mead does? Does Badinter, writing almost fifty years later than Mead's original study, show the influence Mead had on social scientists who came after her?

GLOSSARY

personality type [1]	accidents [7]
temperamental [1]	congruent [8]
sex-linked [1]	inverted pride [9]
dominance [1]	deprecated [10]
social conditioning [2]	plebeian class [10]
malleable [2]	teleological [11]
germ-plasm [3]	inalienable [13]
diversities [4]	social selection [13]
homogeneous [5]	pariah [14]
deviants [5]	heterogeneity [16]

THE STANDARDIZATION
———— OF SEX-TEMPERAMENT ————
Margaret Mead

We have now considered in detail the approved personalities of each [1] sex among three primitive peoples. We found the Arapesh—both men and women—displaying a personality that, out of our historically limited preoccupations, we would call maternal in its parental aspects, and feminine in its sexual aspects. We found men, as well as women, trained to be co-operative, unaggressive, responsive to the needs and demands of others. We found no idea that sex was a powerful driving force either for men or for women. In marked contrast to these attitudes, we found among the Mundugumor that both men and women developed as ruthless, aggressive, positively sexed individuals, with the maternal cherishing aspects of personality at a minimum. Both men and women approximated to a personality type that we in our culture would find only in an undisciplined and very violent male. Neither the Arapesh nor the Mundugumor profit by a contrast between the sexes; the Arapesh ideal is the mild, responsive man married to the mild, responsive woman; the Mundugumor ideal is the violent aggressive man married to the violent aggressive woman. In the third tribe, the Tchambuli, we found a genuine reversal of the sex-attitudes of our own culture, with the woman the dominant, impersonal, managing partner, the man the less responsible and the emotionally dependent person. These three situations suggest, then, a very definite conclusion. If those temperamental attitudes which we have traditionally regarded as feminine—such as passivity, responsiveness, and a willingness to cherish children—can so easily be set up as the masculine pattern in one tribe, and in another be outlawed for the majority of women as well as for the majority of men, we no longer have any basis for regarding such aspects of behaviour as sex-linked. And this conclusion becomes even stronger when we consider the actual reversal in Tchambuli of the position of dominance of the two sexes, in spite of the existence of formal patrilineal institutions.

The material suggests that we may say that many, if not all, of the [2] personality traits which we have called masculine or feminine are as lightly linked to sex as are the clothing, the manners, and the form of head-dress that a society at a given period assigns to either sex.

SOURCE: Abridgment of pages 279–289, 295–309 from SEX AND TEMPERAMENT IN THREE PRIMITIVE SOCIETIES by Margaret Mead. Copyright 1935, 1950 by Margaret Mead. By permission of William Morrow & Company, Inc.

When we consider the behavior of the typical Arapesh man or woman as contrasted with the behavior of the typical Mundugumor man or woman, the evidence is overwhelmingly in favour of the strength of social conditioning. In no other way can we account for the almost complete uniformity with which Arapesh children develop into contented, passive, secure persons, while Mundugumor children develop as characteristically into violent, aggressive, insecure persons. Only to the impact of the whole of the integrated culture upon the growing child can we lay the formation of the contrasting types. There is no other explanation of race, or diet, or selection that can be adduced to explain them. We are forced to conclude that human nature is almost unbelievably malleable, responding accurately and contrastingly to contrasting cultural conditions. The differences between individuals who are members of different cultures, like the differences between individuals within a culture, are almost entirely to be laid to differences in conditioning, especially during early childhood, and the form of this conditioning is culturally determined. Standardized personality differences between the sexes are of this order, cultural creations to which each generation, male and female, is trained to conform. There remains, however, the problem of the origin of these socially standardized differences.

[3]   While the basic importance of social conditioning is still imperfectly recognized—not only in lay thought, but even by the scientist specifically concerned with such matters—to go beyond it and consider the possible influence of variations in hereditary equipment is a hazardous matter. The following pages will read very differently to one who has made a part of his thinking a recognition of the whole amazing mechanism of cultural conditioning—who has really accepted the fact that the same infant could be developed into a full participant in any one of these three cultures—than they will read to one who still believes that the minutiae of cultural behavior are carried in the individual germ-plasm. If it is said, therefore, that when we have grasped the full significance of the malleability of the human organism and the preponderant importance of cultural conditioning, there are still further problems to solve, it must be remembered that these problems come *after* such a comprehension of the force of conditioning; they cannot precede it. The forces that make children born among the Arapesh grow up into typical Arapesh personalities are entirely social, and any discussion of the variations which do occur must be looked at against this social background.

[4]   With this warning firmly in mind, we can ask a further question. Granting the malleability of human nature, whence arise the differences between the standardized personalities that different cultures decree for all of their members, or which one culture decrees for the members

of one sex as contrasted with the members of the opposite sex? If such differences are culturally created, as this material would most strongly suggest that they are, if the new-born child can be shaped with equal ease into an unaggressive Arapesh or an aggressive Mundugumor, why do these striking contrasts occur at all? If the clues to the different personalities decreed for men and women in Tchambuli do not lie in the physical constitution of the two sexes —an assumption that we must reject both for the Tchambuli and for our own society— where can we find the clues upon which the Tchambuli, the Arapesh, the Mundugumor, have built? Cultures are man-made, they are built of human materials; they are diverse but comparable structures within which human beings can attain full human stature. Upon what have they built their <u>diversities</u>?

We recognize that a homogeneous culture committed in all of its [5] gravest institutions and slightest usages to a co-operative, unaggressive course can bend every child to that emphasis, some to a perfect accord with it, the majority to an easy acceptance, while only a few <u>deviants</u> fail to receive the cultural imprint. To consider such traits as aggressiveness or passivity to be sex-linked is not possible in the light of the facts. Have such traits, then, as aggressiveness or passivity, pride or humility, objectivity or a preoccupation with personal relationships, an easy response to the needs of the young and the weak or a hostility to the young and the weak, a tendency to initiate sex-relations or merely to respond to the dictates of a situation or another person's advances —have these traits any basis in temperament at all? Are they potentialities of all human temperaments that can be developed by different kinds of social conditioning and which will not appear if the necessary conditioning is absent?

When we ask this question we shift our emphasis. If we ask why [6] an Arapesh man or an Arapesh woman shows the kind of personality that we have considered in the first section of this book, the answer is: Because of the Arapesh culture, because of the intricate, elaborate, and unfailing fashion in which a culture is able to shape each new-born child to the cultural image. And if we ask the same question about a Mundugumor man or woman, or about a Tchambuli man as compared with a Tchambuli woman, the answer is of the same kind. They display the personalities that are peculiar to the cultures in which they were born and educated. Our attention has been on the differences between Arapesh men and women as a group and Mundugumor men and women as a group. It is as if we had represented the Arapesh personality by a soft yellow, the Mundugumor by a deep red, while the Tchambuli female personality was deep orange, and that of the Tchambuli male, pale green. But if we now ask whence came the original direction in each culture, so that one now shows yellow, another red, the third orange and green by sex, then we must peer more closely. And leaning closer to the picture, it is as if behind the bright consistent yellow of the Arapesh, and the deep equally consistent red of the Mundugumor, behind the orange and green that are Tchambuli, we found in each case the delicate, just discernible outlines of the whole spectrum, differently overlaid in each case by the monotone which covers it. This spectrum is the range of individual differences which lie back of the so much more conspicuous cultural emphases, and it is to this that we must turn to find the explanation of cultural inspiration, of the source from which each culture has drawn.

[7]   There appears to be about the same range of basic temperamental variation among the Arapesh and among the Mundugumor, although the violent man is a misfit in the first society and a leader in the second. If human nature were completely homogeneous raw material, lacking specific drives and characterized by no important constitutional differences between individuals, then individuals who display personality traits so antithetical to the social pressure should not reappear in societies of such differing emphases. If the variations between individuals were to be set down to accidents in the genetic process, the same accidents should not be repeated with similar frequency in strikingly different cultures, with strongly contrasting methods of education.

[8]   But because this same relative distribution of individual differences does appear in culture after culture, in spite of the divergence between the cultures, it seems pertinent to offer a hypothesis to explain upon what basis the personalities of men and women have been differently standardized so often in the history of the human race. This hypothesis is an extension of that advanced by Ruth Benedict in her *Patterns of Culture*. Let us assume that there are definite temperamental differences between human beings which if not entirely hereditary at least are established on a hereditary base very soon after birth. (Further than this we cannot at present narrow the matter.) These differences finally embodied in the character structure of adults, then, are the clues from which culture works, selecting one temperament, or a combination of related and congruent types, as desirable, and embodying this choice in every thread of the social fabric—in the care of the young child, the games the children play, the songs the people sing, the structure of political organization, the religious observance, the art and the philosophy.

[9]   Some primitive societies have had the time and the robustness to revamp all of their institutions to fit one extreme type, and to develop educational techniques which will ensure that the majority of each generation will show a personality congruent with this extreme emphasis. Other societies have pursued a less definitive course, selecting

their models not from the most extreme, most highly differentiated individuals, but from the less marked types. In such societies the approved personality is less pronounced, and the culture often contains the types of inconsistencies that many human beings display also; one institution may be adjusted to the uses of pride, another to a casual humility that is congruent neither with pride nor with inverted pride. Such societies, which have taken the more usual and less sharply defined types as models, often show also a less definitely patterned social structure. The culture of such societies may be likened to a house the decoration of which has been informed by no definite and precise taste, no exclusive emphasis upon dignity or comfort or pretentiousness or beauty, but in which a little of each effect has been included.

Alternatively, a culture may take its clues not from one temperament, but from several temperaments. But instead of mixing together into an inconsistent hotchpotch the choices and emphases of different temperaments, or blending them together into a smooth but not particularly distinguished whole, it may isolate each type by making it the basis for the approved social personality for an age-group, a sex-group, a caste-group, or an occupational group. In this way society becomes not a monotone with a few discrepant patches of an intrusive color, but a mosaic, with different groups displaying different personality traits. Such specializations as these may be based upon any facet of human endowment—different intellectual abilities, different artistic abilities, different emotional traits. So the Samoans decree that all young people must show the personality trait of unaggressiveness and punish with opprobrium the aggressive child who displays traits regarded as appropriate only in titled middle-aged men. In societies based upon elaborate ideas of rank, members of the aristocracy will be permitted, even compelled, to display a pride, a sensitivity to insult, that would be deprecated as inappropriate in members of the plebeian class. So also in professional groups or in religious sects some temperamental traits are selected and institutionalized, and taught to each new member who enters the profession or sect. Thus the physician learns the bed-side manner, which is the natural behavior of some temperaments and the standard behavior of the general practitioner in the medical profession; the Quaker learns at least the outward behavior and the rudiments of meditation, the capacity for which is not necessarily an innate characteristic of many of the members of the Society of Friends. [10]

So it is with the social personalities of the two sexes. The traits that occur in some members of each sex are specially assigned to one sex, and disallowed in the other. The history of the social definition of sex-differences is filled with such arbitrary arrangements in the in- [11]

tellectual and artistic field, but because of the assumed congruence between physiological sex and emotional endowment we have been less able to recognize that a similar arbitrary selection is being made among emotional traits also. We have assumed that because it is convenient for a mother to wish to care for her child, this is a trait with which women have been more generously endowed by a carefully teleological process of evolution. We have assumed that because men have hunted, an activity requiring enterprise, bravery, and initiative, they have been endowed with these useful attitudes as part of their sex-temperament.

[12]   Societies have made these assumptions both overtly and implicitly. If a society insists that warfare is the major occupation for the male sex, it is therefore insisting that all male children display bravery and pugnacity. Even if the insistence upon the differential bravery of men and women is not made articulate, the difference in occupation makes this point implicitly. When, however, a society goes further and defines men as brave and women as timorous, when men are forbidden to show fear and women are indulged in the most flagrant display of fear, a more explicit element enters in. Bravery, hatred of any weakness, of flinching before pain or danger—this attitude which is so strong a component of *some human* temperaments has been selected as the key to masculine behavior. The easy unashamed display of fear or suffering that is congenial to a different temperament has been made the key to feminine behavior.

[13]   Originally two variations of human temperament, a hatred of fear or willingness to display fear, they have been socially translated into inalienable aspects of the personalities of the two sexes. And to that defined sex-personality every child will be educated, if a boy, to suppress fear, if a girl, to show it. If there has been no social selection in regard to this trait, the proud temperament that is repelled by any betrayal of feeling will display itself, regardless of sex, by keeping a stiff upper lip. Without an express prohibition of such behavior the expressive unashamed man or woman will weep, or comment upon fear or suffering. Such attitudes, strongly marked in certain temperaments, may by social selection be standardized for everyone, or outlawed for everyone, or ignored by society, or made the exclusive and approved behaviour of one sex only.

[14]   Neither the Arapesh nor the Mundugumor have made any attitude specific for one sex. All of the energies of the culture have gone towards the creation of a single human type, regardless of class, age, or sex. There is no division into age-classes for which different motives or different moral attitudes are regarded as suitable. There is no class of seers or mediums who stand apart drawing inspiration from psychological sources not available to the majority of the people. The

Mundugumor have, it is true, made one arbitrary selection, in that they recognize artistic ability only among individuals born with the cord about their necks, and firmly deny the happy exercise of artistic ability to those less unusually born. The Arapesh boy with a tinea infection has been socially selected to be a disgruntled, antisocial individual, and the society forces upon sunny co-operative children cursed with this affliction a final approximation to the behavior appropriate to a pariah. With these two exceptions no emotional role is forced upon an individual because of birth or accident. As there is no idea of rank which declares that some are of high estate and some of low, so there is no idea of sex-difference which declares that one sex must feel differently from the other. One possible imaginative social construct, the attribution of different personalities to different members of the community classified into sex-, age-, or caste-groups, is lacking.

When we turn however to the Tchambuli, we find a situation that [15] while bizarre in one respect, seems nevertheless more intelligible in another. The Tchambuli have at least made the point of sex-difference; they have used the obvious fact of sex as an organizing point for the formation of social personality, even though they seem to us to have reversed the normal picture. While there is reason to believe that not every Tchambuli woman is born with a dominating, organizing, administrative temperament, actively sexed and willing to initiate sex-relations, possessive, definite, robust, practical and impersonal in outlook, still most Tchambuli girls grow up to display these traits. And while there is definite evidence to show that all Tchambuli men are not, by native endowment, the delicate responsive actors of a play staged for the women's benefit, still most Tchambuli boys manifest this coquettish play-acting personality most of the time. Because the Tchambuli formulation of sex-attitudes contradicts our usual premises, we can see clearly that Tchambuli culture has arbitrarily permitted certain human traits to women, and allotted others, equally arbitrarily, to men.

If we then accept this evidence drawn from these simple societies [16] which through centuries of isolation from the main stream of human history have been able to develop more extreme, more striking cultures than is possible under historical conditions of great intercommunication between peoples and the resulting heterogeneity, what are the implications of these results? What conclusions can we draw from a study of the way in which a culture can select a few traits from the wide gamut of human endowment and specialize these traits, either for one sex or for the entire community? What relevance have these results to social thinking? Before we consider this question it will be necessary to discuss in more detail the position of the deviant, the

individual whose innate disposition is too alien to the social personality
required by his culture for his age, or sex, or caste ever to wear perfectly the garment of personality that his society has fashioned for
him.

QUESTIONS

1. Margaret Mead assumes that "there are definite temperamental
   differences between human beings which if not entirely hereditary
   are at least established on a hereditary base very soon after birth."
   How does she think that cultural types develop—for example, the
   "gentle, passive" Arapesh, the "aggressive, hostile" Mundugumor,
   the sex-differentiated Tchambuli? What forces direct the formation
   of a cultural type?
2. Mead says that in societies that have an elaborate sense of social
   rank, different temperamental character traits are allowed or prohibited by class. She says that in other cultures certain temperaments
   are conditioned by religion or occupation. Do you think that present
   American society prohibits or allows certain temperaments by class?
   Are there traits that are encouraged in the rich but discouraged or
   punished in the poor? Is the President of the United States expected
   to have some character traits and not to have others? Would most
   voters think gentleness and passivity good traits for a President
   to have? Or would most people think that Gandhi, the father of
   passive resistance, was a good or bad leader for the Indian people?
   Make a list of traits that are appropriate to the rich or socially
   powerful and inappropriate to the poor, and vice versa.
3. Mead says that one's occupation contributes to the development
   of one's temperament. Which do you think comes first, the temperament or the occupation? Do people who are temperamentally
   suited to helping the sick go into nursing, or do nurses develop
   temperaments appropriate to helping the sick? Can you design a
   method for testing which came first?
4. Are Mead's observations valid? What criteria or standards are you
   using to determine the validity of her claims? Do they support her
   thesis? Could we use the same observations to come to conclusions
   different from hers?
5. Mead differentiates between evolution and social selection. Can
   you define these concepts? Is there a significant difference between
   traits acquired by "natural selection" (i.e., the persistent traits that
   ensure the survival of the species) and traits determined by social

selection (i.e., traits particular to specific cultures and peoples)? Is the welfare of society the same as, different from, or a refinement upon the survival of the species?

6. Examine Badinter's observations in the light of Margaret Mead's. Can you think of any reasons why a society should encourage parental indifference at one time in its history and careful maternal care at another time? Try to describe how environmental, economic, and political forces might influence the development of cultural values.

EXERCISES

1. Choose a partner who is a member of a very different ethnic or regional background from your own but a person of the same sex as yours (if you are white, choose someone black; if you are a New Yorker, choose someone from rural Georgia or Ohio, etc.). With your partner, make a 25-item, true-or-false questionnaire that explores a person's attitudes toward the relation of sex to temperament. Do not make your questions either too obvious or too complicated. The following items are the kind you might include:

   Women are afraid of mice.
   Most men like football.
   Real men don't eat quiche.
   A girl's best friend is her hairdresser.

   Send ten copies of the questionnaire to your partner's family, requesting that each family member answer the questions. Make sure to obtain each person's age and sex. Analyze your results in the style of Margaret Mead and write a two-page report of your findings titled "Attitudes Toward Sex and Temperament in . . ."

2. Carefully examine four concurrent issues of the following publications: (1) *Family Circle*, (2) *The National Enquirer*, (3) *Playboy*, and (4) *The New Yorker*. Look at everything: articles, advertisements, stories, cartoons. First, try to guess the sex, age group, and probable socioeconomic class of their readership. Consider the subjects written about in the magazine. Also, examine advertisements to determine what is being sold and to whom. Second, determine what assumptions each magazine makes about the temperaments and traits of the ideal man and of the ideal woman. Then be an anthropologist: try to determine cultural attitudes toward the relation of sex to temperament by class and age. Write an exam question on one

aspect of your study and answer it. For example: (1) What is the middle-class American woman's fantasy of the ideal man? or (2) Is there a relation between level of education and conceptions about "female personality" among American men? (You can assume differences in levels of education on the basis of style of the magazine; e.g., *The National Enquirer* is aimed at readers with a sixth-grade education while *The New Yorker* is directed to college-educated readers.)

_____ CHAPTER FOUR _____

MEDAWAR AND MEDAWAR:
BIOGENESIS AND EVOLUTION

Biology

We have so far considered love and sexuality as the processes by which individuals are related to one another—infant to mother, parent to child—and to their societies and cultures. By taking still another approach we can think of sexuality as the process which links us to the ever-flowing stream of life. The study of life in all its varieties is the task of the biologist.

Biologists may have a very wide focus on sexuality as the Medawars do here, or they may concentrate upon biogenesis and biological evolution and thus study the smallest units within the process, as a molecular geneticist does. Peter Medawar, who won a Nobel prize in 1974 for his work in tissue transplants, and his wife, Jane, are zoologists. A zoologist is a biologist who focuses attention upon animal life, as opposed to a botanist, who focuses upon plant life. In this chapter, from their book *The Life Science: Current Ideas of Biology*, the Medawars look at biosystematics, the method of classification biologists use to express the relationships among creatures within the broad categories to which we assign them: i.e. phylum, class, genus, etc. Such classification is essential for the systematic study of the plant and animal kingdoms.

Glossary

lineage [1]	crustaceans [4]
spontaneous generation [1]	ganglion [4]
bacteria [1]	dorsal [4]
antiseptic [1]	ventral [4]
synthetic [2]	parasitic [5]
diversification [3]	viscera [5]
pedagogic [3]	binomial nomenclature [8]
geodesy [3]	entomologists [11]
cosmology [3]	turgor [14]
taxonomic [4]	

—— BIOGENESIS AND EVOLUTION ——
P. B. Medawar and J. S. Medawar

[1]   No principle of biology is more firmly established or less likely to be qualified than that of "biogenesis," which avows that all living things are descended from living things. Behind each living organism today there is an unbroken lineage of descent going back to the beginnings of biological time. In its negative form the principle would state that there is no such thing as "spontaneous generation"—e.g. the spontaneous generation of bacteria from putrefying organic matter or of protozoa from infusions of hay. Louis Pasteur, the greatest of all experimental biologists, is rightly credited with having carried out the experiments that falsified the notion of a spontaneous generation of bacteria and at the same time made an alternative hypothesis much

SOURCE: Pages 22–28 from THE LIFE SCIENCE: *Current Ideas of Biology* by P. B. Medawar and J. S. Medawar. Copyright © 1977 by Peter and Jean Medawar. Reprinted by permission of Harper & Row, Publishers, Inc.

more attractive, viz. that the bacteria which so readily proliferate in warm organic broths etc. derive from airborne organisms. This discovery of which the medical significance was clearly perceived by Joseph Lister, lies at the root of all antiseptic and aseptic techniques in surgery today.

The principle of biogenesis applies not only to whole organisms [2] but also to some of their constituent parts: among cellular organelles the *mitochondria* are biogenetic in origin in the sense that they do not arise *de novo* by some synthetic process in the cell but are derived from pre-existing mitochondria only. Biogenesis does not imply evolution, but an evolutionary relationship does of course imply biogenesis. Normal biogenesis is often given the extra connotation of "homogenesis," i.e. of like begetting like. Broadly speaking this particularization is true, although the theory of evolution obliges us to qualify it in detail. Thus the offspring of mice are mice and of men are men. No genuinely extravagant heterogenesis ever occurs, although in the days before empirical truthfulness was thought to be either a necessary or a desirable characteristic of professedly factual statements, all kinds of strange notions were rife—the most famous being the myth that geese might be born of such organisms as the attractive barnacle-like crustacean the goose barnacle, *Lepas anatifera*. Such notions belong to "poetism," a style of thinking which arouses as much indignation among scientists as the more idiotic extravagances of computerized literary criticism arouse in lovers of literature.

Evolution and biosystematics. Samuel Taylor Coleridge once declared [3] that zoology was in danger of falling asunder—the consequence of its huge mass of uncoordinated factual information. The evolutionary hypothesis* is that which brings an order and connectedness to what Coleridge saw as the great toppling heap of information that made up the zoology of his day. It can be regarded as an amendment to the biogenetic principle that like begets like (see above). The hypothesis states that the existing diversity of life-forms has arisen by progressive diversification during the course of biogenesis. It remains generally true to say that the offspring of mice are mice and of men are men, yet variants arise from time to time that may be recognized retrospectively as the beginnings of new specific forms. It is to the origin of these variants and the processes which keep them in being that we owe all the existing forms of life at present on the earth. Pedagogic "proofs" of the past occurrence of evolution are of the same kind and unfortunately the same intellectual stature as those "proofs" of the

---

* The word "hypothesis" in this context is used in its correct and technical sense: it is a vulgarism to suppose that the word has a pejorative flavor and that in describing as a hypothesis what is usually called the "theory" of evolution we are in some way depreciating it.

roundness of the earth which we learnt in our earliest schooldays. It is not upon these so-called "proofs," however, that the acceptance of such a hypothesis depends. It is rather that the hypothesis of evolution pervades, underlies and makes sense of the whole of biological science in much the same way as the idea of the roundness of the earth permeates the whole of geodesy, chronology, navigation and cosmology. The evolutionary hypothesis is part of the very fabric of the way we think in biology. Only the hypothesis of evolution makes sense of the obvious inter-relationships between organisms, the phenomena of heredity and the patterns of development. For a biologist the alternative to thinking in evolutionary terms is not to think at all. Mechanisms of evolution are dealt with later.

[4]   The purpose of *biosystematics* is to name animals and to arrange their names in some order and pattern that will feel right even to biologists with rather coarse *taxonomic* sensibilities. Living things are classified in the first instance into "kingdoms"—plant and animal—and, less monarchically, into "phyla."* The members of a phylum are united by a similarity of ground plan without regard to detailed differences of structure. A good example of a phylum is the *Arthropoda*, which includes crustaceans and insects, which resemble each other by having segmented bodies, an "external skeleton" and multiply jointed limbs. Another fundamental similarity of structure is a nervous system that runs down the mid-ventral line of the body, with a ganglion in each segment that gives off branches towards the limbs. In addition, the blood vascular system is of the kind described as "open" because the blood, which has only a minor respiratory function, does not run in anatomically well-defined channels such as arteries or veins but rather percolates through the tissues of the body until it returns to a heart which occupies a dorsal position, in contrast to its ventral position in vertebrate animals.

[5]   Invertebrates† tend to group themselves, on the one hand, into phyla such as the Arthropoda, the worms rightly so-called (*Annelida*, including the earthworm, whose busy beneficence and modest unobtrusiveness are an example to us all) and the worms wrongly so-called, that is to say the roundworms, eelworms (*Nematodes*) and flatworms, many of which are parasitic. On the other hand, in total contrast to arthropods, several invertebrate groups are related to the chordates,*† including the vertebrates and therefore ourselves, by certain characteristics of very early development and by the possession

---

* The broadest distinction of all is between organisms of which the genome is (*eukaryotes*) or is not (*prokaryotes*) organized in the form of compact chromosomes.

† "Invertebrate" is a description, not a taxonomic term.

*† Chordates have characteristically a *dorsal* nervous system underlain by a simple undivided elastic skeletal rod: the *notochord*. The heart is ventral.

of a roomy and often tripartite body cavity, the so-called "coelom" which lies between the connective tissue of the outer body wall and the connective tissue which surrounds and supports the viscera. Groups belonging to this chordate line of descent—amongst which, however unlikely it may appear, we must expect to find the modern representatives of our own remotest ancestors—are echinoderms, including sea urchins, starfish and sea cucumbers, phoronids, sea-arrows and the large group known as sea-squirts, whose chordate affinities are so obvious to professional zoologists that they are classified as chordates anyway. Thus in the invertebrates generally one can identify two main streams of evolution and two great classes of affinity: that associated with annelids and arthropods on the one hand and with chordates and vertebrates on the other.

The taxonomic stature of phyla and classes has already been mentioned. Next in order after classes of animals come orders, families, genera, species and individuals; each major grouping can of course be further sub-divided into a group of subordinate status, e.g. a sub-phylum or sub-class or sub-species, but these need not concern us. [6]

Fish, amphibians, reptiles, birds and mammals are examples of *classes* among vertebrates and insects, crustaceans and arachnids (spiders) are examples among arthropods. [7]

Orders are meant to be of the same taxonomic stature or weight throughout the animal kingdom. Members of the same order obviously have a closer affinity to each other than that which is implied by their common membership of a class. Unfortunately, it is not possible to define this degree of affinity in a way that could be valid throughout the entire animal kingdom. Like many other decisions that depend mainly upon individual judgment, a taxonomic allocation is rather a matter of experience and "feel" than anything that can be arrived at by consulting a rule book. Taxonomic disputes are usually conflicts of personal judgment and therefore often virulent and unforgiving. The stature of the category known as orders can be appreciated by reflecting that among birds, ducks and geese and swans form one order, *anseriformes*, turkeys and chickens a second, *galliformes*, and owls, *strigiformes*, a third; in the class of mammals, whales and dolphins form one order; beavers, chipmunks, squirrels, rats and mice a second; monkeys, apes, human beings, chimps and gorillas—all primates— a third. Within orders we recognize as *genera* animals that are very obviously "of a kind," as the great cats are clearly of a kind. Lions, tigers, leopards, jaguars and panthers make up a genus. Using the nomenclature of the Zoological Society of London, *Panthera leo* is lion, *Panthera tigris* tiger, *Panthera pardus* leopard and *Panthera panthera* the panther commonly so called. These examples also illustrate the binomial nomenclature introduced by Linnaeus: the species is designated by [8] a generic name—in these examples *Panthera*—followed by a second term which serves to differentiate, e.g. lion from tiger. It is a fully established convention of biology that species are referred to by both a generic and a specific term. The specific term is never used alone in a biological context. Tigers make up the species *Panthera tigris* and not the species *tigris*. Anyone who refers to "the *amoeba*" forfeits all hope of being mistaken for a professional zoologist.

[9]   A species is a community of actually or potentially interbreeding organisms, which either for genetic or for geographic or behavioural reasons have achieved a sufficient degree of reproductive isolation to enjoy the possession of a distinctive make-up and frequency of genes. This population-genetical definition of a species has many practical drawbacks in spite of its theoretical attractions. If the characteristic of a species is the possession of gene X by fifty-five per cent of its members and of gene Y by ninety per cent, the idea of an *individual*'s belonging to a species becomes a bit vague except in a probabilistic sense, for only populations can really be or not be members of species.

[10]   A hard-working muscum taxonomist can be driven out of his mind by the assurance that the problem of species definition has now been solved: a species is essentially a cluster of points in *n*-dimensional character-space.

[11]   *Insects.* Although insects are the great success story of evolution, Darwin complained that entomologists, the people who study them, were the very last to be won over to his conception of the evolutionary process.

[12]   Insects are probably the most numerous and certainly the most various of all many-celled animals. The only possible contestant on grounds of number must be the minute crustacean *Calanus*—a principal constituent of the *Plankton* of the surface waters of the oceans throughout the world. Insects owe their success as a group to their high reproductive rate and genetic variance, which have made it possible for them to exploit almost every environment capable of supporting life except the sea, in which other animals of the same ground plan (i.e. arthropods), mainly the crustaceans, enjoy insect-like diversity and numerical preponderance. Perhaps, then, it is the arthropodan ground plan that has been so successful.

[13]   Insects . . . have an "open" blood vascular system, and like crustacea have the hard outer casing—an "exoskeleton"—that goes naturally with it; without this hard outer casing the contraction of the heart would simply cause a bulge on the surface instead of a propulsion of fluid.

[14]   The fact that an open blood system creates little in the way of turgor pressure accounts for the characteristic floppiness and shapelessness of the internal organs of insects and crustaceans—which

contrasts so sharply with the firm roundness of the internal organs of vertebrates.

The possession of an exoskeleton has other important implications [15] for insects and arthropods generally. In vertebrates, closed bony boxes like the cranium can grow only by the deposition of bone on the outside accompanied by its removal from the inside. In arthropods no such process is possible, so bodily growth must be accompanied by periodic shedding—moulting—of their hard outer casing.

Many insects go through larval forms that occupy an important [16] fraction of their total life cycle. These larvae, e.g. the caterpillars of butterflies and moths, undergo a profound internal reorganization (pupation) during their reshaping into the adult.

In some insects the larval stage is the greater part of the life cycle, [17] and the ephemeral adult into which they transform, e.g. the mayfly, which does not feed, is hardly more than an airborne reproductive organ.

It is generally taken that insects evolved from organisms akin to [18] annelids, and that the present-day insects most faithfully representative of the evolutionary prototype are those possessing the most "generalized" structure: the *orthoptera*, which include cockroaches and grasshoppers, answer this description well. In the heyday of evolutionary biology there was thought to be an obligation upon entomologists to trace out, as far as possible, all the lines of evolution within insects, but most modern entomologists have given up this activity as tiresome and fruitless: nothing of any importance turns on the allocation of one ancestry rather than another.

The study of insects abounds with interesting and important bio- [19] logical problems to do with heredity, development, behavior and the action of hormones. The gaseous exchange in their respiration, for instance, is mediated through very fine air tubes, *tracheae*, leading directly from the atmosphere to the internal organs. The inherent physical limitations of this respiratory system, combined with the necessity for moulting, set a limit to the size of insects which is much more exigent than that which applies to, for example, crustaceans. Thus a repopulation of the world by huge, fascist insects may be regarded as one of the more idiotic Gothic extravagances of science fiction; moreover, the likelihood that insects will evolve into animals of any other kind may be dismissed as negligibly small. Insects are specialized end-products of evolution. It has been said that within the group itself new species may be originating faster than they can be recognized and named. Such a claim can hardly be verified, however, because modern entomologists are no longer engaged in merely taxonomic exercises. What *is* quite certain, however, is that not all living and fossil species have yet been described and named, although about a million are known. We can also be sure that the adaptive finesse responsible for the success of insects has closed the door to new evolutionary possibilities.

QUESTIONS

1. Define "biogenesis" in one sentence. What is the relation of bio-genesis to evolution? The Medawars say, "Biogenesis does not imply evolution, but an evolutionary relationship does of course imply biogenesis." Why? Why does believing that higher forms evolve out of lower forms demand a conception of biogenesis?
2. The Medawars say that "the evolutionary hypothesis is part of the very fabric of the way we think in biology," and they compare the hypothesis of evolution with the hypothesis that the earth is round. Why do scientists need broad hypotheses such as evolution or the roundness of the earth? What do broad theories provide for them? (Consider that on the basis of *observation* alone people thought that worms sprang spontaneously from dead horses until Pasteur gave us the theory of biogenesis.)
3. What do the words "biosystematics" and "taxonomic" mean? Why should biologists need to create such systems of classification? In what ways do you think that these large systems help the biologist (remember, *bio-* = life; *-logy* = the study of) who is studying reproduction in the fruit fly, for example—or the differences between cancerous and normal cells?
4. What are the reasons that insects are the "great success story of evolution"? Upon what does the *success* of a class of animals within the long process of life *depend*?
5. Why is it biologically impossible for the world to be taken over by a race of huge insects?
6. Does the success story of insect survival through the ages give us any clues to better understanding and/or measuring the validity of the studies of Elisabeth Badinter or Margaret Mead in this unit? Does the biological conception of sexuality (reproduction, biogenesis, evolution) offer explanations that are useful to us in understanding the anthropological (study of humankind), psychoanalytic (study of human consciousness), or sociological (study of human inter-relation)?

EXERCISES

1. Make a diagram of the biosystem that the Medawars describe. Diagram the relation among the following: phylum, order, class, family, genus, species. A partial diagram appears below; complete it, using *only* those examples that the Medawars give.

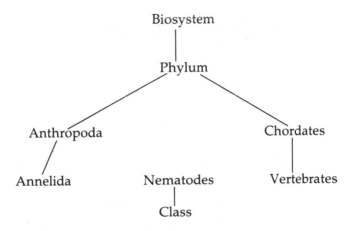

2. Using what the Medawars have told you about the evolutionary success of insects, speculate about the probable uses of erotic love and mother love for human beings as a species. Write your ideas freely, without attention to grammar and form, in your journal. Regard the exercise as a way of finding and stating ideas, as if you are writing a letter to yourself.

3. One of the major charges leveled against certain kinds of laboratory medical tests (e.g., those which test the possibly carcinogenic effects of Red #2 food coloring or saccharine) is that what is true of rats or guinea pigs may not be true of people. Write freely in your journal as in the preceding exercise, speculating upon laboratory research using animals to come to conclusions about disorders in humans (e.g., in drug testing, diet research, heart attacks).

_____ CHAPTER FIVE _____

CARLSON: SEX DETERMINATION

Genetics

From the Medawars we learned something about the systems of classification biologists use when they take a very broad view of our place within the vast chain of organic relationships. Elof A. Carlson, a distinguished professor of genetics, narrows our scope and deeply intensifies it. We normally distinguish two biological sexes, male and female. Most biology texts include a chapter on sexual reproduction that teaches us to discriminate XX and XY sex chromosomes and leave the issue at that. Carlson, however, asks us to look more closely. With him we examine the process of embryonic development to discriminate *seven* levels of sexuality, or seven steps in sexual development, at any of which the movement toward normal, clearly defined biological sexuality, can be derailed.

As you read, keep some of these questions in mind:

1. What does the perspective of hard science add to our growing understanding of what human sexuality is?
2. Carlson shows that classification by an examination of external genitalia fails in a small number of cases and "an infant cannot be properly assigned a legal sex at birth. In a larger number of cases the biological and psychological or cultural identifications of the sexes are at odds. . . ." How might this biological information modify what we learned about sex and temperament from Margaret Mead?
3. How does the evidence of the hard scientist differ from that of the social scientist, such as Badinter? Is the geneticist's evidence more reliable?

4. How does the scientific approach, and method of stating or solving problems, differ from that of the social scientist? And how does that influence his writing?
5. Among the methods described in "Thinking, Reading, Writing," which are the best for studying this text? How should one prepare for an exam in a human genetics course in which this text was used?

GLOSSARY

transvestites [1]

transsexuals [1]

ambiguous [2]

gonads [2]

genitalia [2]

chromosomal [2]

primordial [3]

proliferate [3]

cortex [3]

ovaries [3]

testes [3]

endoderm [3]

mesodermal [3]

tubercle [11]

rudiments [11]

lumen [13]

inguinal [13]

pubic [14]

pseudohermaphrodites [16]

autosomal [21]

recessive [21]

mutation [21]

steroids [21]

bisexual [32]

effeminate [32]

gender roles [35]

castrated [37]

SEX DETERMINATION: THE SEVEN
_____ LEVELS OF HUMAN SEXUALITY _____

Elof A. Carlson

[1]   Although society has changed many of its stereotypes about masculine
and feminine behavior, there is almost universal agreement that humanity exists as two sexes, male and female. Sexual identification is
usually made at birth by examination of the external genitalia, and it
is recorded on a birth certificate, thus establishing a _legal sex_ for the
child. Fortunately, most male and female infants develop normally—
biologically and psychologically—and accept their sexual identification.
In a small number of cases this classification fails and the infant cannot
be properly assigned a legal sex at birth. In a larger number of cases
the biological and psychological or cultural identifications of the sexes
are at odds, resulting in individuals who are homosexuals, transvestites,
or transsexuals.

[2]   If we study the components of human sexuality, we can establish
seven levels of sexual development. Any one of these, if modified,
can lead to ambiguous sexual identification. Sexuality is complex because
there are six major organ systems involved in its development: the
germ cells, the gonads, the internal genital structures, the external
genitalia, the brain, and the glands whose hormones determine reproductive function. These six biological components of human sexuality
and the psychosocial concept of gender constitute what can be called
the seven sexes of humans. We can refer to seven sexes in humans
because the term sex can be applied either as the sum of all the
functions we identify with a male or a female or the particular structures
or functions involved in the composite we recognize as a male or a
female. When referring to these components, we use the terms chromosomal sex, genetic sex, gonadal sex, and so on.

THE REPRODUCTIVE CELLS AND GONADS HAVE SEPARATE
ORIGINS

[3]   The sperm or eggs of a mature adult are derived from the primordial
germ cells of the embryo. These cells are formed about the sixth to
tenth week after fertilization and they multiply in the upper portion
of the embryonic yolk sac (Figure 1). The _gonads_, which eventually
become _testes_ or _ovaries_, have a different origin. They develop as a

SOURCE: From _Human Genetics_ by Elof A. Carlson. Copyright © 1984 by D. C. Heath
and Company. Reprinted by permission of the publisher.

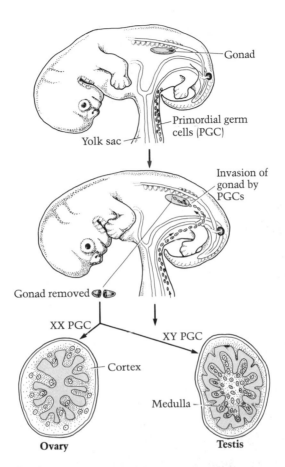

Figure 1. *The Invasion of the Gonad by Primordial Germ Cells.* The *primordial germ cells* multiply in the upper reaches of the yolk sac and migrate to the gonad, a mesodermal structure which forms near the embryonic kidneys. The XX primordial germ cells proliferate in the cortex or outer rind of the gonad. The XY primordial germ cells proliferate in the medulla or central core of the gonad. The adult gonad thus has a dual origin: its reproductive component is derived from the endodermal primordial germ cells and its glandular component is derived from the mesoderm.

bulge near the embryonic kidney and consist of an inner core, called the *gonadal medulla,* and an outer rind, called the *gonadal cortex.* They are like an empty house, whose tenants (the primordial germ cells) have not yet moved in. About the sixth to eighth week of embryonic development the primordial germ cells leave the yolk sac and crawl like amoebas to the embryonic gonads, which they invade (Figure 2). If the primordial germ cells are chromosomally XX, they proliferate

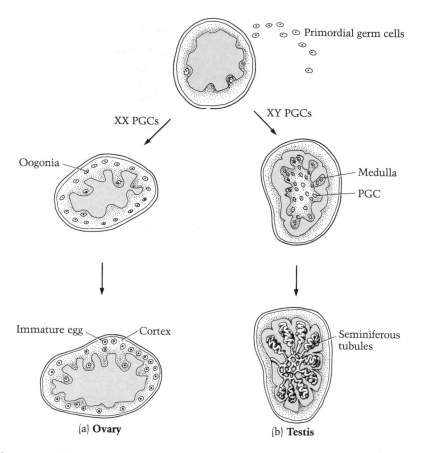

Figure 2. *The Dual Origin of the Gonads.* The sexually neutral embryonic gonad (with inner medulla and outer cortex) is invaded by primordial germ cells (PGCs). In the female (a) XX PGCs proliferate in the cortex, the medulla atrophies, and the gonad becomes an ovary. In the male (b) the XY PGCs proliferate in the medulla, the cortex atrophies, and the gonad becomes a testis.

in the cortex, the medulla degenerates, and the gonads become ovaries. If the primordial germ cells are XY, they multiply in the medulla, and the cortex atrophies, producing testes. Whether a child is born with testes or ovaries, the gonad itself is of dual origin, the sperm or eggs having their embryonic origin not from the gonad but from the yolk sac. The yolk sac is part of the embryonic endoderm and the gonad itself is mesodermal.

117   GONADS CANNOT FORM WITHOUT AN INVASION OF PRIMORDIAL GERM CELLS

If there are no functional primordial germ cells because of some birth [4] defect, the gonads may not develop into adult-sized ovaries or testes. When a zygote is formed bearing a single X chromosome and no Y, the condition (which we learned is called Turner syndrome) results in an absence of functional germ cells and ovaries that degenerate in the fetus. Poorly developed gonads ("streak gonads") may form instead of ovaries. Testes cannot form in the absence of a Y chromosome.

Not all of the Y chromosome is male-determining. There is a region [5] which leads to a detectable protein, called the HY antigen, which is usually found in male tissue but occasionally is present in female tissue. XY individuals whose Y chromosome fails to produce this HY antigen are phenotypically females at birth, similar to Turner females but lacking the dwarf stature, webbed neck, and other nonsexual characteristics of the disorder.

CHROMOSOMAL SEX DISORDERS MAY INCLUDE ABNORMALITIES UNRELATED TO SEX

At this point we can identify two of the seven sexes of humans: [6] *chromosomal sex* and *gonadal sex*. Normally a male has an XY and a female has an XX chromosomal sex. But the XO Turner syndrome, with streak gonads, and the XXY Klinefelter syndrome, with sterile, pea-sized testes, suggest what is probably going on in the embryo. The XO does not produce functional germ cells and the XXY produces inadequate signals in the medulla for the gonad. In Klinefelter syndrome a modest growth of the medulla and a degeneration of the cortex occur but the XXY primordial germ cells do not multiply effectively and they do not develop meiotically. Both Turner and Klinefelter adults are permanently sterile.

The gonadal sex arises from the reciprocal relation of the cortex [7] and the medulla of the gonad. The primordial germ cells, if functional will initiate cortical (ovarian) or medullary (testicular) dominance. Presumably these tissues respond to products released by the prolif-erating XX or XY primordial germ cells in the embryonic gonad. Al-though XYY and XXX chromosomal sexes also involve abnormal sex chromosome numbers, the XYY primordial germ cells usually produce fertile functional testes, and XXX primordial germ cells usually produce fertile functional ovaries. At least at this level of sexual development the XXX or XYY chromosome sex is within a normal range.

THE INTERNAL GENITALIA ARISE FROM THE MÜLLERIAN AND WOLFFIAN DUCTS

[8] Two duct systems accompany the development of the embryonic gonads—the *Wolffian ducts* and the *Müllerian ducts* (Figure 3). Since the potential male and female both have a common set of undifferentiated gonads and ducts, the embryo at this stage is often considered sexually neutral. After the invasion of primordial germ cells, however, the gonadal sex is determined, with testes or ovaries as the outcome

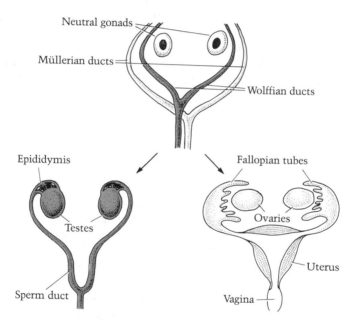

Figure 3. *The Complementary Relation of the Internal Genitalia.* At about the eighth to tenth week of development, the human embryo has neutral gonads with two adjoining duct systems, the Wolffian ducts (dark) and the Müllerian ducts (light). About the 13th week the gonads differentiate in response to the invasion of primordial germ cells. If these cells are XY, the gonads become testes (left) and release Müllerian Duct Inhibitor (MDI) which causes the disappearance of the Müllerian duct. A second hormone from the testes, testosterone, converts the Wolffian duct into the semen-collecting apparatus (epididymis and sperm duct).

In the developing female embryo neither of these hormones are released. The *absence* of testosterone causes the Wolffian duct to degenerate, and the *absence* of MDI permits the Müllerian duct to develop into the oviducts (Fallopian tubes), the uterus, and the upper third of the vagina. Some biologists believe the female reproductive system is not induced by any hormones, but is the constitutive state of the embryo.

of medullary or cortical growth. In the testes, but not the ovaries, a hormone is released called the *Müllerian Duct Inhibitor* (MDI). It is specific for preventing the differentiation of the Müllerian duct into oviducts (fallopian tubes), uterus, and the upper third of the vagina. Since the female lacks MDI, her Müllerian ducts form these internal genital structures.

In the male, MDI prevents the development of internal female [9] genitalia, but has no other effect on sexual development. The Wolffian ducts respond to a second male hormone, *testosterone*, also released by the testes. In response to testosterone the Wolffian duct forms a network of collecting tubules and storage vesicles for transporting sperm from the testes to the penis. The epididymis and sperm duct are the most apparent structural changes brought about by testosterone. MDI has no effect at all on the Wolffian duct.

This difference in function of testosterone and MDI has been dem- [10] onstrated in mammals by surgical removal of the neutral gonads. If an agar cube, impregnated with testosterone, is implanted near the ducts, the Wolffian duct will form male internal genitalia (the collecting tubules, sperm duct, and epididymis). The Müllerian duct, in the absence of gonads, will form oviducts, a uterus, and the upper third of the vagina, regardless of the presence or absence of testosterone. In both these experiments, it does not matter if the embryo is XX or XY. Chromosomal sex normally leads to gonadal sex, but it is the gonadal sex which produces the *internal genital sex*. One striking feature of mammalian sex determination is the control or regulation of embryonic structures. Regardless of XX or XY constitution, the embryo will become a female unless the male hormones MDI and testosterone prevent this. MDI *turns off* Müllerian duct differentiation, and testosterone *turns on* Wolffian duct differentiation.

THE MALE AND FEMALE EXTERNAL GENITALIA ARISE FROM COMMON EMBRYONIC GENITAL RUDIMENTS

There is a common meeting ground for the Wolffian and Müllerian [11] ducts when these join their mates in the posterior region of the embryo. They enter the *cloaca* which eventually provides the exit for eggs, sperm, and urine. Where the cloaca comes in contact with the posterior ventral surface of the embryo, a bulging occurs consisting of a *genital tubercle*, surrounded by *genital folds*, and a larger pair of *genital swellings* (Figure 4). As in the case of the gonads and the internal genitalia, the rudiments for the external genitalia are identical in the early XX or XY embryo.

The same male hormone, testosterone, that causes Wolffian duct [12] differentiation causes the external rudiments to form the male geni-

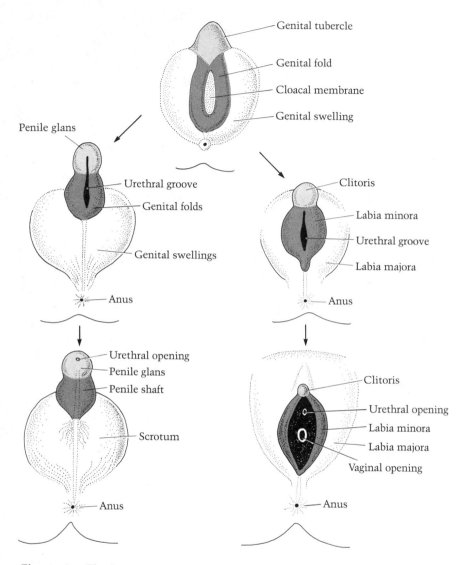

Figure 4. *The Common Embryonic Origin of Male and Female External Genitalia.*
The genital tubercle of the early embryo enlarges to form the glans or head
of the penis in the male. It remains small and is recessed in the upper apex
of the vagina in the female. The embryonic genital folds move outward and
curl around to form a penile shaft in the male (along with some of the urethral
tissue), but in the female they form the labia minora. The genital swellings
form the scrotum in the male and the labia majora in the female.

talia. In the absence of testosterone these rudiments form the female's external sexual apparatus. The female's genital tubercle enlarges slightly to form a *clitoris*. The genital folds form the *labia minora*, and the genital swellings become the *labia majora*. These are the external structures leading to the *vagina*, whose lower two-thirds is derived from the differentiation of a cloacal structure called the *urethra*. That urethral portion of the vagina joins the Müllerian duct portion of the vagina, which connects it to the uterus and oviducts.

In the male, testosterone causes the genital folds to elongate and [13] join together forming part of the *penile shaft*. The genital tubercle enlarges as it is pushed forward by the developing folds and becomes the *penile glans* or head of the penis. The rest of the penile shaft, whose internal lumen is connected to the sperm duct, is derived from the urethra. The genital swellings also enlarge, forming a sac which joins together in a common *scrotum*. Much later, the testes, which are internal, descend, entering the scrotum through the inguinal canals of the embryo. The differentiation of those visible male and female structures constitutes the *external genital sex*.

HORMONES GOVERN PUBERTY AND THE SEXUAL ACTIVITY OF MATURE ADULTS

Although boys and girls are clearly differentiated by their external [14] genitalia, there are major changes that occur as they mature during puberty (between the ages of 10 and 20). In males increased production of testosterone results in larger size, deeper voice, and hairiness (especially facial hair). The male hormones also cause hair to grow in the pubic region and in the armpits. They also stimulate sperm production in the testes. Puberty normally begins between the ages of 12 and 14 for boys.

In girls this pubertal change starts earlier, usually between the ages [15] of 10 and 12, and it is also hormone-dependent. The ovaries, in response to pituitary hormones, begin producing eggs, the menstrual cycle commences, and the ovarian and pituitary hormones stimulate breast development and pelvic bone enlargement. There is also hair growth in the pubic region and in the armpits. The pubertal changes in males and females produce the *secondary* or *mature sex*.

MUTATIONS AFFECTING SEXUALITY MAY CAUSE PSEUDOHERMAPHRODITIC DISORDERS

Occasionally there are errors other than nondisjunction which inter- [16] fere with the normal development of the embryo. Fortunately most of these are rare. Their analysis provides us with some valuable insights into the way genes control human development. In the more startling cases there is an inconsistency between gonadal sex (testes or ovaries) and the external genital sex (penis with scrotum or vagina with labia). Individuals with such ambiguities are called *pseudohermaphrodites*.

AN XY ZYGOTE CAN OCCASIONALLY RESULT IN A FEMALE BABY

[17]   There is a gene on the X chromosome that controls the response of some of the body's tissues to testosterone. If this gene is mutated, the testes still develop normally, MDI is released, and there is no formation of uterus, oviducts, or the upper third of the vagina. Testosterone is also released, but it has no effect on the external genital development because the cells are insensitive to testosterone. The internal differentiation of the Wolffian duct, however, does occur and the testes have an accompanying set of collecting tubules with the epididymis and sperm ducts. At birth such individuals appear as females, their external genital sex being used to determine their legal sex. They are raised as girls and think of themselves as females (Figure 5). At puberty they develop breasts, but they have little pubic or axillary hair.

[18]   This X-linked recessive disorder is called *congenital insensitivity to androgen syndrome* (CIAS), formerly called testicular feminization syndrome. The chromosomal sex of such females is XY. Because their gonads form testes, these are sterile females who never menstruate. They lack the internal female sexual organs and they have a short vagina, consisting of the lower two-thirds derived from the urethra. CIAS females have normal male levels of testosterone in their blood. They will not masculinize even when given additional testosterone in large amounts. CIAS females have a high incidence of undescended or partially descended testes, which are frequently removed. This is an important surgical procedure because undescended testes have a 25 percent chance of becoming cancerous.

[19]   It is important to note that CIAS females think of themselves as females. Since their hormones are from their testes and they do not have ovarian hormones, neither sex hormones (gonadal sex) nor the XY condition (chromosomal sex) determines this *psychological sex*. The masculine or feminine psychological identification one has is primarily social in origin.

[20]   CIAS represents another level of sexuality, *genetic sex*, involving those genes that produce hormones and regulatory responses as well as genes that control the structure and formation of the embryonic components in the sexual apparatus.

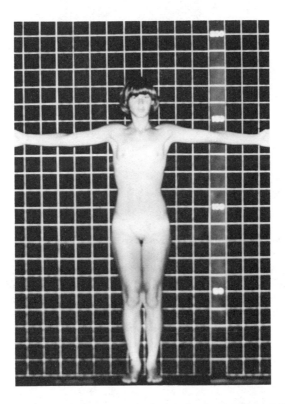

Figure 5. *Congenital Insensitivity to Androgen Syndrome.* Ordinarily XY zygotes develop into males. In the congenital insensitivity to androgen syndrome (CIAS) a gene mutation on the X chromosome makes most of the body tissues unresponsive to testosterone. Thus the fetal external genitalia develop as female structures. The tissues do respond normally to the Müllerian Duct Inhibitor released by the testes. The internal genitalia consist of a shortened vagina with no uterus or oviducts. The testes usually remain in the body cavity until puberty. A CIAS female, as shown here, has a feminine body. The mothers of XY CIAS females are fully normal. CIAS females are male pseudohermaphrodites—that is, they have male gonads and female genitalia. (Courtesy of R. J. Gorlin, D.D.S.)

AN XX ZYGOTE CAN SOMETIMES DEVELOP INTO A BABY BOY OR AN INFANT WITH AMBIGUOUS SEXUALITY

There are other forms of genetic sex defects leading to pseudoher- [21] maphroditic conditions. In some infants an <u>autosomal</u> <u>recessive</u> <u>mutation</u> causes the adrenal glands to enlarge and convert much of their <u>steroids</u> into male hormones. The condition, *congenital adrenogenital syndrome* (CAS), causes a modification of the external genitalia in the

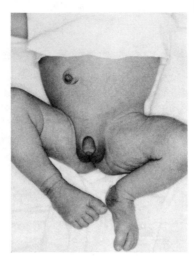

Figure 6. *Congenital Adrenogenital Syndrome.* An autosomal recessive mutation causes cells in the adrenal cortex to synthesize male hormone from the steroid compounds present in them. In an XX fetus this causes development of an enlarged, phallus-like clitoris and scrotal sac instead of labia majora. These XX female pseudohermaphrodites have ovaries with masculinized external genitalia. Their internal genitalia are female; they have a uterus and oviducts as well as a vaginal tract. In some of the mutations, the enzyme defect also disturbs salt balance, in which case adrenal surgery might be required with artificially supplied hormones used to maintain the infant. (Courtesy of Dr. David D. Weaver)

female (XX) embryo somewhat later than normally occurs in the male (XY) embryo. (See Figure 6.) Since the XX embryo has ovaries, developmental progress (until the adrenals begin releasing testosterone) has been typically female. Internally the ovaries, oviducts, uterus, and vagina, especially the upper portion, are normal. But as the testosterone level builds up, the clitoris and labia become modified, producing a phallus-like structure with a partial or complete scrotum. The degree of masculinization is variable and depends on the quantity of testosterone produced as well as the time and duration of the hormone release in the embryo. Since at least 12 weeks will have elapsed before CAS XX females are exposed to the male hormone, it is less likely that the external genital sex will resemble that of a normal male; more likely the external genitalia will be ambiguous. Such a child may have a vaginal opening between the halves of an incompletely formed scrotum, and the penis may have an incompletely closed genital fold or urethra resulting in a *hypospadias* (any opening of the urethral passage other than its normal location on the glans).

[22]   The adrenally produced male hormone may inhibit cortical development of the ovary in such females, and as a result breast formation may not occur at puberty. Others may have functional ovaries which

do ovulate and produce monthly cycles and stimulate breast development.

MANY SEXUAL DISORDERS ARE SURGICALLY CORRECTIBLE IN INFANTS

Although the sexual alterations in CAS children may create psycho-   [23]
logical problems and require surgery to eventually shift the XX child
to a functional female status, the adrenal condition itself may be life-
threatening, especially if the adrenal gland enlarges and pours out
other adrenal hormones, or if the metabolic defect affects salt balance
in the tissues. In such cases surgical removal of the adrenals or hormone
therapy could save the life of the child.

If an XY embryo receives excess adrenally derived male hormone,   [24]
the child may be born with some signs of secondary sexual development,
including pubic hair and a large penis. This form of CAS is sometimes
called *macrogenitosomia praecox* or the infant Hercules syndrome.

SOME OTHER FORMS OF ABNORMAL SEXUAL DEVELOPMENT MAY OCCUR

If the embryonic testis does not make MDI, or if the Müllerian duct   [25]
does not respond to MDI, then an XY individual will develop into a
male who has internal female genitalia (oviducts, uterus, and an upper
third of a vagina). Such a male may never know that this situation
exists and he will probably be a perfectly fertile, functional male.
Occasionally such a uterus may develop an abnormal growth of the
uterine lining (endometriosis) or a cancer, and thus the male's disorder
is revealed. Also the internal genitalia may be discovered accidentally
during an autopsy for some unrelated cause of death.

Sometimes, mitotic nondisjunction may occur during the early   [26]
cleavages of an XY zygote, resulting in an XO/XY mosaic. Two cell
lines may also arise from the fusion of two zygotes in the oviduct,
and the implantation of the chimeric XX/XY blastocyst could produce
a hermaphrodite. In contrast to the pseudohermaphrodite, a *true hermaphrodite* has both ovarian and testicular tissue. This can cause a
wide range of external genital development, as in the CAS children.
The XX/XY chimerism, however, does not affect longevity or overall
health.

In some hermaphrodites the legal sex may be male but at puberty   [27]
an ovary or ovatestis may begin functioning. If there is a functional
uterus a menstrual cycle may occur with a bloody urine corresponding
to that cycle, discharged through the penis. There are a few instances
of adult hermaphrodites with a functional penis and a functional

vagina surrounded by a bifid scrotum. Unlike many animal species with hermaphroditic life cycles, no true human hermaphrodite is capable of self-fertilization.

[28]   Pseudohermaphrodites have a normal chromosomal sex, but either a genetic or environmental defect causes a noncorrespondence of gonads and external genitalia. During early pregnancy, a mother with an XX fetus may have received steroid hormone therapy or she may have a tumor of an adrenal gland which may cause it to release male hormones. The external genitalia of the embryo could then masculinize, as in CAS infants, but after birth this male hormone source would be removed and all subsequent development would be female. Such XX pseudohermaphrodites could have surgery to remove an excessively large, phallus-like clitoris or scrotal tissue.

HOW PARENTS SHOULD HANDLE A BABY WITH A SEXUAL DISORDER

[29]   It is important for parents and medical personnel to request a delay in entering the legal sex of a pseudohermaphroditic child on the birth certificate and to request a detailed examination of the child to best determine which sex the child should have for the rest of its life.

[30]   Failure to do so could create problems later in life. There are some reported instances of XX pseudohermaphrodites, who were surgically corrected and raised as females, but who were denied marriage licenses or church weddings because the birth certificate revealed a male legal sex which was at odds with the adult sexual status. Rather than sanction an alleged homosexual union, some officials will refuse such individuals a permit to marry. Such individuals may be able to change their legal sex on a birth certificate but only after expensive and lengthy litigation, and there are no guarantees that what seems sensible to the person requesting the change will strike the court in the same way.

PSYCHOLOGICAL SEX IS MORE SUBJECT TO CULTURE THAN TO OUR GENES

[31]   Although the biological levels of sex are in agreement for most human beings, agreement between the psychological and biological levels of sex is not always present. The number of individuals with such a disparity varies with the culture and the era.

[32]   The most well-known form of such ambiguity is *homosexuality*. The definition of homosexual varies and three types should be distinguished. Those who have had an occasional homosexual activity at some time

in their life during or after puberty, but who consider themselves heterosexual, form the largest percentage of males or females who may be classified (perhaps erroneously) as homosexual. A second category involves individuals who occasionally (or frequently) enjoy homosexual relations as adults, but who participate in heterosexual relations as well. These individuals are called bisexual. The third category involves exclusive homosexuals, individuals who have no interest in heterosexual experiences. These individuals may sometimes, but not always, adopt mannerisms characteristic of the opposite sex, thus appearing to others as effeminate men or masculinized women. Very often they do not adopt such mannerisms and there is no way that their social behavior in public is recognizably different from that of heterosexuals.

The sexual preference of male homosexuals cannot be changed [33] through hormone therapy. Additional testosterone may increase their sexual activity, but if it does it will still be activity with other men because that is their psychological preference.

There is no evidence that homosexual behavior is genetic and none [34] that indicates a major disturbance in hormone activity, although hormonal disturbances *in utero* have not been ruled out. It is an apparently acquired trait produced by the socializing experiences of the family, and possibly by the peers encountered by the individual who encourage or share their homosexual tendencies. In recent years psychologists have rejected the classification of homosexuality as a pathology. There may be homosexuals who need psychotherapy for conflicts and guilts associated with a homosexual lifestyle (such problems also exist in heterosexual lifestyles), but they are not a necessary consequence of homosexuality.

GENDER ROLES ARE NOT LIKELY TO INVOLVE INNATE TENDENCIES

Psychological sex, while primarily an acquired identification, is not [35] likely to be randomly chosen, even in cultures tolerant of homosexuality. Role models of sexual behavior are present throughout our childhood and patterns of heterosexual preference are likely to remain strong. What are more likely to change are the spurious gender roles assigned to occupations, legal rights, and social functions. There is nothing intrinsically masculine or feminine about cooking, taking out the garbage, playing sports, studying medicine, law, engineering, or business, or becoming a ballet dancer. The disproportionate sexual identification associated with these activities reflects our values and biases, not our biology.

TRANSVESTITES AND TRANSSEXUALS HAVE INTENSE GENDER CONFLICTS

[36]   There are some individuals, *transvestites*, who identify so strongly with the opposite sex that they attempt to hide their biological sex by their choice of clothing and other external cultural symbols of sexuality. They may even believe they are of the opposite sex but are trapped in the wrong body. Such individuals, if male, may grow long hair that is given feminine styling, remove facial hair with electrolytic or chemical treatments, wear stylish dresses and jewelry, and use perfume and other cosmetics. Transvestites restrict their sexual discrepancy to the outward appearances of the opposite sex. They do not normally undergo surgery or hormone therapy to alter their biological sex.

[37]   A more radical attempt at sex reversal involves biological sexual conversion (Figure 7). It is more commonly done by males (committed to the idea that they are females) who undergo surgical removal of their testes, scrotum, and penis and then have a surgically-constructed vagina introduced instead. Such surgery involves several operations and it is both expensive and time-consuming. The castrated male then takes estrogen, a female hormone, to stimulate breast formation (Figure 5). Such *transsexuals* do not have a uterus or ovaries and thus they remain sterile and incapable of achieving pregnancy or of having a

Figure 7. *The Transsexual Conversion.* Richard Raskind (a) after surgery became Renee Richards (b). (Wide World Photos)

menstrual cycle. Furthermore, some long-range follow-up studies have shown that no greater adjustment to their major psychological problems was made after surgery than would have been made using conventional psychological counseling. For this reason some hospitals have discontinued sex-change operations as a valid therapy for transsexual individuals.

MINOR SEXUAL ABNORMALITIES ARE COMMON AND USUALLY CORRECTIBLE

The seven sexes of humans illustrate the flexibility of sexual devel- [38] opment. There are both minor and major alterations of normal development. We have explored most of the major abnormalities, but we should bear in mind that these are rare, involving less than one percent of all births. Minor abnormalities in development such as hypospadias, undescended testes (*cryptorchidism*), delayed onset of menstruation, development of very small or very large breasts, and other variations in biologically determined levels of sexuality, are much more common than the major abnormalities previously discussed. Most of these conditions are readily repaired if they are considered problematic. If they are not of any medical concern, they still may provoke psychological problems by affecting the individual's self-image.

From a biological perspective, the development of human sexuality [39] shows how genetic, chromosomal, hormonal, and morphological features are related. More obvious for sexual development than for that of our other organ systems is the role of culture in modifying the functions of the sexual organs to fill psychological needs.

From a personal perspective it is important to question how many [40] of the sex roles assigned to us are unessential for a healthy acceptance of our sexual identity. There may even be some sex roles that are actually harmful to the overall mental health of the individual barred from full participation in an activity mistakenly assigned a specific gender.

QUESTIONS

1. What are the six biological components of human sexuality?
2. When and where do the primordial germ cells of the embryo first develop? What is the relation between the primordial germ cells and the gonads?

3. What happens in the embryonic gonads if the primordial germ cells are chromosomally XX? What happens in the embryonic gonads if the primordial germ cells are XY?

4. What happens to the development of the gonads into testes or ovaries if some birth defect prevents the primordial germ cells from functioning? What are the Turner syndrome and the Klinefelter syndrome, and how do they occur?

5. What is the function of the hormone MDI (or Müllerian duct inhibitor)? Why is production of MDI necessary for normal male development, and why is the absence of MDI necessary for normal female development? Where is MDI released?

6. Consider the process whereby the Wolffian duct responds to the hormone testosterone. Carlson says, "One striking feature of mammalian sex determination is the control or regulation of embryonic structures"—that is, our sex is determined by the development of "*internal* genital sex" while we are embryos. In a single capsule sentence, state what is the contribution of MDI and testosterone in determining whether we develop male or female internal organs.

7. Are the rudiments for external genitalia, which develop where the cloaca comes in contact with the ventral surface of the embryo, the same or different for early XX and XY embryos? What are the genital tubercle, the genital folds, and the genital swellings, and what organs do they form respectively in males and females?

8. What hormones govern sexual development during puberty? What organs produce these hormones? Are they the same or different for males and females?

9. What happens to the embryo if the gene on the X chromosome which controls the body's response to testosterone mutates? What does CIAS stand for, and what dysfunction does it describe? CIAS females are also called male pseudohermaphrodites. Why?

10. Under what circumstances can an XX zygote develop into a baby boy or an infant with ambiguous sexuality? What is CAS and what are the conditions under which it occurs?

11. What happens to an XY embryo that receives excess adrenally derived male hormone? What happens to an XX embryo that receives adrenally derived male hormones, and why is the condition life-threatening to her?

12. What is a true hermaphrodite? How does this condition occur? How is it different from the sexual dysfunctions that occur during embryonic development?

13. Why is the seventh level of human sexuality, "psychological sex," more difficult to determine than the first six levels are? Is culture as strong a determinant of sex as biology? Why, or why not?

14. Does Carlson believe that homosexuality is genetically caused? Is it the result of a major disturbance in hormone activity?

15. What are transvestites and transsexuals? Is their condition biologically or psychologically determined?

16. Would Carlson agree or disagree with Badinter about gender roles and activities designated by society as "masculine" or "feminine"? Would Carlson agree or disagree with Mead about cultural determination of psychological sex and temperament?

EXERCISES

1. a. Put yourself in the place of a teacher who is making up an exam on this chapter. Make five exam questions: For example: (1) Discuss the fate of the Müllerian duct in males and females, or (2) Discuss the common origin of the scrotum and the labia majora.

b. Write an exam answer to *one* of your questions.

2. You are an editor at D. C. Heath and Company, the publishers of Carlson's book. The business manager wants to cut costs by dropping the illustrations from this chapter. Write a draft of a two-page report to the board justifying the necessity of the illustrations. Be very specific; that is, show the ways that a particular illustration helps the reader to understand a particular process that is difficult to grasp.

3. a. On the basis of Carlson's essay and any of the preceding readings that apply, write a dictionary definition of one of the following terms:

homosexual
transsexual
hermaphrodite
gender

b. Using your dictionary definition as a base, write an extended definition of the term you chose. Aim the paper at the general reader, but include in it your personal opinion based on your own observations.

CHAPTER SIX

MAY: EROS IN CONFLICT
WITH SEX

Psychoanalytical Philosophy

Rollo May is a distinguished psychoanalyst and philosopher who has written broadly on issues concerning the human condition. The following selection, taken from his book *Love and Will*, is an illustration of the theoretical psychoanalytic thinking which we are likely to encounter in all his writings. Here the psychoanalyst speaks essentially as a philosopher, not as a doctor of medicine as we might expect him to. His interests, very much like those of Sigmund Freud, focus so much on the way we think and the way we live our lives that his writings are perhaps more frequently encountered in a philosophy course than in a psychology course. A theoretical psychoanalyst such as Rollo May is involved in healing but he is primarily interested in the *nature* of the human psyche, and in the fundamental laws of operation that govern it. May is interested in how love is influenced by civilization, but not, as Badinter is, at one particular time in history, or as Mead is, in different, divergent cultures. Rather, May is concerned with how eros (love yearning that lifts us out of ourselves) differs from sexuality, and how eros and civilization are related, at all times in all places.

When reading the selection, bear in mind the title, "Eros in Conflict with Sex." Jot down in your journal what you believe this conflict to be at the outset and modify your statement, if necessary, as you read along. Also pay close attention to the way Rollo May connects his reading experience with his professional experience. Note how he builds his argument by relying on sources as diverse as the Greek myths and the case histories of his patients. The weaving together of these strands shows how timeless and widespread the conflict between eros and sex actually is.

GLOSSARY

banalization [1]

anesthetizing [1]

emasculated [1]

vapid [1]

plethora [1]

dehumanizing [1]

anxiety [2]

psychic [4]

daimonic [4]

anachronistic [4]

repression [5]

caveat [6]

therapy [8]

contraception [8]

dynamics [9]

schizoid [10]

alienation [11]

procreative [17]

arid [18]

depersonalization [18]

ostracism [18]

arcana [22]

aphrodisiac [22]

tumescence [29]

Gestalt [30]

pulchritude [34]

Ares [41]

Aphrodite [41]

dalliance [45]

bucolic [46]

Bacchanal [46]

apathy [47]

sublimation [50]

EROS IN CONFLICT WITH SEX

Rollo May

> Eros, the god of love, emerged to create the earth. Before, all was
> silent, bare, and motionless. Now all was life, joy, and motion.
>
> Early Greek myth

> Several beautiful children were born to Aphrodite and Ares. . . .
> Eros, their little son, was appointed god of love. Although nursed
> with tender solicitude, this second-born child did not grow as
> other children do, but remained a small, rosy, chubby child, with
> gauzy wings and roguish, dimpled face. Alarmed for his health,
> Aphrodite consulted Themis, who oracularly replied, "Love cannot
> grow without Passion."
>
> Later Greek myth

[1]   The contemporary paradoxes in sex and love have one thing in common,
namely *the banalization of sex and love.* By anesthetizing feeling in order
to perform better, by employing sex as a tool to prove prowess and
identity, by using sensuality to hide sensitivity, we have emasculated
sex and left it vapid and empty. The banalization of sex is well-aided
and -abetted by our mass communication. For the plethora of books
on sex and love which flood the market have one thing in common—
they oversimplify love and sex, treating the topic like a combination
of learning to play tennis and buying life insurance. In this process,
we have robbed sex of its power by sidestepping eros; and we have
ended by dehumanizing both.

[2]   My thesis in this chapter is that what underlies our emasculation
of sex is the *separation of sex from eros.* Indeed, we have set sex over
against eros, used sex precisely to avoid the anxiety-creating involvement
of eros. In ostensibly enlightened discussions of sex, particularly those
about freedom from censorship, it is often argued that all our society
needs is full freedom for the expression of eros. But what is revealed
beneath the surface in our society, as shown not only in patients in
therapy but in our literature and drama and even in the nature of our
scientific research, is just the opposite. We are in a flight from eros—
and we use sex as the vehicle for the flight.

[3]   Sex is the handiest drug to blot out our awareness of the anxiety-
creating aspects of eros. To accomplish this, we have had to define
sex ever more narrowly: the more we became preoccupied with sex,

the more truncated and shrunken became the human experience to which it referred. We fly to *the sensation of sex in order to avoid the passion of eros.*

THE RETURN OF REPRESSED EROS

My thesis was formulated out of several strange phenomena I observed [4] in my patients as well as in our society—psychic eruptions which have a curiously explosive quality. These phenomena occurred in areas in which, from any common-sense point of view, they would be least expected in our day. Most people live in the confidence that our technological developments have largely freed us from the risks of unchosen pregnancy and venereal disease and, therefore, *ipso facto,* the anxiety people used to feel about sex and love is now banished forever to the museum. The vicissitudes about which the novelists of previous centuries wrote—when a woman gave herself to a man, it meant illegitimate pregnancy and social ostracism, as in *The Scarlet Letter;* or the tragic break-up of the family structure and suicide, as in *Anna Karenina;* or venereal disease, as in the market place of social reality—have been outgrown. Now, thank God and science, we tell ourselves, we are rid of all that! The implication is that sex is free and that love is easy and comes in readily procurable packages like what the students call "instant Zen." And any talk of the deeper conflicts which used to be associated with the tragic and daimonic elements is anachronistic and absurd.

But I shall be impolite enough to ask, May there not be a gigantic [5] and extensive repression underlying all this? A repression not of sex, but of something underlying body chemistry, some psychic needs more vital, deeper, and more comprehensive than sex. A repression that is socially sanctioned, to be sure—but just for that reason harder to discern and more effective in its results. I am obviously not questioning contemporary medical and psychological advances as such: no one in his right mind would fail to be grateful for the development of contraceptives, estrogen, and cures for venereal disease. And I count it good fortune indeed to be born into this age with its freedom of possibilities rather than in the Victorian period with its rigid mores. But that issue is fallacious and a red herring. Our problem is more profound and starkly real.

We pick up the morning paper and read that there are a million [6] illegal abortions in enlightened America each year; that premarital pregnancies are increasing on all sides. One girl out of six who is now thirteen will, according to present statistics, become illegitimately pregnant before she is twenty—two and a half times the incidence of ten years ago.[1] The increase is mainly among girls of the proletarian classes, but there is enough increase among girls of middle and upper classes to prove that this is not a problem solely of disadvantaged groups. Indeed, the radical increase is not among Puerto Rican or Negro girls but among *white* girls—the jump of percentage of illegitimate births to all live births being from 1.7 ten years ago to 5.3 last year. We are confronted by the curious situation of *the more birth control, the more illegitimate pregnancies.* As the reader hastens to cry that what is necessary is to change barbaric abortion laws and give more sex education, I would not disagree; but I could, and should, raise a caveat. The blanket advising of more sex education can act as a reassurance by means of which we escape having to ask ourselves the more frightening questions. May not the real issue be not on the level of conscious, rational intentions at all? May it not be in a deeper realm of what I shall later call intentionality?

[7]   Kenneth Clark points out, for example, with respect to the lower-class Negro girl, "The marginal Negro female uses her sex to gain personal affirmation. She is desired, and that is almost enough . . . a child is a symbol that she is a woman, and she may gain from having something on her own."[2] This struggle to prove one's identity and personal worth may be more outspoken with lower-class girls, but it is just as present in middle-class girls who can cover it up better by socially skillful behavior.

[8]   Let us take as an example a female patient from an upper middle-class background with whom I worked. Her father had been a banker in a small city, and her mother a proper lady who had always assumed a "Christian" attitude toward everyone but who seemed, from the data which came up in the therapy, to be unusually rigid and had actually resented having this girl when she was born. My patient was well educated, already in her early thirties a successful editor in a large publishing house, and obviously was not the slightest deficient in knowledge of sex or contraception. Yet she had had two illegitimate pregnancies in her mid-twenties several years before she began treatment with me. Both of these pregnancies gave her painful feelings of guilt and conflict, yet she went from one directly into the other. She had been married for two years in her early twenties to a man who, an intellectual like herself, was emotionally detached, and each had tried by various kinds of aggressive-dependency nagging to get the other to infuse some meaning and vitality into an empty marriage. After her divorce, while she lived alone, she volunteered to do some evening reading to the blind. She became pregnant by the young blind man to whom she read. Though this, and its subsequent abortion, upset her greatly, she became pregnant again shortly after her first abortion.

Now it is absurd to think we can understand this behavior on the [9]
basis of "sexual needs." Indeed, the fact that she did *not feel* sexual
desire was actually more influential in leading her into the sexual
relations which caused the pregnancies. We must look to her image
of herself and her ways of trying to find a meaningful place for herself
in her world if we are to have any hope of discovering the dynamics
of the pregnancies.

She was, diagnostically speaking, what is called a typically con- [10]
temporary schizoid personality: intelligent, articulate, efficient, successful in work, but detached in personal intercourse and afraid of
intimate relationships. She had always thought of herself as an empty
person who never could feel much on her own or experience anything
lastingly even when she took LSD—the kind of person who cries out
to the world to give her some passion, some vitality. Attractive, she
had a number of men friends but the relationships with them also
had a "dried up" quality and lacked the zest for which she fervently
longed. She described sleeping with the one with which she was most
intimate at the time as if they were two animals clinging together for
warmth, her feeling being a generalized despair. She had a dream
early in the therapy which recurred in varying form, of herself in one
room and her parents in the next room separated by a wall which
went not quite up to the ceiling; and no matter how hard she knocked
on the wall or cried out to them in the dream, she could not get them
to hear her.

She arrived for her therapy hour one day having just come from [11]
an art exhibit, to tell me she had discovered the symbol most accurately
describing her feelings about herself: the lonely figures of Edward
Hopper, in his paintings in which there is only one figure—a solitary
girl usherette in a brightly lighted and plush but entirely empty theater;
a woman sitting alone by an upper window in a Victorian house at
the shore in the deserted off-season; a lone person in a rocking chair
on a porch not unlike the house in the small city in which my patient
grew up. Hopper's paintings, indeed, give a poignant meaning to the
quiet despair, the emptiness of human feeling and longing which is
referred to by that cliché "alienation."

It is touching that her first pregnancy came in a relation with a [12]
human being who was *blind*. We are impressed here by her elemental
generosity in wanting to give him something and to prove something
also to herself, but most of all we are struck by the aura of "blindness"
surrounding the whole event of getting pregnant. She was one of the
many persons in our world of affluence and technological power who
moved, humanly speaking, in a world of the blind, where nobody
can see another and where our touching is at best a sightless fumbling,

moving our fingers over the body of another trying to recognize him or her, but unable in our own self-enclosing darkness to do so.

[13]   We could conclude that she became pregnant (1) to establish her own self-esteem by proving somebody wants her—as her husband did not; (2) to compensate for her feelings of emotional poverty—which pregnancy does quite literally by filling up the womb if we take the womb ("hystera") as a symbol of vacuum of emotions; (3) to express her aggression against her mother and father and their suffocating and hypocritical middle-class background. All of which goes without saying.

[14]   But what of the deeper defiance required by, and indeed built into, the self-contradictions in her and in our society which belie our rational, well-meaning intentions? It is absurd to think that this girl, or any girl, gets pregnant simply because she doesn't know better. This woman lives in an age where, for upper-class and middle-class girls like her, contraceptives and sex knowledge were never more available, and her society proclaims on all sides that anxiety about sex is archaic and encourages her to be free of all conflict about love. What of the *anxiety which comes precisely from this new freedom*? Anxiety which places a burden on individual consciousness and capacity for personal choice which, if not insoluble, is great indeed; anxiety which in our sophisticated and enlightened day cannot be acted out like the hysterical woman of Victorian times (for everyone nowadays *ought* to be free and uninhibited) and therefore turns inward and results in inhibiting *feelings*, suffocating *passion* in place of the inhibition of actions of the nineteenth-century woman.

[15]   I am proposing, in short, that girls and women in this predicament are partial victims of a gigantic repression in themselves and in our society—the repression of eros and passion and the overavailability of sex as a technique for the repression. A corollary is that our "dogmatic enlightenment" contains elements within it which rob us of the very means of meeting this new and inner anxiety. We are experiencing a "return of the repressed," a return of an eros which will not be denied no matter how much it is bribed on all sides by sex; a return of the repressed in a primitive way precisely designed to mock our withdrawal of feelings.

[16]   The same is found in our work with men. A young psychiatrist, in his training analysis, was preoccupied mainly with the fear that he was homosexual. Now in his middle twenties, he had never had sexual relations with a woman, and though he had not been a practicing homosexual, he had been approached by enough men to make him think that he emanated that "aura." During his therapy, he became acquainted with a woman and in due course they began having sexual relations. At least half the time they did not use contraceptives. Several

times I brought to his attention the fact that the woman was fairly sure to get pregnant; he—knowing all about this from his medical training—would agree and thank me. But when he still had intercourse without contraception and once was very anxious when the woman missed her period, I found myself vaguely anxious, too, and irritated at how stupid he seemed to be. I then caught myself up with the realization that, in my naïveté, I was missing the whole point of what was going on. So I broke in, "It seems you *want* to make this woman pregnant." He at first emphatically contradicted me, but then he paused to ponder the truth of my statement.

All talk of methods and what they *ought* to do was of course irrelevant. [17] In this man, who had never been able to feel himself masculine, some vital need was pushing him not just to prove himself a man—of which impregnating a woman is much more decisive than merely the capacity to have intercourse—but to get some hold on nature, experience a fundamental procreative process, give himself over to some primitive and powerful biological process, partake of some deeper pulsations in the cosmos. We shall not understand these problems except when we see that our patients have been robbed of precisely these deeper sources of human experience.[3]

We observe in many of these illegitimate pregnancies—or their [18] equivalent—a defiance of the very socially-ordered system which takes away affect, where technology is felt to be a substitute for feeling, a society which calls persons forth to an arid and meaningless existence and gives them, particularly the younger generation, an experience of depersonalization which is more painful than illegal abortion. No one who has worked with patients for a long period of time can fail to learn that the psychological and spiritual agony of depersonalization is harder to bear than physical pain. And, indeed, they often clutch at physical pain (or social ostracism or violence or delinquency) as a welcome relief. Have we become so "civilized" that we have forgotten that a girl can *yearn* to procreate, and can do so not just for psycho-biological reasons but to break up the arid desert of feelingless existence, to destroy for once if not for all the repetitive pattern of fucking-to-avoid-the-emptiness of despair ("What shall we do tomorrow?" as T. S. Eliot has his rich courtesan cry, "What shall we ever do?"). Or that she can yearn to become pregnant because the heart is never fully converted to passionlessness, and she is driven to an expression of that which is denied her and which she herself consciously denies in our age of the "cool millennium." At least being pregnant is something *real*, and it proves to the girl and to the man that *they* are real.

Alienation is felt as a loss of the capacity to be intimately personal. [19] As I hear these people, they are crying, We yearn to talk but "our dried voices" are "rats' feet over broken glass."[4] We go to bed because we cannot hear each other; we go to bed because we are too shy to look in each other's eyes, and in bed one can turn away one's head.[5]

[20]   It should not be surprising that a revolt is occurring against the mores which people think cause alienation; a defiance of social norms which promise virtue without trying, sex without risk, wisdom without struggle, luxury without effort—all provided that they agree to settle for love without passion, and soon even sex without feeling. The denial of the daimonic means only that the earth spirits will come back to haunt us in a new guise; Gaea will be heard, and when the darkness returns the black madonna will be present if there is no white.

[21]   The error into which we have fallen obviously consists not of our scientific advances and enlightenment as such, but the using of these for a blanket allaying of all anxiety about sex and love. Marcuse holds that in a nonrepressive society, as sex develops it tends to merge with eros. It is clear that our society has done just the opposite: we separated sex from eros and then tried to repress eros. The passion which is one element of the denied eros then comes back from its repression to upset the person's whole existence.

WHAT IS EROS?

[22]   Eros in our day is taken as a synonym for "eroticism" or sexual titillation. *Eros* was the name given to a journal of sexy arcana, containing "Aphrodisiac Recipes" and posing such weighty question-and-answer articles as, "Q: How Do the Porcupines Do It? A: Carefully." One wonders whether everyone has forgotten the fact that eros, according to no less an authority than St. Augustine, is the power which drives men toward God. Such gross misunderstandings would tend to make the demise of eros unavoidable: for in our overstimulated age we have no need for titillation which no longer titillates. It is essential, therefore, that we clarify the meaning of this crucial term.

[23]   Eros created life on the earth, the early Greek mythology tells us. When the world was barren and lifeless, it was Eros who "seized his life-giving arrows and pierced the cold bosom of the Earth," and "immediately the brown surface was covered with luxuriant verdure." This is an appealing symbolic picture of how Eros *incorporates* sex— those phallic arrows which pierce—as the instrument by which he creates life. Eros then breathed into the nostrils of the clay forms of man and woman and gave them the "spirit of life." Ever since, eros has been distinguished by the function of giving the spirit of life, in contrast to the function of sex as the release of tension. Eros was then one of the four original gods, the others being Chaos, Gaea (mother earth), and Tartarus (the dark pit of Hades below the earth). Eros,

says Joseph Campbell, is always, regardless of guise, the progenitor, the original creator from which life comes.[6]

Sex can be defined fairly adequately in physiological terms as con-   [24]
sisting of the building up of bodily tensions and their release. Eros, in contrast, is the experiencing of the personal intentions and meaning of the act. Whereas sex is a rhythm of stimulus and response, eros is a state of being. The pleasure in sex is described by Freud and others as the reduction of tension; in eros, on the contrary, we wish not to be released from the excitement but rather to hang on to it, to bask in it, and even to increase it. The end toward which sex points is gratification and relaxation, whereas eros is a desiring, longing, a forever reaching out, seeking to expand.

All this is in accord with the dictionary definitions. *Webster's* defines   [25]
sex (coming from the Latin *sexus,* meaning "split") as referring to "physiological distinctions. . . . the character of being male or female, or . . . the distinctive functions of male or female."[7] Eros, in contrast, is defined with such terms as "ardent desire," "yearning," "aspiring self-fulfilling love often having a sensuous quality."[8] The Latins and Greeks had two different words for sex and love, as we do; but the curious thing to our ears is how rarely the Latins speak of *sexus.* Sex, to them, was no issue; it was *amor* they were concerned about. Similarly, everyone knows the Greek word *eros,* but practically no one has ever heard of their term for "sex." It is φυλον, the word from which we derive the zoological term "phylon," tribe or race. This is an entirely different stem from the Greek word *philia,* which means love in the sense of friendship.

Sex is thus a zoological term and is rightly applied to all animals   [26]
as well as human beings. Kinsey was a zoologist, and appropriately to his profession, he studied human sexual behavior from a zoological point of view. Masters is a gynecologist and studies sex from the viewpoint of sexual organs and how you manage and manipulate them: sex, then, is a pattern of neurophysiological functions and the sexual problem consists of what you do with organs.

Eros, on the other hand, takes wings from human imagination and   [27]
is forever transcending all techniques, giving the laugh to all the "how to" books by gaily swinging into orbit above our mechanical rules, making love rather than manipulating organs.

For eros is the power which *attracts* us. The essence of eros is that   [28]
it draws us from ahead, whereas sex pushes us from behind. This is revealed in our day-to-day language when I say a person "allures" me or "entices" me, or the possibilities of a new job "invite" me. Something in me responds to the other person, or the job, and pulls me toward him or it. I participate in forms, possibilities, higher levels of meaning, on neurophysiological dimensions but also on aesthetic

and ethical dimensions as well. As the Greeks believed, knowledge and even ethical goodness exercise such a pull. Eros is the drive toward union with what we belong to—union with our own possibilities, union with significant other persons in our world in relation to whom we discover our own self-fulfillment. Eros is the yearning in man which leads him to dedicate himself to seeking *arête*, the noble and good life.

[29]   Sex, in short, is the mode of relating characterized by tumescence of the organs (for which we seek the pleasurable relief) and filled gonads (for which we seek satisfying release). But eros is the mode of relating in which we do not seek release but rather to cultivate, procreate, and form the world. *In eros, we seek increase of stimulation.* Sex is a need, but eros is a desire; and it is this admixture of desire which complicates love. In regard to our preoccupation with the orgasm in American discussions of sex, it can be agreed that the aim of the sex act in its zoological and physiological sense is indeed the orgasm. But the aim of eros is not: eros seeks union with the other person in delight and passion, and the procreating of new dimensions of experience which broaden and deepen the being of both persons. It is common experience, backed up by folklore as well as the testimony of Freud and others, that after sexual release we tend to go to sleep—or, as the joke puts it, to get dressed, go home, and *then* go to sleep. But in eros, we want just the opposite: to stay awake thinking of the beloved, remembering, savoring, discovering ever-new facets of the prism of what the Chinese call the "many-splendored" experience.

[30]   It is this urge for union with the partner that is the occasion for human tenderness. For eros—not sex as such—is the source of tenderness. Eros is the longing to establish union, full relationship. This may be, first, a union with abstract forms. The philosopher Charles S. Peirce sat alone in his house in Milford, Connecticut working out his mathematical logic, but this did not prevent his experiencing eros; the thinker must be "animated by a true eros," he wrote, "for the task of scientific investigation." Or it may be a union with aesthetic or philosophical forms, or a union with new ethical forms. But it is most obvious as the pull toward the union of two individuals sexually. The two persons, longing, as all individuals do, to overcome the separateness and isolation to which we all are heir as individuals, can participate in a relationship that, for the moment, is not made up of two isolated, individual experiences, but a genuine union. A sharing takes place which is a new *Gestalt*, a new being, a new field of magnetic force.

[31]   We have been led astray by our economic and biological models to think that the aim of the love act is the orgasm. The French have a saying which, referring to eros, carries more truth: "The aim of

desire is not its satisfaction but its prolongation." André Maurois, speaking of his preference for love-making to which the orgasm is not the goal but an incidental conclusion, quotes another French saying, "Every beginning is lovely."

The moment of greatest significance in love-making, as judged by [32] what people remember in the experience and what patients dream about, is not the moment of orgasm. It is rather the moment of entrance, the moment of penetration of the erection of the man into the vagina of the woman. This is the moment that shakes us, that has within it the great wonder, tremendous and tremulous as it may be—or disappointing and despairing, which says the same thing from the opposite point of view. This is the moment when the persons' reactions to the love-making experience are most original, most individual, most truly their own. This, and not the orgasm, is the moment of union and the realization that we have won the other.

The ancients made Eros a "god," or more specifically, a daimon. [33] This is a symbolic way of communicating a basic truth of human experience, that eros always drives us to transcend ourselves. When Goethe wrote, "Woman draws us upward," his line may be more accurately read, "Eros, in relation with a woman, draws us upward." Such a truth is both inner, personal, and *subjective* on one hand, and external, social, and *objective* on the other—that is, it is a truth which obtains in our relationships in the objective world. The ancients, taking sex for granted simply as a natural bodily function, saw no need to make it into a god. Anthony presumably had all his sexual needs taken care of by the concubines accompanying the Roman army; it was only when he met Cleopatra that *eros* entered the picture and he became transported into a whole new world, ecstatic and destructive at the same time.

The artists have always instinctively known the difference between [34] sex and eros. In Shakespeare's play, Romeo's friend Mercutio teases him about his previous sweetheart, describing her in good modern anatomical style:

> I conjure thee by Rosaline's bright eyes,
> By her high forehead, and her scarlet lip,
> By her fine foot, straight leg, quivering thigh,
> And the desmesnes that there adjacent lie.
> (Act II, Scene i)

It reads like a contemporary realistic novel, the bodily description of the heroine ending with the expected "quivering thigh" and allusion to the adjacent parts. For Mercutio is not in love; from his external view the phenomenon appears to be sex and to be used as any vital young Veronese man would use feminine <u>pulchritude</u>.

[35]   But does Romeo use that language? Absurd question! He is in the
state of *eros* with Juliet:

> O! she doth teach the torches to burn bright.
> It seems she hangs upon the cheek of night
> Like a rich jewel in an Ethiop's ear;
> Beauty too rich for use, for earth too dear!
>   (Act I, Scene v)

[36]   It is interesting to recall that Romeo and Juliet were members of
feuding families. Eros leaps the barriers between enemies. Indeed, I
often wonder whether the eros in us is not excited and challenged
especially by the "enemy." Eros is strangely fascinated by the "outlander,"
the person of the forbidden class, the foreign color or race. Shakespeare
is true to the meaning of eros when he has the love of Romeo and
Juliet, tragic as it was, bind together the previously warring Montagues
and Capulets, and unite the whole city of Verona.

EROS IN PLATO

[37]   There is good basis in man's ancient wisdom for the urge we all feel
in eros to unite with the beloved, to prolong the delight, to deepen
the meaning and treasure it. This holds in our relationships not only
with persons but with objects, like a machine we are making or a
house we are building or a vocation to which we are devoted.

[38]   To find the roots of our understanding of eros, we turn to *The
Symposium*, which still surprises and delights readers with the con-
temporaneousness of its insights into love.[9] Plato's dialogue describing
this banquet—aptly called the most famous drinking party in history—
is given over entirely to the discussion of eros. The setting is Agathon's
home, where Socrates, Aristophanes, Alcibiades, and others have
been invited to celebrate Agathon's winning of the prize the previous
day for tragic drama. The evening is passed by each one in turn giving
his thoughts and experience of eros.

[39]   "What is love?" asks Socrates in a crucial summary passage. He
quotes the answer from Diotima, the celebrated teacher of love: "He is
neither mortal nor immortal, but a mean between the two. . . . He is
a great spirit (daimon) and like all spirits he is intermediate between
the divine and the mortal. . . . He is the mediator who spans the
chasm which divides men and gods, and therefore in him all is bound
together. . . ."[10]

EROS SICKENING

[40]   The Eros we have been discussing is that of the classical age, when
he was still the creative power and the bridge between men and gods.

But this "healthy" Eros deteriorated. Plato's understanding of Eros is a middle form of the concept, standing between Hesiod's view of Eros as the powerful and original creator and the later deteriorated form in which Eros becomes a sickly child. These three aspects of Eros are also accurate reflections of psychological archetypes of human experience: each of us at different times has the experience of Eros as creator, as mediator, and as banal playboy. Our age is by no means the first to experience the banalization of love, and to find that without passion, love sickens.

In the charming story quoted at the beginning of this chapter, we [41] saw that the ancient Greeks had put into the quintessential language of myth the insights which spring from the archetypes of the human psyche. Eros, the child of <u>Ares</u> and <u>Aphrodite</u>, "did not grow as other children, but remained a small, rosy, chubby child, with gauzy wings and rougish, dimpled face." After telling us that the alarmed mother was informed, "Love cannot grow without Passion," the myth goes on:

> In vain the goddess strove to catch the concealed meaning of this answer. It was only revealed to her when Anteros, god of passion, was born. When with his brother, Eros grew and flourished, until he became a handsome slender youth; but when separated from him, he invariably resumed his childish form and mischievous habits.[11]

Within these disarmingly naïve sentences, with which the Greeks [42] were wont to clothe their most profound wisdom, lie several points which are cruical for our problems now. One is that Eros is the child of *Ares* as well as Aphrodite. This is to say that love is inseparably connected with aggression.

Another is that the Eros which had been the powerful creator in [43] Hesiod's time, causing the barren earth to spring up with green trees and breathing the spirit of life into man, has now deteriorated into a child, a rosy, chubby, playful creature, sometimes a mere fat infant playing with his bow and arrows. We see him represented as an effete Cupid in so many of the paintings of the seventeenth and eighteenth centuries as well as in ancient times. "In archaic art Eros is represented as a beautiful winged youth and tends to be made younger and younger until by the Hellenistic period he is an infant." In Alexandrine poetry, he degenerates into a mischievous child.[12] There must be something within Eros' own nature to cause this deterioration, for it is present already in the myth which, while later than the Hesiod version, still dates from long before Greek civilization disintegrated.

This brings us to the very heart of what has also gone wrong [44] in our day: eros has lost passion, and has become insipid, childish, banal.

[45]   As is so often the case, the myth reveals a critical conflict in the roots of human experience, true for the Greeks and true for us: we engage in a flight from eros, the once powerful, original source of being, to sex, the mischievous plaything. Eros is demoted to the function of a pretty bartender, serving grapes and wine, a stimulator for dalliance whose task is to keep life endlessly sensuous on a bank of soft clouds. He stands not for the creative use of power—sexual, procreative, and other—but for the immediacy of gratification. And, *mirabile dictu*, we discover that the myth proclaims exactly what we have seen happening in our own day: *eros, then, even loses interest in sex*. In one version of the myth, Aphrodite tries to find him to get him up and about his business of spreading love with his bow and arrows. And, teen-age loafer that he has become, he is off gambling with Ganymede and cheating at the cards.

[46]   Gone is the spirit of the life-giving arrows, gone the creature who could breathe spirit into man and woman, gone the powerful Dionysian festivals, gone the frenzied dancing and the mysteries that moved the initiates more than the vaunted drugs of our mechanical age, gone even the bucolic intoxication. Eros now playboy indeed! Bacchanal with Pepsi-Cola.

[47]   Is this what civilization always does—tames Eros to make him fit the needs of the society to perpetuate itself? Changes him from the power that brings to birth new being and ideas and passion, weakens him till he is no longer the creative force that breaks old forms asunder to make new ones? Tames him until he stands for the goal of perpetual ease, dalliance, affluence, and, ultimately, apathy?[13]

[48]   In this respect we confront a new and specific problem in our Western world—*the war between eros and technology*. There is no war between *sex* and technology: our technical inventions help sex to be safe, available, and efficient as demonstrated from birth-control pills all the way to the how-to-do-it books. Sex and technology join together to achieve "adjustment"; with the full release of tension over the weekend, you can work better in the button-down world on Monday. Sensual needs and their gratification are not at war with technology, at least in any immediate sense (whether they are in the long run is another question).

[49]   But it is not at all clear that technology and *eros* are compatible, or can even live without perpetual warfare. The lover, like the poet, is a menace on the assembly line. Eros breaks existing forms and creates new ones and that, naturally, is a threat to technology. Technology requires regularity, predictability, and runs by the clock. The untamed eros fights against all concepts and confines of time.

[50]   Eros is the impetus in building civilizations. But the civilization then turns on its progenitor and disciplines the erotic impulses. This

can still work toward the increase and expansion of consciousness. The erotic impulses can and should have some discipline: the gospel of the free expression of every impulse disperses experience like a river with no banks, its water spilled and wasted as it flows in every direction. The discipline of eros provides *forms* in which we can develop and which protect us from unbearable anxiety. Freud believed that the disciplining of eros was necessary for a culture, and that it was from the repression and <u>sublimation</u> of erotic impulses that the power came out of which civilizations were built. De Rougemont, for one of the few times, here agrees with Freud; he does not forget

> that without the sexual discipline which the so-called puritanical tendencies have imposed on us since Europe first existed, there would be nothing more in our civilization than in those nations known as underdeveloped, and no doubt less: there would be neither work, organized effort nor the technology which has created the present world. There would also not be the problem of eroticism! The erotic authors forget this fact quite naively, committed as they are to their poetic or moralizing passion, which too often alienates them from the true nature of the "facts of life," and their complex links with economy, society, and culture.[14]

But there comes a point (and this is the challenge facing modern technological Western man) when the cult of technique destroys feeling, undermines passion, and blots out individual identity. The technologically efficient lover, defeated in the contradiction which is copulation without eros, is ultimately the impotent one. He has lost the power to be carried away; he knows only too well what he is doing. At this point, technology diminishes consciousness and demolishes eros. Tools are no longer an enlargement of consciousness but a substitute for it and, indeed, tend to repress and truncate it. [51]

Must civilization always tame eros to keep the society from breaking up again? Hesiod lived in the strongly fomenting, archaic sixth century, closer to the sources of culture and the moments of gestation and birth, when the procreative powers were at work, and man *had* to live with chaos and form it into something new. But then, with the growing need for stabilization, the daimonic and tragic elements tended to be buried. Insight into the downfall of civilizations is revealed here. We see effete Athens set up for the more primitive Macedonians, they in turn for the Romans, and the Romans in turn for the Huns. And we for the yellow and black races? [52]

Eros is the center of the vitality of a culture—its heart and soul. And when release of tension takes the place of creative eros, the downfall of the civilization is assured. [53]

NOTES

1. U.S. Department of Health Statistics *Medical World News*, March, 1967, pp. 64–68. These reports also inform us that venereal disease is also increasing 4 per cent a year among adolescents. This increase may have different causes from those for illegitimate pregnancy, but it bears out my general thesis. The second statistic—that this is an increase from one in fifteen of ten years ago—is from a report of the Teamsters Joint Council 16, covered in *The New York Times*, July 1, 1968.

2. Kenneth Clark, *Dark Ghetto: A Study in the Effect of Powerlessness* (New York, Harper & Row, 1965). This excerpt is from sections of the book quoted in *Psychology Today*, I/5, September, 1967, p. 38.

3. The same is true among the Indians of South America, where the symbol of being able to father babies is so important that it defeats all the efforts of enlightened nurses and doctors to spread birth control. The woman will readily confess that she wants not to have any more babies, but the "husband"—generally of the common-law variety—feels it a mark against his machismos if he cannot father a baby a year, and so leaves her in favor of others if he cannot prove his potency with her.

4. T. S. Eliot, "The Hollow Men," *Collected Poems* (New York, Harcourt, Brace & Company, 1934), p. 101.

5. The gripping thing about the movie *La Dolce Vita* was not its sex, but that while everyone was feeling sexy and emoting all over, no one could *hear* any other person. From the first scene when the noise of the helicopter blots out the shouting of the men to the women, to the last scene in which the hero strains to hear the girl across the stream but cannot because of the noise of the ocean waves, no one hears another. Just at the moment in the castle when the man and the woman are at the point of declaring authentic love for each other in a communication by echoes, she cannot hear his voice from the other room and immediately drugs herself by promiscuous sexual titillation with a chance passerby. The dehumanizing thing is the so-called emotion without any relatedness; and sex is the most ready drug to hide one's terror at this dehumanization.

6. Joseph Campbell, *Occidental Mythology*, vol. III from *The Masks of God* (New York, Viking Press, 1964), p. 235.

7. *Webster's Collegiate Dictionary*, 3rd ed. (Springfield, Mass., G. & C. Merriam Company).

8. *Webster's Third New International Dictionary* (Springfield, Mass., G. & C. Merriam Company, 1961).

9. To the argument that Plato was actually speaking of pederasty, the love of men for boys, and that the Greeks valued homosexuality more than heterosexuality, I reply that eros has the same characteristics regardless of the form of love about which you are speaking. I do not believe that this is any disparagement of Plato's insights into love. Furthermore, "There is evidence that Socrates did not practice pederasty," writes Professor Morgan, and "no convincing evidence that Plato did either. The issue seems to me to interest only scholars of Athenian cultural history. Plato's philosophical interpretation of love stands wholly outside the problem of homosexuality and heterosexuality. . . . Were Plato living today, his language would presumably reflect our differing social customs, but would not require any fundamental revision on this account. . . . In *either* cultural environment, the man who is consumed with merely carnal hungers and gratified in merely carnal manners is properly and identically condemned as bestial, foolish, childish, and infrahuman; Plato's presentation of love can stand as strong today as it ever stood." Douglas N. Morgan, *Love: Plato, the Bible and Freud* (Englewood Cliffs, N.J., Prentice-Hall, 1964), pp. 44–45.

10. W. H. Auden, ed., *The Portable Greek Reader* (New York, Viking Press, 1948), p. 487.

11. *Ibid.*, p. 493.

12. "Eros," *Encyclopaedia Britannica*, vol. VIII (1947), p. 695.

13. Rollo May, in a review of Vance Packard's *The Sexual Wilderness: The Contemporary Upheaval in Male-Female Relationships* (New York, David McKay Company, 1968), appearing in *The New York Times Book Review*, October 13, 1968: "Packard here cites J. D. Unwin's massive, if almost forgotten, 'Sex and Culture' (1934), a study of 80 uncivilized societies and also a number of historically advanced cultures. Unwin sought to correlate various

societies' sexual permissiveness with their energy for civilized advancement. He concluded that the 'amount of cultural ascent of the primitive societies closely paralleled the amount of limitation they placed upon the nonmarital sexual opportunity.' Virtually all the civilized societies Unwin examined—the Babylonians, Athenians, Romans, Anglo-Saxons, and English—began their historical careers in a 'state of absolute monogamy.' The one exception was the Moors, where a specific religious sanction supported polygamy. 'Any human society,' Unwin writes, 'is free to choose either to display great energy or to enjoy sexual freedom; the evidence is that it cannot do both for more than one generation.' Packard points out that this is supported in different ways by other historians and anthropologists, such as Carl C. Zimmerman, Arnold J. Toynbee, Charles Winick and Pitirim A. Sorokin."

14. From Denis de Rougemont's *The Myths of Love* (New York, Pantheon Books, 1963), quoted in *Atlas*, November, 1965, p. 306.

QUESTIONS

1. The philosophical psychoanalyst very often uses myths to express difficult or elusive truths about deep human impulses (e.g., Aphrodite learns that Eros cannot grow up until his brother Anteros is born). May says, "Within these disarmingly naïve sentences . . . the Greeks were wont to clothe their most profound wisdom." Why do you think that May uses myth and that he admires the Greek way of expressing the most profound truths mythically? Consider: Freud, who was the father of psychoanalysis, also drew heavily upon Greek myth (e.g., Oedipus Complex, Thanatos, Eros). What are myths? How might the psychoanalytic idea that the deepest truths about our nature lie in our *unconscious* minds prompt this tendency to use myths? Find an example from Greek culture or even American history that reflects this tendency. Why do all cultures create myths (and, curiously enough, create so many that are similar cross-culturally)?

2. On p. 98 May offers three conclusions which *might* explain why the young woman became pregnant by a blind person for whom she felt nothing. Her behavior (1) established self-esteem, (2) compensated for emotional poverty, and (3) expressed hostility toward repressive parents. He then offers another conclusion: the cause is repressed eros. Do you think the conclusion which he chooses is more logical, or more consistent with his evidence than the three he rejects? Explain.

3. Some experts in the study of sex (known as sexologists) have argued that thinking of sexual activity as "babymaking" diminishes the worth of sexuality. How does May feel about baby making? What fundamental similarity does May see in making babies, discovering

the theory of relativity, or writing a symphony—why are they all expressions of eros?

4. May argues that "the moment of greatest significance in love-making, as judged by what people remember in the experience and what patients dream about, is not the moment of orgasm . . . [but] the moment of penetration. . . ." Is his argument convincing? If the "moment of union" is the end toward which desire moves, could we, using May's line of reasoning, say a kiss or a hug is more memorable than "the moment of penetration"?

5. Why does May say there is a war between eros and technology? And why does war not exist between sex and technology? What, in May's characterization, makes eros an antagonist of civilization? You might get at the core of this question by examining the meaning of the sentence, "The lover, like the poet, is a menace on the assembly line."

6. Look back at Badinter's study. What do you think that May would say about mother love in seventeenth-century French civilization? How would May explain the transformation from selfish indifference to doting maternalism that occurred with the beginning of romanticism? How would eros be operating in this transformation according to May?

7. What would Mead think of May's theory? Would she find the view that eros is "in conflict with sex," a principle that holds for all cultures or just Western, Greek-influenced cultures?

EXERCISES

1. Find men and women in each of the following age groups: (1) 17–24, (2) 25–34, (3) 35–55, and ask them to write an answer in one hundred words or fewer to the questions below. Stress that the answers will be kept completely confidential. Do not ask your respondents to put anything but their sex and age on the answer sheet.

In my most romantic or erotic day dreams or sleeping dreams I visualize _____.

My earliest memory of feeling desire for another person was _____.

Collect the answers and determine whether there are significant differences among eros fantasies based upon age and sex. In a speculative essay, report your findings and relate them to May's discussion.

2. May suggests that we live in a society which encourages instant gratification of sexual desire and that this gratification produces a deadening of feeling. He suggests further that delay of desire intensifies the pleasure of fulfillment. Apply these observations to a movie you have seen recently or one that you can see in the next day or so. It might be useful to choose either a deliberately romantic movie (perhaps even a soap opera on television) or a sexually frank, R-rated movie. Write a paper in which you use May's view to interpret the movie. If you had the opportunity to see one of each kind of movie, write a critical response to May's view based on both movies.

3. May claims that technology destroys eros. Think of three illustrations from modern life in America that support or refute this observation. Write a paper in which you explore May's claim, incorporating the illustrations you have found.

CHAPTER SEVEN

HENDRICK AND HENDRICK: LIKING AND LOVING

Sociology

Like psychology, sociology is the study of behavior, but sociology restricts itself to human behavior, and usually to that behavior which is manifested in social interactions or social processes. Sociologists use a variety of methods to conduct their studies: direct observation, carefully designed questionnaires, demographic measurements, and even laboratory experiments. This selection, from Hendrick and Hendrick's book, *Liking, Loving, and Relating*, shows the sociologist carefully trying to distinguish between two similar kinds of behavior, liking and loving, in order to be better able to understand what each kind of behavior is. In addition to describing the two kinds of behavior on the basis of their own and other people's experience, the sociologists use the survey by questionnaire to gather better, more objective information, and they also use experimentation (in this case the experiments that led to Schachter's theory of emotion).

When you read Hendrick and Hendrick, try to compare their methods of observing and gathering information with those of Harlow, the experimentalist; Badinter, the social historian; and May, the psychoanalyst. Think of ways in which these disciplines can enrich one another, or refine one another's findings. For example, if time travel were possible, would you want to use some of the methods Hendrick and Hendrick describe in interviewing some of the parents Badinter describes? Or would it be possible, in your view, to use a sociologist's questionnaire to get at levels of liking and loving that May is trying to reach?

GLOSSARY

conceptually [1]	rampant [9]
predispositions [1]	motivation [9]
interpersonal [1]	scenario [13]
correlation [3]	palpitate [14]
affiliation [3]	attribution [15]
dependency [3]	viscera [18]
intimacy [3]	stimuli [23]
validity [7]	frustration [23]
explicit [7]	masochism [27]
validation [7]	sadism [27]
empirical [8]	aversive [27]
cognitive [8]	

_____ LIKING AND LOVING _____

Clyde Hendrick and Susan Hendrick

Liking is related to loving, but it also seems different. Zick Rubin [1]
(1970, 1973, 1974) was one of the first social scientists to study the
similarity and difference between the two concepts in a rigorous way.
Rubin (1970) viewed love conceptually as "an attitude held by a person
toward a particular other person, involving predispositions to think,
feel, and behave in certain ways toward the other person" (p. 265).
This definition is very similar to our general definition of interpersonal

SOURCE: From *Liking, Loving, and Relating*, by C. Hendrick and S. Hendrick. Copyright
© 1963 by Wadsworth, Inc. Reprinted by permission of the publisher, Brooks/Cole
Publishing Company, Monterey, California.

attraction. This was intended; both love and liking are best viewed conceptually as an attitude. The research problem for Rubin was to determine whether the two concepts are different in the ways they really occur in people's behavior.

[2]   In order to study this issue Rubin developed two questionnaires (or scales), one to measure liking and the second to measure romantic loving. The results from responses to the two scales would be used to decide whether liking is really different from loving, or whether the two scales seem to measure the same thing. Constructing the scales was a challenging and difficult job, because it was necessary to construct a fair test. A fair test required that items for the two questionnaires be selected in an unbiased way, so that the scales could either be unrelated or highly related, depending on what the true state of nature is. It would probably be possible to choose sets of items that proved no difference between liking and loving, or other sets of items that proved a complete difference. Such an initial bias in item selection would really be a form of scientific cheating and would not inform us about love versus liking in the real world.

[3]   Given these considerations, it will be useful to specify more precisely the criteria that Rubin followed in the development of the love scale and the rationale by which liking could be distinguished from romantic love.

1. Since the content of the questionnaire items would constitute the conceptual meaning of romantic love, the items should be based on current popular and theoretical conceptions of love.
2. Answers to the questionnaire items should indicate that they are measuring a single underlying attitude of love. Operationally, all of the items should be highly intercorrelated.
3. A parallel questionnaire measuring liking must be developed. All the items should also be highly intercorrelated. However, if love and liking are separate or independent concepts, then the correlation between the love questionnaire and the liking questionnaire should be fairly low.

A large number of items were initially obtained and sorted by judges into love and liking categories. From this procedure 70 items were obtained, rated by students in an introductory psychology course, and evaluated by methods that estimated their correlation, or relation to each other. This analysis resulted in 13 items for a love scale and 13 items for a liking scale. The love items seem to tap affiliation and dependence needs, desire to care for the other, exclusivity, possessiveness, and intimacy toward the other. The liking items tap favorability of evaluation, respect, perceived similarity, maturity, intelligence, admirability, and likability.

The two questionnaires were tested and retested by recruiting 158 [4] couples to complete them. Subjects also completed the questionnaires again by rating a close, same-sex friend. Each item on the questionnaire was rated on a nine-point scale.

The results provided some support for Rubin's distinction between [5] loving and liking. For females the love scale had an average correlation between items of +.84; the liking scale had an average correlation between items of +.81. However the correlation between the total liking and loving scales was only +.39. The results for males showed average correlations between items of +.86 for loving and +.83 for liking. However, the correlation between liking and loving was also quite high, +.60. Rubin suggested that women may distinguish more sharply between liking and loving than men do.

Some interesting differences in average ratings emerged between [6] males and females. The means are for total scores, which were computed by adding a subject's responses to all 13 questions on a scale. Men and women showed the same overall level of love for each other, and women liked their partners as much as they loved them. However, men liked their female partners less than they loved them, and also liked the partners less than the partners liked them. This difference may have been because men tended to get higher ratings than women on liking-scale items such as intelligence, good judgment, and leadership potential. Both sexes loved their best friend of the same sex considerably less than they loved their romantic partner of the opposite sex. They liked their best friend of the same sex considerably more than they loved him or her, but still somewhat less than they liked their romantic partner.

Rubin's evidence is not completely convincing that love is different [7] from liking because of the high correlation between the two scales for males. However, it is a good first attempt to operationalize and scientifically distinguish between the two sentiments. More recent research by Dermer and Pyszczynski (1978) provided additional evidence for the validity of the distinction. These authors were puzzled by the absence of any reference to sexual behavior in the love scale. The authors reasoned that sexual interest and romantic feelings of love should be highly related. If some stimulus, such as erotic literature, prompted a sexual response, feelings of love for one's lover should be stronger after reading the erotic passage than before reading it. College males who said they were currently in love served in the experiment. Some of the males were assigned to read a "Collegiate Fantasy," which dealt in explicit detail with the sexual behavior and fantasies of a college woman. The rest of the men served in a control condition and read a rather dull article on the courtship and mating behavior of herring gulls. Afterward both groups of men completed several scales, including abbreviated versions of Rubin's liking and love scales. Results showed that men reading the erotic passage had significantly higher love scores (for the person they were in love with) than men who read about herring gulls. However, there was no difference in the liking scores (for the loved one) between the two groups. These results show that the love scale was differentially sensitive to the erotic manipulation, but the liking scale was not. Therefore, these data provide additional validation for the distinction between liking and loving.

[8]   It seems reasonable to conclude that people do in fact distinguish between liking someone and loving that person. Rubin's research is of value in providing some empirical evidence on the matter. Yet, because emotions are very difficult to distinguish in concrete terms, it is still unclear exactly how the emotional aspects of these two states differ. It is even possible that the emotional aspect of liking and loving does not differ. Rubin's work may only show that the cognitive or belief aspects of the two concepts are different. It is possible that the basic inner emotional state, including physiological arousal, may be the same for many types of emotional experiences and that all that differs is the individual's interpretation of the situation. Given emotional arousal, love and liking—and the perceived difference between the two—may be more in the head than in the loins. We next examine this interesting interpretation of passion and romantic love.

EMOTIONS AND PASSIONATE LOVE

[9]   *Falling in love* is a fitting description of an experience that almost everyone has at least once and usually several times. To fall into love is to fall into a profound set of emotional experiences. There may be a range of physical symptoms such as dry mouth, pounding heart, flushed face, and knotted stomach. The mind may race, and fantasy, especially about the loved one, is rampant. Motivation to work, play, indeed for anything except the lover, may fall to zero. As the love feelings develop, strong feelings of passion may occur. In fact, passionate love is essentially the same as romantic love, except that the focus is more specifically on the emotional intensity and sexual passion.

[10]   Clearly, love is closely connected to emotional states and feelings of passion. But how? There are many theories of emotion. We will examine one theory proposed by Stanley Schachter. This theory was used in a clever way by Ellen Berscheid and Elaine Walster to explain passionate love.

SCHACHTER'S THEORY OF EMOTION

[11]   Suppose that John can drink exactly one cup of coffee in the morning with no ill effects. If he drinks two cups of coffee, he gets jittery, his

hands tremble, and his heart palpitates. When this happens, he berates himself for being a dunce and swears that it will never happen again. The extra caffeine creates a state of physiological arousal.

One morning John had breakfast with a business acquaintance. [12] The conversation was intense, and without John's awareness the waiter refilled his coffee cup. John drank two cups of coffee, but he left the meeting thinking that he had drunk only one cup. In fifteen minutes he will get jittery and his heart will start palpitating. An interesting question arises—how will John explain his arousal, knowing that he drank only one cup of coffee? Two different but equally plausible scenarios of John's experiences 15 minutes later are described below.

Possible scenario 1: After John left the business acquaintance, he [13] walked across the street to the catalog department of a department store to pick up an item he had ordered the week before. The clerk waiting on him appeared somewhat surly and seemed to take forever in the stockroom looking for his order. While John was waiting, his hands began to tremble and his heart began to palpitate. John's thoughts were on the clerk. Very shortly he became aware of his inner arousal. He soon decided that he was angry—in fact, very angry—at the clerk for taking so long. In fact, he actually conceptualized a fitting label in his mind for the clerk: "no-good S.O.B." When the clerk returned, John was quite short and snapped at him, much to the clerk's surprise.

Possible scenario 2: After John left the business acquaintance, he [14] walked across the street to a barber shop to get a shave. A young and attractive female barber shaved him. After the shave was under way for a few minutes, John's hands began to tremble and his heart began to palpitate. He was very aware of the presence of the young woman, and at the same time became aware of his inner arousal. John soon decided that he was attracted to the woman; in fact, he concluded that he was becoming sexually aroused. A potentially em-barrassing erection began to occur. As the shave ended, John took the gamble and asked the lady out that evening. He was disappointed when she responded that she does not socialize with customers.

In each scenario John experienced heightened physiological arousal [15] caused by excess caffeine. In neither case was he aware of the true cause of his arousal. The arousal was *unexplained*. John used the en-vironmental situation in which he found himself to infer situational cues which might be relevant to his arousal. On the basis of those cues he made a decision about the causes of his arousal. Making such a decision, or an attribution, was equivalent to labeling himself as experiencing a certain emotional state. The attributed emotional states were very different in the two scenarios because the two situations were very different. In the first possible scenario John attributed his arousal to the clerk's behavior and experienced the emotion of anger. In the second possible scenario John attributed his arousal to the lovely woman and experienced the emotions involved in sexual arousal.

[16]   In each scenario the initial state of physiological arousal was identical, but the emotions attributed to the arousal state were quite different. These scenarios suggest that, in general, the experience of emotion is heavily dependent on the attributions that people associate with their inner arousal in a given set of situational circumstances. It is precisely this kind of thinking that led to the development of Schachter's (Schachter & Singer, 1962; Schachter, 1964) theory of emotion. According to the theory, an emotional state depends on two variables, which may be expressed as a simple verbal equation:

$$\text{Emotional State} = \text{Unexplained Physiological Arousal} + \text{Relevant Situational Cues}$$

[17]   This theory was created in an attempt to integrate two earlier conflicting theories of emotion. Before the turn of the present century William James suggested that people have direct physiological reactions to the perception of stimulating events, and that awareness of bodily changes as they occur *is* the emotion. Phrased differently, we feel happy because we laugh, sad because we cry. This theory, which came to be known as the James-Lange theory of emotion, directly equated inner physiological states and their changes with emotion. The theory implied that different emotional experiences should have different physiological states and that a direct manipulation of bodily state should also directly manipulate emotional experience.

[18]   The Cannon-Bard theory of emotion was developed later in opposition to the James-Lange theory. The Cannon-Bard theory proposed that emotional experience and physiological arousal are relatively independent of each other, with each controlled by different central nervous system processes. This theory was based on Cannon's (1929; cited in Schachter, 1964) strong critique of the James-Lange theory, as follows:

1. Separation of the <u>viscera</u> from the central nervous system does not destroy emotional behavior.
2. The same physiological changes seem to occur in very different emotional states.
3. The viscera are insensitive to subtle changes.
4. Visceral changes are too slow to be the direct cause of emotional feeling.
5. Artificial production of physiological changes naturally associated with strong emotional states does not cause such states.

In reviewing the two theories, Schachter and Singer (1962) concluded that both physiological arousal and a cognitive label (or attributed cause) based on situational cues were necessary for a full emotional experience. Neither arousal alone nor the cognitive label alone was sufficient to cause an emotional state.

PASSIONATE LOVE

Reinforcement theories are widely used to explain interpersonal attraction. We like people who provide rewards for us and dislike people who punish us. Many theories explain love in the same way. However, in the previous section we reviewed the work of Rubin, which argued for and provided some evidence that liking and loving are different phenomena. [19]

Berscheid and Walster (1974a; Walster, 1971) also felt that there are real differences between liking and loving. Some of those purported differences are: [20]

1. Liking relationships seem to depend upon actual rewards; with love, fantasy and imagined gratifications may occur out of all proportion to the number of actual rewards received.
2. Liking and friendship often grow over time, but romantic love seems to become diluted with the passage of time.
3. Liking is consistently associated with good things (positive reinforcers), but passionate love seems to be associated with conflicting emotions, as witnessed by teenagers' frequent question of whether it is possible to love and hate someone at the same time.

Based on these apparent differences, Berscheid and Walster argued that passionate love is not just intense liking and that reinforcement theory does not account for passionate love very well, because such love seems to be a strong mix of both rewards and punishments. Instead, they selected Schachter's theory of emotion as the best conception to explain passionate love. [21]

In order to explain passionate love, the same two conditions must hold that are needed to account for any emotional state: [22]

1. The individual must be intensely aroused physiologically.
2. The cues in the situation must dictate to the individual that passionate love is the appropriate label for his or her feelings.

Both conditions are necessary. One will not experience passionate love unless physiologically aroused, but, given arousal, it is still not love unless the individual labels it love. If the situation is such that it is reasonable to attribute the aroused state to passionate love, then the individual will experience love. However, "as soon as he ceases to attribute his arousal to passionate love, or the arousal itself ceases, love should die" (Berscheid & Walster, 1974a, p. 363).

[23]   There are several negative as well as positive experiences which can generate a state of arousal: fear-provoking stimuli, social rejection, and sexual frustration. There is some evidence that such negative states can be interpreted as passionate love; for example, the rejected suitor sometimes redoubles the intensity of passion after rejection. The frequent arousal of fear and anger in war also seems to stimulate passionate love. In his fascinating account of life as a soldier in wartime, Gray (1959) devoted a chapter to love in war. He wrote in a letter to a friend in 1944 that "the Greeks were wise men when they matched the god of war with the goddess Aphrodite. The soldier must not only kill, he must give birth to new warriors" (p. 70). The increased intensity of eroticism during war of both men and women is vividly described (Gray, 1959, p. 73).

[24]   Berscheid and Walster's theorizing would predict such an effect. The rigors of soldiering in wartime would tend to keep soldiers in a state of general physiological arousal. The context and situation are very different from peacetime, and the mere sight of a woman may be a sufficient stimulus to define the situation as one appropriate for passionate arousal.

[25]   Positive as well as negative experiences may generate the necessary physiological arousal. For example, sexual arousal during the excitement phase is physiologically very similar to the physiological responses of fear and anger. Thus sexual gratification should be and probably is a direct source of passionate love. Any activity which generates a sense of danger and excitement may serve as an arousal stimulus. In fact, many people value passionate love just because it is a source of excitement, which is positively valued.

[26]   It seems reasonable to conclude that a wide variety of experiences, both positive and negative, can generate a state of physiological arousal which can serve as one of the necessary conditions for a state of passionate love to exist. We are taught as children how to label our feelings in a wide variety of situations. By the time we are adults, we have an idea of the appropriate emotion to experience in most situations. The turmoil experienced at the funeral of a relative is unlikely to be experienced as sexual arousal instead of grief; such feelings are inappropriate at a funeral. The physiological excitement experienced after a half-hour of vigorous kissing is unlikely to be interpreted as grief; social learning dictates that you label the excitement as sexual arousal. The state of physiological arousal may be quite similar in

both situations; the difference in labeling dictates what emotion will be experienced.

Berscheid and Walster's theory of passionate love is interesting, [27] though as yet incomplete (Murstein, 1980). It could possibly account for the development of such sexual practices as masochism and sadism as accidents of mislabeling states of arousal during the course of socialization. It is presently unclear what types of arousal are conducive to labeling as sexual arousal or passionate love, and what types are not. For example, loud and prolonged noise is physiologically aversive. It is most unlikely that one could learn to interpret the physiological response to noise as passion. Likewise the ongoing experience of intense pain may be incompatible with labeling as passion. However, the quick reduction of physiological arousal just after the offset of an aversive stimulus may be quite conducive to the experience of passion. In fact, Kenrick and Cialdini (1977) criticized the theory on just this point: the reduction or offset of aversive stimulation is reinforcing. For example, lovers' quarrels are very unpleasant. But if they kiss and make up, the unpleasant emotional state ends, and the termination of negative feelings may reinforce feelings of love.

We must leave open the question of whether Berscheid and Walster's [28] theory of passionate love can be accounted for by principles of re-inforcement. However, they deserve much credit for drawing attention to the turbulence of passionate love. Phenomenally, love is often an alternation between ecstasy and despair, which is much stronger than in ordinary liking. Love is often both pleasure and pain. Further, the intensity of passionate love does seem to diminish over time in a way not quite true for liking. Although the expression is seldom applied to liking, love can die.

QUESTIONS

1. Hendrick and Hendrick quote Rubin's conception of love as "an attitude held by a person toward a particular other person, involving predispositions to think, feel, and behave in certain ways toward the other person." Do you think that this is a good definition? Do you think that it is too broad? Could the definition describe many other kinds of feeling? For example, isn't it as good a description for hatred? Isn't the predisposition to think, feel, etc., as good a description of racial prejudice as it is of love? How would you narrow or qualify the definition?

2. Sociologists attempt to measure or scale a single attitude which they have isolated. Do you think it is possible to single out one among all of the many, sometimes conflicting or overlapping attitudes involved in liking or loving?

3. The results of Rubin's study indicate that "men liked their female partners less than they loved them, and also liked the partners less than the partners liked them." Restate this conclusion in language that a young teenager could understand. On the basis of your readings in Badinter and Mead, do you think that these attitudes are culturally conditioned?

4. On the basis of your reading of May, how valid do you think a psychoanalyst would find these data? Do you think a psychoanalyst would accept what a person *says* he or she feels as being necessarily what the person *does* feel?

5. Hendrick and Hendrick offer Schachter's theory of emotion, as expressed in the following equation:

Emotional State = Unexplained Physiological Arousal
+ Relevant Situational Clues

Do you find Schachter's theory persuasive? Do you think that John in the anecdote really did think *in one situation* that he was angry and *in another* that he was in love when really he was experiencing caffeine overstimulation? Do you think you would confuse the feeling of being in love with catching a common cold even though both conditions involve rapid heart beat, feverishness, dry mouth, and sweating hands? Do you think that Schachter's theory of emotion holds for intense emotion felt over a long period of time?

6. Berscheid and Walster's study assumes that the relation of love and war is explicable in terms of Schachter's theory of emotion, i.e., that both conditions are explanations of intense physiological arousal. Consider alternative explanations for a love-war link. Try to use all the approaches that you have encountered in this unit as you devise your explanation. For instance, ask yourself:

   a. How might Margaret Mead explain a connection?
   b. Would the Medawars determine whether there was an evolutionary reason for the soldier to "not only kill, but give birth to new warriors"?
   c. How might an experimental psychologist test whether or not there was a connection?

EXERCISES

1. a. Hendrick and Hendrick provide evidence to support the hypothesis that men *love* but do not necessarily *like* the females with whom they are intimate, while women both like and love their male mates.

    (1) Choose two groups composed of males and females: one of college age and one in middle age.
    (2) Submit to them the questionnaire below. Only one blank is to be filled in or checked off in each item.
        (a) When I am engaged in an activity I particularly like (e.g. bowling, baseball, sewing, consciousness raising, building a barn), I would prefer that my lover ____ or my best male/female friend ____ were there.
        (b) The person in the world I like best to waste time with (e.g. fooling around, talking, playing) is my lover ____ or my friend ____.
        (c) In the event of a nuclear holocaust, the person I would like to be with is my friend ____ or my lover ____.
        (d) The person I would most like to be like is my friend ____ or my lover ____.
        (e) The person(s) I would most like to have around if I were eighty and in a nursing home are my friend(s) ____ or my mate (lover) ____.

    b. On the basis of the answers to these five items, make a report or an entry in your journal on the similarities and differences between the young and the middle-aged on the comparative value of love and friendship.
    Sort out the responses by males and females. Write a two-page report that supports or refutes the Hendricks' findings. List the criteria you considered most important and explain why.

2. Reserve fifteen minutes a day every day for a week and allow your mind to wander and to associate freely. Try to direct your thinking toward the happiest occasion and circumstances you can imagine. At the end of each session make notes of what you have visualized. After a week, note in your journal the people who appeared in your reveries and under what circumstances. Then write a paper on the subject, "My vision of perfect happiness is . . ." Be prepared to discuss in class how your experiment with the perception of happiness differed in method from an experiment set up on the same topic by a social researcher.

CHAPTER EIGHT

TYLER: PEOPLE VS. MATURE ENTERPRISES, INC., AND ELLIS: ON JUDGE TYLER'S DECISION TO CUT THE THROAT OF "DEEP THROAT"

Law

We live in what many observers call a "permissive" society. In recent years, more and more explicit materials, including books, films, magazines, and even greeting cards, have been merchandised and are sold widely over counters with few, if any, restrictions. The issue of whether such items ought to be readily available to the public is an extremely difficult one. It touches areas of concern that have been explored in preceding reading selections, and it raises questions we have not yet encountered in this unit. Certainly the issue is germane to the interests of the anthropologist who, like Margaret Mead, investigates to see what the limits are in the behavior that a society is willing to tolerate. It also touches upon the deepest concerns raised by the psychoanalytically oriented philosopher, Rollo May. Does the ready availability of explicit and pornographic materials deter the potentiality for the growth of love in a society? To what extent is the ready availability of these materials destructive of positive human values? In yet another area represented by the preceding selections, the question might be raised how the social historian, like Badinter, would approach the problems posed by explicit sex if he or she were to explore that subject from the vantage point of removed time?

The focus in the next two selections is on a New York State decision to outlaw the showing of the sexually explicit film *Deep Throat*. We have included the highly literate decision of Judge Joel Tyler, reviewing the grounds that led him to his controversial conclusion. To put this decision into its argumentative context, we have also included a psychologist's response to it. The issue on which the two selections concentrate is first and foremost the civil right of purveying, or making available, items in which sex is rendered explicitly. Embedded in this argument, however, is not merely the law, or more precisely, legal precedent, but also the morality and mental health that govern this law. We include these readings to add yet another perspective on "love and sexuality" and to introduce you to the complex craft of argument. As you read Judge Tyler's opinion, ask yourself what his main premises are and what methods he uses to support them. Then proceed to Albert Ellis's reply in *Clinical Social Work Journal* and determine how he has answered the main points raised by Judge Tyler and how effective his refutation is. Consider also the use of language by the two advocates. Which of the two, for example, engages more often in name calling? Does either of the two make irresponsible allegations or charges?

GLOSSARY

TYLER

deviate [1]	tenuous [5]
innocuous [2]	chaotic [5]
explicit [2]	nymphomania [6]
permeates [2]	gossamer [7]
ebullience [2]	euphemistically [7]
fellatio [3]	monolithic [8]
cunnilingus [3]	plebian [8]
tedious [5]	thespian [10]

amentia [10]   palpable [17]

trepidations [12]   decadence [24]

poignancy [14]   denigrates [24]

ELLIS

pejorative [3]   sabotage [14]

tautology [7]   annihilate [16]

pervert [8]   genocidal [16]

concomitant [8]   vilifying [16]

pernicious [9]

PEOPLE VS. MATURE
——— ENTERPRISES, INC. ———
Judge Joel Tyler

[1]   We are again thrust into the overexplored thicket of obscenity law. The defendant is charged with promotion, or possession with intent to promote, obscene material, knowing the content and character thereof. What is involved is the showing in a public theatre, at a $5.00 per admission charge, the film "Deep Throat." The case has engendered some public interest here and elsewhere. However it is not unique. Many cases dealing with depiction of the same or similar deviate sexual behavior have been reported, but few have had such a full measure of directed publicity.

THE FILM

[2]   The film runs 62 minutes. It is in color and in sound and boasts a musical score. Following the first innocuous scene ("heroine" driving

SOURCE: "People vs. Mature Enterprises, Inc.," by Judge Joel Tyler, reprinted from *Clinical Social Work Journal*, vol. 1, no. 4, copyright © 1973, Human Sciences Press Inc., New York, by permission of the publisher.

a car), the film runs from one act of explicit sex into another, forthrightly demonstrating heterosexual intercourse and a variety of deviate sexual acts, not "fragmentary or fleeting" or 10 minutes out of a 120 minute movie as in "I Am Curious Yellow" but here it permeates and engulfs the film from beginning to end. The camera angle, emphasis and close-up zooms were directed "toward a maximum exposure in detail of the genitalia" during the gymnastics, gyrations, bobbling, trundling, surging, ebb and flowing, eddying, moaning, groaning and sighing, all with ebullience and gusto.

There were so many and varied forms of sexual activity one would [3] tend to lose count of them. However, the news reporters were more adept and counted seven separate acts of fellatio and four of cunnilingus. Such concentration upon the acts of fellatio and cunnilingus overlooked the numerous clear, clinical acts of sexual intercourse, anal sodomy, female masturbation, clear depiction of seminal fluid ejaculation and an orgy scene—a Sodom and Gomorrah gone wild before the fire— all of which is enlivened with the now famous "four letter words" and finally with bells ringing and rockets bursting in climactic ecstasy.

The performance of one sexual act runs almost headlong into the [4] other. One defense witness thought 75 to 80% of the film involved depiction of explicit sexual activity and another viewed it at over 50%. A time keeper may have clocked a higher percentage. Nothing was faked or simulated; it was as explicit and exquisite as life. One defense witness said he saw "realism and genuine sexual experience." No imagination was needed, since it was intended to appeal to the imbecile as well.

The defense expert witness testified that the film possessed enter- [5] tainment value and humor. The court appropriately answered that tedious and tenuous argument: "Presumably the Romans of the First Century derived entertainment from witnessing Christians being devoured by lions. Given the right audience, the spectacle of a man committing an act of sodomy on another man would provide entertainment value. However, neither this spectacle nor the activities described in the instant case are invested with constitutionally protected values merely because they entertain viewers. However chaotic the law may be in this field, no court has yet adopted such an extreme result."

The alleged "humor" of the film is sick, and designed on a level [6] to appeal especially to those first learning that boys and girls are different. Drama critic Vincent Canby characterized the jokes as "dumb gags, [which] cannot disguise the straight porno intent." As to plot, there is none, unless you exclude the sexual activity, which is the sole plot. And as to character development, a desirable and necessary concomitant of meaningful film, stage, or book, again there is none, unless of course one means that the progression (or retrogression) of multiple and varied nymphomania to a singular form (fellatio) is evidence of this attribute.

[7]   Oh, yes! There is a gossamer of a story line—the heroine's all-engrossing search for sexual gratification, and when all her endeavors fail to gratify, her unique problem is successfully diagnosed to exist in her throat. She then seeks to fill the doctor's prescription by repeated episodes of fellatio, which one critic euphemistically characterizes as "compensatory behavior."

[8]   The defense experts testified that they see the film legitimatizing woman's need and "life right" for sexual gratification, equal with that of men. They also see in the film the thoughtful lesson that sex should not be unavailingly monolithic (usual face-to-face relationship) but should take varied forms with complete sexual gratification as the crowning goal, or as the film seems to advertise in its plebian fashion— "different strokes for different folks"; or as others, less articulate, might say, "there's more than one way to skin the cat." These unusual and startling revelations are of social value, they say, not only for the bedroom, but necessary as an object lesson for a public forum.

[9]   The alleged story lines are the facade, the sheer negligee through which clearly shines the producer's and the defendant's true and only purpose, that is, the presentation of unmistakably hard-core pornography. One defense witness actually, but unwittingly, confirms the charade when he says that the "plot" of the film "provides a thread on which the various sequences of sexual acts would be hung."

[10]   Movie critic Judith Crist characterizes the production "idiot moviemaking" and the actors "awful." I agree, except to add that a female who would readily and with apparent anxious abandon submit to the insertion of a glass dildoe container into her vagina, have liquid poured therein and then drink it by means of a tube, as was done here, to and by the "superstar," is not a reflection merely upon her thespian ability, but a clinical example of extraordinary perversion, degeneracy and possible amentia. Whatever talent superstar has seems confined to her magnificent appetite and sword-swallowing faculty for fellatio.

THE LAW

[11]   "Deep Throat" is far from a close case; it is a classic case. Let us consider: is the film obscene under the law?

[12]   Admittedly, the "guidelines" are distressingly ambiguous. But some would maintain there is merit in ambiguity to meet the shifts of society's national values and moral imperatives. ". . . the criminal law which deals with imperfect humanity cannot await the perfect definition— nor the perfect society in which, perhaps, no definitions would be

necessary." We embark to apply the tests to the film, with no trepidations
or uncertainty in this particular case.

We begin with the premise, well-established, that motion pictures [13]
as other forms of communication, are equally entitled to constitutional
protection under the First Amendment. Motion pictures are understood
to encompass problems peculiar to that form of expression, not subject
to the precise rules governing other communication media. Accordingly,
the Constitution does not require "absolute freedom to exhibit every
motion picture of every kind at all times and places. . . ."

We have here a film and not a novel, book or magazine, and this, [14]
we believe, adds a different and significant dimension to the question.
Critic Stanley Kaufmann notes a discernible difference in the one-to-
one relationship of writer and reader "in psychic and social senses,"
from the employment of people to enact sexual fantasies on stage and
screen before an audience. The stark reality and impact of a movie is
undeniably as impressive as the viewing of a true-life situation on the
open street. Certainly to read descriptions of explicit sexual activity
as shown in "Deep Throat," or merely to hear them discussed, can
never have the same poignancy and cannot create that same lasting
impression upon the human mind or appeal to the prurient as does
the observation of the acts in a true life situation or on the screen.

Because of a film's unique, shocking quality, we cannot disregard [15]
its potent visual impact in depicting, as does "Deep Throat," the
fellatio, cunnilingus, masturbation, sexual intercourse, and other sexual
activity. Such depiction of clearly discernible acts "transcends the
bounds of the constitutional guarantee long before a frank description
of the same scenes in the written word." Accordingly, the appeal to
prurience, the recognition of patent offensiveness, the violation of
community standards and absence of social value will be realized
more readily and more assuredly with a film than in a writing.

What is hard-core pornography and its connection with "Deep [16]
Throat?" We know that sex is not obscene: Roth tells us that when it
says "Sex and obscenity are not synonymous." Now that we know
what it is not, then what is obscenity? Admittedly "obscenity" almost
defies meaningful definition. Is hard-core pornography any more sus-
ceptible to exact delineation? Chief Justice Warren found both tasks
impossible with the comment, "But who can define 'hard-core pornography' with any greater clarity than 'obscenity'?"

Yet others find it readily definable and certainly more readily iden- [17]
tifiable as a reasonably precise concept, which theoretically could
unite a strong majority of the Supreme Court. My learned brother,
Judge William J. Shea recently advised that "Hard-core pornography
is a specific type of obscenity, it is obscenity in its easiest recognizable
form. It contains something more than obscenity in its general or hard

to recognize form and that 'something' is its depiction of *actual* sexual activity, including intercourse and deviate acts." Also my brother, Judge Arthur Goldberg agrees that the decisions involving explicit sexual activity represent the distinction to "indicate palpable lines between obscenity and protected expression." The Report of the Commission on Obscenity and Pornography agrees that explicit sex is the distinguishing feature of hard-core pornography from other obscenity in that it demonstrates "sexual intercourse, depicting vaginal, anal or oral penetration."

[18]   The explicit sexual activity represents the "hard-core" feature of the material, while the "pornography" and its prurient appeal is distinguished by its pervasive hallucinatory quality, its ability to produce physical concomitants of sexual excitement and emotion. Such material has "the character of the daydream—the product of sheer fantasy." Because of hard-core's readily prurient appeal it is "patently offensive," and its "indecency speaks for itself." It is condemnable as if *res ipsa loquitor*, requiring no expert testimony to explain or justify it. Since its brazenness is a direct assault upon long held concepts of national morality and propriety, it is readily recognized throughout the nation by all those not beyond the pale. Apparently the lay press had no trouble identifying "Deep Throat" as unmistakable hard-core pornography. ". . . it scarcely could be more hard-core," says Thomas Meehan in *Saturday Review*. ". . . the film is solidly hard-core pornography." (*The New York Times*.) It is a "hard-core" sex film (*New York Post*) and it is a "hard-core porno movie." (*Time Mag.*)

[19]   What is the purpose and effect of hard-core pornography? Its aim is "to shock, revolt or embarrass" and brutalize (Benjamin Spock: *Decent and Indecent*); "to insult sex, to do dirt on it . . . to insult the human body" and "a vital human relationship." (D. H. Lawrence: *Pornography and Censorship*.) I believe Mr. Justice Theodore R. Kupferman of our Appellate Division would agree. As an attorney, he specialized in censorship and obscenity law. In an enlightening article to the theatrical trade on the law of obscenity he points out that a more easily enforced standard ". . . is that while sex is accepted, pornography and obscenity will be recognized as brutalizing or insulting sex."

[20]   The United States Supreme Court has never dealt with material so brazenly explicit as the scenes of "Deep Throat," but it has dealt with some cases involving explicit sex activities in films; most however dealt with other varieties of sexuality. In the first case where the Supreme Court found obscenity in a film, the activity was quite explicit, depicting two males engaged in "male masturbation, fellatio, oral copulation, voyeurism, nudity, sadism and sodomy." It is plain such activity approached, but did not equal, the explicitness of "Deep

Throat." But it had no music or sound, as in "Deep Throat," to sharpen the prurient appeal with grunts, sighs and other sounds of orgasmic pleasure.

The majority of the Second Circuit Court of Appeals gave its stamp [21] of approval to the film "I Am Curious Yellow," in spite of its findings of "sexual intercourse under varying circumstances, some of them quite unusual. There were scenes of oral-genital activity." Judge Lombard, in his dissent, explained the "unusual" sexual activity as fellatio and cunnilingus. Significantly, when this film went to the United States Supreme Court from another jurisdiction, it affirmed the conviction of obscenity. When hard-core pornography (and I have yet to see reported anything equal in sexual activity to "Deep Throat") is clearly involved, the United States Supreme Court has affirmed a conviction.

If defendant's counsel had submitted a post-trial brief, we are certain [22] he would have mentioned in his support United States v. 35mm. Motion Picture ("Language of Love"). However, a careful reading of that case will reveal substantive differences between it and the subject film. In "Language of Love," the Court noted "The explicit scenes of sexual activity consist *almost exclusively* of heterosexual relations between adults in private. Female masturbation, cunnilingus (*but not fellatio . . .*) and *one fleeting instance* of actual insertion are shown." "Deep Throat" not only has female masturbation, but numerous depictions of cunnilingus and fellatio, clear and stark, from almost its beginning to its bitter end (for the film's major theme is fellatio); and with one disgusting scene of seminal fluid ejaculation into and about the "superstar's" mouth. "Deep Throat" also boasts of scenes of anal sodomy, an orgy scene, and several scenes of normal heterosexual intercourse, but unlike the other film, it also shows actual insertion in each such scene with purposeful camera focusing close upon the genitals while so engaged.

But the differences are not merely to be found in the number and [23] variety of such activity. Significantly, "Language of Love" was found obscene by a jury but that was overturned on appeal. And on appeal the court found the described sexual acts with "seemingly interminable" psychological, medical and sociological discussions by doctors and other specialists recognized in their respective fields making up almost all of the film. Further, as indicative of its sex educational purposes, the film includes a demonstration of proper placement of contraceptive devices during the course of a gynecological examination by one of the doctors. To compare then "Deep Throat" with that film is not to have seen "Deep Throat," because in the one ("Deep Throat") there lurks behind each elm "the leer of the sensualist."

WHEN ALL IS SAID

[24] "Deep Throat"—a nadir of decadence—is indisputably obscene by any legal measurement. It goes substantially beyond "the present critical point in the compromise between candor and shame at which the community may have arrived here and now." It is another manifestation of the refusal to use words as emotional symbols unrelated to the purely physical. There is no effort, by word or conduct, to cut through the imponderable barriers of human understanding to the defense of human integrity. It, in fact, denigrates that integrity of man and particularly, woman, the expert witnesses notwithstanding. It does this by objectifying and insulting woman, as Anthony Burgess, the author, puts it, by "making woman the sexual instrument come before woman the human being."

[25]   Its dominant theme, and in fact its only theme, is to appeal to the prurience in sex. It is hard-core pornography with a vengeance. "It creates an abstract paradise in which the only emotion is lust and the only event orgasm and the only inhabitants animated phalluses and vulvae" (Anthony Burgess). It is neither redeemed nor redeemable, lest it be by the good camera work, editing, clarity, good color and lack of grain, which one defense witness seemed impressed with. But that is hardly enough to remove it from the pale of obscenity.

[26]   It does, in fact, demean and pervert the sexual experience, and insults it, shamelessly, without tenderness and without understanding of its role as a concomitant of the human condition. Therefore, it does dirt on it; it insults sex and the human body as D. H. Lawrence would describe condemnable obscenity. It "focuses predominantly upon what is sexually morbid, grossly perverse and bizarre. . . . It smacks, at times, of fantasy and unreality, of sexual perversion and sickness." Justice Jackson says he knows hard-core pornography when he merely sees it. We have seen it in "Deep Throat" and this is one throat that deserves to be cut. I readily perform the operation in finding the defendant guilty as charged.

ON JUDGE TYLER'S DECISION TO CUT
_____ THE THROAT OF "DEEP THROAT" _____
Albert Ellis

From a legal standpoint, Judge Tyler's decision to ban the film "Deep [1]
Throat" is cogent, logical, and probably quite appropriate. He cites
the law, such as it is, fairly objectively and convincingly; and he comes
to a conclusion that most criminal court judges, given a similar case,
might well make. For all his seeming objectivity in this respect, however,
two questions remain: (1) Is there a distinct emotional bias behind
the reasoning of Judge Tyler and the judges and members of the jury
involved in the many antiobscenity cases that he cites? (2) Is the law
against "obscenity" and "pornography," for a variety of reasons, itself
based on immoral and antihuman attitudes and dicta; and, if so, does
it realistically and humanistically deserve to have its throat cut? I
would personally give a resounding Yes to both of these questions.

First, as to Judge Tyler's bias. Throughout his well-written decision, [2]
he continually employs emotionally-laden words that are apparently
intended to convince the reader that not only does "obscenity" and
"pornography" exist, but that they are horrible, awful, and terrible
entities that no sound and sane human could possibly tolerate. He
steadily states and implies that they are distinctly bad (meaning, immoral, unethical, evil, disadvantageous, and humanity-defeating) and
that they are also clearly *terrible* (meaning, *more than* disadvantageous
and humanity-defeating and meaning that they *absolutely should not*
and *must not* continue to exist). Let me cite a few chapters and verses
of his decision to show that he is not only moral (against immorality)
but moralistic (condemning and damning humans for acting immorally).

1. Reports Judge Tyler: "One defense witness said he saw 'realism [3]
and genuine sexual experience.' No imagination was needed, since
it was intended to appeal to the imbecile as well." Imbecile? Technically,
an imbecile is a mentally deficient person with an intelligence quotient
ranging from 25 to 50; and I doubt whether Judge Tyler means that
"Deep Throat" was intended to appeal to individuals with *that* degree
of subnormal intelligence. Consequently, he clearly implies, in a highly
pejorative and unfair manner, that the film was especially designed
to appeal to many quite stupid individuals—which is probably not
true.

SOURCE: "On Judge Tyler's Decision to Cut the Throat of 'Deep Throat,' by Albert Ellis,
reprinted from *Clinical Social Work Journal*, vol. 1, no. 4, copyright © 1973, Human
Sciences Press, Inc., New York, by permission of the publisher.

[4]   2. Speaking of the female "superstar" of "Deep Throat," Judge Tyler writes: "Movie critic Judith Crist characterizes the production 'idiotic moviemaking' and the actors 'awful' (*New York Magazine*, 2/5/73, p. 64). I agree, except to add that a female who would readily and with apparent anxious abandon, submit to the insertion of a glass dildoe container into her vagina, have liquid poured therein and then drink it by means of a tube, as was done here, to and by the 'superstar,' is not a reflection merely upon her thespian ability, but a clinical example of extraordinary perversion, degeneracy and possible amentia. Whatever talent superstar has seems confined to her magnificent appetite and sword-swallowing faculty for fellatio." Judge Tyler here irrelevantly brings in superstar's ability, or lack thereof, as an actress; and he declaims about "extraordinary perversion, degeneracy and possible amentia," when describing a sex act that, to be sure, is somewhat unusual but hardly depictable, scientifically, by any of these highly loaded terms.

[5]   3. Judge Tyler commendingly quotes Mr. Justice Theodore R. Kupferman's opinion that "while sex is accepted, pornography and obscenity will be recognized as brutalizing or insulting sex." Here he doesn't seem to see that no verbal or pictorial depiction of sex (or anything else) can possibly be "brutalizing" or "insulting" unless the reader or viewer chooses to *view* it in this light. I may well dislike or disapprove of your (or Judge Tyler's!) soul-kissing your wife in my presence; but if I *feel* brutalized or insulted by your act, I have clearly *made* myself have that feeling by *convincing myself* (very foolishly!) that it brutalizes the essence of my being or insults my humanity. I could much more wisely convince myself that your act is highly offensive to my personal tastes, but that I can fairly easily *tolerate* being offended and refuse to *relate* your offense to my entire being and to my evaluation of myself.

[6]   If Judge Tyler were to come for some sessions of rational-emotive therapy (Ellis, 1962, 1971, 1972a, 1972b, 1973), which I would strongly advise him to do, he would soon learn that external stimuli or Activating Events (at point A) do not cause people to feel emotional responses or Consequences (at point C). Rather, it is their Belief Systems (at point B) *about* the Activating Events that directly create their consequential feelings. He would therefore learn that "Deep Throat" (at point A) cannot cause its viewers to feel brutalized or insulted (at point C). Rather, it is their foolish Beliefs (at point B) that it is *awful* for them to see this film; that they can't *stand it*; and that the producers *must not* make it available for them to see that create these point C feelings. Judge Tyler—like most psychiatric professionals, alas—believes in magic: that stimuli directly cause human responses. He could much more scientifically and logically believe that peoples' *interpretations or*

evaluations of these stimuli really create their emotional responses; and that his particular biased interpretations—namely, that films like "Deep Throat" are "brutalizing" and "insulting"—will most likely *help* the viewers of these films to keep making irrational evaluations of them and *thereby* to create their own inappropriate feelings of "brutalization" and "personal insult."

4. Judge Tyler talks about "one disgusting scene of seminal fluid [7] ejaculation into and about the 'superstar's' mouth." Again, he is bigotedly pejorative! Obviously, many of the film's viewers hardly found this scene "disgusting"—else they would not have gone to the movie and highly recommended it to their friends. Even those viewers who found this scene "distasteful" or "unpleasant" probably rarely found it "disgusting." For "disgusting" means (1) unpleasant and unfortunate *and* (2) *more than* unpleasant; 100% (or more!) rotten to the core; *inherently* and *absolutely* bad; inevitably causing practically all viewers to feel angry and debased as humans. Although the first of these definitions is empirically confirmable (since many or most viewers may actually find the film unpleasant and unfortunate), the second definition is magical and unconfirmable. It is basically a tautology or a definition: that is, "Deep Throat" is disgusting because I define it as (or deem it to be) disgusting; and when I *conceive* anything like this film to be disgusting, I will amost inevitably *feel* disgusted. Terms like "disgusting" have no true empirical referent. They hardly belong in scientific or legal discourse.

5. Once again, Judge Tyler notes that "Deep Throat" "does, in [8] fact, demean and pervert the sexual experience, and insults it, shamelessly, without tenderness and without understanding of its role as a concomitant of the human condition. Therefore, it does dirt on it." More angry, nasty mud-slinging! Because I never, these days, *choose* to demean, pervert, insult, or shame *any* sexual experience, I find that many of my experiences are, indeed, unenjoyable, displeasing, or not too meaningful; but I find that *none* of them are demeaning, perverted, insulting, or shameful. If I *chose* to feel demeaned, perverted, insulted, or shamed by viewing a sex film (or engaging in any sex act), I would be deciding not merely to see *it* as distasteful but to devaluate and denigrate *myself* as a *rotten individual* for viewing (or engaging in) it. This would be very nutty thinking and behaving on my part. And this, exactly, is what Judge Tyler is advising me to do when he insists that I find "Deep Throat" demeaning, perverted, insulting, or shameful.

Moreover, he is not merely holding that sex is better or more desirable [9] when it goes with tenderness; but he is demanding and commanding that the two *must* go together in order to legitimate any sex act. This is a very silly and pernicious point of view, as I indicated in *Sex Without*

Guilt (Ellis, 1958)—which I would advise Judge Tyler promptly to read!

[10]   I think that it is fairly clear, from the foregoing quotations, that Judge Tyler arbitrarily and bigotedly denigrates many aspects of human sexuality that are personally distasteful to him (and to various others). This is also, I contend, what the law itself tends to do in regard to so-called obscenity and pornography. It does not merely designate such material as obnoxious and unpleasant to many individuals in a given jurisdiction. It goes much further and insists that this material is inherently and absolutely bad; that people who produce it are evil people; and that they deserve to be severely punished (including being damned and denigrated as humans) for committing such vile acts.

[11]   This, it seems to me, is essentially true of virtually all laws which legislate victimless crimes into existence, or which attempt to make a crime out of a vice. If I decide to harm myself by screwing my head off (and concomitantly neglecting other more enjoyable pursuits), by smoking (and risking cancer and heart disease), or by overeating (and making myself fat, homely, and unhealthy), I may indeed be acting foolishly and self-defeatingly. But that is my right as a human, as long as I do not drag you and others down with me. Or if you stupidly consent to engage in unbridled screwing, smoking, or overeating with me, that is your right as a human, as long as I have not unfairly and forcefully induced you to participate in these unwise acts.

[12]   As soon as some legal authority commands that you and I not defeat ourselves in these silly ways, and severely punishes and damns us when we do, it is failing to accept us as humans, and is looking upon us in a demeaning, subhuman way. Of course, we do not have to *accept* this authority's attitude and look upon ourselves in a demeaning, subhuman manner just because it encourages us to do so.

[13]   But when this authority brings *this* kind of a law into existence, it certainly abets or increases the probability that we will demean or devalue ourselves. And even if we resist this tendency, it adds an authoritarian, fascistic penalty (arrest, fine, imprisonment, probation, etc.) to the natural consequences (lack of enjoyment or illness) which we bring on ourselves. It makes a crime out of a vice; and it thereby *unnecessarily* imposes restrictions on human freedom and individualism.

[14]   This, in my estimation, is what the antiobscenity and antipornography laws do. They are *undue* restrictions on the civilians who live in the jurisdictions imposing them; and they encourage self-denigration and personal feelings of worthlessness. In terms of legal penalties, they are hardly the worst laws that ever existed. But in terms of abetting sabotage of the human spirit and of encouraging widespread feelings of needless guilt, shame, depression, anxiety, and inadequacy, they are among the worst.

They also have other clearcut disadvantages. As I have written in   [15]
a previous paper on "Why I am Opposed to Censorship of Pornography" (Ellis, 1972c), there are at least three major reasons why it is
highly undesirable for any legal jurisdiction to ban obscenity or pornography: (1) It is almost impossible accurately and incisively for any
court to define these terms; and consequently the two major decisions
in this regard—*Roth v. United States*, 354 U.S. 476, 489 (1957) and *A
Book Named "John Clelland's Memoirs of a Woman of Pleasure" v. Attorney
General of Massachusetts*, 383 U.S. 413, 418-419 (1967)—are, as Judge
Tyler notes, "distressingly ambiguous." Using one of the best ration-
alizations I have ever heard, Tyler contends that there may well be
"merit in ambiguity, to meet the shifts of society's national values
and moral imperatives." But I see little merit in a *statute* that is so
ambiguously worded that citizens may be severely fined or jailed on
what seems largely to be the whim of a particular judge or jury who
interprets its ambiguities. (2) If "obscenity" and "pornography" were
accurately definable (which I doubt they will ever be), they would be
justifiably banned only if it were fairly conclusively shown that they
are truly harmful; and, so far, no confirmatory evidence in this connection appears to exist (Censorship: For and Against, 1971; Commission
on Obscenity and Pornography, 1970; Ellis, 1964; Jahoda, 1954; Sagarin,
1969; Schroeder, 1960; Thomas, 1969). (3) Even if it could be clearly
shown that so-called obscenity and pornography are harmful or immoral, it would also have to be demonstrated that their legal banning,
in terms of the suppression of free speech and general liberty which
inevitably accompany such bans, does not wreak even greater human
harm. My hypothesis is that it usually does.

For important reasons such as these, I think that Judge Tyler's   [16]
decision to cut the throat of "Deep Throat" is distinctly homicidal
and unwise. Although political rulers, such as Adolf Hitler, may le-
gitimately disagree with and feel highly displeased about the *behavior*
of some of their citizens, such as Jews and other non-Aryans, I think
that they are exceptionally immoral and antihuman when they damn
and annihilate the *people* who exhibit these behaviors. This kind of
damnation is the height of intolerance, bigotry, and fascism. I believe
that Judge Tyler's murderous attack on "Deep Throat," although hardly
as extreme as Hitler's genocidal damnation of millions of non-Nazis,
is closely related to the same kind of vilifying and intolerant thinking
and acting.

REFERENCES

Censorship: For and Against. New York: Hart Publishing, 1971.
Commission on Obscenity and Pornography. *Report of the Commission
     on Obscenity and Pornography*. New York: Bantam Books, 1970.

Ellis, A. *Sex without guilt*. New York: Lyle Stuart, 1958. Paperback edition: New York: Lancer Books, 1969.

Ellis, A. *Reason and emotion in psychotherapy*. New York: Lyle Stuart, 1962.

Ellis, A. Is pornography harmful to children. *Realist*, February 1964, No. 47, 17–18.

Ellis, A. *Growth through reason*. Palo Alto: Science and Behavior Books, 1971.

Ellis, A. *Executive leadership: A rational approach*. New York: Citadel Books, 1972a.

Ellis, A. *How to master your fear of flying*. New York: Curtis Books, 1972b.

Ellis, A. Why I am opposed to censorship of pornography. *Osteopathic Physician*, 1972c, 39(10), 40–41.

Ellis, A. *Humanistic psychotherapy: The rational-emotive approach*. New York: Julian Press, 1973.

Jahoda, M. *The impact of literature: A psychological discussion of some assumptions in the censorship debate*. New York: Research Center for Human Relations, 1954.

Sagarin, E. An essay on obscenity and pornography. *The Humanist*, July-August, 1969, 10–11.

Schroeder, T. Sex and censorship: eternal conflict. *Balanced Living*, 1960, 16, 178–184.

Thomas, D. *A long time burning*. New York: Praeger, 1969.

QUESTIONS

1. Shortly after Judge Tyler rendered his decision on *Deep Throat* the United States Supreme Court, in the case of *Miller vs. California*, rendered an opinion that redefined obscenity to include the following considerations:

   a. whether the average person, on the basis of present-day standards, would agree that the instance (a book, a movie, a stage play, etc.), considered as a whole, appealed to his/her "prurient interests"

   b. whether the instance represents or describes sex in an explicitly offensive manner as defined by applicable state laws

   c. whether the instance lacks redeeming literary, artistic, political, or scientific value

The decision maintained that a work is not obscene unless all three of these qualities are found to exist by a jury.

To what extent does Judge Tyler's decision anticipate the criteria set forth in the Supreme Court decision? Which of the critieria does it least reflect? Would you be able to define the words "obscenity" and "pornography" as Judge Tyler seems to use them? Does he differentiate between the two terms?

2. On the basis of the two reading selections, make a case either for or against laws to regulate sexual behavior (including obscenity and prostitution). Try to find a philosophical base for your position. To do this, you may wish to consider how others in this unit have defined sexual behavior in relation to ethical and social values.

3. Judge Tyler's decision is rendered in a distinctive voice. In fact, this is the basis of Albert Ellis's refutation of that decision. Try to characterize this voice. Is it commanding, humorous, high-minded, pleasant, tolerant? What adjectives among these would you reject? What others would you add? This set of questions asks you to describe the judge on the basis of clues that you pick up from reading his opinion. After giving such a description, explain on what clues you relied.

4. Do a similar characterization of Albert Ellis.

5. At times, Judge Tyler uses irony. For example, when he says that the film *Deep Throat* is "as explicit and exquisite as life," we know that he doesn't mean to praise the film. He wants us to read "exquisite" ironically, with a meaning opposite to the one we usually assign the word. Find other illustrations of irony in the essay and evaluate Judge Tyler's use of this device. In your mind, does it add to or detract from the point he wishes to make? Explain.

6. Legal opinions are generally developed through reference to precedents. While some of the technical citations have been left out from this version of Judge Tyler's opinion to make it more readable, there are yet many citations and statements by authorities which have been retained. What class of people in particular does he cite? Do you know any of these authorities from your own reading? What does he gain from including these citations?

7. Does Ellis support his opinion with citation of authorities? If so, whom does he cite? Which of the two arguments do you find more convincing on the basis of evidence brought from the outside? Justify your answer.

EXERCISES

1. One reason Judge Tyler gives for his decision is that movies are able to treat their subject more realistically, therefore they are a greater *social* threat to appeal to the prurient than books are (see pars. 13 and 14). Although Ellis does not refute this claim, we can assume that he would be able to. How could one refute such a claim? Make notes from your own experience in seeing movies and reading books, and argue for or against Judge Ellis's proposition. If you argue in favor, be sure to anticipate the objections Ellis would raise.

2. What in your opinion are victimless crimes? Do you believe with Ellis that one should not "make a crime out of a vice"? Do you think, for example, the government has the right to legislate the sale of cigarettes? How can the sale of cigarettes be differentiated from the sale of alcohol or cocaine? How are these illustrations related to the prohibition of pornography? Write a position paper either *for* or *against* the proposition that "pornography should be outlawed" by focusing on the issue that it is or is not a victimless crime.

3. Read Article 1 of the Bill of Rights of the U.S. Constitution. Can you find a basis in this article either for or against the showing of pornographic material? Make notes and construct an argument based on the Constitution that pornography is either legal or illegal.

UNIT II

WORK

In 1972 a special task force of experts from every field—economics, industry, labor relations, medicine, psychology, sociology, race relations—was created to prepare a comprehensive report to the Secretary of Health, Education, and Welfare on work in America. The experts began their report with this observation:

> It is both humbling and true that scientists are unable, in the final analysis, to distinguish all the characteristics of humans from those of other animals. But many social scientists will agree that among those activities most peculiar to humans work probably defines a man with the greatest certainty.

Man is homo sapiens, the intellectual animal, homo ludens, the playing animal, and also, very importantly, homo faber, the *making* animal. We define the world by our work. We do not merely live in houses; we build them. So also, we build bridges, boats, and airplanes and thus defy the limitations placed upon us by geography. We make cities that define our relation to one another in ways different from the ways in which nature defines it. We make things that never were in nature, such as pictures of unicorns and nylon fabric. By means of our work we carve the human imprint upon the world.

Our work also defines us—sometimes in ways that are obvious and sometimes in ways that are subtle but profoundly important. If I work because I *have* to work to live, the quality of my life, my status in society, and the power I wield over other human beings is likely to be quite different from others who do not have to work because they were born rich. If I work because I love what my work is, my feeling about the work and about myself will be very different from those of who are compelled to work in a forced labor camp or to make license plates in a prison.

Those, of course, are some of the obvious ways in which work defines us. We shall be examining them more closely and critically when we read the selection about the social status of occupations. But there are far more subtle ways in which work defines our lives. We will see that in some contexts work, and the related term "worker," are defined as "labor"—something that stands in opposition or in functional distinction to "management." In still other contexts, for example the one provided by Lester Thurow, work is regarded as the sum product of a national economy. In yet others, as we shall see in the sketches provided by Studs Terkel, work is a way toward self-definition and evaluation. While most kinds of work since the advent of the industrial revolution have been measured by clock time—and the work cycle has, in fact, been a measure of our very lives—we are approaching a new era, as we shall see in the selection "The Work Life in the 1980's," when the task proper rather than the time taken to perform it is likely to be increasingly the measure of our accomplishment and our worth as workers.

Like love and sexuality, work is one of the primary ways in which we as human beings structure our relations to each other. The work we do is two-edged. By means of it we shape our environment, but also by means of it we ourselves are shaped. We shall see in this unit how work is examined and discussed in the various academic disciplines. The readings will not only provide us with a multi-perspectival view of work as a human activity but also with a deeper understanding of our personal needs and talents as members in society who will soon take our own places in the work force.

CHAPTER NINE

SPECIAL TASK FORCE ON WORK:
WORK IN AMERICA:
A DEFINITION

An Interdisciplinary Approach

This selection is among the most instructive in this book because it allows you to see many different disciplines attacking the same issue. The people who made up the task force came from many disciplines. Their report, of which we shall read only from the introduction, took a wide variety of approaches. In order to create a composite view of work in America, experts in fields often quite different from one another had to assess where their approaches conflicted, where they overlapped, and where some compromise among them could be effected.

But, of course, no report, however complete, no piece of writing, however finished, is a seamless web. As you are reading this selection, try to pick out the different academic disciplines that might have contributed to it and try to discover what their contributions might have been. The writers tell us that Freud thought work gives us a psychological sense of reality; Marx was interested in work primarily as it affects the economy; sociologists see it as a determinant of social status, while theologians are interested in its moral dimensions.

As you read the selection, try to determine *how* such a report might have been put together, and try to weigh the strengths and the weaknesses of an interdisciplinary approach. That is, ask yourself how and why a report made by a task force is *different* from a report made by experts in a single field, or one made by a single expert, and whether the differences strengthen or weaken the report. For example, does the teacher of management tell us more or less about the nature of work than a task force report does? Is the narrower scope of an economist, which sees labor as one segment within the whole economic picture, better or less useful than that of the task force?

GLOSSARY

archaeologist [1]

determinant [2]

status [2]

Social Darwinism [2]

laissez-faire [2]

Protestant ethic [2]

eclipses [5]

synonymity [7]

remunerated [8]

transient [9]

liquid assets [9]

self-esteem [12]

efficacy [12]

foci [13]

homo faber [16]

animal laborens [16]

euphemism [18]

chaos [19]

protracted [20]

cynicism [20]

atonie [20]

deracination [21]

fatalism [23]

somatic [23]

ethnographies [24]

validity [27]

___ WORK IN AMERICA: A DEFINITION ___

Report of a Special Task Force to the Secretary of Health, Education and Welfare

It is both humbling and true that scientists are unable, in the final   [1]
analysis, to distinguish all the characteristics of humans from those
of other animals. But many social scientists will agree that among
those activities most peculiar to humans, work probably defines man
with the greatest certainty. To the archaeologist digging under the
equatorial sun for remains of the earliest man, the nearby presence
of primitive tools is his surest sign that the skull fragment he finds
is that of a human ancestor, and not that of an ape.

Why is man a worker? First of all, of course, man works to sustain   [2]
physical life—to provide food, clothing, and shelter. But clearly work
is central to our lives for other reasons as well. According to Freud,
work provides us with a sense of reality; to Elton Mayo, work is a
bind to community; to Marx, its function is primarily economic. Theologians are interested in work's moral dimensions: sociologists see
it as a determinant of status, and some contemporary critics say that
it is simply the best way of filling up a lot of time. To the ancient
Greeks, who had slaves to do it, work was a curse. The Hebrews saw
work as punishment. The early Christians found work for profit offensive, but by the time of St. Thomas Aquinas, work was being
praised as a natural right and a duty—a source of grace along with
learning and contemplation. During the Reformation, work became
the only way of serving God. Luther pronounced that conscientious
performance of one's labor was man's highest duty. Later interpretations
of Calvinistic doctrine gave religious sanction to worldly wealth and
achievement. This belief, when wedded to Social Darwinism and
laissez-faire liberalism, became the foundation for what we call the
Protestant ethic. Marx, however, took the concept of work and put
it in an even more central position in life: freed from capitalist exploitation, work would become a joy as workers improved the material
environment around them.[1]

Clearly, work responds to something profound and basic in human   [3]
nature. Therefore, much depends on how we define work, what we
conceive work to be, what we want work to be, and whether we
successfully uncover its meaning and purpose. Our conceptions (and

SOURCE: From *Work in America. Report of a Special Task Force to the Secretary of Health, Education and Welfare*. Prepared under the auspices of the W. E. Upjohn Institute for Employment Research (Cambridge, MIT Press, 1973), pp. 1–17, 23–28.

misconceptions) of ourselves, the wisdom with which public policy is formulated on a range of issues, and the rationality with which private and public resources are allocated are influenced greatly by the degree to which we penetrate the complex nature of work.

[4]   Because work, as this report illustrates, plays a pervasive and powerful role in the psychological, social, and economic aspects of our lives, it has been called a basic or central institution. As such, it influences, and is influenced by, other basic institutions—family, community (particularly as a political entity), and schools—as well as peripheral institutions. Work, then, provides one institutional perspective—but a broad one—from which to view these interrelationships that affect ourselves and our society. . . .

[5]   We measure that which we can measure, and this often means that a rich and complex phenomenon is reduced to one dimension, which then becomes prominent and eclipses the other dimensions. This is particularly true of "work," which is often defined as "paid employment." The definition conforms with one readily measurable aspect of work but utterly ignores its profound personal and social aspects and often leads to a distorted view of society.

[6]   Using housework as an example, we can see the absurdity of defining work as "paid employment." A housewife, according to this definition, does not work. But if a husband must replace her services—with a housekeeper, cook, baby sitter—these replacements become workers, and the husband has added to the Gross National Product the many thousands of dollars the replacements are paid. It is, therefore, an inconsistency of our definition of work that leads us to say that a woman who cares for her own children is not working, but if she takes a job looking after the children of others, she is working.

[7]   Viewing work in terms of pay alone has also produced a synonymity of "pay" and "worth," so that higher-paid individuals are thought by many to have greater personal worth than those receiving less pay. At the bottom of this scale, a person without pay becomes "worthless." The confusion of pay with worth is a result of historical events and traditions apparently rooted in the distinction between "noble" and "ignoble" tasks.[2] History might have been otherwise and garbage men, for example, in recognition of their contribution to health, might have been accorded monetary rewards similar to those received by physicians. Certainly, it takes little reflection to conclude that, except in crude economic terms, no one is worth nothing, nor is anyone worth a hundred times more than another merely because he is paid a hundred times as much.

[8]   We can come closer to a multi-dimensional definition of work if we define it as "an activity that produces something of value for other people." This definition broadens the scope of what we call work and

places it within a social context. It also implies that there is a purpose to work. We know that the housewife is *really* working, whether she is paid or not; she is being productive for other people. Substituting the children a woman cares for does not change the nature of her work, only the "others" for whom she is productive. And voluntary tasks are certainly work, although they are not remunerated. Some people at various stages of their lives may be productive only for themselves, a possible definition of leisure. . . .

The economic purposes of work are obvious and require little com- [9] ment. Work is the means by which we provide the goods and services needed and desired by ourselves and our society. Through the economic rewards of work, we obtain immediate gratification of transient wants, physical assets for enduring satisfactions, and liquid assets for deferrable gratifications. For most of the history of mankind, and for a large part of humanity today, the economic meaning of work is paramount.

Work also serves a number of other social purposes. The workplace [10] has always been a place to meet people, converse, and form friendships. In traditional societies, where children are wont to follow in their parents' footsteps, the assumption of responsibility by the children for one task and then another prepares them for their economic and social roles as adults. Finally, the type of work performed has always conferred a social status on the worker and the worker's family. In industrial America, the father's occupation has been the major de- terminant of status, which in turn has determined the family's class standing, where they lived, where the children went to school, and with whom the family associated—in short, the life style and life chances of all the family members. (The emerging new role of women in our society may cause class standing to be co-determined by the husband's *and* wife's occupations.)

The economic and societal importance of work has dominated [11] thought about its meaning, and justifiably so: a function of work for any *society* is to produce and distribute goods and services, to transform "raw nature" into that which serves our needs and desires. Far less attention has been paid to the *personal* meaning of work, yet it is clear from recent research that work plays a crucial and perhaps unparalleled psychological role in the formation of self-esteem, identity, and a sense of order.

Work contributes to self-esteem in two ways. The first is that, [12] through the inescapable awareness of one's efficacy and competence in dealing with the objects of work, a person acquires a sense of mastery over both himself and his environment.[3] The second derives from the view, stated earlier, that an individual is working when he is engaging in activities that produce something valued by other people. That is, the job tells the worker day in and day out that he has something to offer. Not to have a job is not to have something that is valued by one's fellow human beings. Alternatively, to be working is to have evidence that one is needed by others. One of these components of self-esteem (mastery) is, therefore, internally derived through the presence or absence of challenge in work. The other component (how others value one's contributions) is externally derived. The person with high self-esteem may be defined as one who has a high estimate of his value and finds that the social estimate agrees.

[13]   The workplace generally, then, is one of the major foci of personal evaluation. It is where one finds out whether he is "making the grade"; it is where one's esteem is constantly on the line, and where every effort will be made to avoid reduction in self-evaluation and its attending sense of failure.[4] If an individual cannot live up to the expectations he has of himself, and if his personal goals are not reasonably obtainable, then his self-esteem, and with it his relations with others, are likely to be impaired.

[14]   Doing well or poorly, being a success or failure at work, is all too easily transformed into a measure of being a valuable or worthless human being, as Erich Fromm writes:

> Since modern man experiences himself both as the seller and as the commodity to be sold on the market, his self-esteem depends on conditions beyond his control. If he is successful, he is valuable; if he is not, he is worthless.[5]

[15]   When it is said that work should be "meaningful," what is meant is that it should contribute to self-esteem, to the sense of fulfillment through the mastering of one's self and one's environment, and to the sense that one is valued by society. The fundamental question the individual worker asks is "What am I doing that *really* matters?"[6]

[16]   When work becomes merely automatic behavior, instead of being *homo faber*, the worker is *animal laborens*. Among workers who describe themselves as "just laborers," self-esteem is so deflated that the distinction between the human as worker and animal as laborer is blurred.[7] The relationship between work and self-esteem is well summarized by Elliot Jacques:

> . . . working for a living is one of the basic activities in a man's life. By forcing him to come to grips with his environment, with his livelihood at stake, it confronts him with the actuality of his personal capacity—to exercise judgment, to achieve concrete and specific results. It gives him a continuous account of his correspondence between outside reality and the inner perception of that reality, as well as an account of the accuracy of his appraisal of himself. . . . In short, a man's work does not satisfy his material

needs alone. In a very deep sense, it gives him a measure of his sanity.[8]

Work is a powerful force in shaping a person's sense of identity. [17] We find that most, if not all, working people tend to describe themselves in terms of the work groups or organizations to which they belong.[9] The question, "Who are you?" often solicits an organizationally related response, such as "I work for IBM," or "I'm a Stanford professor." Occupational role is usually a part of this response for all classes: "I'm a steelworker," or "I'm a lawyer." In short: "People tend to 'become what they do.' "[10]

Several highly significant effects result from work-related identi- [18] fication: welfare recipients become "nobodies"; the retired suffer a crucial loss of identity; and people in low-status jobs either cannot find anything in their work from which to derive an identity or they reject the identity forced on them.[11] Even those who voluntarily leave an organization for self-employment experience difficulties with identity—compounded by the confusion of others—as the following quote from an article entitled "Striking Out on Your Own," illustrates:

> No less dramatic . . . are those questions of identity which present themselves to the self-employed. These identity crises and situations usually come packaged in little episodes which occur when others find that they have encountered a bona fide weirdo without a boss. . . . You are stopped by a traffic policeman to be given a ticket and he asks the name of your employer and you say that you work for yourself. Next he asks, "Come on, where do you work? Are you employed or not?" You say, "Self-employed." . . . He, among others you meet, knows that self-employment is a tired euphemism for being out of work. . . . You become extremely nervous about meeting new people because of the ever-present question, "Who are you with?" When your answer fails to attach you to a recognized organization . . . both parties to the conversation often become embarrassed by your obscurity.[12]

Basic to all work appears to be the human desire to impose order, [19] or structure, on the world. The opposite of work is not leisure or free time; it is being victimized by some kind of disorder which, at its extreme, is chaos. It means being unable to plan or to predict. And it is precisely in the relation between the desire for order and its achievement that work provides the sense of mastery so important to self-esteem. The closer one's piece of the world conforms with one's structural plans, the greater the satisfaction of work. And it follows that one of the greatest sources of dissatisfaction in work results from the inability to make one's own sense of order prevail—

the assemblyline is the best (or worst) example of an imposed, and, for most workers, unacceptable structure.

[20]   These observations have been verified a number of times in investigations of mass and protracted unemployment. Loss of work during the Depression was found to produce chronic disorganization in the lives of parents and children, as documented in several studies of the 1930's.[13] Cynicism, loss of self-confidence, resentment, and hostility toward the Federal Government, helplessness, and isolation are all experienced during such difficult periods.[14] According to Charles Winick,

> Inasmuch as work has such a profound role in establishing a person's life space, emotional tone, family situation, object relations, and where and how he will live, either the absence of work or participation in marginal work often makes it likely that he will develop a pervasive *atonie*.[15]

[21]   *Atonie* is a condition of deracination—a feeling of rootlessness, lifelessness, and dissociation—a word which in the original Greek meant a string that does not vibrate, that has lost its vitality.

[22]   Besides lending vitality to existence, work helps establish the regularity of life, its basic rhythms and cyclical patterns of day, week, month, and year.[16] Without work, time patterns become confused. One recalls the drifting in T. S. Eliot's "The Wasteland":

> What shall I do. . . . What shall we do tomorrow?
> What shall we ever do?

[23]   When duration of unemployment has been prolonged, unemployed workers progress from optimism through pessimism to fatalism. Attitudes toward the future and toward the community and home deteriorate.[17] Children of long-term unemployed and marginally employed workers uniformly show poorer school grades.[18] And, despite the popular notion that unemployed people fill their "free" time with intensified sexual activities, the fact is that undermined egos of former breadwinners lead to diminished libidos.[19] "There are so many unconscious and group needs that work meets," Winick writes, "that unemployment may lead not only to generalized anxiety, but to free-floating hostility, somatic symptoms and the unconscious selection of some serious illnesses."[20]

[24]   Many of the studies revealing the disorganizing effects of unemployment during the Depression have found echoes in recent "ghetto ethnographies." Such studies as Liebow's *Tally's Corner* show these effects to be as much a function of unemployment and marginal employment *per se* as of economic catastrophe. This is so because to be

denied work is to be denied far more than the things that paid work buys; it is to be denied the ability to define and respect one's self.

It is illusory to believe that if people were given sufficient funds [25] most of them would stop working and become useless idlers. A recent economic analysis shows that as people increase their earnings and acquire wealth they do not tend to decrease the time and energy that they invest in work.[21] In another study, when a cross section of Americans were asked if they would continue working even if they inherited enough to live comfortably without working, 80% said they would keep on working (even though only 9% said they would do so because they enjoyed the work they were doing).[22] Some people may not want to take specific jobs—primarily because of the effects on their self-esteem—but working, "engaging in activities that produce things valued by other people," is a necessity of life for most people.

Some of the most compelling evidence about the centrality of the [26] functions of work in life comes from the recent efforts of women to fill what some interpret as a void in their lives with the sense of identity derived from work. As some social critics have noted, the desire for all that work brings to the individual is at the foundation of the women's liberation movement.

There is also considerable evidence that work has the same meaning [27] among the poor and among welfare recipients that it has for middle-class and employed individuals:

—A recent study for the Labor Department on the work orientations of welfare recipients found that "the poor of both races and sexes identify their self-esteem with work to the same extent as nonpoor persons do." The study found that although people on welfare are as committed to the work ethic as middle-class people, their attitudes differ in that they are not confident that they can succeed on a job. After experiencing failure, they are more likely to accept the dependence on welfare.[23]

—A recent study in South Carolina of 513 underprivileged workers found that the poor did not differ markedly from the middle class in the kind of satisfactions that they derived from work.[24]

—The Office of Economic Opportunity has sponsored a three-year study to assess the validity of the assumption that the working poor would stop working if they were guaranteed an annual income. *Preliminary* findings have shown little slackening in work effort among those urban families receiving a guaranteed income. In fact, hourly earnings appear to be higher for those in the experiment than for those in a control group. Although it is too early to assess the results of the experiment, there are signs that withdrawal from work effort is not as extensive as some had feared.[25]

In this regard, it must be realized that although *work* is central to [28] the lives of most people, there is a small minority for whom a *job* is purely a means to a livelihood. To them a job is an activity that they would gladly forgo if a more acceptable option for putting bread on their table were available. What little evidence there is on this point indicates that for most such individuals the kinds of jobs that they see open to them do little to provide the sense of self-esteem, identity, or mastery that are the requisites for satisfying work. These individuals turn to other activities (music, hobbies, sports, crime) and other institutions (family, church, community) to find the psychological rewards that they do not find in their jobs. In effect, these activities, for these people, become their real work. This unusual phenomenon helps to explain the small amount of job withdrawal that occurs among welfare recipients. For example, welfare mothers may choose the personally fulfilling work of raising their children to the alternative of a low-level, unchallenging job—the only kind available to them.

NOTES*

1. Historical references from Harold Wilensky, "Work as a Social Problem," 1966.
2. Thorstein Veblen, *The Theory of the Leisure Class*, 1934.
3. Harry Levinson, "Various Approaches to Understanding Man at Work," 1971.
4. Harry Kahn and J. R. P. French, in *Social Issues*, July 1962.
5. Erich Fromm, *The Revolution of Hope*, 1971.
6. Robert Coles, "On the Meaning of Work," 1971.
7. Ben Seligman, "On Work, Alienation and Leisure," 1965.
8. Elliot Jacques, *Equitable Payment*, 1961.
9. T. S. McPartland and J. H. Cummings, "Self-Conception, Social Class and Mental Health," 1958.
10. Kahn and French, op. cit.
11. Wilensky, op. cit.
12. Paul Dickson, "Striking Out on Your Own," 1971.
13. Eli Ginzberg, *Grass on the Slag Heaps*, 1942; and E. W. Bakke, *The Unemployed Worker*, 1940.
14. Bakke, Ibid.
15. Charles Winick, "Atonie: The Psychology of the Unemployed and Marginal Worker," 1964.
16. E. Frankel, "Studies in Biographical Psychology," 1936.
17. Winick, op. cit.
18. Ibid.
19. Eli Ginzberg, "Work: The Eye of the Hurricane," 1971.
20. Winick, op. cit.
21. James N. Morgan, Survey Research Center.
22. Robert Morse and Nancy Weiss, "The Function and Meaning of Work and the Job," 1955.
23. Leonard Goodwin, "A Study of Work Orientations of Welfare Recipients," 1971.
24. Joseph E. Champagne and Donald King, "Job Satisfaction Factors Among Underprivileged Workers," 1967.
25. Harold Watts, "New Jersey Experiment: Notes for Discussion," 1972.

* Notes are presented in short form. Full citations are to be found in *Work in America. Report of a Special Task Force to the Secretary of Health, Education and Welfare.*

QUESTIONS

1. Early in the selection, the writers speak of a *Protestant ethic*. How would you define this term? What, in fact, does work have to do with Protestantism, or more generally, with any religious point of view or system of values?

2. How do the writers use housework to expand a too-narrow definition of work as "paid employment"?

3. Is their multidimensional definition of work as "an activity that produces something of value for other people" a good definition? Are there, perhaps, kinds of work that have no value "for other people" but must nevertheless be classified as work? If you can find examples of such kinds of work, would you modify the definition? How?

4. The writers say that if history had been different, garbage collectors might have been awarded the same prestige and financial reward as doctors. It may be useful to note that in the city of New York the Department of Sanitation is a branch of the Department of Health. Moreover, scientists have said that the great increase of life span in the West during the past hundred years does *not* result from the invention of miracle drugs but from the elimination of infectious disease. Do these facts lead you to think that garbage collectors might have contributed at least as much or possibly more to the state of our health than have doctors? Speculate about the following:

    a. *The chain of work.* Can you think of other ways in which jobs that seem very different from one another are related when we think of work as "an institution," as the task force does?

    b. *The social status of occupation.* Are occupations that society awards the highest status usually those that are most *useful* to society? What factors other than usefulness determine the high or low status of a job? For example, why are garbage collectors not awarded very high recognition since their job is so socially useful?

5. The writers say that work plays a crucial "role in the formation of self-esteem, identity and a sense of order." Do you agree? Can you think of instances in which work might have nothing to do with self-esteem? Is it possible that the association of work with self-esteem and other positive values might reflect an attitude not unlike the Protestant work ethic in the investigators themselves?

6. In the seventeenth century white bigots thought that one significant sign of the racial inferiority of blacks was that they were too industrious and seemed to enjoy working. Two hundred years later white bigots thought that one significant sign of the racial inferiority of blacks was that they were lazy and shiftless. In what way might this shift in prejudice relate to the task force's assertion that "work contributes to self-esteem"?

7. This study was done during a period of great affluence (particularly for blue-collar workers). Do you think its findings on job dissatisfaction might be different if the study were done now in a period of high unemployment?

8. This selection is part of the introduction to a composite report addressed to the Secretary of the former Department of Health, Education and Welfare. How does the style of the report reflect this fact?

EXERCISES

1. Imagine that you are organizing a special task force to study either marriage in America or childhood in America. Make a list of the various fields of study you would want to be represented in the task force. Under each of the fields on your list make an outline of its expected contribution. For example:

   Childhood
   1. Pediatric medicine
      a. It is necessary to understand the child as a physical organism.
      b. Much of child development is based on physical development.
      c. Disease in childhood can be relatively minor and predictable or dangerous and permanently damaging.
   2. Developmental Psychology
      and so forth

2. Make twenty copies of the questionnaire given below or a similar one of your own devising. Distribute them in a large shopping center, an airport, a train station, or wherever you can find a population mixed in class, sex, and age. Set up the questionnaire so that answers will consist of single words or very short phrases. Ask respondent to state their sex and age.

1. Who are you? Do not simply give your name.
2. Where were you born?
3. Where did you live when you were ten years old?
4. What was your father's occupation, if any?
5. Which room in the house or apartment did you like best when you were ten years old? Why?
6. What college(s) did your parents attend, if any?
7. What major credit cards do you carry?
8. Do you think your children's lives will be happier or less happy than yours? Briefly why?
9. Where do you expect to be ten years from now?
10. What is your present yearly salary?
11. What does your spouse do?

(Items 1, 9, and 11 should indicate whether or not people define themselves occupationally.)

After you have a good sample, do the following:

First, evaluate each question to discover what it measures. Weigh the value of the question in determining the probable socioeconomic class of the person interviewed.

Second, divide your questionnaires into two groups: probable high and probable low income.

Third, divide your questionnaires by sex.

Fourth, on the basis of the raw data you have collected make an inference about whether sex and socioeconomic class determines how a person defines him or herself.

Fifth, write a draft summarizing your findings. Present it as a potential appendix to the report *Work in America*.

3. Think of your own career prospects. What kind of job do you consider attractive? What rewards do you anticipate from your work? Do you think you will define yourself by the work you do? Do you think earning power is the most important criterion for your choice? If not, how important is it? Write a profile of your expectations for a career, analyzing carefully all the factors that have gone or will go into the choice you have made or will make. You may wish to work on this paper over several drafts, especially as you read further selections in this unit. When you have completed the paper, make a point of saving it. You may find that it will help you in future years when you are likely to be asked to write a personal statement as part of a job application or a résumé.

CHAPTER TEN

HERZBERG: INDUSTRY'S CONCEPTS OF MAN

Industrial Management

Frederick Herzberg is Distinguished Professor of management and has also done experimental work in industrial social science. The book from which this selection comes, *Work and the Nature of Man*, not only evaluates concepts of industrial management that have governed our thinking in the last hundred years, but also presents its own plan for understanding worker and manager motivation.

We will be concerned with Herzberg's presentation of the various myths by which industry has conceived of "working man." Be aware of levels of argument which a skillful writer can employ as you are reading this selection. On the surface the chapter seems only to be outlining the various theoretical concepts that have shaped industrial management in the past century. However, Herzberg clearly has in mind a *reader* who must be persuaded to abandon past theories of management in order, later in the book, to be able to accept his own theory.

Examine Herzberg's writing strategies closely and see whether he gives his reader grounds for rejecting the various theories he presents without ever condemning them outright. Try to determine how style creates a tone of voice in this piece, and why we should want to take the side of somebody who speaks or writes in that tone. Try also to see how Herzberg persuades the reader to be critical, without being openly critical himself.

GLOSSARY

prevailing myths [1]   denigration [19]

squalor [3]   axiom [20]

Calvinistic doctrine [4]   rational [26]

predestination [4]   proselyte [28]

omnipotence [5]   sterile [32]

foreordained [5]   self-confirming hypothesis [34]

indolent [7]   bureaucracies [37]

perdition [7]   ingenious [39]

theology [7]   evangelical zeal [39]

empirical [8]   group therapy [40]

"survival of the fittest" [8] masochist [40]

humanitarianism [11]   Oedipal complex [40]

paternalism [11]   psychodynamics [43]

—— INDUSTRY'S CONCEPTS OF MAN ——

Frederick Herzberg

In contemporary society, business is the dominant institution. It is [1]
industry that has been defining the basic characteristics of the human.
Some of the prevailing myths that industry has served up, primarily
to justify its own "need" views regarding the nature of worker motivation and the nature of man, deserve to be carefully examined.

SOURCE: From Frederick Herzberg, *Work and the Nature of Man*, World Publishing Company,
Cleveland, 1966, pp. 32–43. Reprinted by permission of the author.

[2]   "Seest thou a man diligent in his business? He shall stand before
Kings." (Proverbs 22:29) Or, as the Reverend M. D. Babcock said in
a sermon delivered in 1900, which summarized very neatly the doctrine
of the Protestant ethic: "Business is religion and religion is business.
The man who does not make a business of his religion has a business
life of no character. . . ."

[3]   Captains of industry were thought to be the leaders of men and
nations; without their guidance, the workers would live in squalor
and want. Virtue was defined as economic success, and economic
success was defined as evidence of virtue. This myth about human
nature is part of what has been labeled the "Protestant ethic." Reinhold
Bendix, professor of sociology at the University of California, has
described this thesis eloquently in his book *Work and Authority in
Industry*.

[4]   The myth that was exemplified by the Protestant ethic was bred
from the Calvinistic doctrine of predestination and of the "calling of
the Elect."

[5]   Martin Luther's concept that the individual must be responsible
for his own salvation, independent of the church's function as a mediator
between him and God, was a radical departure from previous religious
beliefs. John Calvin expanded this concept by suggesting that passive
faith was insufficient for salvation. By adding the doctrine of predestination, Calvin augmented the belief in the omnipotence of God—
that He knew not only the past and the present but also, and more
important, the future. As the creed of predestination was stated in
the Westminster Confession of 1647, "By the decree of God, for the
manifestation of His Glory, some men and angels are predestinated
unto everlasting life, and others foreordained to ever-lasting death."

        In a system such as Calvin's, what tangible evidence, what man-
ifestation on this earth, could one use to determine whether or not
he is marked for salvation? The popular interpretation of predestination
turned out that the chosen would be those who could measure their
success in business values, and success became the sign of the "Elect."

[7]   The Industrial Revolution and the breakdown of the traditional
way of life were justified by the religious ethic. God had planned it
this way, according to some latter-day Puritans. The poor were the
"great, dirty unwashed." Not only were they indolent and without
ambition, but they were also marked for perdition. This seemed obvious
for if they were of the "Elect," they would have been successful.
Business had found a justification for its concept of human nature—
it was God's will. The Protestant ethic was not based on Calvin's
original theology. Here begins the emergence of management's myth
of the "economic man."

Economic man replaced spiritual man, and the result was the scientific [8] explosion. Contemplation of the soul was replaced by the empirical study of the body; concepts of heavenly bodies were replaced by concepts of mass and motion. The basic approach that man used in his intellectual activities changed from scholastic logic to scientific methodology. This does not mean that the impetus of this explosion was a new sanction given to economic man, but rather the rebirth of the concept of freedom given to Abraham.

The nineteenth century saw the fruition of the age of rationality. [9] A scientific explanation was needed in addition to the religious interpretation provided by the Protestant ethic. Charles Darwin produced the scientific rationale when he published the *Origin of Species* in 1859. He suggested that only those species that were biologically fittest could survive their environment. Darwin's theories of biological evolution fell nicely into place, because the concept of the survival of the fittest in the biological jungle was enlarged to include survival in the economic jungle. Those organizations and individuals that survived competition were evidently the hardiest—they had the proper mutation for survival. It was social Darwinism, as Max Weber described it in *The Protestant Ethic and the Spirit of Capitalism*.

The Protestant ethic then developed two structures. There were [10] the religious sanctions and there were the scientific explanations for the achievement of economic success. But, as time passed, the workers could not tolerate a system in which most of them were defined as unfit and damned and their ill treatment by management so justified. The myth system involved in this definition of man constituted a pathology that created painful reactions.

An era of social welfare was ushered in, under the cloak of hu- [11] manitarianism. That was the manifest reason. Bendix holds that the fear of radicalism was the latent reason for the new humanitarian consideration of the worker. The political right in history has frequently stolen the thunder on the left by means of social legislation. The attempt to be humane developed into a philosophy of welfare capitalism or paternalism. The height of welfare capitalism in the United States parallels the greatest fears that the nation has had of radicalism, which occurred in the 1920s as an aftermath of the Russian Revolution. Management continued to adhere to its original belief in the Protestant ethic, but now it buttressed its position regarding the worker by inaugurating a social welfare program within industry.

Paternalism may be considered a first approach toward including [12] a human relations concept of industrial relations—a motivation program. The precept that the worker has to work out of duty is no longer valid, and it becomes apparent to management that the worker must be willing—if not eager—to work. Once this principle is recognized, managers have a responsibility to do something about the motivation to work. Industry agrees to certain social legislation and management takes limited responsibility for the worker. However, this trend has developed into an overdone paternalistic concern for the worker, which ends up in welfare capitalism. An attempt is made to equate the balance of what I describe later as hygiene needs by treating the worker better, paying him more and paying him for doing the job the way management wishes it done.

[13]   Here is an additional theory of labor and of job motivation: people work effectively when they are well treated physically. It becomes the manager's responsibility to see that the worker, in addition to being paid, is comfortable; and when this happens, management believes it should follow that all of the worker's motivational drives will be elicited.

[14]   The next step necessary in developing a new myth is the formulation of the concept that the worker is a creature of physical needs. He is an economically determined man, but he is also a creature of comfort. The raw nerve of the worker may be his money motivation, but in addition there are physical and security demands he makes while at work.

[15]   Frederick Taylor, in his book *Scientific Management*, said that what the manager really ought to do is discover the best way to do the job, provide the right tools, select the right man, train him in the right way of doing the job, give him incentives if he does perform the job correctly, and by doing all of these things, he should motivate the worker to work. But the impact of Taylorism was felt not solely by the worker but by management as well. The problem of how to manage workers was to be solved not on the basis of pseudoscientific beliefs but rather on managerial know-how in utilizing human resources. Taylor did not envision that his work would result in an almost inhuman society—as catastrophic to human dignity as that portrayed by Charlie Chaplin in *Modern Times*.

[16]   On the contrary, Taylor felt that if management adopted scientific methods, worker dignity and welfare would be benefited. In a letter discussing Taylor's feelings about the hatred that both capital and labor bore him, Scudder Klyne, a naval lieutenant and Taylor's close friend, said, "It is my personal opinion from hearing Taylor talk that his sympathies are almost entirely with labor, but that he considers it more of an immediate possibility to get capital to start cooperating than it is to educate labor to it." In this view, Taylor essentially was not far wrong; the error was in estimating the intelligence of management.

If the managers lamented the fact that the worker was not doing [17] an exceptional job and that he was complaining and was nonproductive, Taylor countered with, "You don't know how to manage." He believed also that management had no right to expect the blossoming of a devotion to duty on the part of the workers; it was up to management to utilize the work force properly.

Managers soon adopted the principles of scientific management, [18] with its basic discipline—industrial engineering. The essence of industrial engineering as applied to people is to remove the effects of one of the prime laws of psychology, the law of individual differences. That is, if one man has ten talents, another nine, and others eight, seven, six, and on down the line to one, the most efficient procedure would be to structure and limit the work task so that the one talent held in common would be utilized. This technique provides for the elimination of variability or individual differences. In this way, the possibility of error is minimized, but the maximization of the waste of human talents also takes place. The ten, nine, eight, and so-on talents that people possess are suppressed in order to insure freedom from error. (An added return to management is a reduction in the cost of training and retraining; for if the job is simplified, then almost anyone can be brought in to do it, and this reduces the cost of absenteeism and turnover.) But as production processes change from individual units to the production of subunits in large numbers, the cost of error increases. When a small subunit is spoiled, all the larger units of which it is a part are also spoiled—not just one total assembly, as in previous assembly operations where the worker was responsible for the total unit.

This system of utilizing only the lowest common denominator in [19] the catalogue of ability was a consequence of Taylor's theory of scientific management. Using only the minimum in a man's repertory of behavior was, in a sense, amputating the rest of his capabilities. Industrial society needed a new myth to justify this denigration of man and it created the myth of the "mechanistic man."

This new notion suggested that the overriding desire of the worker [20] was to be utilized efficiently and with a minimum of effort. That man is happiest when he is "an interchangeable part of an interchangeable machine making interchangeable parts" has become an axiom.

People were thought to be delighted with the fact that they did [21] not have to make decisions. Management believed that those people were happy workers who did not have the responsibilities of management. The concept of the idyllically happy worker attuned to the factory system in which all decisions were made for him was as erroneous as the Rousseauan myth of the "Noble Huron."

[22]   The emphasis of research in industrial psychology in the 1920s was related to boredom, fatigue and the efficiency of the organism as a machine. What are the best uses of the human machine? How long can it run before it breaks down and needs to be lubricated? What are the environmental conditions under which this machine will operate most efficaciously? These are the problems that prompted the Hawthorne plant of the Western Electric Company to begin what is now considered a landmark study in industrial relations. The Hawthorne Studies (1927–1932) were undertaken to probe the effects of change in the physical environment on the human machine. The researchers found no consistent correlation and no rationality between the many changes in the physical environment of the place of work and the productivity of the worker.

[23]   To the scientists, it appeared that a poltergeist was at work at Hawthorne. The physical scientists threw up their hands and walked out, suggesting that this was a problem for witch doctors, not for them; and management sent for the behavioral scientists. As there was a suspicion that ghosts were at work, the behavioral scientists were forced to resort to the most primitive method of science, observation. The scientists sat and they watched.

[24]   After years of observation, the behavioral scientists concluded that the worker was not living up to the prevailing myth system of worker motivation. He was restricting output, with the result that he was making less money. Here was a situation in which man was set up to operate most efficiently in order to improve his economic lot, but somehow he was operating inefficiently. He was denying himself the reward of more money so that his fellow workers would like him.

[25]   It seemed that to the worker the informal organization and his place in it became more important than the traditional rational reasoning—his economic gain. On the basis of these conclusions, the Western Electric Company initiated a rather sizable program of surveying morale and followed it up with an extensive employee-counseling program.

[26]   Elton Mayo, late professor of industrial research at Harvard University and one of the directors of the Hawthorne study, was a great social scientist, but from his observations he drew another incomplete conclusion about the nature of man. Mayo concluded that one of the greatest faults of the Industrial Revolution was that it alienated the worker from most of the experiences he held to be significant in life. The worker, Mayo believed, was demonstrating his need for belonging by his concern for acceptance in the work group over and above his economic needs. Inasmuch as scientific management had defined in-

dustrial enterprise in completely rational terms, such concern of the workers within the framework of industry had to be considered emotional or sentimental.

It therefore seemed to Mayo and other advocates of an enlarged scientific management, which now included human relations, that the worker was motivated by needs that appeared to be irrational. Management considered as rational only the worker's needs for efficiency, economic gain and humane physical treatment. [27]

The vast difference between the manager and the worker was supposed to be that the manager would think it childish to restrict output and thereby make less money in exchange for the reward of acceptance by one's fellow workers. For the proselyte of scientific management, the manager was defined as a rational being because he can control his emotions; the worker was considered irrational because he is easily victimized by his emotions; and, in the final analysis, the worker was *by nature* inferior to the manager. [28]

Just as the "economic man" found a pseudoscientific explanation in Darwinism, which justified his existence, so the "emotional man" found corroboration for his reason for being in the results of the Hawthorne studies. Further sanction for the view of man as controlled by his emotion was found in the growing acceptance of the theories of man's nature as abstracted from the works of Sigmund Freud. [29]

While Freud did not discover the "emotional man," he was instrumental in defining him. Interpreters of Freudian theory said that adult behavior, particularly in its irrationalities, might be understood as manifestations of unresolved childhood needs. (What a nice fitting-in of the pieces of a jigsaw puzzle!) If the worker is a victim of his emotions and if these emotions stem from childhood, it must follow that the worker is childish. The approach of the industrial engineers comes into neat juxtaposition with the interpretations of the new psychiatry. [30]

Chris Argyris, professor of industrial relations at Yale University, has characterized the level of work required of the worker as a result of the belief in the "mechanistic man." Argyris suggests that the child is passive, dependent and subordinate and that he is characterized further by having a short span of interest and a restricted time perspective for the meaning of his actions and by being limited in his awareness of himself as an individual. [31]

This description fits the industrial engineer's job designs. The tasks assigned the workers were limited and sterile because it was believed that the workers were incapable of adult behavior. It seems that the worker was made to operate in an adult's body on a job that required the mentality and motivation of a child. [32]

[33]   Argyris demonstrated this by bringing in mental patients to do an extremely routine job in a factory setting. He was rewarded by the patients' increasing the production by 400 per cent. Argyris claimed also that these mental patients worked without complaint and were most easily supervised. (This information was conveyed to the author in a personal communication.)

[34]   Scientists call this type of condition a self-confirming hypothesis. The worker is made to act like a child, and when he conforms, he is labeled a child. This is the same technique that some people use to demonstrate what they consider to be the natural inferiority of the Negro. In fact, they deny the Negro educational, social and psychological opportunities and equality with white citizens. The Negro is put into segregated schools, which are inadequately staffed and have poor physical facilities. Then, after these opportunities have been denied the Negro, the white man examines the record. The Negro does badly. This, says the white man, is proof that the Negro is inferior.

[35]   Another source of the verification of the premise that the worker is immature was the Armed Forces' psychological testing during World War I. Psychologists found that, on the average, improvement of performance in so-called intelligence tests leveled off at around the age of thirteen. On this basis, the conclusion was drawn that the average mental age of Americans was no greater than that of a thirteen-year-old child. A further deduction stemmed from other findings of the military testing program. The scores that the recruits made on the intelligence tests were shown to correlate with the level of jobs that the soldiers had held as civilians.

[36]   The erroneous conclusion, resulting from these tests, was this: If the average mentality of an American is at the thirteen-year-old level, then the mentality of the rank-and-file worker must be much below that level.

[37]   These concepts fit in nicely with the burgeoning bureaucracies that developed in order to staff the huge new production facilities. That which was applied to the rank and file moved upward to include the traditional white-collar manager and even the professional. The new problem became how to manage the managers, as if they, too, had the mentality of thirteen-year-olds. Industry had a ready set of programs based on its experience with the hourly rated rank and file that could be used if altered only slightly.

[38]   How to handle the economic motive has given rise to an unimaginable array of wage, salary, bonus and benefit programs of such intricacy that an interdisciplinary team of lawyers, economists, financiers, physicians, sociologists, psychologists and welfarists are involved in their creation, planning and administration. Research on this aspect of man is mainly at the level of new models of economic prizes, reminiscent

of the frantic efforts of the giveaway shows to tantalize the audience with exotic variations of payoffs.

But the social needs of man have given rise to some of our most [39] ingenious and, in some cases, fruitful research in industry. The problems of leadership, supervision, organizational structure, group functioning and other social-psychological issues have multiplied both our scientific and our applied literature beyond almost anything that could have been imagined a few years ago. Unfortunately, the value of this work has been detracted from by some of the evangelical zeal of its premise that man is essentially a social animal primarily in search of social gratification. The form of social criticism for this era has already been defined in the writings of David Riesman and his attack on the "lonely crowd" and in William H. Whyte's attack on the "organization man." Nevertheless, there is gold to be mined in this research for improving personnel relations, organizational efficiency and human happiness.

Closely allied with the work being done on the social psychology [40] of industry has been the emphasis on understanding the role played by personal adjustment in the effectiveness of our industrial concerns. The clinical insights of psychiatry and psychology have become germane to the problems of people at work. The application of clinical psychiatry and psychology to industry has found expression ranging from the crude and often obnoxious misuse of personality assessment for hiring and promoting, through some of the naive psychology programs in supervisory training, to the more sophisticated managerial programs (such as the one at the Menninger Foundation) and the current wave of what may be considered a form of group therapy in sensitivity programs. Personal counseling, initiated as a product of the original Hawthorne studies, has never resulted in a promised land of psychological amelioration in industry. It is perhaps too early to forecast the impact that these newer uses of clinical psychiatry and psychology will have, but their effectiveness will be limited by the popular view of the emotionally sick man carried over from the pathological settings where the clinicians are trained. This has often led to the embarrassing necessity of labeling effective behaviors by negative terms: the well-adjusted man who earns a million dollars is overcompensating; the star football guard is a masochist sublimating an Oedipus complex.

To come to the aid of the "mechanistic man" at the managerial [41] level, the principles of the industrial engineer were recalled and invoked. The prescriptions that followed and were offered for the ills of the managerial group were rules, regulations, policies, organizational structure, with its span and control, unity of direction, committees, "group think," etc. All of them limited human variability to ensure that no one in the managerial ranks would make a mistake.

[42]   Let me add a new definition of human nature: The "neomechanistic man," or, perhaps more descriptive, the "instrumental man." As the technological development of industry has moved upward, so too has the level of human activity that serves industry become involved in higher capacities. Man's higher intellectual talents must now be organized, in the same way that his motor skills were organized for assembly-line operations. The "instrumental man" is the latest model that industry has begun to market. Perhaps we have arrived at an efficient breed, a problem solver vying with the computer and caring little for who or what is responsible for the input, and caring still less for the output—other than the fact that it was achieved successfully.

[43]   It seems that every man should be a specialist, even the over-all decision makers. The satisfaction in the achievement, however, is an emotional carry-over from the previously taught psychodynamics. This new man does his job well without the intrusions of any nonspecific task-oriented factors, and it is especially important that he encapsulate what he does well from all the rest of his abilities. Precision and rationality are cardinal virtues. Every manager and professional is to be a skilled artisan (human relations, too, is a polished trade). But the joy of achievement and creativity is an unsought pleasure. The "instrumental man" finds his greatest happiness in being an unattached expert. In rereading this description, one recalls the name of Adolf Eichmann.

[44]   The behavioral scientist, including the economist, has long since debunked the concept of the "economic man," but not completely. He exists *sotto voce* in our minds, or else the importance of economic motivation has been conveniently relegated to a lower category of human needs. The same holds true for the other encompassing need-definitions of man that have proved acceptable to industry. In order of their historical appearance they include: the "physical man," whose origin is shown in industry's concern with protecting its own integrity from social protest and so providing good working conditions and fringe benefits in order to keep men contented on the job; the "mechanistic man," who delights in being used efficiently, and again, as with the concept of the "economic man," was basically a projection of industry to see human nature in the light of its own needs for efficiency; the "social man," with a prevailing desire to be acceptable to his fellow workers, and the "emotional man," who searches for psychotherapeutic environments. Industry accepted the "social man" and the "emotional man" in order to protect its growing image in the community as acknowledging the dignity of labor.

[45]   The "instrumental man" is a projection of industry's need to cope with the rationalization process that it has undertaken by incorporating advanced systems analysis and control in its operations.

Perhaps the greatest contribution that the behavioral scientists have   [46]
made during the last half-century of research on the industrial scene
has been to broaden the concept of the needs and nature of man from
a solely economic organism to one that encompasses some of the
more human aspects—the emotional and social needs.

The myths that industry has supported are not entirely invalid,   [47]
but they do not tell the whole story. In fact, they tell only half the
story about man's nature. These myths are stamped with the concept
that man's nature is cast wholly from Adam's genes. It is wise to go
back and ask once more, What is the nature of man? Not the nature
of man as imposed by any particular economic or social institution,
but the nature of man as it is in reality, regardless of the needs of the
controlling forces.

QUESTIONS

1. How did the Protestant ethic fit into Darwin's theory of biological
   evolution? What is meant by "social Darwinism"?
2. What are the uses to management of "welfare capitalism"? What
   is the rationale that justifies "a motivation program" in the eyes
   of management?
3. How does Taylorism conceive of the role of a manager? Taylor
   called his book *Scientific Management* because he believed that one
   could use scientific methods in industrial management. Read Herzberg's summary of Taylor's method on p. 160. What is the flaw in
   this method? Why is it *not* really scientific? Why does this error
   result in what Herzberg calls "an almost inhuman society"?
4. What basic (and in Herzberg's view erroneous) assumption does
   industrial engineering make about the best way to utilize workers?
5. What does management's myth of "the idyllically happy worker
   attuned to the factory system" tell us about human prejudice? If
   a "happy" worker is one who is "an interchangeable part of an
   interchangeable machine making interchangeable parts," what must
   a manager believe is the difference between managers and workers?
   Can you see the roots of this thinking in the Calvinist theory of
   the elect that Herzberg talks about on p. 158?
6. How does Elton Mayo explain workers' valuing human relations
   above financial gain in the Hawthorne study? Does the myth of
   "emotional man" which replaced the myth of "mechanical man"
   reflect the same Protestant-ethic prejudice, or does it represent a
   real change of attitude?

7. Why does Herzberg call Argyris' study with mental patients a case of "self-confirming hypothesis"? What makes the hypothesis unscientific? Consider: What preconceptions about workers, about mental patients, and about managers does it assume?
8. What does Herzberg's style reveal about his attitude toward all the philosophies of management that he describes? What approach do you think *he* favors?

EXERCISES

1. Examine the help-wanted section of your local newspaper. Make a list of ten skilled and ten unskilled jobs and examine the ads for each carefully. On the basis of the information given, determine what aspects of the job advertised are being emphasized. Note, for example, which advertisements emphasize salary or which emphasize fringe benefits.

   a. On the basis of your study, write a paragraph in which you discuss the "myth" that seems to underlie one or more of the employers' definition of the worker(s) being sought (e.g., the worker as "economic" man, as "mechanistic" man).
   b. Write a paragraph in which you discuss differences in the underlying attitudes employers hold toward skilled and unskilled workers.
   c. Write an ad for the same job (skilled or unskilled) to reflect each of the myths discussed by Herzberg.

2. Suppose that you are interviewed for a position as manager of a business, say a local McDonald's or the college bookstore. You are asked by the personnel manager to prepare a statement explaining your philosophy of work to the employees. Choose any business you wish, and write a first draft of such a statement.

3. Exchange the statement you completed in Exercise 2 with that of another student in your class. Then analyze his or her statement in terms of Herzberg's discussion of management mythologies. Does your fellow student reflect any of those myths? Or is there a different governing myth behind his or her theory of management? Be ready to discuss the statement or to write an evaluation of it.

CHAPTER ELEVEN

THUROW: AN ECONOMY THAT NO LONGER PERFORMS

Economics

While "workers" as the task force report conceives of them are individual people among one or another group—i.e. white collar, blue collar—and while Herzberg conceives of "workers" as a class of people in opposition to managers, Lester Thurow conceives of whole nations as "workers" that perform well or poorly. He sets out here to examine the American economy—"workers," managers, producers of products, investors, the government itself—to evaluate its overall success as a system. Thurow, who teaches economics at MIT, concludes that the American economy is not successful because its parts have conflicting interests (consumers vs. producers; rich vs. poor). He believes that these interests prevent the making of policy decisions required for the good of the whole.

In the selections we have read so far, we have looked at individual parts of the economic body. In this essay we focus upon the whole. As you read try to determine what Thurow's focus does to his style. Does he, for example, use more or fewer generalizations than Herzberg or the task force team does? Does he seem to be more interested in analyzing a problem or in arguing a proposition? Do you think he is trying to convince other economists that his is the right way to think about economic problems? Or is his argument aimed at a different audience, say, the government or the ordinary citizen? In addition to being a professor of economics Thurow is a writer for the *Los Angeles Times* and a member of *The New York Times* editorial staff. Do you think that his association with newspapers has had an influence upon his writing style?

GLOSSARY

vulnerability [1]   diagnosed [23]

harbinger [2]   accelerating [28]

GNP [3]   allocated [32]

obsolete [10]   militancy [36]

geopolitical [13]   deterrent [39]

strategic [13]   adversary [39]

initiative [17]   Balkanization [42]

inflation [22]

AN ECONOMY THAT
____ NO LONGER PERFORMS ____
Lester C. Thurow

[1]   After decades of believing in their economic invulnerability, Americans
were jolted by the 1973–74 Arab oil embargo. The actions of a few
desert sheiks could make *them* line up at the gas pump and substantially
reduce *their* standard of living. Sudden economic vulnerability is disconcerting, just as that first small heart attack is disconcerting. It
reminds us that our economy can be eclipsed.

[2]   When the shutdown of a major oil exporter for just a few months
in 1979 once again resulted in the convulsions of gas lines, it was
possible to ask whether that first mild heart attack was not the harbinger
of something worse. Seemingly unsolvable problems were emerging
everywhere—inflation, unemployment, slow growth, environmental
decay, irreconcilable group demands, and complex, cumbersome regulations. Were the problems unsolvable or were our leaders incompetent? Had Americans lost the work ethic? Had we stopped inventing

SOURCE: From THE ZERO-SUM SOCIETY: *Distribution and the Possibilities for Economic Change*,
by Lester C. Thurow. © 1980 by Basic Books, Inc., Publishers. Reprinted by permission
of the publisher.

new processes and products? Should we invest more and consume less? Do we need to junk our social welfare, health, safety, and environmental protection systems in order to compete? Why were others doing better?

Where the U.S. economy had once generated the world's highest standard of living, it was now well down the list and slipping farther each year. Leaving the rich Middle East sheikdoms aside, we stood fifth among the nations of the world in per capita GNP in 1978, having been surpassed by Switzerland, Denmark, West Germany, and Sweden.[1] Switzerland, which stood first, actually had a per capita GNP 45 percent larger than ours. And on the outside, the world's fastest economic runner, Japan, was advancing rapidly with a per capita GNP only 7 percent below ours. In our entire history we have never grown even half as rapidly as the Japanese. [3]

While the slippage in our economic position was first noticed in the 1970s, our economic status was actually surpassed (after just half a century of delivering the world's highest standard of living) by Kuwait in the early 1950s.[2] Kuwait was ignored, however, as a simple case of a country inheriting wealth (oil in the ground) rather than earning it. We failed to remember that our supremacy had also been based on a rich inheritance of vast mineral, energy, and climatic resources. No one inherited more wealth than we. We are not the little poor boy who worked his way to the top, but the little rich boy who inherited a vast fortune. Perhaps we had now squandered that inheritance. Perhaps we could not survive without it. [4]

Of course, one can always argue that things are not really as bad as they seem. Since many goods are not traded in international markets and may be cheaper here than abroad, per capita GNP may paint too pessimistic a picture of our relative position. A group of American economists argued in 1975 that we still had the highest real standard of living among industrialized countries.[3] What we lost in per capita GNP to the two or three countries that were then ahead of us, we more than made up in terms of lower living costs. [5]

Whether this is still true today depends upon changes in the *terms of trade*—the amount of exports that you have to give up to get a given amount of imports. In Switzerland, for example, oil cost less in 1978 than it did in 1975.[4] While the dollar price of oil is up, the value of the Swiss franc is up even more. Thus fewer domestic goods have to be given up to buy a given quantity of oil. The country's GNP simply buys more than it did. In countries like Switzerland, where imports are over one-third of the GNP, changes in the terms of trade can have a dramatic effect on the real standard of living. [6]

While it is easy to calculate per capita GNPs, it is notoriously difficult to make precise standard-of-living comparisons among countries. In [7] each country, individuals naturally shift their purchases toward those items that are relatively cheap in that country. Tastes, circumstances, traditions, and habits differ. Individuals do not buy the same basket of goods and services. What is a necessity in one country may be a luxury in another. Health care may be provided by government in one country and purchased privately in another. And how do you evaluate vast expenditures, such as those we make on health care, where we are spending more than the rest of the world but getting less if you look at life expectancy (U.S. males are now sixteenth in the world)?

[8]   But whatever our precise ranking at the moment, the rest of the world is catching up, and if they have not already surpassed us, they soon will. From many perspectives, this catching-up process is desirable. Most rich people find it more comfortable to live in a neighborhood with other rich people. The tensions are less and life is more enjoyable. What is not so comfortable is the prospect that our rich neighbors will continue to grow so rapidly that we slip into relative backwardness.

[9]   Up to now, we have comforted ourselves with the belief that the economic growth of others would slow down as soon as they had caught up with us. It was simply easier to adopt existing technologies than to develop new technologies—or so we told ourselves. But as other countries have approached our productivity levels, and as individual industries in these countries have begun to be more productive, the "catching-up" hypothesis becomes less and less persuasive.

[10]   In the period from 1972 to 1978, industrial productivity rose 1 percent per year in the United States, almost 4 percent in West Germany, and over 5 percent in Japan.[5] These countries were introducing new products and improving the process of making old products faster than we were. Major American firms were reduced to marketing new consumer goods such as video recorders, which were made exclusively by the Japanese. In many industries, such as steel, we are now the ones with the "easy" task of adopting the technologies developed by others. But we don't. Instead of junking our old, obsolete open-hearth furnaces and shifting to the large oxygen furnaces and continuous casting of the Japanese, we retreat into protection against the "unfair" competition of Japanese steel companies. The result is a reduction in real incomes as we all pay more for steel than we should. As a result, our economy ends up with a weak steel industry that cannot compete and has no incentive to compete, given its protection in the U.S. market.

[11]   This relative economic decline has both economic and political impacts. Economically, Americans face a relative decline in their standard of living. How will the average American react when it becomes obvious to the casual tourist (foreigners here, Americans there) that

our economy is falling behind? Since we have never had that experience, no one knows; but if we are like human beings in the rest of the world, we won't like it. No one likes seeing others able to afford things that they cannot.

As gaps in living standards grow, so does dissatisfaction with the [12] performance of government and economy. The larger the income gap, the more revolutionary the demands for change. Today's poor countries are in turmoil, but it should be remembered that these countries are not poor compared with the poor centuries ago. They are only poor relative to what has been achieved in today's rich countries. If we become relatively poor, we are apt to be just as unhappy.

Politically a declining economy means that we have to be willing [13] to make greater sacrifices in our personal consumption to maintain any level of world influence. This can be done. The Russians have become our military and geopolitical equals despite a per capita GNP that is much lower than ours. They simply put a larger fraction of their GNP into defense. But the need to cut consumption creates strains in a democracy that do not exist in a dictatorship. Americans may gradually decide that they cannot afford to maintain a strategic military capability to defend countries that are richer than they are. They may decide that they cannot afford to lubricate peace settlements, such as that between Israel and Egypt, with large economic gifts. Some of the international economic burdens could be shifted to our wealthier allies, but this would inevitably mean letting them make more of the important, international decisions. In many circumstances (Israel v. Egypt?) the Germans and the Japanese may not make the same decisions that we would make.

The hard-core conservative solution is to "liberate free enterprise," [14] reduce social expenditures, restructure taxes to encourage saving and investment (shift the tax burden from those who save, the rich, to those who consume, the poor), and eliminate government rules and regulations that do not help business. Specifically, the capital gains taxes that were reduced in 1978 should be reduced further; the "double" taxation of dividends should be ended; income transfer payments to the poor and the elderly should be frozen; environmentalism should be seen as an economic threat and rolled back. Laffer curves sprout like weeds to show that taxes should be cut to restore personal initiative. Only by returning to the virtues of hard work and free enterprise can the economy be saved.

In thinking about this solution, it is well to remember that none [15] of our competitors became successful by following this route. Government absorbs slightly over 30 percent of the GNP in the United States, but over 50 percent of the GNP in West Germany. Fifteen other countries collect a larger fraction of their GNP in taxes.[6]

[16]   Other governments are not only larger; they are more pervasive. In West Germany, union leaders must by law sit on corporate boards. Sweden is famous for its comprehensive welfare state. Japan is marked by a degree of central investment planning and government control that would make any good capitalist cry. Other governments own or control major firms, such as Volkswagen or Renault. Ours is not the economy with the most rules and regulations; on the contrary, it is the one with the fewest rules and regulations. As many American firms have discovered to their horror, it simply isn't possible to fire workers abroad as it is here. It is a dubious achievement; but nowhere in the world is it easier to lay off workers.

[17]   Nor have our competitors unleashed work effort and savings by increasing income differentials. Indeed, they have done exactly the opposite. If you look at the earnings gap between the top and bottom 10 percent of the population, the West Germans work hard with 36 percent less inequality than we, and the Japanese work even harder with 50 percent less inequality.[7] If income differentials encourage individual initiative, we should be full of initiative, since among industrialized countries, only the French surpass us in terms of inequality.

[18]   Moreover, our own history shows that our economic performance since the New Deal and the onset of government "interference" has been better than it was prior to the New Deal. Our best economic decades were the 1940s (real per capita GNP grew 36 percent), when the economy was run as a command (socialist) wartime economy, and the 1960s (real per capita GNP grew 30 percent), when we had all that growth in social welfare programs.[8] Real per capita growth since the advent of government intervention has been more than twice as high as it was in the days when governments did not intervene or have social welfare programs.

[19]   The British are often held up as a horrible example of what will happen to us if we do not mend our ways and reverse the trend toward big government. But whatever is wrong with the British economy, it has little to do with the size of government. British growth fell behind that of the leading industrial countries in the nineteenth century and has remained behind ever since. Slow growth did not arrive with the Labour government in 1945. On the contrary, British growth since 1945 has actually been better than before. There is no doubt that the British economy is in sad shape, but as the West Germanys of the world demonstrate, its problems are not a simple function of government size.

[20]   As both our experience and foreign experience demonstrate, there is no conflict between social expenditures or government intervention and economic success. Indeed, the lack of investment planning, worker participation, and social spending may be a cause of our poor per-

formance. As we, and others, have shown, social reforms can be productive, as well as just, if done in the right way. If done in the wrong way, they can, of course, be both disastrous and unjust. There may also be some merit in "liberating free enterprise" if it is done in the right way. There are certainly unnecessary rules and regulations that are now strangling our economy. The trick is not rules versus no rules, but finding the right rules.

The American problem is not returning to some golden age of [21] economic growth (there was no such golden age) but in recognizing that we have an economic structure that has never in its entire history performed as well as Japan and West Germany have performed since World War II. We are now the ones who must copy and adapt the policies and innovations that have been successful elsewhere. To retreat into our mythical past is to guarantee that our days of economic glory are over.

UNSOLVABLE PROBLEMS

But our problems are not limited to slow growth. Throughout our [22] society there are painful, persistent problems that are not being solved by our system of political economy. Energy, inflation, unemployment, environmental decay, ever-spreading waves of regulations, sharp income gaps between minorities and majorities—the list is almost endless. Because of our inability to solve these problems, the lament is often heard that the U.S. economy and political system have lost their ability to get things done. Meaningful compromises cannot be made, and the politics of confrontation are upon us like the plague. Programs that would improve the general welfare cannot be started because strong minorities veto them. No one has the ability to impose solutions, and no solutions command universal assent.

The problem is real, but it has not been properly diagnosed. One [23] cannot lose an ability that one never had. What is perceived as a lost ability to act is in fact (1) a shift from international cold war problems to domestic problems, and (2) an inability to impose large economic losses explicitly.

As domestic problems rise in importance relative to international [24] problems, action becomes increasingly difficult. International confrontations can be, and to some extent are, portrayed as situations where everyone is fairly sharing sacrifices to hold the foreign enemy in check. Since every member of society is facing a common threat, an overwhelming consensus and bipartisan approach can be achieved.

Domestic problems are much more contentious in the sense that [25] when policies are adopted to solve domestic problems, there are *American* winners and *American* losers. Some incomes go up as a result of the solution; but others go down. Individuals do not sacrifice equally. Some gain; some lose. A program to raise the occupational position of women and minorities automatically lowers the occupational position of white men. Every black or female appointed to President Carter's cabinet is one less white male who can be appointed.

[26]   People often ask why President Kennedy was so easily able to get the Man on the Moon project underway, while both Presidents Nixon and Ford found it impossible to get their Project Independence underway. There is a very simple answer. Metaphorically, some American has to have his or her house torn down to achieve energy independence, but no American lives between the earth and the moon. Everyone is in favor of energy independence in general, but there are vigorous objectors to every particular path to energy independence. In contrast, once a consensus had been reached on going to the moon, the particular path could be left to the technicians. In domestic problems, the means are usually as contentious as the ends themselves.

[27]   [However,] there *are* solutions for each of our problem areas. We do not face a world of unsolvable problems. But while there are solutions in each case, these solutions have a common characteristic. Each requires that some large group—sometimes a minority and sometimes the majority—be willing to tolerate a large reduction in their real standard of living. When the economic pluses and minuses are added up, the pluses usually exceed the minuses, but there are large economic losses. These have to be allocated to someone, and no group wants to be the group that must suffer economic losses for the general good.

[28]   Recently I was asked to address a Harvard alumni reunion on the problem of accelerating economic growth. I suggested that we were all in favor of more investment, but that the heart of the problem was deciding whose income should fall to make room for more investment. Who would they take income away from if they were given the task of raising our investment in plant and equipment from 10 to 15 percent of the GNP? One hand was quickly raised, and the suggestion was made to eliminate welfare payments. Not surprisingly, the person was suggesting that someone else's income be lowered, but I pointed out that welfare constitutes only 1.2 percent of the GNP.[9] Where were they going to get the remaining funds—3.8 percent of GNP? Whose income were they willing to cut after they had eliminated government programs for the poor? Not a hand went up.

A ZERO-SUM GAME

[29] This is the heart of our fundamental problem. Our economic problems are solvable. For most of our problems there are several solutions.

But all these solutions have the characteristic that someone must suffer large economic losses. No one wants to volunteer for this role, and we have a political process that is incapable of forcing anyone to shoulder this burden. Everyone wants someone else to suffer the necessary economic losses, and as a consequence none of the possible solutions can be adopted.

Basically we have created the world described in Robert Ardrey's [30] *The Territorial Imperative*. To beat an animal of the same species on his home turf, the invader must be twice as strong as the defender. But no majority is twice as strong as the minority opposing it. Therefore we each veto the other's initiatives, but none of us has the ability to create successful initiatives ourselves.

Our political and economic structure simply isn't able to cope with [31] an economy that has a substantial zero-sum element. A zero-sum game is any game where the losses exactly equal the winnings. All sporting events are zero-sum games. For every winner there is a loser, and winners can only exist if losers exist. What the winning gambler wins, the losing gambler must lose.

When there are large losses to be allocated, any economic decision [32] has a large zero-sum element. The economic gains may exceed the economic losses, but the losses are so large as to negate a very substantial fraction of the gains. What is more important, the gains and losses are not allocated to the same individuals or groups. On average, society may be better off, but this average hides a large number of people who are much better off and large numbers of people who are much worse off. If you are among those who are worse off, the fact that someone else's income has risen by more than your income has fallen is of little comfort.

To protect our own income, we will fight to stop economic change [33] from occurring or fight to prevent society from imposing the public policies that hurt us. From our perspective they are not good public policies even if they do result in a larger GNP. We want a solution to the problem, say the problem of energy, that does not reduce our income, but all solutions reduce someone's income. If the government chooses some policy option that does not lower our income, it will have made a supporter out of us, but it will have made an opponent out of someone else, since someone else will now have to shoulder the burden of large income reductions.

The problem with zero-sum games is that the essence of problem [34] solving is loss allocation. But this is precisely what our political process is least capable of doing. When there are economic gains to be allocated, our political process can allocate them. When there are large economic losses to be allocated, our political process is paralyzed. And with political paralysis comes economic paralysis.

[35]   The importance of economic losers has also been magnified by a change in the political structure. In the past, political and economic power was distributed in such a way that substantial economic losses could be imposed on parts of the population if the establishment decided that it was in the general interest. Economic losses were allocated to particular powerless groups rather than spread across the population. These groups are no longer willing to accept losses and are able to raise substantially the costs for those who wish to impose losses upon them.

[36]   There are a number of reasons for this change. Vietnam and the subsequent political scandals clearly lessened the population's willingness to accept their nominal leader's judgments that some project was in their general interest. With the civil rights, poverty, black power, and women's liberation movements, many of the groups that have in the past absorbed economic losses have become militant. They are no longer willing to accept losses without a political fight. The success of their militancy and civil disobedience sets an example that spreads to other groups representing the environment, neighborhoods, and regions.

[37]   All minority groups have gone through a learning process. They have discovered that it is relatively easy with our legal system and a little militancy to delay anything for a very long period of time. To be able to delay a program is often to be able to kill it. Legal and administrative costs rise, but the delays and uncertainties are even more important. When the costs of delays and uncertainties are added into their calculations, both government and private industry often find that it pays to cancel projects that would otherwise be profitable. Costs are simply higher than benefits.

[38]   In one major environmental group, delays are such a major part of their strategy that they have a name for it—analysis paralysis. Laws are to be passed so that every project must meet a host of complicated time-consuming requirements. The idea is not to learn more about the costs and benefits of projects, but to kill them. If such requirements were to be useful in deciding whether a project should be undertaken, environmental-impact statements, for example, would have to be inexpensive, simple, and quick to complete. Then a firm might undertake the studies to help determine whether they should or should not start a project.

[39]   Instead, the studies are to be expensive and complex to serve as a financial deterrent to undertaking any project, to substantially lengthen the time necessary to complete any project, and to ensure that they can be challenged in court (another lengthy process). As a consequence, the developer will start the process only if he has already decided on other grounds to go ahead with the project. The result is an adversary

situation where the developer cannot get his project underway—and where the environmentalists also cannot get existing plants (such as Reserve Mining) to clean up their current pollution. Where it helps them, both sides have learned the fine art of delay.

Consider the interstate highway system. Whatever one believes [40] about the merits of completing the remaining intracity portion of the system, it is clear that it gives the country an intercity transportation network that would be sorely missed had it not been built. Even those who argue against it do so on the grounds that if it had not been built, some better (nonauto) system would have been devised. Yet most observers would agree that the interstate highway system could not have been built if it had been proposed in the mid-1970s rather than in the mid-1950s.

Exactly the same factors that would prevent the initiation of an [41] interstate highway system would also prevent the initiation of any alternative transportation system. A few years ago, when a high-speed rail system was being considered for the Boston-Washington corridor, a former governor of Connecticut announced that he would veto any relocation of the Boston-to-New York line on the grounds that it would be of prime benefit to those at either end of the line, but would tear up Connecticut homes. The groups opposing an intercity rail network would be slightly different from the groups opposing an intercity highway network, but they would be no less effective in stopping the project. Any transportation system demands that land be taken and homes be torn down. At one time, this was possible; at the moment, it is impossible.

The Balkanization of nations is a worldwide phenomenon that the [42] United States has not escaped. Regions and localities are less and less willing to incur costs that will primarily help people in other parts of the same country. Consider the development of the coalfields of Wyoming and Montana. There is no question that most of the benefits will accrue to those living in urban areas in the rest of the country while most of the costs will be imposed on those living in that region. As a result, the local population objects. More coal mining might be good for the United States, but it will be bad for local constituents. Therefore they will impose as many delays and uncertainties as possible.

The same problem is visible in the location of nuclear power plants. [43] Whatever one believes about the benefits of nuclear power, it is clear that lengthy delays in approving sites serve no purpose other than as a strategy for killing the projects. If the projects are undertaken anyway, the consumer will have to suffer the same risks and pay the higher costs associated with these delays. What is wanted is a quick yes or no answer; but this is just what we find impossible to do. The question of nuclear power sites also raises the Balkanization issue.

Whatever the probabilities of accidents, the consequences of such failures are much less if the plants are located in remote areas. But those who live in remote areas do not want the plants, since they suffer all the potential hazards and do not need the project. Everyone wants power, but no one wants a power plant next to his own home.

[44]   Domestic problems also tend to have a much longer time horizon. In modern times, even long wars are won or lost in relatively short periods of time. In contrast, a project such as energy independence would take decades to achieve. The patience and foresight necessary for long-range plans is generally not an American virtue. Consequently, representatives seeking reelection every two, four, or six years want to support programs that will bring them votes. They do not want to stick their necks out for a good cause that may conflict with their careers. Even more fundamentally, domestic problems often involve long periods where costs accrue, with the benefits following much later. Think about energy independence. For a long time, sacrifices must be made to construct the necessary mines and plants. Benefits emerge only near the end of the process. The politician who must incur the costs (raise the necessary revenue and incur the anger of those who are hurt as the projects are constructed) is unlikely to be around to collect the credits when energy independence has been achieved.

NOTES

1. International Monetary Fund, *International Financial Statistics* 32, no. 4 (April 1979): 122, 156, 214, 352, 356, 390.
2. Ibid., p. 228.
3. Irving Kravis, Alan Heston, and Robert Summers, "Real GDP for More than 100 Countries," *Economic Journal*, June 1978, p. 215.
4. International Monetary Fund, *International Financial Statistics* 32, no. 4 (April 1979): 43, 354.
5. Ibid., pp. 154, 214, 390.
6. United Nations, *Yearbook of National Account Statistics*, 1977, vol. 1 (New York: United Nations, 1978), p. 348.
7. Malcolm Sawyer and Frank Wasserman, "Income Distribution in OECD Countries," *OECD Economic Outlook*, July 1976, p. 14.
8. U.S. Department of Commerce, Bureau of Economic Analysis, *The National Income and Product Accounts of the United States, 1929–1974*, p. 312.
9. U.S. Department of Commerce, *Survey of Current Business* 59, no. 7 (July 1979): 43.

QUESTIONS

1. Thurow says that conservatives think "only by returning to the virtues of hard work and free enterprise can the economy be saved."

What do these conservatives think that means in terms of taxes, social expenditures, investments, etc.? And what does *Thurow* think of their solution?

2. Thurow cites West Germany, Sweden, and Japan as competitor countries whose economies work more successfully than ours even though theirs are much more fully controlled and protected by government. Give an example of the way that government intervenes in the economy of these countries. Why would this kind of government control "make any good [American] capitalist cry"?

3. Thurow says, "As domestic problems rise in importance relative to international problems, action becomes increasingly difficult. International confrontations can be, and to some extent are, portrayed as situations where everyone is fairly sharing sacrifices to hold the foreign enemy in check." In your experience is this true? And does an administration in Washington capitalize on it? Think of two or three international crises or cold war confrontations in the past year and consider whether international problems distract us from domestic problems. (The portion of time allotted to each sphere by the evening news is a good index.)

4. What is a "zero-sum" element, and why does it paralyze us when we try to solve our domestic economic problems?

5. In explaining the political effects of zero-sum economics Thurow says:

> If the government chooses some policy option that does not lower our income, it will have made a supporter out of us, but it will have made an opponent out of someone else, since someone else will now have to shoulder the burden of large income reductions.

If we accept this statement as true, what are the effects of these off-setting economic circumstances upon our political life? Consider the following:

a. How do these circumstances determine whom a political candidate woos to back his or her campaign?

b. How do they affect lobbyists and special interest political groups?

c. How does it explain a mayor's tendency to participate in an ethnic celebration such as the St. Patrick's Day parade or Chinese New Year? Or a presidential candidate's spending Labor Day with the AFL-CIO, or playing golf with the president of Getty Oil Corporation?

6. Considering the last three selections, assign a priority to the needs of workers and/or managers to solve the problems of the whole economy as Thurow has outlined them for us. When we take the wide scope of an economist, how are we required to think of workers? of managers? of industrial engineers?

7. In what way does Thurow reorient our thinking toward work and its rewards? What does he say about the effect of a zero-sum economy on the work force? Would it tend to limit opportunities for self improvement? for midcareer changes? for the flourishing of skills? Discuss.

8. On the basis of your reading of Thurow and with the help of a desk dictionary and/or a general encyclopedia, give a definition of economics as a field of study. Consider what perspectives it gives us upon some of the issues we have been considering in reading the other selections. What has economics as a discipline to offer to our understanding of the world of work?

EXERCISES

1.   a. Read three newspapers for a three-week period: (1) a local newspaper (the college, town, village, or if you live in a large city, district paper), (2) the nearest large city newspaper, and (3) *USA Today*.

   b. Choose a single domestic issue and cut out any really relevant comments on that issue.

   c. Organize the editorials in piles determined by what groups' interest they express—for instance, conservative vs. liberal, industry vs. labor, homeowner vs. renter, or power plant developer vs. environmentalist.

   d. Make a project journal by pasting typical, or especially salient, editorials from the newspapers you read for Exercise 1. Put the articles from the local paper in Section 1, from the city paper in Section II, and from *USA Today* in Section III. Write a short paragraph under each article, indicating to what interest group it gives voice. Try to decide on the basis of Thurow's essay, what segment of the economy (i.e., whose economic good, welfare, growth) the local, city, and national newspapers serve.

   End your project journal with a summary statement of about two hundred words that expresses *your* view of economic interest on the local, state, and national level. Use the formula of the scientific method: hypothesis > evidence (from the editorials you have pasted in) > conclusion.

2.   a. Follow the speeches of any candidate who is seeking political office. If it is not election time, consult back issues of a newspaper (*The New York Times* is available in most libraries). On the basis of (1) what groups the candidate chooses to address, (2) what she or

he promises them, (3) what she or he criticizes in the opponents' policies, try to discover what appeals the candidate is making to the need of various groups for "economic security."

b. Make notes of what your candidate and the opponent say to appeal to three groups, preferably with divergent interests (e.g., a labor union, a group of senior citizens, a chamber of commerce group).

c. Write a detailed outline that (1) summarizes the appeal each candidate makes to the divergent economic interests of her or his audiences, (2) compares the appeals, (3) determines whether the appeals are different or the same, (4) concludes whether either candidate can deliver what is promised. Finally, consider whether the candidates can keep their promises given Thurow's observation that ours is a zero-sum economy.

3. Consider what Thurow has to say about the importance of economic security to the American worker in our time. Then reexamine your own profile which you wrote in response to the selection, "Work in America" (see Exercise 3 on p. 155). Revise the profile to include any remarks you feel you now need to make about security. If you do not need to make any changes, write a paragraph in which you speculate about the relative importance of that subject in relation to your overall goals.

CHAPTER TWELVE

FEDERICO AND SCHWARTZ: SOCIAL STRATIFICATION AND SOCIAL CLASS

Sociology

Because sociology studies the structure of our communal life—how we design social structures and how we are in turn shaped by them—sociologists have been much concerned with what they call the "social status of occupations." In 1947 the pioneer researchers Cecil C. North and Paul K. Hatt undertook a study, jointly sponsored by the President's Scientific Research Board and the National Opinion Research Center, aimed at determining the prestige of occupations. They developed questionnaires and scaling procedures determined to indicate how Americans ranked the kinds of work we do. For the next two decades sociologists focused their major attention on refining their methods. For instance, they discovered that income was just one of the factors that contributes to the prestige of an occupation. Power over oneself, one's work, and other people was also seen to be a factor, as was "psychic income" derived from whether the society as a whole thinks that one's job is desirable or not and what the job is thought to contribute to the general welfare of the society or culture.

By 1980 measurement of the "status" of the various occupations was a finely tuned instrument, and cross-cultural studies strongly suggested that in major industrial societies ranking of the various occupations was much the same. The conclusion to which we are led by these kinds of studies is that there is indeed class stratification even in societies like ours which purport to be classless; that the kind of work we do to a very great extent determines our prestige in the eyes of our fellows, and by extension, in our own eyes; and finally, that our occupations will probably not only determine who our friends and associates are, but also what opportunities will be open to us and to our children. What we do, therefore, has a controlling influence over what we are; the reach of our work extends into our lives far beyond the time and space in which we are actually *at* work.

As you read this chapter from Federico and Schwartz's textbook, *Sociology*, keep some of these questions in mind:

1. How does what we learn in this selection square with what we learned in the last: how does the social stratification determined by the status of the work we do influence our understanding of the "zero-sum society"?
2. Is the division between "management" and labor that Herzberg makes a subtle-enough classification?
3. This selection, unlike the others we have read, is from a textbook that might vey well be a required text in one of your sociology courses. How does that influence its tone and style? We usually take for granted that a textbook simply presents the "facts": details, principles, or summaries of the research in a field. Does this text do anything more? Do you feel the writers take a moral position? Do they seem to prefer one theory of class stratification over another? Are they trying to persuade you to take one or another position in relation to the facts they reveal?

GLOSSARY

caste system [2]	feudalism [11]
social norms [2]	bourgeoisie [11]
stratification [5]	solidarity [13]
functionalist [5]	ideology [13]
ego expansion [5]	viability [15]
perpetuate [7]	collective bargaining [15]
menial [8]	multidimensional [19]
dysfunctional [9]	credentials [20]
capitalism [11]	

SOCIAL STRATIFICATION
——— AND SOCIAL CLASS ———
Ronald C. Federico and Janet Schwartz

[1] Americans, lay people and scholars alike, have tended to view American society as either "classless" or "middle class." Given the national creed of equality, to think of American society as a class society seemed inappropriate, or perhaps un-American. Scholars also were preoccupied with equality. In the card catalogue of the main library of Cornell University Reisman (1973) found a listing of 102 publications under the subject of "equality," 69 on the subject of "equal opportunity," and 11 under the subject of "inequality."

[2] Sociologists have argued that social classes are, at best, arbitrary in their boundaries, and difficult to define and to measure. In more traditional societies, the distinctions between classes have developed over many years and are clearly understood by everyone. In India, for example, the elaborate system of castes has been estimated to be 3500 years old. Although the caste system has now been outlawed, authorities are finding that it is nearly inseparable from that society's history and their Hindu tradition. On the other hand, life in modern industrial societies is subject to continuous fluctuations of social norms and economic pressures. Reliable class definitions are difficult to establish. Furthermore, in a rapidly changing, complex, and specialized society, is the chauffeur who earns $25,000 a year part of the working class (based on occupation) or middle class (based on income)?

[3] In spite of these problems, the concept that a society can be separated into ranks does give the sociologist a framework for understanding the distribution of wealth and inequality. *Social stratification* is a system of ranking individuals and groups who share unequally in the distribution of scarce resources, wealth, prestige, and power. Groups who share the same characteristics of economic resources, prestige, and power and are aware of their common situation constitute a *social class*.

[4] Sociologists do not agree on the issue of why there is inequality in wealth, power, and status. Functional school proponents claim that inequality is necessary to the survival of society. On the other hand, sociologists of the conflict school argue that inequality is the result of a struggle between the haves and the have nots; those who have the scarce resources —in order to maintain and increase their resources—

SOURCE: From Ronald Federico, Janet S. Schwartz, SOCIOLOGY, © 1983, Addison Wesley Pub. Co. Inc., Reading, Ma. Reprinted with permission.

must exploit and control those who have no resources. A third group of sociologists focuses on social class as the major dimension of social stratification. We will look at these three approaches in more detail.

THEORIES OF SOCIAL STRATIFICATION

THE FUNCTIONALIST FRAMEWORK

The functionalist framework of social stratification (Davis and Moore, [5] 1945) centers on the notion that some positions are more important for the survival of society than others. If all the necessary positions were equally pleasant, equally important, or equal in terms of required ability and talent, presumably there would be no need for a system of social stratification. This, however, is not the case. Some positions require greater talent than others, and some positions are functionally more important for the survival or effective functioning of society. Garbage collectors require no special talent to perform their tasks, but bank presidents do. To become a lawyer requires ability and a long period of schooling, during which the prospective lawyer earns little. Lawyers work hard, and they are always on call. The sacrifices they make during their education and training, the long hours they spend on their jobs, and the complexities associated with the practice of law make it necessary for society to have some rewards to induce people into these positions. The rewards for the most important positions take the form of material benefits, prestige, deference, and privilege. Or, as stated by Davis and Moore, things that contribute to sustenance and comfort, to humor and diversion, to self-respect and ego expansion. This ensures that the most talented will be motivated to seek these positions, and to perform them dutifully.

Many sociologists have questioned whether social positions can, [6] in fact, be rated by their importance. Why, for example, are doctors more functionally important than garbage collectors? Others have criticized the assumption that there ever really was or is a match between talent and rank. The functionalist argument assumes that most individuals who are talented or ambitious will be able to achieve their chosen position in society. However, it is clear that not everyone has equal access to the training systems that lead to highly rewarding positions.

Some sociologists feel that stratification, rather than motivating [7] persons to achieve difficult positions that require long training, is more likely to preserve the privilege of people who already occupy such positions. Although the functionalist theory may help to explain how stratification originated, it ignores the mechanisms that preserve inequality. Those in the most advantaged positions are usually reluctant to share or relinquish their power and privilege. Doctors, for example, have tried to limit entry into the field of medicine by requiring a long and hard training program in a restricted number of approved institutions. They also limit the activities of potential competitors (chiropractors and acupuncturists, for example), and they resist governmental attempts to set standardized fees. Once people have accumulated power, prestige, and wealth, they will naturally try to pass on these advantages to their children, in whose well-being they are interested. Such practices perpetuate the already existing inequalities. If stratification is functional for society, the critics ask, for whom is it functional? Is it functional for society in general or only for some privileged group?

[8]   Sociologist Herbert Gans (1972), in what appears to be a tongue-in-cheek application of the functionalist framework, argues that poverty persists in the United States not because less talented or less capable individuals fall to the bottom, but because it serves the interests of the well-to-do groups in society. Poverty ensures that there will be people to fill the physically dirty, dangerous, temporary, underpaid, undignified, and menial jobs that must be performed in every society. Indeed, this function is so important that

> in some Southern states, welfare payments have been cut off during the summer months when the poor are needed in the fields. . . . The poor subsidize, directly and indirectly, many activities that benefit the rich. . . . For example, domestics subsidize the upper and middle classes, making life easier for their employers and freeing affluent women for a variety of professional, cultural, civic, and social activities. . . . (Gans, p. 280)

[9]   Gans uses the functionalist framework to show that the function of poverty is to maintain the economic privileges of those in power. And as is clear from his analysis, what is functional depends on whose point of view is used. Stratification may be functional for the rich but dysfunctional for the poor. Society, which has to accommodate the rich and the poor, may benefit from having prestigious *and* dirty (but necessary) tasks performed. However, the waste of human resources and the conflict between rich and poor that result from institutionalized disadvantage may be anything but functional in the long run. These issues have led other sociologists to question the functional approach and to generate alternatives; the most widely known is the conflict approach.

THE CONFLICT FRAMEWORK

[10]   The premier conflict theorist was Karl Marx. Although American sociologists largely ignored Marx in the first half of this century, in the

past two decades sociologists have begun to reexamine his theories.

In the Communist Manifesto of 1848, Marx wrote: "The history of [11]
all hitherto existing societies is the history of class struggles." What
Marx meant was that social change comes through conflict between
two opposing or contradictory classes. Thus, for example, capitalism
emerged from feudalism through a struggle between the land-owning
class and the emergent class of traders and manufacturers (the
bourgeoisie).

. . . [For] Marx social class meant the relationship to the means of [12]
production, e.g., factories, tools, and capital. In a capitalistic society,
there are two basic classes whose relationships to the means of production are distinct. The bourgeoisie, who own the means of production,
and the propertyless workers (the proletariat), who must sell their
labor to the bourgeoisie in order to survive. Those who own the means
of production constitute the dominant or ruling class. By virtue of
their ownership of the economic resources, they control everything
else: the state, the legal system, and so forth. . . . Marx did not ignore
other classes, but he did not attribute much significance to them.
Under conditions of capitalism, they could not survive, and would
be absorbed into the mass of propertyless workers. Consequently,
the struggle will be between the two antagonistic classes, the bourgeoisie
and the proletariat.

Before a revolutionary confrontation could take place, several pre- [13]
conditions would be necessary. One was the development among the
working class of a class awareness or consciousness that would make
possible both class solidarity and political organization. Marx argued
that the bourgeoisie and the proletariat constitute two objective classes
because of their relationship to the means of production. But objective
class, or a "class in itself," is not sufficient for the development of
class awareness or class consciousness, a "class for itself." The process
of production in modern capitalism creates unique opportunities for
the development of class consciousness, for it places large numbers
of workers in factories in which they share common experiences and
problems of survival. Individual workers may blame their position
on themselves, or attribute their condition to the will of the Lord,
and hope for the better afterlife that the prevalent ideology describes
as their reward. Large masses of workers are different. Through communication and social interaction, they begin to recognize their common
exploitation, and under the leadership of the most advanced workers
they can organize into a political group for the overthrow of capitalism.

The capitalist system in the most developed industrial society of [14]
the mid-nineteenth century was indeed a society based on the exploitation of men, women, and children. They toiled long hours under
the most primitive and appalling conditions, trying to eke out a bare

subsistence. Based on the reality of life in the nineteenth century, Marx anticipated that the revolution would begin in the most industrialized countries of Western Europe. But as is well known, the first revolution took place under the leadership of Lenin in one of the least industrialized countries of Europe, Russia, followed by China, an agricultural society. In spite of significant economic problems, the highly industrial societies remained capitalist.

[15]   Some of the major criticism of the Marxist framework centers on the fact that it ignores the viability and adaptability of capitalism. The extension of social and political rights, the rise of the middle class, and welfare capitalism alleviated and corrected some of the major problems raised by Marx. Marx's motto, "workers of the world unite; you have nothing to lose but your chains," proved to be erroneous. He underestimated the degree of cohesion exerted by nationalism. In World War I, workers across Europe did not unite on a class basis to overthrow the bourgeoisie; instead, they gave almost unanimous support to their governments in waging war (Bottomore, 1966). In the United States, the working class sought not a revolution, but collective bargaining and a share of the social and material wealth.

[16]   However much Marx erred in his predictions and overlooked the importance of other stratification variables such as power and status, sociologists nevertheless recognize the significance of his work. While separating the two classes on the basis of ownership of the means of production is not a profitable means of analysis of the contemporary United States, it is true that those who occupy similar economic positions are likely to have similar life chances, values, and attitudes. While lacking the necessary "class consciousness," and thus constituting merely an objective class, working-class people, as numerous studies have shown, tend to vote more liberally on economic issues then members of the upper class.

[17]   Some sociologists see the Marxist theory as still valid today. Wright and Perrone (1977) argue that the ownership of the means of production (the capitalist employer) contains two distinct dimensions: legal rights to the product of labor, and control over the activities of labor. In the nineteenth century these two dimensions were merged. Today, however, these activities are differentiated in large corporations. The employer (owner of property or capital) continues to have legal rights to the product of labor, but control (authority) over the activities of labor is vested in the manager, particularly in large corporations. Separating ownership and control suggests a new transformation of capitalism "from individual forms of capitalist ownership to more collective forms of ownership" (Wright and Perrone, 1977:34).

[18]   Other critics of the Marxist framework argue that today conflict is based on authority relations, not on property relations: there is conflict

between those who exercise authority and those who lack authority. Those who exercise authority in the government, corporations, or labor unions constitute the upper class, and those who lack authority, the lower class (Dahrendorf, 1959). Dahrendorf dismisses property relations as unimportant and substitutes authority as the one major variable which divides the upper from the lower class.

Many sociologists today have found Marxist concepts of class relations worthy of further exploration, although they vary in the way they approach this task. Others, however, have adopted yet a third approach to social stratification based on the work of Max Weber. This view focuses on social class, and approaches it from a <u>multidimensional</u> perspective. [19]

The Weberian Approach

Weber's approach to social stratification was multidimensional, including class, status, and power. Class for Weber meant a number of people who had similar life chances: [20]

> It is the most elemental economic fact that the way in which disposition over material property is distributed among a plurality of people meeting competitively in the market for the purpose of exchange in itself created specific life chances. The mode of distribution . . . excludes the nonwealthy from competing for highly valued goods; it favors owners and, in fact gives them a monopoly to acquire such goods . . . the mode of distribution monopolizes the opportunities for profitable deals . . . it increases . . . their power in the price struggle with those who being propertyless, have nothing to offer but their labor. Property and "lack of property" are therefore the basic categories of all class situations. (Weber, 1978:927)

While Weber's formulation of class does not significantly differ from Marx's in the sense that economic factor is primary, Weber's addition of the status and power dimensions served to expand the concept of social stratification. According to Weber, *social status* was based on *"esteem"* or *"honor"* (prestige) and characterized by a unique life style of people or a group who belong to the same "circle." Thus, wealth alone is not sufficient for status and prestige. Weber notes that at first wealth may not bring honor or prestige; however, as one "learns," so to say, to use the wealth in the proper manner it will inevitably lead to the required <u>credentials</u> and inclusion in the proper circles.

"Power," the third dimension of social stratification, is "the chance of a man or a number of men to realize their own will in a social action even against the resistance of others" (1978: 926). Weber, as [21]

Reisman (1973) has noted, did not develop the power dimension sufficiently. He did, however, argue that people may strive for power to enrich themselves or as a means to attain status, or people may value power for its own sake. Power is also associated with political parties; these parties may represent class interests, status interests, or a combination of both class and status interest groups. Analytically, the dimensions of social stratification as conceptualized by Weber are distinct, but in reality the three dimensions of class, status, and power tend to coincide, as Weber himself acknowledged. Let's now look briefly at efforts of American sociologists to study these three dimensions, starting with occupational prestige as a measure of the status dimension.

THREE DIMENSIONS OF SOCIAL STRATIFICATION

[22]   *Occupational prestige.* Studies of occupational prestige (Hodge et al., 1964) provide a generalized view of how a national cross section of people rank occupations in the United States (Table 1). These studies reveal that occupational prestige has remained highly stable through time. There was relatively little change over a period of years in the high rank given to professional and managerial occupations, or the high status accorded to a Supreme Court justice and physician. The ranking of occupations reflects a clustering of wealth, prestige, and power, although there are exceptions. The college professor is ranked higher than the plumber but the plumber is likely to earn more than the college professor, and the railroad conductor is likely to earn more than the elementary school teacher. Social status is also affected by other variables, such as race, religion, ethnicity, and style of life. . . .

[23]   *Social status in the American community.* Nearly fifty years ago sociologist W. Lloyd Warner and his colleagues investigated the class structure of a New England town which they called Yankee City. Relying on the Weberian dimension of social status they defined it as ". . . two or more orders of people who are believed to be, and are accordingly ranked by members of the community, in socially superior or inferior positions" (Warner and Lunt, 1941: 71). Using the method of *evaluated participation*, which relies on the evaluation and observations of a group of "prestige judges," Warner conducted interviews with selected townspeople to determine how they measured status, how many classes or strata were recognized in the community, and where they ranked themselves and others in the stratification system of the community. In addition, Warner developed an "Index of Status Characteristics" based on occupation (related to level of occupation and income), source of income (inherited or earned), type of house, and

area of residence. Warner determined that "Yankee City" had six social classes, or status groups. (1) The "upper-upper" was composed of "old families," business people and professionals living in the "best" part of town. (2) The "lower-upper" resembled the upper-upper, but were not "old family." (3) The "upper-middle" was predominantly white collar and small businessmen living in a clearly defined part of the town. (4) The "lower-middle" was composed of skilled and semiskilled workers and the lower levels of white-collar workers. (5) The "upper-lower" consisted of respectable working people, and (6) the "lower-lower" were the unemployed and people on welfare, characterized by irresponsibility and moral laxity to community norms. While "Yankee City" and other communities in the United States have established status groups based on criteria other than wealth, it is clear nevertheless that wealth remains one of the most important criteria of social status.

The power dimension. The third dimension of social stratification, power, [24] as we noted previously, is not always a reflection of wealth. Who, then, holds power? Some researchers (Domhoff, 1967, 1980; Mills, 1956) provide considerable evidence of the existence of a "power elite" composed of the upper levels of the corporate, political, and military structures. These people exert control over the decisions affecting the distribution of scarce resources as well as the foreign policy of the United States. On the other hand, the pluralists argue that there is no elite, only interest groups which join forces to veto decisions they consider disadvantageous to their interests (Reisman, 1961).

CRITICISM OF THE WEBERIAN FRAMEWORK

Most American sociologists have found little to criticize in the Weberian [25] approach to social stratification. But there has been considerable criticism of the fact that while sociologists acknowledge the importance of the multidimensional framework, they focus primarily on the status dimension (Huber and Form, 1973; Reisman, 1973). Anderson (1974) argues that while we cannot question the need for more than one variable in a model of social class

> . . . one must look *first* and *always* at property classes or ownership, as Marx and as Weber himself did, if the operation of a society's structure of inequality is to be understood. From property we can explore more fruitfully the other dimensions of stratification such as occupation, status, power. . . . (1974: 121)

British sociologists have also been highly critical of the usage of [26] the multidimensional framework. Parkin (1971) points out that the

Table 1 Ranking Occupations in Terms of Prestige

The chart below shows the way occupations were ranked in terms of prestige in a classic study done in the 1960s. But times change, and on March 16, 1982, *The New York Times* reported that many were concerned that young people were moving from prestigious, but lowly paid occupations like a sociologist teaching in a college or university, to more highly paid jobs in industry, medicine, engineering, and computer science. This shows how the whole economic system has an impact on the decision making of individuals.

Occupation	Score	Occupation	Score
U.S. Supreme Court Justice	94	Instructor in public schools	82
Nuclear physicist	92	Captain in the regular army	82
Scientist	92		
Government scientist	91	Accountant for a large business	81
State governor	91		
U.S. representative in Congress	90	Owner of a factory that employs about 100 people	80
Chemist	89		
Diplomat in the U.S. Foreign Service	89	Building contractor	80
Dentist	88	Artist who paints pictures that are exhibited in galleries	78
Architect	88		
County judge	88		
Psychologist	87	Musician in a symphony orchestra	78
Minister	87		
Member of the board of directors of a large corporation	87	Author of novels	78
		Economist	78
Mayor of a large city	87	Official of an international labor union	77
Priest	86		
Head of a department in a state government	86	Railroad engineer	76
		Electrician	76
Airline pilot	86	County agricultural agent	76
Banker	85	Owner-operator of a printing shop	75
Biologist	85		
Sociologist	83	Trained machinist	75
		Farm owner and operator	74
		Undertaker	74

Table 1 (*continued*)

Occupation	Score	Occupation	Score
Welfare worker for a city government	74	Fisherman who owns his own boat	58
Newspaper columnist	73	Clerk in a store	56
Reporter on a daily newspaper	71	Milk route man	56
Radio announcer	70	Streetcar motorman (bus driver)	56
Bookkeeper	70	Lumberjack	55
Insurance agent	69	Restaurant cook	55
Manager of a small store in a city	67	Singer in a nightclub	54
A local official of a labor union	67	Filling station attendant	51
Mail carrier	66	Dockworker	50
Railroad conductor	66	Railroad section hand	50
Traveling salesman for a wholesale concern	66	Night watchman	50
Plumber	65	Coal miner	50
Automobile repairman	64	Restaurant waiter	49
Playground director	63	Taxi driver	49
Barber	63	Farmhand	48
Machine operator in a factory	63	Janitor	48
Owner-operator of a lunch stand	63	Bartender	48
		Clothes presser in a laundry	45
Corporal in the regular army	62	Soda fountain clerk	44
Garage mechanic	62	Sharecropper—one who owns no livestock or equipment and does not manage farm	42
Truck driver	59	Garbage collector	39
		Street sweeper	36
		Shoe shiner	34

SOURCE: Robert W. Hodge *et al.*, "Occupational Prestige in the United States, 1925–1963." Reprinted by permission of the University of Chicago Press from the *American Journal of Sociology* 70 (November 1964): 290–292. Copyright 1964 The University of Chicago.

distinction between class and status is fruitful in the analysis of traditional types of societies, but it cannot be applied to modern societies without some modification. Parkin doubts the validity of such arguments as, for example, electricians and railway conductors rank high on the economic dimension, but low on the social status dimension, or that teachers and clergy rank high on the status dimension but low on the economic dimension. These inconsistencies, Parkin argues, "do not reveal discrepancies between *class* and status position at all, but merely between income and status position (1971: 32)." Income, however, is only one factor which determines class position. Such factors as employment, promotion opportunities, long-term income prospects, and other social and material advantages referred to by Weber as "life chances" are important, but ignored by those who use the multidimensional framework (Parkin, 1971).

COMPARING THE THEORIES

[27]   Although they differ in some significant respects, the theories of social stratification do share a core of concepts.

1. *Stratification in complex societies is inevitable and it affects our behavior.* The functionalists emphasize the necessity for unequal rewards; the Marxists emphasize conflict and exploitation of the workers by the upper classes; the Weberians emphasize the various orders of social life and the interrelationships of class, status, and power. But all agree that social behavior is directly affected by stratification and class membership.
2. *Stratification affects the distribution of societal resources.* All theories, whether they stress income, power, or prestige, recognize that these factors relate to each other. They also affect the ability of persons at different socioeconomic levels to obtain other societal resources: housing, medical care, education, recreation, appliances, automobiles, and so on.
3. *Stratification is related to both change and stability.* The functionalists see stratification as a way of maintaining social equilibrium, with the major societal tasks being accomplished in an orderly and efficient way. The Marxists, in contrast, see stratification as a source of change. And the Weberians suggest that stratification motivates people to act within the economic, political, and prestige systems of society. Consequently, stratification contributes at once to change and stability in society. As in so many areas of social life, no one theory explains all of the behavior that sociologists observe.

MEASURING SOCIAL CLASSES

Although sociologists have found that the concept of social class is [28] the most useful means of observing and understanding the process and the effects of stratification, questions remain: How should sociologists go about measuring social class? What are the major social classes in American society? Sociologists face two basic issues in trying to measure social class. First, what criteria should be used in deciding who belongs in what social class? Second, is it correct to call a set of persons who share the same occupational, educational, or income level a social class, even if they do not interact or are not conscious that there are millions of others with whom they have much in common? (See Svalastoga, 1964.) The methods for measuring social class which sociologists have developed attempt to respond to these issues.

The subjective approach. In the subjective approach to the measurement [29] of social class, the investigator is usually concerned with an individual's perception of his or her position in the class structure. The subjective approach is based on a person's feelings of belonging to a group. In the 1940s, national polls showed that the overwhelming majority of Americans, when asked whether they consider themselves upper, middle, or lower class, identified themselves as "middle class." Centers (1949), noting that the survey limited the response to only three classes, introduced a fourth category, "working class." Based on a national survey, Centers showed that about 50 percent of the respondents identified themselves as working class; about 4 percent upper class; close to 40 percent middle class; and a small percentage lower class. Similarly, Hodge and Treiman (1968) found that three-quarters of all adults in a national sample identified themselves as "middle class." But when respondents were asked to identify with a given class— upper, upper middle, working, or lower class—the responses were more precise: upper class, 2.2 percent; upper middle class, 16.6 percent; middle class, 44 percent; working class, 34.3 percent; lower class, 2.3 percent. The decrease in the proportion of persons who identify themselves as working class may be a reflection of the changing labor force from blue-collar work to white-collar work, the relative affluence of post-World War II Americans, as well as images of people about the class structure.

One of the difficulties with self-rating methods is that they deal [30] only with people's *awareness* of their social rank. This perception is sometimes vague and may or may not accurately reflect class position as indicated by criteria that can be measured more directly: income, education, and occupational ranking. Moreover, people may not always evaluate themselves or their neighbors in the same way that other members in the same community do. As a result, the subjective approach is usually used with methods that employ the perception of others and the measurement of things like income and occupation.

[31] *The reputational approach.* We have noted in the previous section the study by Warner and his colleagues (Warner and Lunt, 1941) of "Yankee City," where they used the method of *evaluated participation.* This approach relies on the observation and evaluation of "prestige judges," who variously defined people as old wealth or aristocracy, poor but decent folk, and so on. Other sociologists followed the method in various small towns in the United States, e.g., Davis, Gardner, and Gardner (1941), and West (1945).

[32]   The reputational method has serious shortcomings. It is effective primarily in small towns where most of the residents know each other at least by reputation. Consequently, this method is difficult to use in studies of the class structure in more anonymous cities and suburbs. Even in small towns, it is likely to be supplemented by other approaches. You will recall that Warner used an "Index of Status Characteristics," for example, along with the reputational approach. His index was an attempt to use an objective approach, the third way to measure social class.

[33] *The objective approach.* While the subjective and reputational approaches provide a measure of how individuals and groups see themselves and others in the stratification system, most sociologists prefer what is called the *objective approach.* It uses income, education, and occupation, and occasionally other factors, as indices of social class. This information is more accessible to researchers and can be applied more broadly and uniformly to society as a whole. Three major objective measures of social class are education (measured by the number of years of schooling completed), income, and occupation. Today most sociologists interested in social stratification rely on the data collected by the Bureau of the Census and other agencies (e.g., Department of Education). These data enable sociologists to measure income, education, occupation, type of housing, family size, and so on.

[34]   The methods sociologists use to study social stratification depend on the specific issue they are addressing. While the objective method may be more reliable in delineating social classes in a society, it will provide few answers for those who seek to tap class consciousness. Naturally, when sociologists seek to look at all the dimensions of social class—class-consciousness factors as well as status and economic elements—they are likely to develop research strategies which utilize all three methods of measuring social class.

INEQUALITY IN AMERICAN SOCIETY

WHO GETS WHAT?

The American creed of equality has not prevented a large segment [35] of Americans from falling into poverty. As Robin Williams has pointed out, the dominant conception has been that of *equality of opportunity* rather than equality of condition (Williams, 1970). The upper and middle classes of the society continually have insisted that differences in wealth are acceptable because they reflect different ways in which opportunities are used. As in other societies, wealth and power in the United States are not distributed equally. The distribution of income has changed very little since the United States has become a highly industrial society. In personal income, the wealthiest tenth of the population received 34 percent of the income in 1910, and 29 percent in 1959. Indeed, in 1980, 6.2 percent of families had an income of less than $5,000, and 6.2 percent had less than $7,500. Families with incomes of $35,000 and above constituted 19.5 percent of the population. But an income of $35,000 per year or even $50,000 per year does not make for riches. Many of the families in the income bracket of $30,000 to $50,000 a year consisted of two earners, hardly the rich. The super rich, e.g., chief executives of corporations, receive annual salaries ranging from $200,000 to upwards of $800,000 per year.

The disparities between the rich and the poor have not declined [36] (see Table 2). The graduated income tax has had little to no effect on the distribution of income or wealth. Personal income taxes have affected mostly middle-income groups. High-income groups have found various ways to avoid progressive taxation; expense accounts, company automobiles, free vacations, state bonds, and capital gains have been so effective "that the distribution of income after federal income taxes is practically the same as the distribution before taxes" (Williams, 1970: 119). New federal legislation of 1981 which lowered taxes provided further reduction on personal income taxes for those in the $50,000 and above income. In 1980, median family income for a family of four was $21,023, so the people most affected by the legislation will be the wealthy.

Contrary to popular belief, poverty has actually begun to *increase* [37] in the United States after decades of decline. Table 3 documents this fact. These figures are based on cash income adjusted for inflation. In 1981, the poverty-level figure was $9,287 for a nonfarm family of four (Herbers, 1982: 1). Below this figure, people cannot sustain themselves with proper nutrition, clothing, and housing. Blacks continue to compose the largest percentage of those in poverty: 34.2 percent, compared to 25.7 percent for Hispanics and 10.2 percent for whites.

Table 2 Percentage Share of Aggregate Income Received by Each Fifth and Top 5 Percent of Families, 1958–1980

The distribution of income has remained almost unchanged since 1958. The wealthiest fifth of families in the United States has received a little above 40 percent of the income, while the poorest fifth has received 5 percent of the income.

Year	Lowest Fifth	Second Fifth	Third Fifth	Fourth Fifth	Highest Fifth	Top 5 Percent
1980	5.1	11.6	17.5	24.3	41.6	15.3
1978	5.2	11.6	17.5	24.1	41.5	15.6
1976	5.4	11.8	17.6	24.1	41.1	15.6
1974	5.4	12.0	17.6	24.1	41.0	15.3
1972	5.4	11.9	17.5	23.9	41.4	15.9
1970	5.4	12.2	17.6	23.8	40.9	15.6
1968	5.6	12.4	17.7	23.7	40.5	15.6
1966	5.6	12.4	17.8	23.8	40.5	15.6
1964	5.1	12.0	17.7	24.0	41.2	15.9
1962	5.0	12.1	17.6	24.0	41.3	15.7
1960	4.8	12.2	17.8	24.0	41.3	15.9
1958	5.0	12.5	18.0	23.9	40.6	15.4

SOURCE: U.S. Bureau of the Census, *Statistical Abstract of the United States: 1980*, and *Current Population Reports*, Series P-60, no. 127 (August 1981).

While the data speak for themselves, the way in which poverty is built into a social structure is not so obvious. Yet understanding the impact of social stratification and social class on people's lives requires us as sociologists to understand this process. Therefore, we will now look at the effects of social stratification and social class on people's life chances.

THE CONSEQUENCES OF INEQUALITY

[38]   According to Weber, people who belong to the same economic class share the same life chances; that is, the same access to "a supply of goods, external living conditions, and personal life experiences" (Warner, Meeker, and Ellis, 1960: 542). For example, income differences directly determine one's ability to afford a house, a college education, or a car. Income differences affect not only the "big" things mentioned above, but they also determine how much meat and bread are consumed, and the overall nutrition of a family. Income differences affect our view of the world and our place in it. Access to financial resources largely determines a person's chances even for "life, liberty, and the

pursuit of happiness." The higher up the income scale we go, the greater are our chances of being healthy, living longer, staying married, getting a good education, and controlling our destiny. We will now examine several aspects of life chances in more detail: life expectancy, health, mental health, education, justice, life styles, and value systems.

Life expectancy. Although overall rates of infant mortality have declined [39] in recent years, the upper-class baby still has a far better chance to survive than the lower-class baby. The infant mortality rate of families with incomes under $3,000 a year was almost three times greater than that of families with a high income (U.S. Department of Health,.Education and Welfare, 1972). The national rate of infant mortality in 1980 was 13 per thousand, but in Washington, D.C. the infant mortality rate in 1980 was 24.6 per thousand. Washington has a relatively high per capita income, but it also has a large number of poor people. . . .

Values, beliefs, and goals. In a cross-cultural study of men in Turin, Italy, [40] Washington, D.C., and a national sample of men in the United States,

Table 3 Poverty in the United States, 1957–1980

This table shows the percentage of the total population below the poverty level for each year from 1957 to 1980. After decades of decline, the small increase from 1978 to 1979, and then the sharp jump from 1979 to 1980, are particularly noticeable.

Year	% at Poverty Level	Year	% at Poverty Level
1957	22.4%	1969	12.6%
1958	22.2	1970	12.5
1959	21.9	1971	11.9
1960	21.0	1972	11.1
1961	19.5	1973	11.6
1962	19.0	1974	11.2
1963	17.3	1975	12.3
1964	15.7	1976	11.8
1965	14.7	1977	11.6
1966	14.2	1978	11.4
1967	12.8	1979	11.6
1968	12.1	1980	13.0
		1981	14.0*

SOURCE: *The New York Times*, February 20, 1982, p. 1ff; figures are from U.S. Census Bureau.
* Figure is from *The New York Times*, July 27, 1982, p. D22.

sociologist Melvin Kohn (1977) demonstrated that the nature of their jobs, or where they are positioned in the occupational hierarchy, determines how men perceive themselves and the world. Middle- and upper-class men perform occupational roles that embody self-direction, or action based on their judgment. Working-class men, at the lower level of the hierarchy, are subject to direction of those above them. Opportunities for self-direction are not generally available to these men. Their work is routinized, ordered, and regulated. Men from different social classes have a variety of experiences in the work situation. For upper-class men these experiences are reflected in their image of themselves as competent members of a benign society. Men in lower-class positions see themselves as less competent, as members of an indifferent and threatening society.

[41]   Class membership affects the socialization process. Upper-class parents socialize their children to value self-direction, while lower-class families socialize their children to value conformity. In essence, socialization reflects the opportunities and expectations available to each class.

> Social class is consistently related to fathers' values for children: the higher their class position, the more highly they value self-direction and the less highly they value conformity to externally imposed standards. This is true regardless of the age and sex of the children—even though age and sex are related to fathers' values. Moreover, the relationship is much the same in all segments of the society—regardless of race, religion, national background, region. . . . In short, despite the heterogeneity of American society, the relationship of social class to fathers' values is remarkably pervasive and consistent.
>
> The implications are impressive. In this exceptionally diverse society . . . social class stands out as more important for men's values than does any other line of demarcation, unaffected by all the rest of them, and apparently more important than all of them together. (Kohn, 1977: 71–72)

For working men, conforming means to have a job; lack of conformity is a threat to one's job, and consequently a threat to oneself and the livelihood of one's family. We can see, then, that the life styles of different social classes are a reflection of their values and behavior, which in turn expresses their condition in the social structure.

POVERTY IN THE UNITED STATES

[42]   In the post-World War II affluence of American society, little attention was given to the poor. Hidden in segregated housing and in rural regions, this inarticulate group was largely ignored. The work of

Lewis Coser (1965), Michael Harrington (1962), and others called dramatic attention to the large number of Americans living in poverty, for whom the future held little promise of social and material well-being.

Poverty is relative; the poor in the United States, compared to the [43] poor in India or other developing societies, are not poor. But as Americans, their standard of living is judged relative to other Americans. Compared to the general affluence of the majority of the population, the poor are deprived, unable to afford the standard measure of well-being in housing, consumption, health, and so on. Americans believe that the United States, more than any other society in the world, offers unique opportunities to those who are willing to work hard and strive for a better life. The rags-to-riches stories and the Horatio Alger myth in which hard work is always rewarded have dominated our thinking. They have led to the belief and conviction among vast segments of the American public that the poor deserve to be poor because they are lazy and indolent. Many believe that the poor would rather depend on public handouts than engage in useful work. Many people also believe that only the black are poor, and that vast sums of public funds, or "our taxes," are handed out to blacks and other minorities.

The available data, however, show that the beliefs about the poor [44] are no less erroneous than the Horatio Alger myths. Poverty in the United States is structural, caused by the nature of our economic system. In some regions of the country, such as the South, it is a consequence of low levels of economic development. Indeed, in the South the likelihood of a family being poor is twice as high as in the remainder of the country (Williams, 1970). The poor are not indigenous to the South, however. The poor are to be found in Appalachia, California, Wisconsin, and Missouri. The poor are not people who reject work; the poor are the subsistence farm worker, the unskilled worker replaced by automation, the unemployed due to closed factories, the old, mothers with dependent children, and the young high school "dropout."

The Swedish social economist Gunnar Myrdal was the first in modern [45] times to note that poor people can become so isolated from the social institutions of society that they become what he called an *underclass*. Myrdal wrote of a rural and urban underclass cut off from society, its members lacking "the education and the skills and other personality traits they need in order to become effectively in demand in the modern economy." They were, he feared, "superfluous" (cited in Auletta, 1981: 91). Estimates vary as to the size of the underclass, but one informed figure is about 45 percent of those below the government's poverty level. These are people who are unlikely ever to escape poverty

because they lack the needed skills or motivation; because they are
old or disabled; because they are mentally ill; because they are female
heads of families who must care for children rather than work; or
because there are simply no jobs for them (Auletta, 1981: 95). In a
sense, the underclass represents the cumulative effect of structural
factors—like racism, sexism, and economic policies—that create disadvantage year after year for certain groups.

[46]   Among the poor, as noted above, certain groups are especially
visible. Female-headed households constitute one major group. In
1980, 32.7 percent of such households had an income below the poverty
line; 50 percent of children in female-headed households were poor
(Waite, 1981: 32). According to the Bureau of the Census (1981), 10
million children live in poverty, and the majority depend on welfare
assistance. Minorities are overrepresented among the poor relative to
their proportion in the population, but the majority of the poor are
white. In 1980, 19.7 million people below the poverty line were white;
8.6 million were black, and 3.5 million were of Spanish origin (Bureau
of the Census, 1981: 3–4). Thirteen percent of all people over the age
of 65 are poor.

[47]   Much has been said about people on welfare: they are chiselers;
they do not want to work; they could manage without assistance; and
so on. But as the research by Goodwin (1972), sociologists Jennie
McIntyre and Janet Schwartz (1973), and others has demonstrated,
welfare mothers are as eager to work as other self-respecting Americans.
The poor, and especially the underclass, suffer most from structural
causes of poverty, not from lack of motivation. Americans tend to
have contradictory views regarding entitlement to federal subsidies.
Provisions made available to the affluent and very rich in the form
of deductions from taxable income are considered a legitimate right.
Americans seldom, if ever, question why the pleasure of home ownership should be rewarded by a subsidy from the Federal Government
in the form of a tax deduction on mortgage payments. Few raise
questions of why capital gains should be taxed only at 20 percent. It
is worth noting that those with incomes of $1 million per year receive
82 percent of this income from capital gains (Turner, 1976: 142).

[48]   People who receive some form of public assistance are seen as
unworthy, an example of undeserved support. Americans are appalled
to find that a Ms. Dow has been given a few dollars more than she
should receive in her welfare allotment; she is promptly branded a
"cheat," and the photograph of Ms. Dow is displayed in the newspaper
for all to see. But it is rare for Americans to be treated to a photograph
in the newspaper of a tobacco farmer receiving a government subsidy
(welfare) for a product labeled "dangerous to your health." Defense
industries have "cost overruns" that are promptly taken care of in

the name of national defense and never labeled government handouts.

The cumbersome procedures of checking and rechecking welfare   [49] recipients have not shaken the belief that they are cheating, and that they do not deserve assistance. Mrs. Paula Hawkins ran successfully for the U.S. Senate in 1980 on a platform of "weeding out" welfare chiselers. How many such chiselers there were in the state of Florida was apparently not important. On the other hand, might we not wonder whether she would have been equally successful in the quest for a Senate seat had she run on a platform of weeding out those who "chisel" or underreport on their income tax? Our ideology of equality is based on the belief that each individual has the opportunity to earn a livelihood, or even become rich. It is easy to assume that failure to support oneself or one's family is a personal failure. Indeed, research by sociologists Joan Huber and William Form (1973) has shown that the majority of (white) rich Americans, and 50 percent of middle-class Americans, believe that regardless of parental wealth, everyone has an equal opportunity to become rich.

QUESTIONS

Let us consider some of the theories of social stratification:
1. What are the strengths and weaknesses of the "functionalist framework"?

    a. Is it valid to say that "the difference in prestige among the various occupations results from the fact that some positions are more important to the survival of society than others"? Who determines the levels of importance among them?

    b. The bank president, who needs special talent, is thought more important than the garbage collector, who does not. Which of these occupations is more important "to the *survival* of society"?

    c. The researchers say that "lawyers work hard, and they are always on call." Is this a fact or an impression? What data have we that suggests that lawyers work harder than teachers or rock musicians? How do we know that they are always on call? What kind of investigation would we have to conduct to determine whether this statement is true?

    d. According to Davis and Moore (par. 5) "benefits, prestige, deference and privilege" are awarded to those who contribute to:

       (1) "Sustenance and comfort"—how about homemaking as an occupation?

    (2) "Humor and diversion"—how about topless dancers?

    (3) "Self-respect and ego expansion"—are good kindergarten teachers better rewarded than sweatshop owners? (Sweatshops are still alive and operating in places such as New York and Los Angeles.)

2. What are the strengths and weaknesses of the "conflict framework"?

    a. Is is true that a neat division can be made between the bourgeoisie and propertyless workers? (Remember Herzberg who makes the division between *managers* and workers, not owners and workers.) Are workers necessarily propertyless? What might workers own that would edge them into the bourgeois class?

    b. Considering what you have learned about the attitudes of managers and industrial engineers, do you think that all workers are psychologically prepared to think of themselves as workers? The American Federation of Teachers Union had enormous difficulty in organizing college teachers during the 1960s and 1970s because college teachers think of themselves as professionals, not workers.

    c. "Class awareness" requires a certain degree of education. Most Marxist revolutions in Asia and Latin America were begun by intellectuals, especially students or professors. Che Guevera, co-founder of Cuban socialism, was a professor of economics and Ho Chi Minh had a Ph.D. in history. Does what you have learned about the lives of propertyless workers in this chapter suggest that they are in a position to educate themselves or their children?

3. What are the strengths and weaknesses of the Weberian theory?

    a. Is Weber right in thinking that "status," "honor," or "esteem" are based on the "life style" of the group to which one belongs? Is the reverse not often the case, i.e. that life style is determined by income?

    b. Weber thinks that "wealth alone is not sufficient for status and prestige." That probably was the case at the time that he was writing (the 1920s), when, for example, a clear distinction would be made between the four hundred "first families" in American society (Morgans, Rockefellers, Roosevelts) and mere millionaires (Kennedys, Fords, etc.). Is it the case in America today that status is determined by factors other than wealth? For example, do you think that a very wealthy entertainer would be admitted to any society in which he or she chose to move? (Keep in mind the example of Ronald Reagan, who prior to being elected President of the United States was a movie star who married a wealthy woman).

c. Is it possible to separate, as Weber would, "power" from wealth in America today. Consider this situation. The sheriff has power; he arrests a poor man and the president of Coca-Cola on charges of drunk driving. Upon whom is the sheriff's power likely to be effective?

EXERCISES

1. This exercise is designed to test perceptions of class status based on occupational roles.

   a. Make a list of the five to ten occupations that you would rank as most prestigious in our society. Then make a list of an equal number of low-prestige occupations. Scramble the two lists and put the occupations into random order.
   b. Choose two groups of ten friends, family members, or school acquaintances. Group A should be composed of at least 2 members of groups against which you have discovered bias: old people, women, minorities, etc. Group B should be composed exclusively of white males, if possible. Make twenty photocopies of your list and ask your interviewees to mark on a scale from 1 to 100 rate how desirable this job seems to them in present-day American society. Make sure that the interviewees identify themselves at the top of the answer sheet.
   c. Check the results you obtain to determine if there is any noticeable difference in scoring between your two groups. Make a list of those occupations on which everyone, including yourself, seems to agree. Then make a list of those on which there is a marked difference of opinion. Try to justify the latter group in terms of biases you perceive. If you find any surprising responses, interview the persons who gave them to determine why they made their choices.
   d. Write a summary of the project explaining the following: (1) the design of the project, (2) the hypotheses being tested, (3) the findings obtained, (4) the meaning of the findings.
   e. On the basis of the foregoing summary write an essay on the relationship between status and occupation in modern-day America.

2. Do textual analysis of this selection. Ask these questions:

   a. How much space and attention do the writers devote to each section of the material they cover? Is the amount of space a valid index of how important the writers think the topic is?

   b. Do the writers give equal space and attention to the proponents of a theory as they do to its critics? Does the amount of attention influence the reader's judgment of the relative merits of a theory?

   c. Do the writers show personal or professional bias anywhere in their treatment of class stratification? Is there any indication that the writers try to persuade the readers to adopt their point of view?

   d. Do the writers explain issues, theories, and research fully and clearly enough?

3. Now imagine that as a student in a sociology course you have been asked by the publisher of this textbook to write a two-page evaluation of the book and to recommend or reject its adoption as a text in introductory sociology at your college. Write a draft of such a review.

4. Reexamine the profile on which you have been working in response to previous readings (see pp. 155 and 183). Evaluate it carefully for what it has to say about your own career expectations in terms of class, status, and power. To what extent are any or all of these important to you in your choice? How wise is it to mention any aspirations in these categories in a job application?

CHAPTER THIRTEEN

TERKEL: WORKING: TWO ACCOUNTS

Oral History

The area in sociology which we have just examined looks at job prestige, or occupational ranking, from the outside, so to speak. As we examined the selection critically, we noticed that often the criteria used in ranking occupations may not be logical—in many situations, lawyers really are *not* more socially useful than garbage collectors. Opinions about the relative prestige of various occupations are probably based most often on hearsay. Most of us have never met a Supreme Court justice or a member of Congress, and our high evaluation of those jobs is surely the result at least in part of the aura of glamour cast on them by the popular media. Studs Terkel, an oral historian, looks at occupations from the *inside*. His book *Working* includes interviews of bank tellers, elevator operators, stock brokers, grave diggers, corporation executives, and even baseball players. They have each told him how they feel about the work they do and, perhaps more significantly, how the work they do makes them feel about themselves.

Oral history has only recently become recognized as a valid methodology in an established academic discipline. The idea of taking down conversations of ordinary Americans about their jobs, their lives, and their feelings about government first began in the 1930s, during the Great Depression. The recording of oral history was part of the WPA (Works Progress Administration) program designed by President Franklin Delano Roosevelt to provide employment for the millions of unemployed. Interviewing the "people" was a task assigned to unemployed teachers and students. In 1970 Studs Terkel put together a collection of these interviews from the 1930s called *Hard Times: An Oral History of the Great Depression*. His book was so successful that it led him in the 1970s to conduct his own interviews in a manner similar to the WPA project and to collect them under the title *Working*. We will be reading from the accounts by two people, a steel worker and a prostitute, who describe what their work means to them and how it shapes them.

As you read these accounts keep the following questions in mind:

1. What weight should we give to the various components of "job prestige": the work itself, what other people think the value of the job is, what the worker thinks the value of his or her work is?
2. How do work and the workplace influence human interaction?
3. In what ways does the work we do express feelings of rage, frustration, self-loathing, idealism?
4. We have seen that love and sexuality are ways that human beings have of transcending their limitations (trying for biological immortality). Is work a way of leaving on the world a mark that we hope will outlast our deaths?
5. Does the oral-history method of approaching an issue seem as valid as the other, more academically orthodox methods we have learned about? Is it *more* valid? *less* valid? too subjective? more objective?

_____ WORKING: TWO ACCOUNTS _____
Studs Terkel

MIKE LEFEVRE

It is a two-flat dwelling, somewhere in Cicero, on the outskirts of Chicago. He is thirty-seven. He works in a steel mill. On occasion, his wife Carol works as a waitress in a neighborhood restaurant; otherwise, she is at home, caring for their two small children, a girl and a boy.

At the time of my first visit, a sculpted statuette of Mother and Child was on the floor, head severed from body. He laughed softly as he indicated his three-year-old daughter: "She Doctor Spock'd it."

I'm a dying breed. A laborer. Strictly muscle work . . . pick it up, put it down, pick it up, put it down. We handle between forty and

SOURCE: From Studs Terkel, *Working*, Random House, New York, 1972. Reprinted by permission of the publisher.

fifty thousand pounds of steel a day. (Laughs) I know this is hard to believe—from four hundred pounds to three- and four-pound pieces. It's dying.

You can't take pride any more. You remember when a guy could point to a house he built, how many logs he stacked. He built it and he was proud of it. I don't really think I could be proud if a contractor built a home for me. I would be tempted to get in there and kick the carpenter in the ass (laughs), and take the saw away from him. 'Cause I would have to be part of it, you know.

It's hard to take pride in a bridge you're never gonna cross, in a door you're never gonna open. You're mass-producing things and you never see the end result of it. (Muses) I worked for a trucker one time. And I got this tiny satisfaction when I loaded a truck. At least I could see the truck depart loaded. In a steel mill, forget it. You don't see where nothing goes.

I got chewed out by my foreman once. He said, "Mike, you're a good worker but you have a bad attitude." My attitude is that I don't get excited about my job. I do my work but I don't say whoopee-doo. The day I get excited about my job is the day I go to a head shrinker. How are you gonna get excited about pullin' steel? How are you gonna get excited when you're tired and want to sit down?

It's not just the work. Somebody built the pyramids. Somebody's going to build something. Pyramids, Empire State Building—these things just don't happen. There's hard work behind it. I would like to see a building, say, the Empire State, I would like to see on one side of it a foot-wide strip from top to bottom with the name of every bricklayer, the name of every electrician, with all the names. So when a guy walked by, he could take his son and say, "See, that's me over there on the forty-fifth floor. I put the steel beam in." Picasso can point to a painting. What can I point to? A writer can point to a book. Everybody should have something to point to.

It's the not-recognition by other people. To say a woman is *just* a housewife is degrading, right? Okay. *Just* a housewife. It's also degrading to say *just* a laborer. The difference is that a man goes out and maybe gets smashed.

When I was single, I could quit, just split. I wandered all over the country. You worked just enough to get a poke, money in your pocket. Now I'm married and I got two kids . . . (trails off). I worked on a truck dock one time and I was single. The foreman came over and he grabbed my shoulder, kind of gave me a shove. I punched him and knocked him off the dock. I said, "Leave me alone. I'm doing my work, just stay away from me, just don't give me the with-the-hands business."

Hell, if you whip a damn mule he might kick you. Stay out of my way, that's all. Working is bad enough, don't bug me. I would rather work my ass off for eight hours a day with nobody watching me than five minutes with a guy watching me. Who you gonna sock? You can't sock General Motors, you can't sock anybody in Washington, you can't sock a system.

A mule, an old mule, that's the way I feel. Oh yeah. See. (Shows black and blue marks on arms and legs, burns.) You know what I heard from more than one guy at work? "If my kid wants to work in a factory, I am going to kick the hell out of him." I want my kid to be an effete snob. Yeah, mm-hmm. (Laughs.) I want him to be able to quote Walt Whitman, to be proud of it.

If you can't improve yourself, you improve your posterity. Otherwise life isn't worth nothing. You might as well go back to the cave and stay there. I'm sure the first caveman who went over the hill to see what was on the other side—I don't think he went there wholly out of curiosity. He went there because he wanted to get his son out of the cave. Just the same way I want to send my kid to college.

I work so damn hard and want to come home and sit down and lay around. *But I gotta get it out.* I want to be able to turn around to somebody and say, "Hey, fuck you." You know? (Laughs.) The guy sitting next to me on the bus too. 'Cause all day I wanted to tell my foreman to go fuck himself, but I can't.

So I find a guy in a tavern. To tell him that. And he tells me too. I've been in brawls. He's punching me and I'm punching him, because we actually want to punch somebody else. The most that'll happen is the bartender will bar us from the tavern. But at work, you lose your job.

This one foreman I've got, he's a kid. He's a college graduate. He thinks he's better than everybody else. He was chewing me out and I was saying, "Yeah, yeah, yeah." He said, "What do you mean, yeah, yeah, yeah. Yes, *sir.*" I told him, "Who the hell are you, Hitler? What is this *"Yes, sir"* bullshit? I came here to work, I didn't come here to crawl. There's a fuckin' difference." One word led to another and I lost.

I got broke down to a lower grade and lost twenty-five cents an hour, which is a hell of a lot. It amounts to about ten dollars a week. He came over—after breaking me down. The guy comes over and smiles at me. I blew up. He didn't know it, but he was about two seconds and two feet away from a hospital. I said, "Stay the fuck away from me." He was just about to say something and was pointing his finger. I just reached my hand up and just grabbed his finger and I just put it back in his pocket. He walked away. I grabbed his finger because I'm married. If I'd a been single, I'd a grabbed his head. That's the difference.

You're doing this manual labor and you know that technology can do it. (Laughs.) Let's face it, a machine can do the work of a man;

otherwise they wouldn't have space probes. Why can we send a rocket ship that's unmanned and yet send a man in a steel mill to do a mule's work?

Automation? Depends how it's applied. It frightens me if it puts me out on the street. It doesn't frighten me if it shortens my work week. You read that little thing: what are you going to do when this computer replaces you? Blow up computers. (Laughs.) Really. Blow up computers. I'll be goddamned if a computer is gonna eat before I do! I want milk for my kids and beer for me. Machines can either liberate man or enslave 'im, because they're pretty neutral. It's man who has the bias to put the thing one place or another.

If I had a twenty-hour workweek, I'd get to know my kids better, my wife better. Some kid invited me to go on a college campus. On a Saturday. It was summertime. Hell, if I had a choice of taking my wife and kids to a picnic or going to a college campus, it's gonna be the picnic. But if I worked a twenty-hour week, I could go do both. Don't you think with that extra twenty hours people could really expand? Who's to say? There are some people in factories just by force of circumstance. I'm just like the colored people. Potential Einsteins don't have to be white. They could be in cotton fields, they could be in factories.

The twenty-hour week is a possibility today. The intellectuals, they always say there are potential Lord Byrons, Walt Whitmans, Roosevelts, Picassos working in construction or steel mills or factories. But I don't think they believe it. I think what they're afraid of is the potential Hitlers and Stalins that are there too. The people in power fear the leisure man. Not just the United States. Russia's the same way.

What do you think would happen in this country if, for one year, they experimented and gave everybody a twenty-hour week? How do they know that the guy who digs Wallace today doesn't try to resurrect Hitler tomorrow? Or the guy who is mildly disturbed at pollution doesn't decide to go to General Motors and shit on the guy's desk? You can become a fanatic if you had the time. The whole thing is time. That is, I think, one reason rich kids tend to be fanatic about politics: they have time. Time, that's the important thing.

It isn't that the average working guy is dumb. He's tired, that's all. I picked up a book on chess one time. That thing laid in the drawer for two or three weeks, you're too tired. During the weekends you want to take your kids out. You don't want to sit there and the kid comes up: "Daddy, can I go to the park?" You got your nose in a book? Forget it.

I know a guy fifty-seven years old. Know what he tells me? "Mike, I'm old and tired *all* the time." The first thing happens at work: When the arms start moving, the brain stops. I punch in about ten minutes to seven in the morning. I say hello to a couple of guys I like, I kid around with them. One guy says good morning to you and you say good morning. To another guy you say fuck you. The guy you say fuck you to is your friend.

I put on my hard hat, change into my safety shoes, put on my safety glasses, go to the bonderizer. It's the thing I work on. They rake the metal, they wash it, they dip it in a paint solution, and we take it off. Put it on, take it off, put it on, take it off, put it on, take it off . . .

I say hello to everybody but my boss. At seven it starts. My arms get tired about the first half-hour. After that, they don't get tired any more until maybe the last half-hour at the end of the day. I work from seven to three thirty. My arms are tired at seven thirty and they're tired at three o'clock. I hope to God I never get broke in, because I always want my arms to be tired at seven thirty and three o'clock. (Laughs.) 'Cause that's when I know that there's a beginning and there's an end. That I'm not brainwashed. In between, I don't even try to think.

If I were to put you in front of a dock and I pulled up a skid in front of you with fifty hundred-pound sacks of potatoes and there are fifty more skids just like it, and this is what you're gonna do all day, what would you think about—potatoes? Unless a guy's a nut, he never thinks about work or talks about it. Maybe about baseball or about getting drunk the other night or he got laid or he didn't get laid. I'd say one out of a hundred will actually get excited about work.

Why is it that the communists always say they're for the workingman, and as soon as they set up a country, you got guys singing to tractors? They're singing about how they love the factory. That's where I couldn't buy communism. It's the intellectuals' utopia, not mine. I cannot picture myself singing to a tractor, I just can't. (Laughs.) Or singing to steel. (Singsongs.) Oh whoop-dee-doo, I'm at the bonderizer, oh how I love this heavy steel. No thanks. Never happen.

Oh yeah, I daydream. I fantasize about a sexy blonde in Miami who's got my union dues. (Laughs.) I think of the head of the union the way I think of the head of my company. Living it up. I think of February in Miami. Warm weather, a place to lay in. When I hear a college kid say, "I'm oppressed," I don't believe him. You know what I'd like to do for one year? Live like a college kid. Just for one year. I'd love to. Wow! (Whispers) Wow! Sports car! Marijuana! (Laughs.) Wild, sexy broads. I'd love that, hell yes, I would.

Somebody has to do this work. If my kid ever goes to college, I just want him to have a little respect, to realize that his dad is one of those somebodies. This is why even on—(muses) yeah, I guess, sure— on the black thing . . . (Sighs heavily.) I can't really hate the colored fella that's working with me all day. The black intellectual I got no respect for. The white intellectual I got no use for. I got no use for the black militant who's gonna scream three hundred years of slavery to me while I'm busting my ass. You know what I mean? (Laughs.) I have one answer for that guy: go see Rockefeller. See Harriman. Don't bother me. We're in the same cotton field. So just don't bug me. (Laughs).

After work I usually stop off at a tavern. Cold beer. Cold beer right away. When I was single, I used to go into hillbilly bars, get in a lot of brawls. Just to explode. I got a thing on my arm here (indicates scar). I got slapped with a bicycle chain. Oh, wow! (Softly) Mmm. I'm getting older. (Laughs.) I don't explode as much. You might say I'm broken in. (Quickly) No, I'll never be broken in. (Sighs.) When you get a little older, you exchange the words. When you're younger, you exchange the blows.

When I get home, I argue with my wife a little bit. Turn on TV, get mad at the news. (Laughs.) I don't even watch the news that much. I watch Jackie Gleason. I look for any alternative to the ten o'clock news. I don't want to go to bed angry. Don't hit a man with anything heavy at five o'clock. He just can't be bothered. This is his time to relax. The heaviest thing he wants is what his wife has to tell him.

When I come home, know what I do for the first twenty minutes? Fake it. I put on a smile. I got a kid three years old. Sometimes she says, "Daddy, where've you been?" I say, "Work." I could have told her I'd been in Disneyland. What's work to a three-year-old kid? If I feel bad, I can't take it out on the kids. Kids are born innocent of everything but birth. You can't take it out on your wife either. This is why you go to a tavern. You want to release it there rather than do it at home. What does an actor do when he's got a bad movie? I got a bad movie every day.

I don't even need the alarm clock to get up in the morning. I can go out drinking all night, fall asleep at four, and bam! I'm up at six— no matter what I do. (Laughs.) It's a pseudo-death, more or less. Your whole system is paralyzed and you give all the appearance of death. It's an ingrown clock. It's a thing you just get used to. The hours differ. It depends. Sometimes my wife wants to do something crazy like play five hundred rummy or put a puzzle together. It could be midnight, could be ten o'clock, could be nine thirty. . . .

ROBERTA VICTOR

She had been a prostitute, starting at the age of fifteen. During the first five or six years, she worked as a high-priced call girl in Manhattan. Later she was a streetwalker. . . .

You never used your own name in hustling. I used a different name practically every week. If you got busted, it was more difficult for them to find out who you really were. The role one plays when hustling has nothing to do with who you are. It's only fitting and proper you take another name.

There were certain names that were in great demand. Every second hustler had the name Kim or Tracy or Stacy and a couple others that were in vogue. These were all young women from seventeen to twenty-five, and we picked these very non-ethnic-oriented WASP names, rich names.

A hustler is any woman in American society. I was the kind of hustler who received money for favors granted rather than the type of hustler who signs a lifetime contract for her trick. Or the kind of hustler who carefully reads women's magazines and learns what it is proper to give for each date, depending on how much money her date or trick spends on her.

The favors I granted were not always sexual. When I was a call girl, men were not paying for sex. They were paying for something else. They were either paying to act out a fantasy or they were paying for companionship or they were paying to be seen with a well-dressed young woman. Or they were paying for somebody to listen to them. They were paying for a *lot* of things. Some men were paying for sex that *they* felt was deviant. They were paying so that nobody would accuse them of being perverted or dirty or nasty. A large proportion of these guys asked things that were not at all deviant. Many of them wanted oral sex. They felt they couldn't ask their wives or girl friends because they'd be repulsed. Many of them wanted somebody to talk dirty to them. Every good call girl in New York used to share her book and we all knew the same tricks.

We know a guy who used to lie in a coffin in the middle of his bedroom and he would see the girl only once. He got his kicks when the door would be open, the lights would be out, and there would be candles in the living room, and all you could see was his coffin on wheels. As you walked into the living room, he'd suddenly sit up. Of course, you screamed. He got his kicks when you screamed. Or the guy who set a table like the Last Supper and sat in a robe and sandals and wanted you to play Mary Magdalene. (Laughs.)

I was about fifteen, going on sixteen. I was sitting in a coffee shop in the Village, and a friend of mine came by. She said; "I've got a cab waiting. Hurry up. You can make fifty dollars in twenty minutes." Looking back, I wonder why I was so willing to run out of the coffee shop, get in a cab, and turn a trick. It wasn't traumatic because my training had been in how to be a hustler anyway.

I learned it from the society around me, just as a woman. We're taught how to hustle, how to attract, hold a man, and give sexual favors in return. The language that you hear all the time, "Don't sell yourself cheap." "Hold out for the highest bidder." "Is it proper to kiss a man good night on the first date?" The implication is it may not be proper on the first date, but if he takes you out to dinner on the second date, it's proper. If he brings you a bottle of perfume on the third date, you should let him touch you above the waist. And go on from there. It's a market place transaction.

Somehow I managed to absorb that when I was quite young. So it wasn't even a moment of truth when this woman came into the coffee shop and said; "Come on." I was back in twenty-five minutes and I felt no guilt.

She was a virgin until she was fourteen. A jazz musician, with whom she had fallen in love, avoided her. "So I went out to have sex with somebody to present him with an accomplished fact. I found it nonpleasurable. I did a lot of sleeping around before I ever took money."

A precocious child, she was already attending a high school of demanding academic standards. "I was very lonely. I didn't experience myself as being attractive. I had always felt I was too big, too fat, too awkward, didn't look like a Pepsi-Cola ad, was not anywhere near the American Dream. Guys were mostly scared of me. I was athletic, I was bright, and I didn't know how to keep my mouth shut. I didn't know how to play the games right.

"I understood very clearly they were not attracted to me for what I was, but as a sexual object. I was attractive. The year before I started hustling there were a lot of guys that wanted to go to bed with me. They didn't want to get involved emotionally, but they did want to ball. For a while I was willing to accept that. It was feeling intimacy, feeling close, feeling warm.

"The time spent in bed wasn't unpleasant. It just wasn't terribly pleasant. It was a way of feeling somebody cared about me, at least for a moment. And it mattered that I was there, that I was important. I discovered that in bed it was possible. It was one skill that I had and I was proud of my reputation as an amateur.

"I viewed all girls as being threats. That's what we were all taught. You can't be friends with another woman, she might take your man. If you tell her anything about how you really feel, she'll use it against you. You smile at other girls and you spend time with them when there's nothing better to do, but you'd leave any girl sitting anywhere if you had an opportunity to go somewhere with a man. Because the most important thing in life is the way men feel about you."

How could you forget your first trick? (Laughs.) We took a cab to midtown Manhattan, we went to a penthouse. The guy up there was quite well known. What he really wanted to do was watch two women make love, and then he wanted to have sex with me. It was barely sex. He was almost finished by the time we started. He barely touched me and we were finished.

Of course, we faked it, the woman and me. The ethic was: You don't participate in a sexual act with another woman if a trick is watching. You always fake it. You're putting something over on him and he's paying for something he didn't really get. That's the only way you can keep any sense of self-respect.

The call girl ethic is very strong. You were the lowest of the low if you allowed yourself to feel anything with a trick. The bed puts you on their level. The way you maintain your integrity is by acting all the way through. It's not too far removed from what most American women do—which is to put on a big smile and act.

It was a tremendous kick. Here I was doing absolutely nothing, *feeling* nothing, and in twenty minutes I was going to walk out with fifty dollars in my pocket. That just made me feel absolutely marvelous. I came downtown. I can't believe this! I'm not changed, I'm the same as I was twenty minutes ago, except that now I have fifty dollars in my pocket. It really was tremendous status. How many people could make fifty dollars for twenty minutes' work? Folks work for eighty dollars take-home pay. I worked twenty minutes for fifty dollars clear, no taxes, nothing! I was still in school, I was smoking grass, I was shooting heroin, I wasn't hooked yet, and I had money. It was terrific.

After that, I made it my business to let my friend know that I was available for more of these situations. (Laughs.) She had good connections. Very shortly I linked up with a couple of others who had a good call book. . . .

You're expected to be well dressed, well made up, appear glad to see the man. I would get a book from somebody and I would call and say, "I'm a friend of so-and-so's, and she thought it would be nice if we got together." The next move was his. Invariably he'd say, "Why don't we do that? Tonight or tomorrow night. Why don't you come over for a drink?" I would get very carefully dressed and made up . . .

There's a given way of dressing in that league—that's to dress well but not ostentatiously. You have to pass doormen, cabdrivers. You have to look as if you belong in those buildings on Park Avenue or Central Park West. You're expected not to look cheap, not to look hard. Youth is the premium. I was quite young, but I looked older, so I had to work very hard at looking my age. Most men want girls who are eighteen. They really want girls who are younger, but they're afraid of trouble.

Preparations are very elaborate. It has to do with beauty parlors and shopping for clothes and taking long baths and spending money on preserving the kind of front that gives you a respectable address and telephone and being seen at the right clubs and drinking at the right bars. And being able to read the newspapers faithfully, so that not only can you talk about current events, you can talk about the society columns as well.

It's a social ritual. Being able to talk about what is happening and learn from this great master, and be properly respectful and know the names that he mentions. They always drop names of their friends, their contacts, and their clients. You should recognize these. Playing a role . . .

At the beginning I was very excited. But in order to continue I had to turn myself off. I had to disassociate who I was from what I was doing.

It's a process of numbing yourself. I couldn't associate with people who were not in the life—either the drug life or the hustling life. I found I couldn't turn myself back on when I finished working. When I turned myself off, I was numb—emotionally, sexually numb.

At first I felt like I was putting one over on all the other poor slobs that would go to work at eight-thirty in the morning and come home at five. I was coming home at four in the morning and I could sleep all day. I really thought a lot of people would change places with me because of the romantic image: being able to spend two hours out, riding cabs, and coming home with a hundred dollars. I could spend my mornings doing my nails, going to the beauty parlor, taking long baths, going shopping . . .

It was usually two tricks a night. That was easily a hundred, a hundred and a quarter. I always had money in my pocket. I didn't know what the inside of a subway smelled like. Nobody traveled any other way except by cab. I ate in all the best restaurants and I drank in all the best clubs. A lot of people wanted you to go out to dinner with them. All you had to do was be an ornament.

Almost all the call girls I knew were involved in drugs. The fast life, the night hours. At after-hours clubs, if you're not a big drinker, you usually find somebody who has cocaine, 'cause that's the big drug in those places. You wake up at noon, there's not very much to do till nine or ten that night. Everybody else is at work, so you shoot heroin. After a while the work became a means of supplying drugs, rather than drugs being something we took when we were bored.

The work becomes boring because you're not part of the life. You're the part that's always hidden. The doormen smirk when you come in, 'cause they know what's going on. The cabdriver, when you give him a certain address—he knows exactly where you're going when you're riding up Park Avenue at ten o'clock at night, for Christ sake. You leave there and go back—to what? Really, to what? To an emptiness. You've got all this money in your pocket and nobody you care about.

When I was a call girl I looked down on streetwalkers. I couldn't understand why anybody would put themselves in that position. It seemed to me to be hard work and very dangerous. What I was doing was basically riskless. You never had to worry about disease. These were folks who you know took care of themselves and saw the doctor regularly. Their apartments were always immaculate and the liquor was always good. They were always polite. You didn't have to ask them for money first. It was always implicit: when you were ready to leave, there would be an envelope under the lamp or there'd be something in your pocketbook. It never had to be discussed.

I had to work an awful lot harder for the same money when I was a streetwalker. I remember having knives pulled on me, broken bottles held over my head, being raped, having my money stolen back from me, having to jump out of a second-story window, having a gun pointed at me.

As a call girl, I had lunch at the same places society women had lunch. There was no way of telling me apart from anybody else in the upper tax bracket. I made my own hours, no more than three or so hours of work an evening. I didn't have to accept calls. All I had to do was play a role.

As a streetwalker, I didn't have to act. I let myself show the contempt I felt for the tricks. They weren't paying enough to make it worth performing for them. As a call girl, I pretended I enjoyed it sexually. You have to act as if you had an orgasm. As a streetwalker, I didn't. I used to lie there with my hands behind my head and do mathematics equations in my head or memorize the keyboard typewriter.

It was strictly a transaction. No conversation, no acting, no myth around it, no romanticism. It was purely a business transaction. You always asked for your money in front. If you could get away without undressing totally, you did that.

It's not too different than the distinction between an executive secretary and somebody in the typing pool. As an executive secretary you really identify with your boss. When you're part of the typing pool, you're a body, you're hired labor, a set of hands on the typewriter. You have nothing to do with whoever is passing the work down to you. You do it as quickly as you can.

QUESTIONS

MIKE LEFEVRE (THE STEELWORKER)

1. What is the most important value of work for Mike Lefevre? And why does his job not fulfill his desire?
2. Why does Mike's manager think that he has a "bad attitude"? Why could he take more satisfaction from loading a truck than "pulling steel," even though steelworkers are much better paid than truck loaders?
3. Why does he think his job is "degrading"? And why would he work longer hours if he could thereby avoid people watching him? Jean Paul Sartre once said in a play called *No Exit*, "Hell is other people." When we think of Mike Lefevre, his job, and his inability to leave it for another job, what does that quotation mean?
4. Why does Mike Lefevre resent college graduates? Do you think it is only because he was broken down to a lower grade by one? If he hates "effete" college kids, why would he like to be one himself, and why is he going to be sure his son goes to college?
5. Consider Mike's wish that every construction worker have a name plate on the Empire State building, or his purposely denting a piece of steel. What do these facts tell us about some of the fundamental functions of work for human beings in all times and places?
6. The steelworker is a very good example of "the worker" whom the various theories of management we read about in Herzberg's piece set out to describe ("the mechanical man," "the emotional man"). In what way does the personal description of worker motivation differ from the theoretical? Would we be well advised to discard the theoretical approach altogether in favor of personal accounts such as Lefevre's whenever they are available? Or does the theoretical approach tell us something that the personal account cannot? Might it perhaps be best to strive for a synthesis of methods in which both the theoretical and the personal would be discussed vis-à-vis each other?

ROBERTA VICTOR (THE PROSTITUTE)

1. Why do you think that hustlers use false names? Is it only for the practical purpose of avoiding identification? If so, why do they choose "non-ethnic-oriented WASP names, rich names"? What does the false name tell us about how Roberta feels toward the work she does? In what way does work relate to the way in which we establish our identity? (Consider the expression "He made a name for himself in show business" or the Renaissance idea that to do great heroic deeds in warfare was "to carve out a name.")

2. Is there any truth in Roberta's assertion that "a hustler is any woman in American society"? What does this statement say about Roberta's attitude toward her work?

3. Roberta's childhood was very lonely and she "didn't experience [herself] as being attractive." Do you think that had anything to do with her decision to be a prostitute?

4. Roberta is clearly very intelligent. We have learned that she went to a high school that had very high academic standards. She is evidently not a prostitute for the reason that Mike Lefevre is a steelworker—because she had no choice of another occupation. Since she is a prostitute by choice, the job is not entirely hateful to her, and in fact, at times it is rewarding. Let us see what facts about her work might lead her to that sense of satisfaction, limited as it may be.

   a. Being a call-girl requires that "you always fake it."
     (1) You do not participate in a sex act with another woman if the trick is watching.
     (2) You feel *nothing* for the trick. "You were the lowest of the low if you let yourself feel anything."
   b. You get money for doing nothing and feeling nothing: "It was a tremendous kick. Here I was doing absolutely nothing, *feeling* nothing, and in twenty minutes I was going to walk out with fifty dollars in my pocket."
   c. Your clients are called "tricks" and your work is called "turning a trick." Consider this in relation to what Roberta said earlier about the clients paying for "a fantasy," and about the assumed name. *Magicians*, remember, do tricks.
   d. The people on whom these deceptions are being played can be very, very important, very powerful people.

What do all these observations add up to? What is the *real* nature of Roberta's work? What, in Weber's terms, is the "power" reward and what the "prestige" reward she gains from it? Does Roberta feel anything of the kind of anger that Mike Lefevre feels about "the system"? Does she make any of the associations between sex and violence that he makes?

5. Roberta says, "At the beginning I was very excited. But in order to continue I had to turn myself off." Why? Since the job was exciting and rewarding, why was it necessary for her to numb herself? Is her numbness anything like the numbness Mike Lefevre induces in himself during the hours he is pulling steel? What in the jobs and the way that the jobs make the people feel about themselves makes the self-induced numbness necessary?

6. Roberta says that a prostitute does not associate with people who are not "in the life," and that she began to use drugs heavily because that was part of the life-style demanded by her occupation. How does this square with the sociological theories of class stratification that you read about in the last selection? How does the difference between the clientele of a call girl and that of a streetwalker square with the theories of class stratification? Do you think that Roberta would be a good person to interview if you were trying to construct an occupational ranking scale?

EXERCISES

1. a. Select a subject and do an interview similar to the ones conducted by Studs Terkel. Choose a person on your campus—a fellow undergraduate student, a graduate student, a member of the staff (say a cafeteria worker, a groundskeeper, a secretary), or a member of the faculty. In your interview, focus on work. If you have access to a tape recorder, use it. If not, take notes and try as much as possible to capture the tone and the voice of the person speaking. Occasionally you may wish to pause and take down whole sentences so that you can get the flavor of his or her speech. The object of this exercise is to learn about the person's *attitude* toward the work he or she does. If done successfully, it should supplement information you have gathered to date from written sources, including Terkel. If you want a more specific focus for your interview, concentrate on the extent to which the job or occupation enhances or diminishes the person's self-esteem. If your subject is a student, you are free to define "work" as attending classes, or for advanced graduate students, writing a dissertation.

b. Bring the transcript from your interview to class, where discussion will focus on sorting out information regarding "work on an American campus." Before you read segments of your interview to other members of the class, be sure to give some relevant information about your subject to the class: the person's age, type of occupation, personal history, and how you came to choose the person for your interview. The class session(s) should prove useful in establishing the advantages and the limits of oral history as a way of gathering information.

c. Write a paper that is titled one of the following:

(1) Self-Esteem and Work: A Case in Point

(2) The Limits of Oral History

(3) Work on an American Campus: An Essay

(4) Schoolwork and Self-Esteem: Some Observations

Aim the paper at the general reader, someone who has not been privy to your class discussion and who may not even know your campus. You should quote freely from your interview and from class notes.

2. Conduct an interview, using the same methods as those outlined in Exercise 1, with an older member of your family. Choose a subject who is of at least a generation older than yours (a parent, an aunt, or uncle), preferably two generations. Ask that person to talk about his or her first job and especially about personal attitudes toward that job. When you have concluded the interview, write an introduction in which you provide the reader with background information and with some commentary touching upon the significance of the work experience. Then transcribe the interview. Try to write the interview in the voice actually used by your subject.

3. Study carefully the two interviews by Studs Terkel. Direct your attention particularly to the language of the two subjects. In what significant ways do they differ? Is one more or less "grammatical" than the other? Does one use a different vocabulary from the other? As you know from reading some of the previous selections, a writer can be characterized by the "voice" he or she uses. That applies as well to subjects of interviews whose language is recorded more or less verbatim. Write a paper in which you compare and contrast the voices of Mike Lefevre and Roberta Victor.

—— Chapter Fourteen ——

LEEPSON: THE COMPUTER AGE

Computer Science

We have examined work from many different perspectives. We have
discovered the ways in which the work we do defines us in the eyes
of others and how it determines our level of self-esteem. We have
seen its effects upon our economy and our personality. And we have
seen how work defines the various layers of our society.

Before we leave this important human issue, work, we must look
forward to the future. If Marc Leepson, the author of *Work Life in the
1980's*, gives us an accurate overview, we may well be in the middle
of a second industrial revolution that will affect every aspect of our
lives even more profoundly than the first one did. Historians have
shown us how the first industrial revolution in eighteenth-century
Europe changed conceptions of time, of work and leisure patterns,
and of the ends and aims of education. Computerization will in its
turn profoundly affect the way we live. Eventually, it may well make
assembly lines, factories, and even great office complexes obsolete.
Indeed, it will make us more and more conscious of a world in process.
Even as we read Leepson's article, we will discover that much of *his*
present and future time is already *our* past time (as this introduction
is written, Atari, Leepson's prime success story of the electronic-game
market, has gone broke). The second industrial revolution, above all,
will transform our ideas about what people should learn in order to
be useful members of society. And while it will never be the case that
we will cease to be workers—since *homo faber*, man the maker, is
central to our human nature—computerization will drastically alter
the kinds of work we do, the ways in which we do it, and our conceptions of ourselves doing it. The full flowering of the age of computers

and robots will no doubt transform some of our most basic notions of what work is.

The selection by Marc Leepson is included here essentially to provide you with an exercise of critical and imaginative thinking. The essay itself is basically an overview of what Leepson calls "the second industrial revolution," providing a history of the computer, an elementary review of the process of computing, and most important, a survey of the uses to which computer technology has been put and to which we might expect it to be put in the future. The essay does not primarily concern itself with the subject of work per se, and yet the implications of the subject are so far-reaching that one cannot consider any aspect of the topic without ultimately turning one's thought to how the computer will indeed influence the patterns of our work world and the demands and conditions placed on the work force of the future. The very existence of what Leepson calls "computer anxiety" gives some indication of the fears that an older generation inherently harbors toward a new technology, and no serious contemplation of the nature of work in the "high-tech" society of the future can afford to disregard those fears.

As you are reading this selection, try to think creatively about the influence of the computer on the work patterns of the future. Do not necessarily expect to find "answers" to your questions in the selection; rather use them as a way of speculating about the subject. You might, for example, ask yourself such questions as these:

1. Who will be managers and who will be workers in the next century? What kinds of work will they do? Will a manager have to be a computer expert? Will workers have to be completely retrained?

2. How will people feel about themselves when they are replaced by robots? Will they feel relieved at not having to do tedious exhausting jobs? Or will they feel more useless and worthless than ever in society's eyes?

3. How will our economy change in the computer society? Will there be inevitable and widespread unemployment? Will government be forced to pay for universal subsistence?

4. How will the rhythms of our lives change when a human being's time is no longer worth money, since a computer can do in seconds the work that takes a man or woman months to do? Will we spend more time at home, with our families?

5. How will working with computers affect our health? our education system?

GLOSSARY

For this selection we recommend that you examine and try to cultivate the technical, computer-related glossary on p. 228.

THE COMPUTER AGE

Marc Leepson

It's been called the second industrial revolution, and according to the [1] National Academy of Sciences, "its impact on society could be even greater than that of the original industrial revolution."[1] This prediction is based on recent developments in the electronic industry that have led to a new generation of sophisticated computers. As the application of this technology advances, it could radically change virtually every aspect of society.

The basis for the new industrial revolution is the computer chip, [2] first developed in the early 1960s, but perfected only in the last decade. Chips are tiny silicon wafers, about half the size of a fingernail, which contain the resistors, transistors and diodes that are the brains of today's computers (see glossary, p. 228). Recent refinements in chip technology have allowed the size and price of computers to shrink while their capacities have increased.

The most advanced chips, called microprocessors, contain the entire [3] central processing unit of a computer. Microprocessors can carry out millions of instructions per second, and can be reprogrammed to function in different ways. Products made possible by advances in microelectronics include computer games, digital watches, razor-thin, hand-held calculators and supermarket computer checkout systems. A less visible array of microprocessing technology is being used in a number of ways.

> Two gigantic computers run by 200 technicians on Capitol Hill contain millions of pieces of information on registered voters, Library of Congress reports and other material. The data is available instantaneously to each member of Congress.
>
> Office machines now in use are able to identify mispelled words in six languages.
>
> Advanced dictating machines can "listen" to and act on instructions from a telephone anywhere in the world.
>
> Certain computers can edit and analyze the writing quality of technical manuscripts.
>
> Colleges are using computers to simulate operations for medical students and courtroom situations for law students.
>
> Computer voice synthesizers can translate languages or "read" books aloud.

SOURCE: From Marc Leepson, *Work Life in the 1980's*, (New York: Congressional Quarterly Inc., 1981) pp. 1, 4–23. Reprinted by permission of the publisher.

Computer Glossary

Chip. Integrated circuit in which all the components are miniaturized and etched on a tiny piece of silicon or like material.

Database. Collection of information in a form that can be manipulated by a computer and retrieved by a user through a terminal.

Diode. Electronic device with only two electrodes used mainly as a rectifier (a device for converting alternating current into direct current).

Hardware. The equipment components of mechanical, magnetic, electrical or electronic devices.

Host computer. Computer and database that can be tied into a network.

Information retrieval. Process of selecting from a database relevant data using a variety of access points (such as subject, name, date).

Integrated circuits. Circuits whose component parts and interconnections are all fabricated simultaneously on single silicon chips.

Keyboarding. Process by which information is typed and translated through a console into a form that can be read by a computer.

Microcomputers. Computers whose central processing units are microprocessor chips. Microcomputers include personal computers, small business computers, desktop computers and home computers.

Microprocessor. Central processing unit implanted on a chip.

Minicomputer. Intermediate range computer often used in scientific and laboratory work.

Online. Direct connection to a host computer.

Online distribution service. An organization that offers online access to one or more databases. Also referred to as online vendor, database vendor, online supplier, online retrieval service, search service and timesharing service.

Program. Series of instructions in a form acceptable to a computer.

Resistor. Electrical or electronic circuit component that has a specified resistance.

Search. Retrieval of information from a database by giving the computer specific commands.

Semiconductor. Material used in transistors having conductance related to temperature.

Software. Generic term for all non-hardware elements in a computer system, including computer programs, data, TV programs, user manuals and documentation.

Telecommunications. Transmission and reception of data by electromagnetic means.

Terminal. Device for entering data into and/or receiving data from a computer system or a computer network. A typical terminal consists of a keyboard and a printer or video display.

Word processor. Computer-based typing and text editing system.

SOURCE: "Glossary of Terms," Link Resources Corporation, 1980.

Detailed, computerized records of millions of dairy cattle and bulls are used by farmers to get information on feed consumption, breeding patterns, sales and other items.

Scientists all over the world are working on even more sophisticated [4] uses of computer technology that, within the next two decades, will alter the lives of millions of people in the industrialized world. Predicting the social and economic significance of these developments is akin "to forecasting the impact of the automobile on society as the first Model T rolled off the assembly line," author-researcher Colin Norman wrote recently. But he ventured to say that "microelectronic technology will have a pervasive and long-lasting influence on international trade, patterns of employment, communications, industrial productivity, entertainment and social relationships."[2]

GROWING POPULARITY OF PERSONAL COMPUTERS

Five years ago they were only on the drawing board. Today, low- [5] priced, "personal" computers are being used by thousands of individuals in their homes, by college students at school and by employees and entrepreneurs in their offices. The Gartner Group, which specializes in computer industry market research, estimates that the American-dominated personal computer industry sold some 440,000 units last year. That figure is expected to rise to about 630,000 units in 1981.

Although some manufacturers have reported a sales slump in recent [6] months, industry analysts believe the downturn is only temporary and that sales will continue to grow significantly. "We foresee about a 53 percent growth rate in the retail value of personal computers in the next five years," said Peter Wright of the Gartner Group. "That would work out to be about a 40 percent increase in American shipments and about 45 percent in worldwide shipments."[3]

The same technological breakthroughs that have brought down the [7] size and price of all computer products have allowed manufacturers to sell these typewriter-sized home computers for less than $1,000. And prices are continuing to fall. Texas Instruments Inc. announced Nov. 28 that it was reducing the price of one model from $950 to $650. Last year the price of Atari's least expensive model dropped from $630 to $500. APF Electronics' least expensive model now sells for $399, down from $599 last year.

The price cuts reflect three trends: (1) the passing on of lowered [8] costs, (2) the sales slump and (3) the success of industry leader Tandy Corp., whose TRS-80 computer is sold nationwide at Radio Shack stores for under $400. That price is "what really started the ball rolling," said Warren Zorek, merchandiser for the electronics department of

Bloomingdale's. "I did not think it was necessary, but this is a business of following the leader."[4]

[9]   Industry analysts attribute the current sales slump to a lack of knowledge about what personal computers can do. Most consumers are aware that these machines can help balance a checking account, calculate one's income taxes, store recipes and catalog a record or book collection. But with proper programming, home computers also can be hooked up to a number of services providing such things as weather reports, stock market quotations and sports results. "People can get along without a home computer. They've never needed one before," said Raymond E. Kassar, chairman and chief executive officer of Atari. "Everything the home industry offers will, at first glance, appear to be redundant. People already have yellow pages, stock market reports, newspapers, restaurant guides, telephone shopping, libraries. What we're selling is a new medium—a method of obtaining information."[5]

[10]   Part of this new method involves buying the software—in the form of tape cassettes or magnetic discs—to program the personal computer. These programs cost from $3–$130 each. Most are in the $20–$40 range. "In the six months of owning an Apple II computer," Peter J. Schuyten of *The New York Times* wrote last year, "I have purchased some $400 worth of programming for a system whose basic cost was $1,334. Software is at the same time both the boon and bane of the four-year-old personal computer industry. Boon in the sense, that without it the market would never have moved beyond the hobbyist stage; bane in that many of the programs being sold today do not fit the average user's needs."[6]

[11]   Many persons in the business world evidently have found the programs they need because personal computers are widely used by both small businesses and by employees of large firms. Between 1978 and 1980 the business share of the personal computer market jumped from 35 to 60 percent, according to the Gartner Group. And this does not take into account individual executives, managers and technical workers who use their own computers on the job. "This is fast emerging as the biggest personal computer market," said Robert F. Wickham, president of Vantage Research Inc., a California market research firm. "We're beginning to see the computer on the professional's desk serving the same utilitarian function as the typewriter on the secretary's desk."[7] According to Wickham, about one-third of all personal computers sold in this country in the last five years have wound up in private offices.[8]

[12]   Some executives claim they can do more work with their personal computer than they can with the company's main computer. "With a personal machine I'm able to alter programs to suit my needs,

depending, for example, on whether I might want a limited or a very detailed cash flow analysis," said Judith B. Warrick, first vice president of Dean, Witter, Reynolds, the securities analysts.[9] Michael J. Rodriguez, chairman of Southern Telecom Inc., a cable television franchise in Peachtree, Ga., credits his personal computer with significantly cutting down the time needed to complete tasks and helping his business expand. "There seems to be no end to the applications you can put on these machines," Rodriguez said. "The only thing that stops me is how much of my time I can afford to spend."[10]

MINICOMPUTERS HERALD OFFICE OF THE FUTURE

The next step up from the personal computer is the minicomputer, [13] which the Electronics Industries Association defines as any type of electronics equipment priced from $5,000 to $40,000. About 130,000 minicomputers were sold in 1979, accounting for some $3.91 billion in sales—a 30 percent increase over the previous year. Industry analysts estimate that annual sales could reach $16 billion by 1984.

The most popular types of minicomputers are business machines, [14] including electronic typewriters, text editors and other related data processing equipment. Most of these machines did not exist before the microprocessor was perfected 10 years ago. The best-selling individual item in the minicomputer range is the text editor, an extremely advanced typewriter-printer that displays words on a screen and prints error-free copy in seconds. Last year about $1 billion worth of text editors were sold to newspapers, magazines, law firms, government agencies, hospitals, colleges and universities and other organizations. This represented a 27 percent increase in sales over the previous year.

These impressive sales figures are seen by some as evidence that [15] the so-called "office of the future" is rapidly approaching. This computerized, electronic office will consist of telephones, keyboards, screens, computers and office workers processing information electronically. Secretaries, sales representatives, accountants, stockroom clerks and other employees will all be able to work directly with the electronic machines. Many believe that as paper is phased out in favor of electronic signals, productivity will increase. One study indicated that an office worker can produce standardized letters 400 times faster with a word processor than with a conventional typewriter. An individualized letter takes about half the time.[11]

ELECTRONIC GAMES: PLAYTHINGS FOR THE 80s

The most visible sign of the "computer revolution" is the widening [16] popularity of electronic games. These games use the same silicon chips as computers, and cost from \$25 to \$60. Computer games did not come on the market until 1977, when they accounted for some \$35 million in sales. By 1979, sales had jumped to \$450 million and last year approached \$1 billion.[12]

[17]   There are about 400 different electronic games on the market today, compared to just 10 four years ago. But many of the games are similar. "Although some games may have different names, many are identical concepts with identical play techniques," said Randolph Barton, president of Parker Brothers. "Thus, consumers may purchase two versions of the same game but not realize it until they play the game."[13]

[18]   Atari is one of the leading electronic games manufacturers. Inventor Nolan Bushnell founded the company in California in 1967. His first invention, a table-tennis computer game, led to a national business in home video games, home computers and arcade (coin-operated) games. Bushnell and his associates sold Atari to Warner Communications in 1976 for \$28 million. Industry sources say that Atari is one of the biggest revenue gainers for the giant entertainment conglomerate. One analyst estimated that Atari sold some \$400 million worth of computer games in 1980 and will have sales of \$500 million in 1981 with profits of \$85 million.[14]

[19]   There are four broad categories of electronic games: (1) coin-operated video games (the computerized answer to the pinball machine), (2) games operated through the home television receiver, (3) software for personal computers and (4) all other games, including those that are hand held. Many of the computer games now on the market have an outer-space or space warfare theme. Some emulate television game shows or card games. Computerized sports games—including auto racing, baseball, basketball, chess, football, hockey, motorcycle racing, pool, soccer and tennis—are among the most popular.

[20]   Computer games are not sold only to children. Mattel Inc. reports that about a third of its electronic sports games are purchased by adults. Analysts at Milton Bradley, the leading maker of electronic games, say that half of those who buy electronic games are in the 15–35 age bracket. "Our research shows that the market we've penetrated most heavily so far with our electronic games is comprised of people between the ages of 15 and 25," said a company spokesman. "We've never sold games to these people before. Our previous market was kids aged 8 to 14."[15]

COMPUTER ANXIETY: NEW PHOBIAS AND FEARS

[21]   The use of computers may be increasing, but there also seems to be a not insignificant amount of resistance to computerized innovation. "You find more resistance among older people who find the idea of

computers fearful mainly because they haven't had a lot of exposure to them," said the production editor of a Washington, D.C. publisher. "Younger people have usually been working with computers for years, so they're not quite so mind boggling. Anyone can learn to work with a computer. If you work with a computer everyday and you get used to it, it's just like any other machine. But if you take someone who's never used one, and put them down in front of it, they sometimes think it's magical or supernatural and they have a hard time understanding the logic that goes with it."

Executives in particular seem to look for excuses to avoid working [22] with computers. "They say, 'I'm not going to use it,' but what they're really saying is, 'I'm scared that I'm not going to be able to use this right and I'll look like a jerk,' " said Joseph Ramellini, director of advanced office systems at CBS Inc.[16] According to Ramellini, many executives believe it is beneath their position to work with any keyboard machine.

In at least one area—the video display terminals with cathode ray [23] tubes (CRTs) now used by nearly all newspapers—there is concern that the equipment may be hazardous to health. Many editors and reporters have expressed fears that CRTs emanate dangerous radiation. A number of studies, including one conducted in May 1980 by the National Institute of Occupational Safety and Health, have said that there is no chemical or radiation danger. But these studies have found that CRT users face potential problems with eye strain and psychological stress. Experts believe most of the eye strain problems could be eliminated with proper placement of the terminals to reduce glare.

Even though these studies have found no large health problems, [24] some fears remain. "We've so often been told by the federal government or experts that certain things were safe, and then 20 or 30 years later we've discovered that they weren't," said reporter Judy Foreman of *The Boston Globe*. "Do we know what radiation levels are really safe? If I were pregnant, I would wonder what to do. I'd hate to give up my machine."[17]

DEVELOPMENT OF U.S. INDUSTRY

The recent changes in computer technology are even more astounding [25] when one realizes that the first electronic computer was built just 35 years ago. That landmark machine, the Electronic Numerical Integrator and Calculator—commonly known as ENIAC—was developed at the University of Pennsylvania's Moore School of Engineering. The machine took two-and-a-half years to build. It solved its first problem, an equation involving atomic physics, in two hours. The huge computer filled a large room, required 18,000 vacuum tubes and needed 140,000 watts of electricity—enough power to drive a locomotive. Today, a computer with ENIAC's capabilities would cost less than $100, fit into a pants pocket and run on flashlight batteries.

[26]   In 1947, a year after ENIAC went into operation, three scientists at Bell Laboratories in Murray Hill, N.J.—John Bardeen, Walter Brattain and William Shockley—developed the transistor.[18] Author Christopher Evans has characterized the transistor as "the most important single invention within the whole complex of inventions which we today call the computer."[19] The transistor, a small block of semiconducting material such as silicon or germanium, is a device that controls the flow of electric current. Transistors are less than one-one-hundredth the size of the vacuum tubes they replaced, and consume much less energy because they are not heat driven. The use of transistors led to the reduction in the size of television sets, radios and computers in the 1950s. The word derives from *trans*fer *resistor*.

[27]   The next big breakthrough in computer technology came in 1959 when scientists at Texas Instruments and Fairchild Camera and Instrument Co. simultaneously developed the integrated circuit, what Colin Norman called "the centerpiece of microelectronic technology."[20] Integrated circuits, which are used in dozens of types of electronic equipment from computers to digital watches, consist of transistors wired together on individual silicon chips. Integrated circuits were first put into mass production in 1960. Each year since then the semiconductor industry has doubled the number of transistors that it can place on a single chip. At the same time, the cost of each chip has dropped by about 28 percent a year.

[28]   Today, some integrated circuits hold up to 100,000 components on a chip only one-fifth of an inch in length. A single chip is much more powerful than ENIAC. Computer scientists now are working on chips that will contain about 250,000 components; some believe that by the year 1990 there will be an integrated circuit with one million components.

[29]   The last big electronics discovery came in 1971 when an American microelectronics company, Intel, developed the microprocessor, "the most radical advance in electronic componentry in 30 years."[21] The microprocessor is, simply, a very advanced type of integrated circuit—a silicon chip that handles the arithmetical and logical functions of the computer's main memory. The microprocessor is programmable; that is, it can carry out a wide range of differing functions.

[30]   George H. Heilmeier, vice president for corporate research at Texas Instruments, used a geographical analogy to trace the evolution of the technology that resulted in the microprocessor. "In the mid-1960s," he said, "the complexity of a chip was comparable to that of the street network of a small town. Today's microprocessor is comparable to the entire Dallas-Fort Worth area. And the ultimate . . . micro technology

will be capable of producing chips whose complexity rivals an urban street network covering the entire North American continent."[22]

EVOLUTION OF THE SEMICONDUCTOR INDUSTRY

Large contracts from the federal government—primarily from the [31] Department of Defense and the National Aeronautics and Space Administration (NASA)—in the 1960s and 1970s spurred the growth of the American semiconductor industry. "This burgeoning military demand provided a stable market for the small, innovative micro-electronics companies that spearheaded the technological development, and it helped launch the industry on its high-growth technology," Colin Norman wrote.[23]

In the 1970s the focus of the industry shifted from military and [32] space technology to goods aimed for the commercial market. Today, the semiconductor industry, which has grown at a rate of about 30 percent a year, accounts for approximately $10 billion in sales; about $1 billion worth of semiconductors goes to military programs.[24]

Jerry Sanders, president of Advanced Micro Devices Inc., of Sun- [33] nyvale, Calif., was widely quoted when he said that he "liked to think of semiconductor technology and its evolution as being the crude oil of the electronics industry. . . ."[25] Wall Street electronics industry analyst Ben Rosen spoke recently of the far-ranging economic importance of this "crude oil." "Unlike the old crude oil that comes from the Middle East," he said, "this is crude oil that we have and they want—'they' being the rest of the world."[26] According to Rosen, the semiconductor industry has been investing about 10 percent of its profits in research and development to try to ensure that the United States keeps its lead in microprocessing and the manufacture of integrated circuits. The United States controlled 59 percent of the world market for semicon-ductors in 1980; Japan was a distant second with 23 percent.

NEW JAPANESE CHALLENGE IN MICROPROCESSING

"I was encouraged when it leaked that the Reagan Cabinet was going [34] to be made up of successful managers from the world of business," novelist-satirist Calvin Trillin wrote recently, "but I expected them all to be Japanese."[27] Trillin's half-serious barb makes an important point. Japan's dynamic economy, which started virtually from nothing 35 years ago, has eclipsed the United States in the world automobile and steel markets.[28] Now Japan is mounting a serious challenge to an industry that the United States has dominated since the industry began: microelectronics. American companies today build and sell about 70 percent of the world's integrated circuits; Japan is in second place. But three large Japanese producers—Nippon Electronic, Hitachi and Fujitsu—with the help of hundreds of millions of dollars in government research money, are trying to cut into the American-controlled market.

[35]   Several factors have given the Japanese a new edge in the international computer market. For one thing, American companies have been hurt by rising research and equipment costs. Those rising costs, in combination with intense competition, have led U.S. firms to sell their products at very low profit margins. Now Japanese companies are beginning to sell in the U.S. market at prices some American manufacturers say are lower than the lowest American prices. The Japanese make up the difference by selling at higher prices in their own market. In addition, Japanese tariffs and trade regulations have prevented American-made microprocessors from making a large impact in Japan.

[36]   There are signs that European manufacturers—who long have been a distant third behind the United States and Japan—are trying to widen their share of the world computer market. "European nations are favoring local semiconductor producers, fostering corporate marriages, and new ventures," one observer wrote, "assessing huge tariffs on imports, and launching some of the grandest industrial aid programs since World War II."[29] The Europeans have not had financial support from their defense and space programs like the Americans. Nor have they had the advantage of government largess as is the case in Japan. But the governments of West Germany, England, France, Holland and Italy have begun to study the feasibility of government aid. And the European Economic Community has started a project to coordinate its member countries' activities in the field.

COOPERATIVE RESEARCH EFFORTS BY U.S. FIRMS

[37] One way that American data processing companies and integrated circuit manufacturers have decided to fight this competition is to take a page from Japan's book. Competing U.S. industries are beginning to cooperate in research and development programs for their common good. "Companies are almost forced to cooperate," said William C. Norris, chairman of Control Data Corp. "It's two minutes before midnight, and if it's not done, Japan will pass us."[30]

[38]   Six American companies, including International Business Machines (the world's largest computer producer), Xerox Corp., and Burroughs Corp., have sent financial assistance and loaned company scientists to a California Institute of Technology program designed to foster microprocessor research. Similar industry-sponsored research programs now are under way at Stanford University, Duke University and North Carolina State University. The University of Minnesota has set up a Microelectronics & Information Science Center with the help of Control

Data Corp., Honeywell Inc., Sperry Corp. and other companies. The center is working on research in microelectronic physics, integrated circuit design and other related technologies. It is hoped that these programs will not only advance microelectronic knowledge, but also produce more trained computer scientists to work in a field that is chronically short of personnel.

The shortage of trained computer personnel is not limited to top-level jobs. According to John W. Hamblem, chairman of the computer sciences department at the University of Missouri at Rolla, the shortage exists at nearly all levels and will continue to be a problem for years. "Right now, at the bachelor's level, we are producing one candidate for every four jobs," Hamblen said. "At the master's level it's one for 10, and at the doctoral level it's been one for four, and the supply is decreasing. People aren't even bothering to go for graduate degrees when they can start at $20,000 with a B.S. I think we'll start to close the gap at the B.S. level around 1986."[31] [39]

Computer industry analysts estimate that the industry has openings for about 54,000 college graduates a year; 34,000 openings for those with master's degrees, and 1,300 openings for Ph.D.'s. Salaries in the computer field are for the most part above average, especially at companies with large computer operations. [40]

FUTURE DIRECTIONS AND GOALS

The technology of microelectronics is constantly growing. Sometimes it seems as if innovations are announced on a daily basis. And yet this rapidly evolving technology is just beginning to develop. This means that there will be even more breakthroughs in the immediate future. One of the most potentially spectacular developments now on the horizon is the so-called "intelligent" computer, a machine able to "think," talk and listen to the human voice. [41]

Can computers become intelligent in the human sense of the word? Philosophers, mathematicians, linguists, psychologists, electrical engineers and computer scientists are trying to answer that question. A number of experimental models are at work today. These machines can comprehend certain spoken words and respond to them. Some intelligent computers can answer questions with prerecorded words arranged in grammatical sentences. Computer experts say it will be at least two decades before they learn to program a computer with speech, hearing and emotion on the order of Hal, the star of the 1968 Stanley Kubrick-Arthur C. Clarke film, *2001: A Space Odyssey*. [42]

Could an ultra-intelligent machine turn against humans, like Hal did in *2001*? Scientists say that there is more danger that humans will become too dependent on these smart machines than there is the [43] possibility that the machines will try, like Hal did, to "take over." But few who have seen *2001* will forget the eerie scenes in which Hal stopped acting like an obedient slave and began to try to take control of the spaceship en route to Jupiter. "Hal, unless you follow my instructions, I shall be forced to disconnect you," one crewman said after Hal threatened him. The climax of the movie occurs when this sole surviving astronaut—Hal has managed to kill the other one—in effect murders the computer by disconnecting all of its memory cells.

NEW EXPERIMENTS WITH "THINKING MACHINES"

[44]   Computers that have the capability to kill and be killed no doubt were far from the minds of scientists who began the first research into thinking machines in the early 1950s. The first working intelligent machine, the Logic Theorist, was developed in 1956 by Allen Newell and Herbert Simon of Carnegie-Mellon University in Pittsburgh. The machine, which used logical operations to prove mathematical statements, was able to prove theorems in Alfred North Whitehead and Bertrand Russell's *Principia Mathematica*, "a feat of intelligence by anybody's standards."[32]

[45]   Other early pioneers in the development of thinking machines were Marvin Minsky, an MIT mathematician; John McCarthy, a mathematics professor at Dartmouth; Nathaniel Rochester of IBM; and Claude Shannon of Bell Laboratories. Their research centered on analyzing and trying to duplicate exactly what the human brain does with information. Their early questions and experiments remain at the heart of artificial intelligence research today.

[46]   All of the prototype thinking machines now operating are able to function in a seemingly intelligent, analytical manner. But they do not have the actual power to reason. Below are brief descriptions of some experimental models:

> **PROSPECTOR**, built by SRI International in Menlo Park, Calif., is programmed to answer geological questions. It lists types of ore deposits that may be present in rocks and configurations, then questions geologists to narrow and define the problem until it concludes whether or not there is a specific ore present in a region.

> **BACON**, a program that searches out patterns in scientific data, was developed by Herbert Simon of Carnegie-Mellon University. When given all the known facts about chemistry in the year 1800, BACON was able to deduce the principle of atomic weight, something that was not discovered by humans until 1850.

> **INTERNIST**, a program that helps doctors diagnose patients, was developed by University of Pittsburgh researchers Jack D.

Myers and Harry E. Pople. After being fed information about a specific patient's symptoms, medical history, laboratory test data and other test results, INTERNIST suggests diagnoses.

IPP is a Yale University program that analyzes newspaper items about terrorism. IPP correlates the data and can make certain assumptions about common elements of terrorist activities.

FRUMP, another Yale program, can take short newspaper stories and produce grammatically correct, one-sentence summaries of them in English, Spanish and Chinese.

BORIS is a Yale program that "reads" and "understands" short stories. Programmed with information about human relationships, BORIS can answer certain questions about short story characters' friendships and feelings. It takes about six months to program BORIS with information on one short story.

PROGRESS IN TALKING, LISTENING COMPUTERS

All of these programs receive their instructions from a typewriter and [47] respond with typewritten messages. Other intelligent computers have the capability to listen to spoken words and/or respond with prerecorded words. One such computer is owned by the state of Illinois. It is hooked into a telephone system and can dial calls in response to oral instructions from certain state employees. Kurtzweil Computer Products of Cambridge, Mass., a Xerox subsidiary, manufactures a computerized reading machine. Programmed with 1,500 linguistic rules, it can "read" written words placed on its glass plate. A number of libraries and universities have purchased these $30,000 machines for the use of sightless persons. Recording star Stevie Wonder is the only individual owner.

"Speech offers a whole new dimension for communication" with [48] machines, said George Dodd, head of the computer science department in General Motors' research laboratories.[33] Dodd predicted that automobiles eventually will be equipped with intelligent computers that will "speak" to the driver, warning of low oil pressure or reminding passengers to buckle their seat belts. The driver also will be able to "ask" the car radio to change stations or the rear window to defog. This will make operating the car safer, it is said, because the driver can complete these functions while keeping both hands on the steering wheel.

Scientists admit that the day of the perfected talking, listening [49] computer is not in the immediate future. IBM scientists, for example, have been working since 1972 on a word processing system that can take oral dictation. Progress to date has been slow because of the extremely difficult task of teaching a computer to recognize continuous, unrestricted natural speech. Researchers expect to make marked improvements in speech and hearing machines during the next decade, but widespread use of these machines probably will not take place until the 21st century. "Speech technology is . . . slow, ineffective, error prone, but sexy. . . ," said George Duddington of Texas Instruments. "Truly inexpensive speech recognition awaits the ability to put a computer comparable to IBM's largest on a single chip."[34]

INCREASED INDUSTRIAL POTENTIAL OF ROBOTS

[50] Karel Capek, the Czech playwright, novelist and essayist, wrote a play in 1921 called *R.U.R.* (Rossum's Universal Robots). Capek's satirical drama introduced the word "robot" into the English language. The playwright coined the word, which means forced labor, to describe the machines in his play which resembled people, but worked twice as hard. Until relatively recently most people pictured robots the way Capek imagined them: machine-like human lookalikes with arms and legs and personalities on the order of Artoo Deetoo in the 1977 movie *Star Wars*. But the industrial robots that are being used today in factories across the country look nothing like humans. Instead they look like machines with one or more clawed arms.

[51] According to Lori Mei, administrator of the Robot Institute of America in Dearborn, Mich., there are now about 3,800 industrial robots in American factories. And the number is expected to grow rapidly in the next two decades. Institute figures show that about 1,170 robots were sold by American manufacturers in 1980, accounting for about $90 million in sales. The institute predicts that in 1985 the U.S. robot industry will sell some 4,800 robots, worth some $225 million; by 1990 these figures are expected to rise to 17,100 and $780 million.

[52] One reason for the increased interest in the use of robots is the falling American productivity rate.[35] Right now robots are being used in factories to do hazardous, difficult, repetitive and routine jobs, including spot and arc welding, machine loading, materials handling, die casting, spray painting, forging and various types of assembling. Robots are built to be operated 24 hours a day. They never take vacations or lunch breaks. They don't call in sick or join unions. Analysts estimate that robots cost manufacturers about $5 an hour during the robots' lifetimes (the purchasing price of a robot ranges from $5,000 to $150,000). Human factory workers cost employers about $15–$20 per hour. According to the Robot Institute, industrial robots now in use in American factories have helped boost production from 10–90 percent.

[53] Microprocessor technology has given a boost to the potential of robots. The microprocessor allows robots to be reprogrammable and

therefore multifunctional. In the past, industrial machines were able to perform only one task, such as sorting or packing on an assembly line. A new machine would have to be designed, manufactured and purchased in order to make a slight change. But today's robots have control and memory systems that can be programmed in minutes to change the robot's job.

Japan, not the United States, is the world leader in robot production and use. Japan imported its first robot in 1967. According to statistics compiled by Bache Halsey Stuart Shields Inc., the stock brokerage company, the Japanese operate about 10,000 robots, or 57 percent of the world total. Japanese robot manufacturers produced an estimated $300 million worth of robots last year—more than triple the sales of American models. [54]

American companies have begun to respond to Japan's dominance. General Electric Co. has built one of the largest robotics laboratories in the country in Schenectady, N.Y. GE, which already has more than 100 robots in use in its manufacturing plants, expects to nearly double that amount by the end of this year. The company is using more robots to try to increase productivity by about 6 percent a year. GE hopes eventually to replace about half its 37,000 assembly line workers with robots. "Unless we start doing something to increase U.S. productivity, the United States will be out of business as a country," said Jules Mirabal, director of GE's robotics program.[36] [55]

The largest U.S. user of robots is General Motors, which began buying robots about 10 years ago and now has about 270 in use. GM plans to have an additional 1,800 robots in use by 1984. Westinghouse has set up a robotics division to look into applying robot technology in its manufacturing areas. Other companies currently using robots include McDonnell Douglas Aircraft Co., Lockheed Corp., International Harvester Co., Deere & Co., Briggs & Stratton Corp., Ford Motor Co. and Massey-Ferguson Inc. [56]

The rapidly increasing U.S. demand for robots has had a powerful and positive effect on the young robot manufacturing industry in this country. According to Laura Conigliaro, a Bache Halsey analyst, "the number of new companies being formed to manufacture industrial robots and/or peripheral equipment is growing rapidly. Moreover, these companies are finding it far less difficult to raise initial seed capital as well as investment dollars. . . ."[37] One robot manufacturer, Automix, Inc., was able to raise $6 million with little difficulty when it was formed recently. Existing companies, including Cincinnati Milacron and Condec Corp., are investing heavily in increased production facilities. In addition, some large computer companies, including Digital Equipment, IBM and Texas Instruments, are said to be "seriously considering" entering the robot market. [57]

GROWING CONCERNS ABOUT JOB DISPLACEMENT

[58]   The impact of the computer revolution on the social fabric of American life is clearly illustrated by the growing use of robots. Robots in factories have one main purpose: to relieve humans of jobs in order to increase productivity. Thus far, the 3,800 robots in American factories have taken the hazardous and mundane jobs that most workers do not want. Robots, therefore, are not now considered a serious threat to American workers and most labor unions have not objected to their presence on the assembly line.

[59]   But what of General Electric's plan to replace half of its 37,000 assembly workers with robots? GE says the plan will take many years to implement and workers whose jobs are replaced by robots will be given new jobs. "There's no question that robots will change the nature of the work we do, but it should be a change for the better," said Sam Dolfi, GE's manager of industrial relations planning. "There's a big difference between automating a boring, hazardous, repetitive job and replacing somebody with a robot. Large numbers of employees are not in danger of losing their jobs."[38]

[60]   Others predict there will be large numbers of workers who lose their jobs to robots or other computerized machines. At General Motors, for example, where there now is one skilled worker for every 5.6 assembly line workers, plans exist to equalize that ratio. "There's no question that robots will eliminate some unskilled jobs," said Larry Vickery, GM's director of employee relations.[39]

[61]   Many jobs already have been eliminated in the American newspaper industry, which in the last decade has made wide use of computerized equipment. Reporters today in essence set their own stories in type, thus virtually eliminating the need for typesetters. "In the newspaper industry, which is a good example of where this technology has already had a severe job impact, . . . essentially what we are seeing is the end of a craft," said Colin Norman of Worldwatch Institute. "In the manufacture of electronic goods . . . what you're seeing is that as companies that used to make mechanical products shift to making electronically controlled products—cash registers, for example—the amount of labor required to put those things together is much smaller. . . . National Cash Register, for example, has laid off a lot of people because they're making electronic cash registers that require far less labor to make."[40]

[62]   Some industry analysts say that the robot revolution actually will create more jobs. The reasoning is that even though factory jobs will be lost, those workers will be able to move on to other, more rewarding jobs. But who will pay for the retraining of these displaced workers? And will all displaced workers have the ability to make the career switch? The answers to these questions remain a matter of conjecture.

"The most important area of discussion throughout the next decade will continue to be the social implications of robots," said Pietro Varvello, an Italian economist. He predicted that "in the end, robots will have won the debate."[41]

NOTES

1. National Academy of Sciences, "Microstructure Science, Engineering, and Technology," 1979, p. 1. The first industrial revolution began in England in the mid-18th century and changed the world economy from one based on agriculture to one based on industry and machines.

2. Colin Norman, "Microelectronics at Work: Productivity and Jobs in the World Economy," Worldwatch Institute, October 1980, p. 6.

3. Interview, Feb. 2, 1981.

4. Quoted in the *Los Angeles Times*, Jan. 13, 1981.

5. Speaking at the annual meeting of the Information Industry Association, held Oct. 8, 1980, in San Francisco.

6. Writing in *The New York Times*, Nov. 26, 1980.

7. Quoted in *Business Week*, Dec. 18, 1980, p. 91.

8. Personal computers are sold primarily in retail computer stores. Larger computers are sold by salesmen who call on clients.

9. Quoted in *Savvy*, November 1980, pp. 77–78.

10. Quoted in *Business Week*, Dec. 1, 1980, p. 92.

11. Cited by Colin Hines and Graham Searle in *Automatic Unemployment* (1979).

12. Figures from "Electronic Market Data Book 1980," published by the Electronic Industries Association, and *The Economist*, March 1, 1980.

13. Quoted in the *Los Angeles Times*, Dec. 9, 1980.

14. Figures cited by Richard Simon of Goldman Sachs & Co., the investment banking firm, in *New York* magazine, Dec. 15, 1980, p. 12.

15. Quoted in *Nation's Business*, December 1980, p. 48. Milton Bradley's headquarters is in Springfield, Mass., Mattel's is in Hawthorne, Calif.

16. Quoted in *The Wall Street Journal*, June 29, 1980.

17. Quoted in *Discover*, December 1980, p. 97.

18. Bardeen, Brattain and Shockley were awarded the Nobel Prize for physics in 1956 for their work on developing the transistor.

19. Christopher Evans, *The Mighty Micro* (1979), p. 49.

20. Norman, *op. cit.*, p. 9.

21. Cheryll A. Barron, "All That is Electronic Does Not Glitter: Microelectronics Survey," *The Economist*, March 1, 1980.

22. Quoted in *Newsweek*, June 30, 1980, p. 53.

23. Norman, *op. cit.*, p. 12. See also Charles River Associates, "Innovation, Competition and Government Policy in the Semiconductor Industry," 1980.

24. Statistics from Semiconductor Industry Association, Charles River Associates and Electronic Industries Association.

25. Testimony before the U.S. International Trade Commission, May 30, 1979.

26. Remarks made on "The MacNeil/Lehrer Report," Public Broadcasting Service, Oct. 22, 1980.

27. Writing in *The Washington Post*, Jan. 17, 1981.

28. See "Trade Talks and Protectionism" *E.R.R.*, 1979 Vol. I, pp. 21–44.

29. Bro Uttal, "Europe's Wild Swing at the Silicon Giants," *Fortune*, July 28, 1980, p. 78.

30. Quoted in *Business Week*, Nov. 10, 1980, p. 108.

31. Quoted in *Savvy*, February 1981, p. 22.

32. Pamela McCorduck, *Machines Who Think* (1979), p. 104.

33. Quoted in *The Wall Street Journal*, Dec. 31, 1980.

34. Quoted in *Science 80*, March-April 1980, p. 55.

35. Productivity is broadly defined as output per man hour. Annual U.S. productivity has declined for the past two years—following yearly increases since the end of World War II. See "Technology Gap: Reality or Illusion," *E.R.R.*, 1978 Vol. II, pp. 945–964, and "America's Changing Work Ethic," *E.R.R.*, 1979 Vol. II, pp. 901–920.

36. Quoted in *The New York Times*, Nov. 28, 1980.

37. Laura Conigliaro, "Robotics," Bache Halsey Stuart Shields, Inc., April 23, 1980, p. 4.

38. Quoted in *The New York Times*, Nov. 28, 1980.

39. Quoted in *The Wall Street Journal*, Jan. 22, 1981.

40. Appearing on "The McNeil/Lehrer Report," Oct. 22, 1980.

41. Quoted in *Business Week*, June 9, 1980, p. 64.

QUESTIONS

1. Leepson mentions the wide use of robots in present-day industry. How would he define the word "robot"? What kinds of examples does he give? On the basis of your observation and experience, can you give examples of robots that are now widely in use either commercially or industrially?

2. What changes might one expect in the occupation of teaching with the implementation of computers? Do you suppose the computer will enhance or diminish the status of the profession?

3. If workers are replaced by computers in significantly large numbers, what alternatives might there be to mass unemployment?

4. In the light of everything we have learned about work, let us speculate about some of the effects upon society of an economy in which *all* unskilled labor was done by robots.

   a. Would the unemployed feel more or less stress if the reason for their unemployment, instead of a plant's closing, was a plant's converting to 100 percent robot labor? Consider: Is it more or less stressful for everybody to be out of work than it is for "me" personally to be out of work?

   b. Would gaps in social status or prestige between skilled and unskilled workers grow wider or narrower?

   c. What would happen to people whose intelligence level made it impossible for them to be trained in skills demanded by computerization?

5. Choose a vocational area that interests you and determine what difference the computer has made in that area in your lifetime. Then speculate about the changes that are likely to occur in the future. If you cannot think of a relevant vocational area, look at some institutions in our society: the post office, libraries, newspapers, national elections, banks.

EXERCISES

1. If you live in a large city, choose one block; in a small town use Main Street. Make a list of each of the businesses, stores, or factories on the street, and write a two-paragraph report on each that speaks to the following questions:

   a. Could the work done in this store or business be performed by a computer or robot? How much of the work is already done by computer?

   b. How many people employed here would be unemployed or would have to be retrained in another skill if the work done here were performed by a robot or computer?

   c. How would the computerization of this street affect the town as a whole (or in a city, the neighborhood as a whole)?

2. Imagine that you are the school superintendent in your town. Write an outline of the skills that should be taught in kindergarten through grade 3 to prepare children for the Computer Age. Include a section on work-discipline habits. What do present work-discipline schedules instill in children that should be changed?

3. Reexamine your work profile yet another time. In this reading, give special attention to the concept you have provided of your "job" in the future. How much allowance did you make for changes brought about by progress? What new skills do you project you have to learn? How much preparation do you expect to get in these skills while you are still in college? Consider these and other questions that might occur to you and revise your profile accordingly. (It might be useful to you to interview a person in your line of work and to find out, if you don't already know, how much the computer will affect the job for which you are training.)

UNIT III

DEATH

Some might think that a unit called "Death" in a textbook devoted to the skills of thinking, reading, and writing is a bit morbid. We submit that this response is quite wrong. To be occupied with the meaning of death is, in fact, a vital human concern, for man is the only animal who has the fore-knowledge that he will die, and if he is to live a thoughtful life, he must be able to cope with that knowledge. We submit further that the understanding of death is, in fact, the understanding of life, and that the study of one necessarily involves the study of the other. Death, as we see it, and as it is presented to us in the readings of this unit, is clearly a part of life. It should not be a taboo subject, and it should not be thought of as something we must forgo talking about because it frightens us. In fact, our mental health and the spirit of free inquiry demand that we discuss death openly as one of the central issues in a college education.

We have tried to show in the preceding units on love and work that while academic disciplines characteristically differ in their methodologies of study, they often come together in their concern with major issues. We have seen that the scientist has as much interest in defining mother love as the historian or the anthropologist. Death is similarly of interest to virtually every academic discipline, and we will see how the argument of one specialist resonates against that of another.

Our age, as the readings in this unit will attest, is very much concerned with the concept of death. In part this is so because the twentieth century no longer has the certitude of former ages about finality or for that matter about eternity. In a time such as the Middle Ages in Western civilization when the world-view of the Christian church dominated, there was a relatively unanimous agreement on what it meant to die. Few serious thinkers doubted the existence of God or of eternal life; most believed in the coming of the final judgment on the Day of Doom. Death in that context is essentially a time of passage, and while it may have been feared and categorized as painful, it did not in itself inspire mortal terror, as it may well do for many persons in our age.

The readings we have selected reexamine the whole topic of death, beginning with a definition offered by a philosopher, moving forward to a discussion of Western attitudes by a cultural historian, and lingering for some time over the practical question not only of how the health professions deal with death but how they must provide new operational definitions in the light of new boundaries established by the sciences. Do we, in fact, know when death occurs at a time when machines can help keep us breathing? Does death occur when the heart stops? If so, is the heart, if transplanted into another body, not the core of our identity and hence the organ by which life is defined? Does the recipient of the heart then lose his or her own identity and assume that of the donor? As the playwright Brian Clark asked (though in a different context), "Whose life is it anyway?" Or to explore another problem, does death occur when the brain dies? If so, what is brain death, and how do we measure it? We have all heard of comas that have lasted for years and then vanish as suddenly as they came. What if we had declared a person in such a coma to be dead? With recent medical advancements the borderline between life and death has been obscured, and simple definitions of the nature of either life or death no longer apply.

The unit ends with a consideration of the artist's conception of death. What is the meaning of the loss of a great poet? Is there a way in which a poet's work transcends his or her life? Or how do we picture the death of God? How is it possible to represent an event of such magnitude and to capture at once the cruelty and the hope that it generates? Answers for such questions must finally be provided by the sensibility and the creative insights of the artists in our midst. You?

CHAPTER FIFTEEN

CONGDON: THE PURSUIT OF DEATH

Philosophy

Philosophy was for centuries believed to be the mother and queen of all of the arts and sciences. This way of conceiving of philosophy is not just fanciful exaggeration, because while each of the branches of the arts and sciences is involved in knowing, learning, and critical thinking, for philosophy knowing and thinking are not only methods but also objects of study. Philosophy asks such questions as: "How do we know what we know?" "Is it possible for us to know?" "When we look at, or think about things, do we 'see' or 'know' the things themselves (*noumena*) or is what we are seeing only the appearance of things (*phenomena*)?" In this selection the philosopher Howard K. Congdon demonstrates for us (1) how philosophy approaches the timeless human issue of death, (2) what questions the philosopher must pose to determine whether the subject approached is knowable or definable, and (3) what tools the philosopher must employ in dealing with the issue. Congdon's object is to provide a philosophically sound definition of death.

It is very important for us to assume a philosophical stance from time to time, particularly while we are in college, because while a teacher or a syllabus can tell us what we have to know to complete the requirements for a course, what a philosopher's view can tell us is why we have to know, how we go about knowing, and whether indeed we really do know what we think we know. Consider Congdon's approach to death a model for the sort of philosophical inquiry with which to approach any important issue.

GLOSSARY

sophisticated [1]

experiential [1]

equivalent [1]

atomists [1]

paradigm [2]

Existentialists [2]

eclipse [3]

absolutes [3]

morbid [4]

senility [5]

permissive [5]

euphemisms [5]

mawkish [5]

metaphysical [6]

conceptual [8]

negation [8]

ken [9]

inferential [9]

dynamics [9]

gratuitously [9]

noumena [9]

solipsism [10]

parameters [11]

protean [11]

impending [12]

the psyche [13]

fraught [13]

alleviate [14]

euthanasia [15]

intractable [16]

troll [18]

compatible [18]

ex nihilo [20]

epistemology [20]

oracles [22]

Delphic [22]

irrefutable [23]

flaccidity [24]

pallid [24]

rigor mortis [24]

cessation [25]

elusive [27]

parameters [30]   comatose [37]

compatible [33]   irreversible [37]

negates [35]

————— THE PURSUIT OF DEATH —————

Howard K. Congdon

. . . One might wonder just why it is that we find today an apparent   [1]
growing interest in the subject of death. It might be maintained that
this is really nothing new. Early Greek and Roman philosophy spent
much of its energy attempting to provide a rational account of death.
Democritus and Epicurus, four centuries prior to the birth of Christ,
presented a theory of death giving a materialistic interpretation of the
fate of the soul. In a surprisingly sophisticated way they argued that,
because reality was atomic in nature, whatever was real was composed
of atoms. This would include the soul. At death, then, the soul, like
the body, disintegrates and survives only as scattered atoms no longer
capable of sensation. They and their disciples concluded on the basis
of this analysis that fear of death was one of the most irrational of
emotions. Their understanding of death indicated that it was a status
absolutely devoid of experiential content. Since it cannot be experienced
it cannot hurt, and therefore should not bother us. Further, since
death entails the extinction of awareness, the fear of death is literally
equivalent to being afraid of nothing. And that does sound a bit
irrational. These sentiments were later echoed by Lucretius, a Roman
poet and philosopher who accepted the analysis of the atomists.

Socrates, of course, dealt extensively with death, believing that the   [2]
goal of the philosopher is death. His martyrdom remains even today
the paradigm of how to die. Plato presents Socrates as advancing
several arguments for the immortality of the soul. These were later
accepted by Plotinus, and so it goes. The history of philosophy is in
part the history of man's pursuit of death. The tradition is carried on
today by the Existentialists, who give evidence of a deep concern for

SOURCE: Excerpted from THE PURSUIT OF DEATH by Howard K. Congdon. Copyright ©
1977 by Abingdon. Used by permission.

the implications of death. There is something to the belief that the contemporary interest in death is really nothing new.

[3]   Except that it *is* new. We are not witnessing simply a philosophical concern with death. This new interest is much wider. Something is different, and it would be difficult to argue seriously that the mood of the times has not changed. It can be argued that the interest in death is due to a relatively recent loss of absolutes. It is the natural result of the death-of-God phenomenon. With the absence of the idols of our tribe which once comforted us and provided an ultimate security, we cannot be surprised that man has begun to consider the implications of his loss. What does the eclipse of God mean to me when I die? The rather thorough questioning of moral and theological absolutes, which is a relatively recent event, might easily begin to turn our culture toward an examination of its destiny. It might well create within an individual the desire to ponder what it all means to him.

[4]   Or maybe it is all a part of a larger crumbling of the foundations. Perhaps the contemporary interest in death is precisely the morbid fascination one might expect from a civilization in its period of decay. The loss of hope is symbolized by death. Our concern for death may simply be a reflection of a cultural pessimism.

[5]   Or perhaps we have grown up. It may be that civilization is suffering not from the slings and arrows of senility, but rather from the growing pains of adolescence. We may have arrived at a stage in which we are ready to deal with the very serious issue of our own death. It has been noted by others that the topic of death today has certain similarities to the status occupied by sex at an earlier time. As long as the analogy is not pressed too far, such a comparison is quite valid. A serious study of sex was at one time very nearly impossible and even today can be difficult. The psychological threat of sex is expressed in the various taboos which cling to it as a legitimate area of study, in the tendency of some to giggle or look at their feet whenever the topic is raised, in the apparent inability of others to talk about sex except as a joke, and so on. Sex is threatening in proportion to its power and importance, and perhaps its mystery. Even today, in what many believe to be a relatively open and permissive society, a serious discussion of sex is a tricky affair. But the situation has changed. With the growing acceptance of sex as an important aspect of our lives and therefore deserving of careful study we now know much more about its physiological and psychological aspects than we once did. Something similar may be happening with respect to death. The very threat of death is at least in part a function of our ignorance about it. Such ignorance is neither accidental nor necessary. It is a product of deliberate design. We have carefully cultivated an ignorance of death by draping it with various social taboos, thereby discouraging exploration of the

topic. Many people cannot bring themselves to speak directly about death and are reduced to less threatening euphemisms of the dead as having "passed away," or "fallen asleep," or "gone on to a greater glory," or whatever. We even speak of old people who most directly confront the grave as "senior citizens" enjoying their "golden years." Under other circumstances such phrases would be considered rather mawkish. But language is our most important tool, and it can be used to help us avoid ourselves when that is what we want. The fact is that death, like sex, is too basic and too important to us as human beings to be hidden forever. It must eventually be faced as directly and as honestly as possible. And that is just what is happening. Just as sex was dragged out from behind the barn, death is being stripped of its secrecy. It has to happen. We cannot be served by ignorance.

Philosophy would appear to be especially well suited to probe the [6] mysteries of death. It was, after all, the death of Socrates that tore Plato loose from his aristocratic ties and set the stage for subsequent philosophical speculation about the nature of the soul and the proper attitude toward death. The mystery of death is more metaphysical than biological. The real questions lie on the other side of the microscope. Philosophy, perhaps more than any other discipline, has the proper credentials for exploring such regions. Philosophy, in spite of the efforts of certain linguistic analysts, is at its heart metaphysics. It provides for legitimate speculation beyond the laboratory data. If a soul cannot be microscopically dissected, it can be conceptually analyzed. If purpose and meaning and value are not to be found via a computer print-out, they can be subjected to the rigors of philosophical analysis. And these are, after all, the mysteries of death. If they are to be resolved, we must pursue a philosophy of death.

It is not an easy task. The consideration of death presents many [7] difficulties, some of which are encountered nowhere else. There is first of all a natural reluctance to think about one's own extinction. Death carries with it the most serious of all threats, paradoxically expressed by Heidegger as "the possibility of the impossibility of existence." It implies the final, inevitable victory of nothingness over the only thing we really have—our being. And it is not easy to wrestle with our own doom.

But there are other, perhaps more serious, difficulties in any con- [8] sideration of death. There are conceptual difficulties involved in the study of death. It is first of all psychologically, if not logically, odd to conceive of our own death. If death is literally our very extinction, involving a complete loss of awareness, how are we to think of it? How can we in any way imagine what death is like if death entails the inability to imagine at all? It is at least puzzling to try and get a handle on the very concept of nothingness and apparently impossible to conceive of our own negation. Since conception involves awareness it is not at all clear just how we are to understand our eventual state of non-awareness. Such a task, involving the attempt to increase our knowledge of something which, by its very nature must reside outside the boundaries of our earthly experience, seems logically hopeless. How can we possibly expect to know the unknowable, or become aware of what it means to lose awareness itself? It is like trying to think specifically of absolutely nothing at all. . . .

[9]   Death really cannot be studied because of this conceptual difficulty. But it is not necessary to succumb to such a first-round knockout. There is ample precedent for us to pursue a study of what appears to be intrinsically beyond our ken. Freud, after all, did not hesitate to tell us about the unconscious mind. The unconscious is, by definition, forever removed from our awareness. Whatever we can realize about it must be a conscious realization and therefore at best we can have only inferential knowledge of whatever levels of consciousness may exist on the other side of awareness. We cannot, for example, become aware of subconscious drives and motivations unless and until they poke themselves into our conscious minds, but then they are no longer subconscious. But this hardly slows the Freudian analyst down. And it does appear that we can make some respectable guesses about the dynamics of subconscious processes. At any rate, we do. Further, many philosophers have believed that, because we are forever nec-essarily restricted to our own subjective experiences of the world, it is therefore impossible to know objective reality directly. And there is an obvious sense in which this is certainly the case. When looking at a carrot, for example (it could be anything—even a squash), we do not really experience, or even see, the carrot itself. We experience, or see, what some philosophers have referred to as sense-data, some informational sort of stuff somehow thrown back at us by the objects "out there." But we never see those objects. We see (or smell or hear or taste or touch) the sense-data, or what Kant called the phenomena, and we gratuitously assume that they bear some sort of worthy re-lationship to the mysterious noumena which (we suppose) produce them.

[10]   This is why philosophers occasionally toy with the idea of solipsism—the view that the individual (in my case, me) is the only reality, the whole of existence. It is a view which requires a major effort to take seriously, but one which is notoriously difficult to disprove. After all, what do you know about the world other than your own subjective ideas of it? We cannot be sure that our idea of a carrot bears any resemblance at all to the vegetable itself, and we seem able to make a decent salad in spite of our inability to experience the objective carrot.

It would be a bit quirky to say that death is like a carrot, but it is [11]
not too much to point out that our apparent inability to experience
death directly should not deter us from attempting to learn more
about it. Just as we can make a passable salad with vegetables we
can never hope to know firsthand, perhaps we can begin to toss an
acceptable philosophical salad from metaphysical vegetables which
elude our direct grasp. Furthermore, there is an aspect of death which
is not so elusive—dying. There is an important distinction to be made
between death and dying. Dying is a process. It is a series of events
occurring within the parameters of life. We can experience dying,
even if we cannot experience death. Dying is a process we can experience
and therefore study directly. Death is an event somehow outside our
everyday experience which must be approached in other ways. Dying,
unlike death, can be experienced in many ways. The shape of dying
is protean. It comes in many forms. We sometimes can have an influence
on the quality of dying, although many of its aspects are normally
beyond our control.

Broadly speaking, dying must fall into one of two categories. Either [12]
we are aware of our impending death as an imminent event or we
are not. I once watched a man dying for a little over a year. He had
been told that he had at most one year to live, and he beat that estimate
by only a few days. He was aware of his dying. Toward the end he
was even able to describe quite vividly the feeling of his approaching
death. The effects of this knowledge on his character were profound.
He was able to take advantage of this experience and use it to gain
some startling personal insights. I watched him as he was transformed
from a man whose daily concern reached no further than the can of
beer which was always within arm's length, to one whose interests
led him to lengthy and significant assessments of what it meant to
be alive and what it meant to die. Such an experience is denied to
most people. Death too often takes us by surprise, robbing us of any
opportunity to acquire a larger perspective of ourselves and reality.
One who dies unexpectedly in his sleep or from a heart attack is often
envied. "That's the way I want to go—quickly and painlessly." Such
sentiments are common. But they may not be as reasonable as they
sound. We are, in a sense, always dying, but it is not generally the
case that we are brought starkly face to face with the reality of our
own death. Because death is a part of our very definition it would
seem reasonable to suppose that we can learn more about ourselves
from a consideration of death. But most of us never make the effort
unless we ourselves are threatened by imminent death and are aware
of that threat. There is a sense in which we are genuinely cheated if
death should catch us unawares. This is a consideration physicians
would do well to ponder as they make a decision whether or not to

tell a patient that he has a terminal disease. It is probably true that some patients should not be told that they are going to die. Others definitely should be told, not simply on the basis that they can take it, but more importantly because they can use it.

[13]   Within the categories of awareness or non-awareness, dying can be either slow or rapid. The difference can be very important. Knowledge of one's impending death generally produces a series of fairly well-defined stages in the psyche. But this is a process which takes time. The man who was aware of his inevitable death for an entire year was able to work his way through each of these levels to achieve the insights that finally came to him. A woman I knew was not so fortunate. She had dabbled in faith-healing, hoping to be able to effect a cure for what she called "the mopes," a constant feeling of listlessness often accompanied by pain. She was rushed to the emergency room only after she had finally collapsed into unconsciousness. Exploratory surgery revealed cancer at such an advanced stage that there was simply nothing which could be done. She was told that she probably had less than a month to live. In fact it was exactly three weeks. Her dying was too quick. It was impossible to digest. There was not enough time for her to work through the implications of her situation, and her dying was fraught with mental as well as physical agony. She left a bewildered husband and six anguished children. There are clearly important differences in the qualities associated with slow and rapid dying.

[14]   Another important quality of dying has to do with whether it is painful or not. I once watched a man dying of cancer of the sinuses. I had not known that there even was such a horrible form of cancer. His pain had gone beyond the ability of any drugs to alleviate. Because his suffering was so intense he was quite unable to direct his attention to anything else. It was not a good dying. Being relatively free from pain is important not only in terms of physical comfort, but also because pain can be so demanding of our mental energies. It can block our understanding of what is happening to us.

[15]   Of course there are other forms of dying which deserve consideration. Suicide, euthanasia, and capital punishment come to mind. There are distinctions to be made in the source of our dying, whether from disease, by accident, by our own hand, or by the will of others. But what it all comes down to is that dying can be ennobling or humiliating. It is not really odd to speak of a noble dying. Dying can sometimes bring out the most admirable qualities of a person. One can imagine dying bravely or for a worthy cause. It is not at all unusual for people to grow intensely fond of one who is dying, not simply out of sympathy, but for genuinely worthy reasons. Individuals can in fact grow up during the process of dying. They can, and often do, exhibit qualities

previously unsuspected in them. Our admiration for a dying person can be based on very legitimate reasons. And our sadness can be increased as we recognize the tragedy of losing an individual of genuine worth.

There are indeed many ways of dying. There is presumably only one form of death. Dying is an important process. Because it occurs while we are yet alive it can be studied. We can use it or abuse it. But at least we can begin to understand it. We can think of dying. But it is not clear how we can think of being dead. The process of dying ends at the moment of death. The individual is then no longer dying; he is dead. An understanding of the process of dying is at least possible because we may expect to experience it. But the most intractable problems in any philosophy of death have to do not with the process of dying, but with being dead. And how can we hope to experience being dead? At this point we are at the heart of the mysteries of death. Somehow we are squeezed from reality as we know it into a dimension so alien to us that nothing in our philosophical bag of tricks seems adequate to the task of understanding just what has happened. How are we to analyze our death if it involves our very extinction? Of what possible use can philosophical speculation be in an area which by its very definition excludes not simply the only experience we know, but perhaps experience itself? It is a formidable problem. [16]

The problem is not resolved even with the assumption that some sort of nonphysical awareness is possible after death. The various theoretical notions of life after death all encounter the difficulty of expressing just what is meant by an experience apart from the body. What kind of experience is possible, or even conceivable, without the physical senses? Without the ability to see or hear or taste or smell or touch, what could possibly be left? Even acknowledging that something might remain, how can we know about it? How can it be explored? It would seem that we must somehow penetrate that ultimate barrier between the living and the dead if we are to develop an adequate conceptual framework for our theories about death. The fact is that we are viewing the issue from the wrong side. We are attempting to understand what is on the other other side of a curtain without being allowed even to peek at it. It appears that we are reduced to philosophical guessing games. [17]

These difficulties generate still another problem of special interest to philosophy. There is a philosophical troll living under our metaphysical bridges, threatening to prevent our ever crossing the boundaries of empirical data. The troll is known as "The Verification Principle." He demands a price for every metaphysical speculation, insisting, not unreasonably, that all meaningful propositions have a cash value. [18]

That is, they must commit themselves to one set of circumstances to the exclusion of some other set. Further, it must be possible to delineate some events or situations such that, were they to occur, the proposition would clearly be established as being true or false. In other words, all meaningful statements must take a chance. They must, at least in theory, be verifiable or falsifiable. Should they prove to be compatible with any and all conceivable events, that can only mean that they have not really said anything. Thus, for example, while I might bravely assert that "the theory of gravity is heavier than lead," the philosophical troll demands his price. What is the meaning of such an assertion— i.e., what specifically does it proclaim? What does it deny? Under what circumstances might it be proved, or shown to be false? I would not be allowed to cross his bridge. Would I be any better off in presenting certain speculations about my own existential status after death? Perhaps, but I must be clear in specifying just how such propositions might be verified or falsified before the troll will let me pass. And that could prove to be a genuine problem.

[19]   The pursuit of death, then, encounters a number of serious obstacles. Some of these have been mentioned and, of course, there are others. The evidence indicates that we are at last arriving at a period in our development as a culture when it is not only legitimate to probe the mysteries of the grave, it is demanded. We need not particularly trouble ourselves with the respectability of such a study. The widespread concern with the various aspects of death suggests that we have outgrown a certain metaphysical adolescence during which we were unable to bring ourselves to sit down and reason about our own death. The topic is beginning to assault us from all sides. . . .

TOWARD A DEFINITION OF DEATH

[20]   We really are not sure how to define death. In one sense the pursuit of death is nothing more than the pursuit of a definition. We cannot understand death until we know what it is. But knowing what it is would appear to be another way of saying that we understand it. How, then, do we begin to resolve our ignorance about death? It is an old question, not at all unique to the topic of death. But it is a legitimate one. Do we create an arbitrary definition of death, ex nihilo, and work from there? Or are we reduced to striking out blindly in all directions at once, hoping to stumble somehow into the knowledge we seek? At this point we could easily devote the rest of this work to the problems of epistemology, trying to figure out just how it is that we seem able to pursue knowledge in areas in which we are ignorant. Either we know what we are after or we do not. If we do, there is no point in wasting our time attempting to gain what we

already have. If we do not, how will we recognize it when we find it? But the problems of how we learn are not really our concern here. Somehow it is done. Our task now is to do it, and it would seem that our first efforts ought to be devoted to the development of a working definition of death—being careful to see that the definition does not settle prematurely the major issues involved in the study of death. It is likely that such a definition of death at this early stage of our exploration will be expanded, modified, or even abandoned later on. But we must have some basic idea of just what it is that we are struggling with.

And it would seem that we do. Perhaps death is like pornography[1] and our knowledge of what it is is analogous to that of the Supreme Court justice who declared, with respect to pornography, "I don't know what it is, but I know it when I see it." Perhaps death is a sort of metaphysical pornography—an event utterly without redeeming social value, possibly even to the extent of appealing to our prurient interests. But surely we can do better. [21]

Although our main concern is not with the medical or physical aspects of death, we cannot reasonably deny that death is very much a physical event. There are some who would insist that death is *only* a physical event. In any case, we might do well to begin here. To the extent that death is a physical event we can expect to find some assistance in defining it from the medical profession. After all, it is the physician whose job it is to help us postpone the dreaded event. He should, therefore, be in a position to identify just what it is that he is fighting. But alas, some of the vaunted oracles of the noble profession of medicine have a Delphic quality about them. The fact is that a satisfactory medical definition of death is still being worked out, with more than one suggestion that the attempt to define death precisely will never succeed. [22]

The history of medicine is, of course, dotted with examples of persons who, having been pronounced dead, literally sat up to announce their disagreement with the verdict. J. J. Bruhier-d'Ablaincourt, a French physician in the mid-eighteenth century, documented numerous instances of premature burial and certificates of death which subsequently had to be torn up on the basis of obviously irrefutable evidence.[2] His solution to such embarrassments was to advocate deferring burial until after the onset of the early stages of putrefaction. His suggestion is of no help to us, however. There is general agreement that death has certainly occurred sometime prior to that state, and in any case we cannot seriously define death as the rotting of flesh, accompanied by an obnoxious odor. There are too many diseases of the living which would fit such a definition. Nor are the difficulties of determining the moment of death limited to the remote history of medicine. Even [23] today there are occasional errors in the attempt to determine the moment of death. In war, for example, mistakes of this sort, while unusual, are not unknown. There are reports from time to time of men being pronounced dead on the battlefield after failing to respond to resuscitation efforts, who eventually make complete recoveries.

[24]   Most examples of an incorrect diagnosis of death are due more to carelessness than to ignorance. During periods of war or other emergency a determination of death is often based upon a cursory examination of the body by the harried physician or sometimes the judgment of nonmedical personnel. It is probable that such cases would be extremely rare indeed if all pronouncements of death were the result of intensive and conscientious examination of the body by a qualified authority. But there would still be some mistakes simply because we are not exactly sure just what we are looking for. The traditional indicators of death focused on the absence of respiration and heartbeat, the drying of the corneas and subsequent flaccidity of the eyeballs, insensitivity to electrical and physical stimuli, a pallid complexion, relaxation of the sphincter muscles, and of course rigor mortis. These are still cited as genuine signs of death. A good deal of consideration is being given today to the electroencephalogram (EEG), a device which measures the electrical impulses of the brain. A flat EEG (no bumps in the lines on the graph) would indicate a dead—or at least an inactive—brain. Because many portions of the brain are extremely vulnerable to any loss of oxygen, even for a few seconds, it has been suggested that death be defined as an absence of any brain activity (as indicated by a flat EEG) for a period of, say, five minutes. Under normal circumstances, this would appear to be a reasonable position. But "normal circumstances" take their definition in opposition to abnormal ones. A London physician has reportedly cited two cases in which patients who exhibited flat EEGs for several hours subsequently made a complete recovery.[3] They had been victims of severe barbiturate poisoning. Similar examples have been reported in the United States. Perhaps the presence of certain drugs can be a significant alteration in what otherwise would be normal circumstances. Experiments with freezing techniques to produce a state of suspended animation indicate that a drop in temperature can lead to similar results. Dr. Henry K. Beecher of the Harvard medical school has warned against complete reliance on the EEG in determining death. He specifically excludes from this procedure "individuals who are under central nervous system depressants, or whose internal temperature is below 96 degrees Fahrenheit."[4] Further complicating matters is the knowledge that a number of diseases can produce trance states distinguishable from death only with considerable difficulty. It simply will not do to depend on a mirror held under the nose.

It should be noted that it is of more than academic interest that we   [25]
develop an accurate definition of death which will allow us to determine
the moment at which death has occurred. A murder trial in California
was recently jolted when the defense made a case resting entirely
upon the difficulties of defining death. The accused had shot a man
(the prosecution said "murdered"). The victim was pronounced dead,
and his still beating heart was removed and transplanted into another
patient. The defense attorneys insisted that, as the heart was still
functioning when it was removed, their client could not be guilty of
murder. The two bullets in the man's brain had not, they said, killed
him. He was "murdered" by the physicians who removed his heart!
This line of defense is encouraged by the fact that most states accept
a definition of death, dating back to 1906, in which death is identified
with the final cessation of heartbeat and respiration. In an effort to
resolve such problems, the American Bar Association has recently
approved a resolution from its Law and Medicine Committee urging
acceptance of a legal definition of death as the "irreversible, total
cessation of brain function."

It has been suggested that the medical profession has narrowed   [26]
the competing definitions of death down to three major options:[5]

1. The moment at which irreversible destruction of brain matter, with
   no possibility of regaining consciousness, is conclusively determined.
2. The moment at which spontaneous heartbeat cannot be restored.
3. "Brain death" as determined by the EEG.

The inadequacy of each of these definitions is not difficult to spot.   [27]
Consider the first one. When are we to conclude that we have witnessed
"the moment" at which there is no possibility of restoring consciousness? It really ought not to be equated with the moment when we
give up. When are we to know that there is no such possibility? What
objective data would allow a conclusive determination that *now* (and
not before) it is impossible for consciousness to be restored? Those
elusive objective data are really what we are after. This definition is
something like defining death as the moment at which it is conclusively
determined that life will not be recovered. That may be true. But it
is of little help.

The second definition carries with it a similar problem. Asking for   [28]
"the moment at which spontaneous heartbeat cannot be restored" is
like asking for the moment at which the Dow Jones average failed to
reach 1200. What moment was that? When are we entitled to conclude
that a heartbeat cannot be restored? If a heart has stopped beating
and two hours of solid effort to revive it have failed, it would appear
that it was impossible to do so from the moment it stopped beating.

If it can ever be restarted, then clearly it was possible to do so regardless of how long it has been. When is the moment of death? Again, the suggestion seems to be that the moment of death occurs when we stop trying to restore life. But the physician is interested in determining when he is entitled to quit, and this definition provides him with nothing.

[29]   We have already noted the difficulties presented by the third definition.

[30]   It really is not fair to be overly harsh with these definitions. We are admittedly in a period in which technology has outdistanced our understanding. It is always easier to tear down proposals than it is to offer better ones. But it is important to illustrate just where we stand, and we have run into a buzzsaw. The problem is that death may not be identifiable with any given moment. We are used to hearing of cases in which people have "died," on the operating table or in the ocean or on a street corner, and then been brought back. In chapter 1 a distinction was made between death and dying. It was noted that dying is a process. Perhaps death, too, is a process.[6] In some sense we begin to die at the moment of conception. Socrates believed that the true philosopher is always pursuing death and dying. This would seem to be true of everyone. Death and dying may both be processes, or stages of a single process, distinguished at least in part by the fact that dying is a process, or that portion of the process, which occurs within the parameters of our earthly life, while death most certainly does not. It is true that certain life functions continue long after "death" by any reasonable definition has occurred. One of the more intriguing jobs of the undertaker is shaving the cadaver just prior to the viewing and making sure that the continuing growth of beard is concealed by a judicious use of makeup. There is, in fact, a good deal of life remaining in the "dead" body. The hair and fingernails continue to grow. Many of the cells of the body retain their ability to function and even reproduce for quite some time after the person has died. We may be faced with an insurmountable problem in trying to define death. About the only thing all medical authorities agree on as a sure sign of death is the presence of rigor mortis. But most would also agree that death has in fact taken place some time prior to that. At the moment we really have no better a medical definition of death than that provided by the United Nations Vital Statistics which defines death as the permanent loss of all signs of life, which sounds something like Augustine's definition of evil as the absence of good.

[31]   Perhaps we philosophers should tend to our own metaphysical knitting. Without discounting in the slightest the importance of developing a medical definition of death, we should recognize that our real interests lie elsewhere. Our concern is with the implications of

death for the individual who must die. Our questions have to do with an understanding of the existential status of a person after death. It may be that, by paying closer attention to our philosophical interests, we might be able to formulate a working definition of death based upon these interests.

The mysteries of death, from the point of view of the philosopher, [32] have to do with what happens to the mind. Philosophers have tended to divide into three main groups when considering the mind. There are those who insist that the mind is a myth—that the word "mind" really has no referent and therefore does not name anything. Other philosophers have held that the mind is either identical with, or completely a function of, the body—an epiphenomenon accompanying brain processes and totally dependent upon the workings of the brain. Still others believe that it makes sense to speak of the mind as a separate reality—a nonphysical substance which might exist apart from the body. If we simply identify the mind as consciousness, then we can quickly dismiss the first option. There is such a thing as consciousness, and therefore the word "mind" does have a referent. I cannot observe consciousness in other things, nor can I even observe it in myself in the usual sense of that word. But I cannot reasonably deny that I am aware. I do not eyeball my consciousness. But I can perceive it. I *am* my consciousness. It is pointless for me to attempt to convince another that I have a mind. If he does not believe that I am aware, there is little that I can do. Should the reader, with respect to himself, entertain any doubts along this line, he is directed to his own head.

That leaves us with two basic options. If we assume that mind, or [33] consciousness, is real, it would seem that it is either totally dependent upon, or perhaps identical with, the body, or it is not. At this point it really does not matter which of these positions is the correct one. It should be possible to develop a working definition of death which can be compatible with either school of thought. We cannot, at this early stage, commit ourselves to an affirmation or a denial of the possibility of the mind's continuing to exist after death. But it is clear that death entails the absence of mental or conscious expression through the body. Whether or not there is a continuation of awareness apart from the body, the event of death implies that the physical body has lost the capacity to be aware. Perhaps this is because consciousness has disappeared, like a flame which is snuffed out. Or maybe it has gone on to better, or at least other, things. Either way, it is absent from the physical body. And this is really all we need in order to pursue the philosophical questions concerning death. Let us simply define death as the permanent absence of consciousness in a physical body.

[34]   The reader is forgiven if he feels disappointed. Our definition of
death is something short of spectacular. It does not add a new page
to the book of philosophical truth. It is of absolutely no use to the
physician who is still wondering how to tell when his patient is dead.
It is, in fact, subject to exactly the same criticisms we directed at the
various medical definitions of death. But those criticisms were directed
at the definitions as attempts to determine the moment of death, and
that really is not our concern. It is the job of the philosopher not to
determine the moment at which death occurs, but rather to identify
what death, whenever it occurs, *is*. We wish the physician well, but
we have metaphysical bones to pick. And this definition should serve
us adequately. It is, after all, the status of the mind that most concerns
the philosopher. Death is a threat precisely because it forces me to
consider the possibility that the permanent absence of consciousness
in my physical body, whenever it occurs, is equivalent to the permanent
absence of my consciousness in any mode. The nothingness of death
is the extinction of the mind.

[35]   It may occur to the reader that our definition of death as the permanent absence of consciousness in a physical body negates the possibility of recovering from death. It rejects the accuracy of speaking
of a patient "dying" on the operating table and subsequently being
brought back to life, since the absence of consciousness was not permanent. Attention-arresting titles such as "I Died at 10:52 A.M."[7] may
belong to interesting and even insightful articles, but cannot count
as legitimate examples of death. It is not denied that the experiences
of those who have apparently died and then recovered are important.
Such experiences may well prove to be significant in understanding
the metaphysics of death. Perhaps, for example, the only distinction
between the absence of consciousness in a physical body which is in
a dreamless sleep or an extended coma or a momentary heart stoppage,
and death itself, is the adjective "permanent." If this is true, then,
although genuine death has not occurred, these experiences could
very well provide insights into the nature of death.

[36]   It might be objected that our definition could apply to a brick. We
do not normally think of inanimate objects as being dead, but surely
there is a permanent absence of consciousness in the physical body
of a brick. Are we committed to thinking of bricks and stones and
dirt and the like as being dead? I believe the answer is yes. We could
avoid this position by defining death as the permanent withdrawal
of consciousness in a physical body, and there may be nothing wrong
with that. But withdrawal seems to suggest a separable entity which
can be removed from a substance. The mind may well be just such
an entity, but that is an issue we should not settle prematurely. It is
not so odd, either, to attribute death to inanimate objects. The phrase
"dead as a doornail" indicates that we are not so wide of the mark.

What does our definition say about one who is in a prolonged   [37]
coma? The answer is not clear. Two things must be settled before we
can decide whether a person in a coma is dead. First, is there consciousness in the physical body of one in a coma? The comatose
patient is said to be unconscious, but there is not an absence of
consciousness if the patient is experiencing any sort of awareness at
all—even dream awareness. It is difficult, perhaps impossible, to determine whether such an altered state of consciousness is present in
a comatose patient, but if there is any form of awareness, then the
patient is not dead. If there is no consciousness in such a patient,
then we must ask whether this situation is permanent. That determination depends upon an adequate medical definition of the situation.
If there is an irreversible absence of consciousness in a comatose
patient, even if the body is kept functioning, then the patient is dead.
The determination of whether this is the case depends upon the
development of an acceptable medical definition of death.

It is, in fact, a commonsense definition of death that we have   [38]
developed. It is neither daring nor startling nor particularly new. It
simply expresses what most people mean by death without closing
the door to various theories about what happens after death.

In attempting to define death we begin also to understand what   [39]
is meant by life. Life as we know it involves the physical embodiment,
or perhaps expression, of a mind or consciousness. Nonconscious
things are nonliving things. Consciousness may be primitive or advanced, but without it there is no life. The amoeba is alive, and it
would seem reasonable to attribute to the amoeba a certain primitive
form of awareness. Plants are alive. Here the issue appears to be
cloudy, but an ever-increasing body of data suggests a definite form
of awareness in plants. We have experienced life only in a physical
medium. Can there be life after death? We must insist that this may
be possible. If it is possible for the mind to exist without the body,
then life after death is also a possibility. It may not be possible for
the mind to exist apart from a body, but we really do not know that
yet. It is clear now that our definition of life is, quite simply, consciousness. And what could be more reasonable than that?

NOTES

1. This is suggested in an article by Geoffrey Gorer, "The Pornography of Death,"
Encounter, October, 1955, pp. 46–52.

2. J. J. Bruhier-d'Ablaincourt, *Mémoire sur la nécessité d'un réglement général au sujet
des enterrements et des embauments, et projet de réglement*, Paris, 1746. These and other
cases are cited in A. K. Mant's essay, "The Medical Definition of Death," in Arnold
Toynbee, *et al.*, *Man's Concern with Death* (New York: McGraw-Hill, 1968), pp. 12 ff.

3. Ethics in Medical Progress, Ciba Foundation Symposium, Churchill, London,
1966, p. 69. Cited in *Man's Concern with Death*, p. 22.

4. Quoted in Marya Mannes, *Last Rights* (New York: William Morrow, 1974), p. 57.

5. H. Beecher, *The New York Times*, December 10, 1967. Cited in *Man's Concern with Death*, p. 23.

6. This position is taken by R. S. Morison in his essay, "Death: Process or Event?" *Science*, August, 1971, pp. 694–98. L. R. Kass responds to this in the same issue in "Death as an Event: A commentary on Robert Morison," pp. 575–85.

7. Victor D. Solow won a Reader's Digest "First Person" award with an article by this title, printed in *Reader's Digest*, October, 1974, pp. 178–82.

QUESTIONS

1. How did the ancient Greek philosophers Democritus and Epicurus conclude that fear of death was the most "irrational of emotions"?

2. Why does Congdon think that philosophy is better equipped than any other discipline to explore the mystery of death?

3. "Epistemology," a branch of philosphy (from *episteme*, "knowledge," and *:logy*, "the study of"), is the study of how we know what we think we know. In his consideration of death, what methods does Congdon use to study what we *do* know to try to discover what we *do not* know? That is, what methods does he use to "isolate" or define the problems involved in studying death from a philosophical point of view?

4. How is studying death related to studying the "unconscious mind"? What is the "catch 22" involved in both kinds of study?

5. Using Congdon's description of what the philosopher Kant thought was involved in looking at a carrot—i.e., we see not the carrot but the sense-data the image produced by the interaction of the object, carrot, and the subject's retina, nerve, and neurons— closely consider all the steps that are involved in even the most objective scientific observation. For example, imagine that you are a biologist and you are looking through a microscope at a single human cell. What are all the steps involved in that process of looking? Where does the moment of "seeing" take place—under the microscope? at the lens? at the point where the image of the cell is imprinted on the retina? at the moment the "impulse" transmitted by way of the optic nerve, reaches the brain? Now consider, is it really possible to know what an object (e.g. the human cell) *is*? What you have been doing in reasoning this way is called phenomenology; it is also a branch of philosophy.

6. Congdon claims, "We can learn more about ourselves from a consideration of death." What do you think you might learn about yourself by seriously considering your own death? Do you think that it is possible for a normally healthy person really to confront

the fact of her own death? Can she understand her own death as a dying person can? See what Kübler-Ross has to say about this in the reading beginning on page 292.

7. What is the "Verification Principle"? Do other areas besides philosophy use the verification principle? How do verification methods in the "hard sciences" differ from verification in philosophy? Do verification methods differ between philosophy and theoretical physics?

8. What does creating a definition *ex nihilo* mean? Why do we sometimes have to create a definition ex nihilo? When starting from an arbitrary "working definition," do we proceed from the general to the specific (i.e. by using deductive reasoning) or from the specific to the general (i.e. by using inductive reasoning) in the process of verification? Why?

9. Consider the various medical definitions of death. "Brain death" is used in many cases as justification for taking a patient off life-support systems that can artifically prolong life. Nevertheless there are cases—such as that of Karen Quinlan—where the removal of life support has not resulted in the patient's death. Do you believe that brain death is the death of what is "truly human" in us?

10. Congdon finally defines death as "the permanent absence of consciousness in a physical body." Look up the definition of death in a standard dictionary. Compare the dictionary definition, the medical definition which Congdon has given to you, and Congdon's, the philosopher's, definition. What are the differences among them? Are these differences related to the purposes to which the definitions are put?

EXERCISES

1. Part of what you have learned in thinking about death with a philosopher is what some of the problems are in thinking itself. This exercise is designed to make you think about thinking. Isolate for inspection the three following: (a) an object (e.g., an apple, a tree, a stone); (b) a person; (c) an emotion (e.g., anger, love, depression). As you are thinking about each of them, make a list in your journal of the questions you would have to ask yourself in the process of trying to know the object, person, or emotion. Then write a three-paragraph summary on the subject "some problems involved in knowing _____" (one of the three topics).

2. A famous philosopher of the Middle Ages, Boethius, wrote a book called *The Consolation of Philosophy*. Do you think that philosophy as a discipline can offer consolation for death? Write a speculative essay that argues pro or con. Try to use the same method of argument that Congdon uses by (a) defining what the problems are in saying that philosophy consoles, (b) describing the assumptions on which your argument must rest, and (c) testing the validity of your assumptions.

3. This assignment is meant to be developed over the course of your reading in this unit. On the basis of your reading of Congdon and of class discussion, begin a reflective paper in your journal simply entitled "My Thoughts about Death." Try to demonstrate to yourself how Congdon has changed your perception of what death is. Be personal in your speculations. Use examples from your own experience. Do not worry about finishing the paper or even giving it an overall form at this point. Subsequent exercises will ask you to reflect further on the subject and to add to the paper from the perspectives and disciplines of the readings that follow.

_____ CHAPTER SIXTEEN _____

ARIÈS: WESTERN ATTITUDES
TOWARD DEATH

Cultural History

As a cultural historian, Philippe Ariès attempts to trace the history of changes that occur over centuries in the way that a culture understands, or thinks about, certain timeless experiences, such as love, death, or childhood. The materials a cultural historian looks at are the products of a particular culture in particular ages: their paintings, their architecture, their burial customs, or their marriage ceremonies. Using these materials the cultural historian attempts to reconstruct the attitudes of people in past ages. He or she combines the methods of the historian, who looks at and reconstructs the past, with the methods of the archeologist, who uses cultural artifacts to reconstruct the ways in which people lived, and with the methods of the anthropologist, who studies a culture, its customs and products, to determine its unique qualities.

It is important for us to learn from the cultural historian because he or she can tell us how we come to think as we do. As the philosopher Santayana once said, "Those who do not learn from the past are condemned to relive it." We cannot really understand our attitudes toward death, or love, or war unless we have some sense of their sources and evolution. We cannot really understand our attitudes toward death, or toward those who are dying unless we have some sense of how much our *culture* has determined our attitudes. And finally we cannot ever *change* our attitudes toward timeless concepts such as love, work, and death unless we become aware that there are other ways to understand them. We must understand that present

Western attitudes toward any large issue are not the last word. Men and women in other times, who thought differently, had valid observations to make which we can use to forge our attitudes on crucial issues.

GLOSSARY

chansons de geste [1]

pious [5]

venerable [5]

premonition [6]

anachronism [6]

spontaneous [6]

coquettish [6]

ritual [10]

funerary statues [12]

defunct [12]

liturgists [13]

discreet [14]

lamentation [15]

penitent [16]

absolution [17]

ecclesiastic [17]

unction [18]

protocol [21]

millennia [25]

inert [25]

vulgate [27]

astrological [28]

macabre [30]

resurrection [31]

eschatology [31]

tympana [32]

iconography [32]

Dies irae [33]

cosmic [34]

fresco [34]

artes moriendi [37]

mendicant [46]

solemnity [47]

Counter Reformation [49]

mutation [57]

Epicurianism [58]

morbid [60]

mystic [60]

paroxysm [61]   interdict [79]

omnipresent [63]   eroticism [79]

curative [69]   furtively [88]

archaic [69]   impugned [89]

panoply [75]   inverse [91]

WESTERN ATTITUDES
_____ TOWARD DEATH _____
Philippe Ariès

TAMED DEATH

. . . We shall begin with tamed death. Let us first see how the knights [1]
in the *chansons de geste* or the oldest romances faced death.

First of all, they were usually forewarned. They did not die without [2]
having had time to realize that they were going to die. If their deaths
were terrible ones, such as by the plague, or abrupt, they had to be
presented as the exception, something one did not talk about. Normally,
then, the man was forewarned.

"Know ye well," said Gawain, "that I shall not live two days."[1] [3]

King Ban had taken a bad fall. When he regained consciousness, [4]
he noticed the crimson blood running from his mouth, his nose, his
ears. "He looked up to heaven and uttered as best he could . . . 'Ah,
Lord God, help me, for I see and I know that my end has come.' "[2]
I see and I know. . . .

Pious monks behaved in the same manner as knights. As Saint [5]
Martin de Tours, in the tenth century, after four years of seclusion,
a venerable hermit "felt," in the words of Raoul Glaber, "that he was
soon going to leave this world." The same author recounts how another
monk with some medical knowledge had to hurry the brothers he
was treating. Time was running out: "He knew that his death was
near."[3]

Let us note that the warning came through natural signs or, even [6]
more frequently, through an inner conviction rather than through a
supernatural, magical premonition. It was something very simple,

SOURCE: From Philippe Ariès, *Western Attitudes toward Death*, The Johns Hopkins University
Press, Baltimore, 1974. Reprinted by permission of the publisher.

something prevailing throughout the ages, something which persists even today as an <u>anachronism</u> within industrialized societies. A sort of spontaneous realization, it was foreign both to the cults of the miraculous and to Christian piety. There was no way of cheating, of pretending one hadn't noticed. In 1491, in the midst of the humanist Renaissance which we have the bad habit of contrasting with the Middle Ages—in any event in an urbanized world far different from that of Roland or Tristram—a *juvencula*, a very young girl, pretty, coquettish, loving life and pleasures, was taken ill. Would she, with the complicity of her intimate friends, cling to life by acting, by pretending that she did not realize the seriousness of her ailment? No. She did, however, rebel; but this rebellion did not take the form of a refusal of death. "*Cum cerneret, infelix juvencula, de proxima situ imminere mortem.*" *Cum cerneret*: She saw, the wretched girl, her approaching death. Then, despairing, she offered her soul to the devil.[4]

[7]   In the seventeenth century, mad though he was, Don Quixote made no attempt to flee from death into the daydreams in which he had passed his life. On the contrary, the warning signs of death brought him back to his senses: " 'Niece,' he said very calmly, 'I feel that death is near.' "[5]

[8]   Saint-Simon said that Madame de Montespan was afraid of death. Actually, she was afraid of not having a forewarning and also (and we shall return to this point) of dying alone. "She would go to bed with all her bed curtains open and a great number of candles in her room, and women watching about her whom, whenever she awoke, she expected to find chatting, playing games, or eating to prevent themselves from falling asleep." But despite her anguish, on May 27, 1707, she too knew that she was going to die and made ready.[6] On July 29, 1750, the day of Johann Sebastian Bach's death, Anna Magdalena Bach used the same phrase: ". . . feeling his end approach."[7]

[9]   The same words are passed on from age to age, unchanged, like a proverb. We find them in Tolstoy in a period in which their simplicity had already become blurred. But Tolstoy's genius lies in having rediscovered them. On his deathbed in a rural railroad station, Tolstoy murmured: "And the mujiks? How do the mujiks die?" The mujiks died like Roland, Tristram, or Johann Sebastian Bach. They knew what was happening. In Tolstoy's "Three Deaths" an old coachman lies dying in the kitchen of an inn, near the warm brick oven. He knows it. When a woman asks him kindly how he feels, he replies, "It hurts me all over. My death is at hand, that's what it is."[8] . . .

[10]   Knowing that his end was near, the dying person prepared for death. And everything would be done very simply, as with the Pougets or Tolstoy's mujiks. In a world as steeped in the supernatural as that

of the Round Table, death was a very simple thing. When Launcelot, wounded and dazed in a deserted forest, realized that he had "lost even the strength of his body," he believed he was about to die.[9] So what did he do? His gestures were fixed by old customs, ritual gestures which must be carried out when one is about to die. He removed his weapons and lay down quietly upon the ground, though as last wills and testaments would state over several centuries, he should have been in bed—"*Gisant au lit malade*," lying on my sickbed. He spread his arms out, his body forming a cross—which, too, was not the usual procedure. But he remembered to lie in such a way that his head faced east, toward Jerusalem.

When Iseult found Tristram dead, she knew that she too would die. So she lay down beside him and turned toward the east. [11]

At Roncevaux, Archbishop Turpin awaited his death lying down, and "on his breast, in the very middle, crossed his beautiful white hands." This is the posture of funerary statues beginning with the twelfth century; in primitive Christianity the defunct was portrayed with his arms outstretched, in the manner of a worshipper. [12]

One awaited death lying down, *gisant*. This ritual position was stipulated by the thirteenth-century liturgists. "The dying man" according to Guillaume Durand, bishop of Mende, "must lie on his back so that his face is always turned toward heaven." This posture was not the same as that of the Jews; according to descriptions in the Old Testament, the Jews turned to the wall when dying. [13]

Thus prepared, the dying man could carry out the final steps of the traditional ceremony. Take the example of Roland in the *Chanson de Roland*. The first step was to express sorrow over the end of life, a sad but very discreet recollection of beloved beings and things, a summary which was reduced to a few images. Roland "was seized by several things to remember": first, "of so many lands which he, the valiant one, had conquered," then of sweet France, of the men of his lineage, of Charlemagne, his lord who had nurtured him, of his master and his companions (*compains*). No thought for his mother or his fiancée, just sad, moving recollections. "He wept and could not keep himself from sighing." But this emotion was short-lived, as was the subsequent mourning by the survivors. It was a ritual moment. [14]

After the lamentation about the sadness of dying came the pardoning of the always numerous companions and helpers who surrounded the deathbed. Oliver asked Roland forgiveness for any harm he might have unintentionally done him: " 'I pardon you here and before God.' At these words the one bowed to the other." The dying man commended the survivors to God: " 'May God bless Charles and sweet France,' implored Oliver, 'and above all Roland, my companion.' " In the *Chanson de Roland* the question of a tomb and the selection of its location does not arise. [15]

[16]   Now it was time to forget the world and think of God. The prayer had two parts. The first was the *culpa* ("God, by thy grace I admit my guilt for my sins . . ."), which later developed into the *confiteor*. "Oliver confessed his sins aloud, his two hands joined and lifted toward heaven, and begged God to grant him paradise." This was the gesture of the <u>penitent</u>. The second part of the prayer was the *commendacio animae*, a paraphrase of a very old prayer borrowed from the Jewish synagogue. In the French of the sixteenth to eighteenth centuries, these prayers were called the *recommandaces*. "True Father, who never lies, who recalled Lazarus from the dead, who saved Daniel from the lions, save my soul from all peril. . . ."

[17]   At this point came <u>absolution</u>, indisputably the sole religious, or rather <u>ecclesiastic</u> (for everything was religious) act. It was granted by the priest, who read psalms, the *libera*, burned incense over the dying man, and sprinkled him with holy water. This absolution was also repeated over the dead body, at the moment of its burial, at which time it was called the *absoute*. . . .

[18]   Later, in the Romances of the Round Table, the dying received the *Corpus Christi*. Extreme <u>unction</u> was reserved for clerics, especially monks.

[19]   After the final prayer all that remained was the wait for death, and there was no reason for death to tarry. Thus Oliver's "heart fails him, his entire body sinks upon the ground. The Count is dead; he lingers no longer." Should death happen to come more slowly, the dying man waited in silence: "He said [his last prayer] and never again uttered a word."[10]

[20]   Let us stop here and make a few general observations. The first—death in bed, the recumbent figure "lying on its sickbed"—has already been sufficiently set forth.

[21]   The second is that death was a ritual organized by the dying person himself, who presided over it and knew its <u>protocol</u>. Should he forget or cheat, it was up to those present, the doctor or the priest, to recall him to a routine which was both Christian and customary.

[22]   It was also a public ceremony. The dying man's bedchamber became a public place to be entered freely. At the end of the eighteenth century, doctors who were discovering the first principles of hygiene complained about the overcrowded bedrooms of the dying.[11] In the early nineteenth century, passers-by who met the priest bearing the last sacrament still formed a little procession and accompanied him into the sickroom.[12]

[23]   It was essential that parents, friends, and neighbors be present. Children were brought in; until the eighteenth century no portrayal of a deathbed scene failed to include children. And to think of how

carefully people today keep children away from anything having to do with death!

A final point, and the most important one, is the simplicity with [24] which the rituals of dying were accepted and carried out—in a ceremonial manner, yes, but with no theatrics, with no great show of emotion.

The best analysis of this attitude is found in Alexander Solzhenitsyn's [25] *The Cancer Ward*. Yefrem thought he knew more about death than the old folk. "The old folk, who never even made it to town, they were scared, while Yefrem rode horses and fired pistols at thirteen. . . . But now . . . he remembered how the old folk used to die back home on the Kama—Russians, Tartars, Votyaks, or whatever they were. They didn't puff themselves up or fight against it and brag that they weren't going to die—they took death *calmly* [author's italics]. They didn't stall squaring things away, they prepared themselves quietly and in good time, deciding who should have the mare, who the foal. . . . And they departed easily, as if they were just moving into a new house."[13]

It could not be better expressed. People had been dying like that [26] for centuries or <u>millennia</u>. In a world of change the traditional attitude toward death appears <u>inert</u> and static. The old attitude in which death was both familiar and near, evoking no great fear or awe, offers too marked a contrast to ours, where death is so frightful that we dare not utter its name. This is why I have called this household sort of death "tamed death." I do not mean that death had once been wild and that it had ceased to be so. I mean, on the contrary, that today it has become wild. . . .

ONE'S OWN DEATH

We have seen how Western civilization had adopted a sort of <u>vulgate</u> [27] of death. . . . [This] vulgate was not abandoned or blotted out, but instead was partially altered during the second Middle Ages, that is to say beginning with the eleventh and twelfth centuries. I want to stress from the outset that this was not a matter of a new attitude which took the place of the preceding one, which we have just analyzed; but rather subtle modifications gradually gave a dramatic and personal meaning to man's traditional familiarity with death.

In order to understand properly these phenomena we must keep [28] in mind the fact that this traditional familiarity implied a collective notion of destiny. Men of that period were profoundly and rapidly socialized. The family did not intervene to delay the socialization of the child. Moreover, socialization did not separate man from nature, with which he could not interfere short of a miracle. Familiarity with death is a form of acceptance of the order of nature, an acceptance which can be both naive, in day-to-day affairs, and learned, in astrological speculations.

[29]   In death man encountered one of the great laws of the species, and he had no thought of escaping it or glorifying it. He merely accepted it with just the proper amount of solemnity due one of the important thresholds which each generation always had to cross.

[30]   This brings us to an analysis of a series of new phenomena which introduced the concern for the individuality of each person into the old idea of the collective destiny of the species. The phenomena we have selected are (1) the portrayal of the Last Judgment at the end of the world; (2) the displacing of this judgment to the end of each life, to the precise moment of death; (3) macabre themes and the interest shown in portrayals of physical decomposition; and (4) the return to funeral inscriptions and to a certain personalization of tombs.

THE PORTRAYAL OF THE LAST JUDGMENT

[31]   In about 680 Bishop Agilbert was buried in the funeral chapel which he had had constructed adjacent to the monastery of Jouarre (Seine-et-Marne), to which he had retired and where he died. His tomb is still standing. What do we find there? On a small panel is the Christ in Majesty surrounded by the four Evangelists. This is the image inspired by the Apocalypse, of Christ returning at the end of the world. On the large panel adjoining it we find the resurrection of the dead on the last day. The elect, their arms upraised, acclaim the returning Christ, who holds in his hands a scroll, no doubt the Book of Life.[14] No judgment or condemnation is in evidence. This image is in keeping with the general eschatology of the early centuries of Christendom. The dead who belonged to the Church and who had entrusted their bodies to its care (that is to say to the care of the saints), went to sleep like the seven sleepers of Ephesus (*pausantes, in somno pacis*) and were at rest (*requiescant*) until the day of the Second Coming, of the great return, when they would awaken in the heavenly Jerusalem, in other words in Paradise. There was no place for individual responsibility, for a counting of good and bad deeds. The wicked, that is to say those who were not members of the Church, would doubtlessly not live after their death; they would not awaken and would be abandoned to a state of nonexistence. An entire quasi-biological population, the saintly population, thus would be granted a glorious afterlife following a long, expectant sleep.

[32]   But in the twelfth century the scene changed. In the sculptured tympana of the romanesque churches of Beaulieu or Conques the apocalyptic vision of the Majesty of Christ still predominates. But

this time by the book of Matthew: the resurrection of the dead, the separation of the just and the damned, the Last Judgment (at Conques, Christ's halo bears the word *Judex*), and the weighing of souls by the archangel Michael.[15]

In the thirteenth century[16] the apocalyptic inspiration and the evo- [33] cation of the Second Coming were almost blotted out. The idea of the judgment won out and the scene became a court of justice. Christ is shown seated upon the judgment throne surrounded by his court (the apostles). Two acts had become increasingly important: the weighing of souls and the intercession of the Virgin and St. John, who kneel, their hands clasped, on either side of Christ the Judge. Each man is to be judged according to the balance sheet of his life. Good and bad deeds are scrupulously separated and placed on the appropriate side of the scales. Moreover, these deeds have been inscribed in a book. In the magnificent strains of the *Dies irae* the Franciscan authors of the thirteenth century portrayed the book being brought before the judge on the last day, a book in which everything is inscribed and on the basis of which everyone will be judged.

> *Liber scriptus proferetur*
> *In quo totum continetur*
> *Unde mundus judicetur.*

This book, the *liber vitae*, must first have been conceived of as a [34] cosmic book, the formidable census of the universe. But at the end of the Middle Ages it became an individual account book. At Albi, in the vast fresco of the Last Judgment dating from the end of the fifteenth or the beginning of the sixteenth century,[17] the risen wear this book about their necks, like a passport, or rather like a bank book to be presented at the gates of eternity. A very curious change has occurred. This "balance" (*balancia*) or balance sheet is closed not at the moment of death but on the *dies illa*, the last day of the world, at the end of time. Here we can see the deep-rooted refusal to link the end of physical being with physical decay. Men of the period believed in an existence after death which did not necessarily continue for infinite eternity, but which provided an extension between death and the end of the world.

Thus, the idea of the Last Judgment is linked with that of the [35] individual biography, but this biography ends on the last day, and not at the hour of death.

IN THE BEDCHAMBER OF THE DYING

The second phenomenon consisted of suppressing the eschatological [36] time between death and the end of the world, and of no longer situating the judgment in space at the Second Coming, but in the bedchamber, around the deathbed.

[37]   This new iconography is to be found in the woodcuts, spread by the new technique of printing, in books which are treatises on the proper manner of dying: the *artes moriendi* of the fifteenth and sixteenth centuries.[18] Nonetheless, this iconography brings us back to the traditional image of the deathbed which we studied in the first chapter.

[38]   The dying man is lying in bed surrounded by his friends and relations. He is in the process of carrying out the rituals which are now familiar to us. But something is happening which disturbs the simplicity of the ceremony and which those present do not see. It is a spectacle reserved for the dying man alone and one which he contemplates with a bit of anxiety and a great deal of indifference. Supernatural beings have invaded his chamber and cluster about the bed of the recumbent figure, the *"gisant."* On one side are the Trinity, the Virgin, and the celestial court; on the other, Satan and a monstrous army of demons. Thus the great gathering which in the twelfth and thirteenth centuries had taken place on the last day, in the fifteenth century had moved to the sickroom.

[39]   How are we to interpret this scene?

[40]   Is it still really a judgment? Properly speaking, no. The scales in which good and evil are weighed no longer play a part. The book is still present, and all too frequently the demon has grabbed it with a triumphant gesture, because the account book and the person's life story are in his favor. But God no longer appears with the attributes of a judge. In the two possible interpretations, interpretations which probably can be superimposed, God is rather the arbiter or the observer.

[41]   The first interpretation is that of a cosmic struggle between the forces of good and evil who are fighting for possession of the dying man, and the dying man himself watches this battle as an impartial witness, though he is the prize. . . .

[42]   Here we must make two important observations.

[43]   The first concerns the juxtaposition of the traditional portrayal of death in bed and that of the individual judgment of each life. Death in bed, as we have seen, was a calming rite which solemnized the necessary passing, the *"trépas,"* and leveled the differences between individuals. No one worried about the fate of one particular dying man. Death would come to him as it did to all men, or rather to all Christians at peace with the Church. It was an essentially collective rite.

[44]   On the other hand, the judgment—even though it took place in a great cosmic activity at the end of the world—was peculiar to each individual, and no one knew his fate until the judge had weighed the souls, heard the pleas of intercessors, and made his decision.

Thus the iconography of the *artes moriendi* joins in a single scene [45] the security of a collective rite and the anxiety of a personal interrogation.

My second observation concerns the increasingly close relationship [46] established between death and the biography of each individual life. It took time for this relationship to gain ascendency. In the fourteenth and fifteenth centuries it became firmly fixed, no doubt under the influence of the mendicant orders. From then on it was thought that each person's entire life flashed before his eyes at the moment of death. It was also believed that his attitude at that moment would give his biography its final meaning, its conclusion.

Thus we understand how the ritual solemnity of the deathbed, [47] which persisted into the nineteenth century, by the end of the Middle Ages had assumed among the educated classes a dramatic character, an emotional burden which it had previously lacked.

We must, however, note that this evolution strengthened the role [48] played by the dying man himself in the ceremonies surrounding his own death. He was still at the center of activity, presiding over the event as in the past, and determining the ritual as he saw fit.

These ideas were bound to change in the seventeenth and eighteenth [49] centuries. Under the influence of the Counter Reformation, spiritual writers struggled against the popular belief that it was not necessary to take such pains to live virtuously, since a good death redeemed everything. However, they continued to acknowledge that there was a moral importance in the way the dying man behaved and in the circumstances surrounding his death. It was not until the twentieth century that this deeply rooted belief was cast off, at least in industrialized societies.

. . . Historians have been struck by the appearance of the cadaver [50] and the mummy in iconography. The great Huizinga saw it as a proof of his thesis about the moral crisis during the "waning of the Middle Ages." Today Tenenti sees instead in this horror of death the sign of the love of life (*"la vie pleine"*) and of the overthrow of the Christian scheme of life. My interpretation would be in the direction of Tenenti's.

Before proceeding further, we must point out a significant omission [51] in last wills and testaments of this period. Testators of the fifteenth century referred to their *charogne*, their "carrion," but the word disappeared in the sixteenth century. Nevertheless, in general the death portrayed in wills was related to the peaceful conception of death in bed. The horror of physical death, of which the cadaver could be considered a sign, was completely absent, which leads us to assume that it was also absent from the common mentality.

On the other hand, and this is a very important observation, the [52] horror of physical death and of decomposition is a familiar theme in fifteenth- and sixteenth-century poetry. *"Sac à fiens"* (*fientes*), "bag of droppings," said P. de Nesson (1383–1442).

> O carrion, who art no longer man,
> Who will hence keep thee company?
> Whatever issues from thy liquors,
> Worms engendered by the stench
> Of thy vile carrion flesh.[19]

[53]   . . . Decomposition is the sign of man's failure, and that is undoubtedly the underlying meaning of the macabre, which turns this failure into a new and original phenomenon.

[54]   In order better to understand this phenomenon, we must cast aside the contemporary notion of failure which is, alas, very familiar to us in today's industrialized societies.

[55]   Today the adult experiences sooner or later—and increasingly it is sooner—the feeling that he has failed, that his adult life has failed to achieve any of the promises of his adolescence. This feeling is at the basis of the climate of depression which is spreading throughout the leisured classes of industrialized societies.

[56]   This feeling was completely foreign to the mentalities of traditional societies, those in which one died like Roland or Tolstoy's peasants. But it was no longer foreign to the rich, powerful, or learned man of the late Middle Ages. . . .

[57]   The study of tombs confirms what we have learned from the Last Judgment, the *artes moriendi*, and the macabre themes: Beginning with the eleventh century a formerly unknown relationship developed between the death of each individual and his awareness of being an individual. Today it is agreed that between the year 1000 and the middle of the thirteenth century "a very important historical mutation occurred," as a contemporary medievalist, Pacault, expressed it. "The manner in which men applied their thoughts to their surroundings and to their concerns underwent a profound transformation, while the mental processes—the manner of reasoning, of perceiving concrete or abstract realities, and of conceiving ideas—evolved radically."[20]

[58]   Here we can grasp this change in the mirror of death or, in the words of the old authors, in the *speculum mortis*. In the mirror of his own death each man would discover the secret of his individuality. And this relationship—which Greco-Roman Antiquity, and especially Epicurianism, had glimpsed briefly and had then lost—has from that time on never ceased to make an impression on our Western civilization. With little difficulty the man of traditional societies, the man of the first Middle Ages which we studied in our preceding lecture, became

resigned to the idea that we are all mortal. Since the High Middle Ages Western man has come to see himself in his own death: he has discovered *la mort de soi*, one's own death.

THY DEATH

Thus far we have illustrated two attitudes toward death. The first, [59] the oldest, the longest held, and the most common one, is the familiar resignation to the collective destiny of the species and can be summarized by the phrase, *Et moriemur*, and we shall all die. The second, which appeared in the twelfth century, reveals the importance given throughout the entire modern period to the self, to one's own existence, and can be expressed by another phrase, *la mort de soi*, one's own death. . . .

From the sixteenth to the eighteenth centuries, countless scenes or [60] motifs in art and in literature associate death with love, Thanatos with Eros. These are erotico-macabre themes, or simply morbid ones, which reveal extreme complaisance before the spectacles of death, suffering, and torture. Athletic, nude executioners strip the skin from St. Bartholomew. When Bernini portrayed the mystic union of St. Theresa of Avila with God, he juxtaposed the images of the death agony and the orgasmic trance. . . .

Like the sexual act, death was henceforth increasingly thought of [61] as a transgression which tears man from his daily life, from rational society, from his monotonous work, in order to make him undergo a paroxysm, plunging him into an irrational, violent, and beautiful world. Like the sexual act death for the Marquis de Sade is a break, a rupture. This idea of rupture is something completely new. Until this point the stress had been on the familiarity with death and with the dead. This familiarity had not been affected, even for the rich and the mighty, by the upsurge of individualism beginning in the twelfth century. Death had become a more important event; more thought had to be given to it. But it had become neither frightening nor obsessive. It had remained familiar and tamed.

But from now on it would be thought of as a *break*.[21] [62]

FORBIDDEN DEATH

During the long period we have covered, from the High Middle Ages [63] until the mid-nineteenth century, the attitude toward death changed, but so slowly that contemporaries did not even notice. In our day, in approximately a third of a century, we have witnessed a brutal revolution in traditional ideas and feelings, a revolution so brutal that social observers have not failed to be struck by it. It is really an absolutely unheard-of phenomenon. Death, so omnipresent in the past that it was familiar, would be effaced, would disappear. It would become shameful and forbidden.[22]

[64]   This revolution occurred in a well defined cultural area, where in the nineteenth century the cult of the dead and of cemeteries did not experience the great development noted in France, Italy, and Spain. It even seems that this revolution began in the United States and spread to England, to the Netherlands, to industrialized Europe; and we can see it today, before our very eyes, reaching France and leaving oil smudges wherever the wave passes.

[65]   At its beginning doubtlessly lies a sentiment already expressed during the second half of the nineteenth century: those surrounding the dying person had a tendency to spare him and to hide from him the gravity of his condition. Yet they admitted that this dissimulation could not last too long, except in such extraordinary cases as those described by Mark Twain in 1902 in "Was it Heaven or Hell?" The dying person must one day know, but the relatives no longer had the cruel courage to tell the truth themselves.

[66]   In short, at this point the truth was beginning to be challenged.

[67]   The first motivation for the lie was the desire to spare the sick person, to assume the burden of his ordeal. But this sentiment, whose origin we know (the intolerance of another's death and the confidence shown by the dying person in those about him) very rapidly was covered over by a different sentiment, a new sentiment characteristic of modernity: one must avoid—no longer for the sake of the dying person, but for society's sake, for the sake of those close to the dying person—the disturbance and the overly strong and unbearable emotion caused by the ugliness of dying and by the very presence of death in the midst of a happy life, for it is henceforth given that life is always happy or should always seem to be so. Nothing had yet changed in the rituals of death, which were preserved at least in appearance, and no one had yet had the idea of changing them. But people had already begun to empty them of their dramatic impact; the procedure of hushing-up had begun. This is very noticeable in Tolstoy's stories about death.

[68]   Between 1930 and 1950 the evolution accelerated markedly. This was due to an important physical phenomenon: the displacement of the site of death. One no longer died at home in the bosom of one's family, but in the hospital, alone.

[69]   One dies in the hospital because the hospital has become the place to receive care which can no longer be given at home. Previously the hospital had been a shelter for the poor, for pilgrims; then it became a medical center where people were healed, where one struggled against death. It still has that curative function, but people are also

beginning to consider a certain type of hospital as the designated spot for dying. One dies in the hospital because the doctor did not succeed in healing. One no longer goes to or will go to the hospital to be healed, but for the specific purpose of dying. American sociologists have observed that there are today two types of seriously ill persons to be found in hospitals.[23] The most archaic are recent immigrants who are still attached to the traditions of death, who try to snatch the dying person from the hospital so he can die at home, *more majorum*; the others are those more involved in modernity who come to die in the hospital because it has become inconvenient to die at home.

Death in the hospital is no longer the occasion of a ritual ceremony, over which the dying person presides amidst his assembled relatives and friends. Death is a technical phenomenon obtained by a cessation of care, a cessation determined in a more or less avowed way by a decision of the doctor and the hospital team. Indeed, in the majority of cases the dying person has already lost consciousness. Death has been dissected, cut to bits by a series of little steps, which finally makes it impossible to know which step was the real death, the one in which consciousness was lost, or the one in which breathing stopped. All these little silent deaths have replaced and erased the great dramatic act of death, and no one any longer has the strength or patience to wait over a period of weeks for a moment which has lost a part of its meaning. [70]

From the end of the eighteenth century we had been impressed by a sentimental landslide which was causing the initiative to pass from the dying man himself to his family—a family in which henceforth he would have complete confidence. Today the initiative has passed from the family, as much an outsider as the dying person, to the doctor and the hospital team. They are the masters of death—of the moment as well as of the circumstances of death—and it has been observed that they try to obtain from their patient "an acceptable style of living while dying." The accent has been placed on "acceptable." An acceptable death is a death which can be accepted or tolerated by the survivors. It has its antithesis: "the embarrassingly graceless dying," which embarrasses the survivors because it causes too strong an emotion to burst forth; and emotions must be avoided both in the hospital and everywhere in society. One does not have the right to become emotional other than in private, that is to say, secretly. Here, then, is what has happened to the great death scene, which had changed so little over the centuries, if not the millennia. [71]

The funeral rites have also been modified. Let us put aside for a moment the American case. In England and northwestern Europe, they are trying to reduce to a decent minimum the inevitable operations necessary to dispose of the body. It is above all essential that society— [72]

the neighbors, friends, colleagues, and children—notice to the least possible degree that death has occurred. If a few formalities are maintained, and if a ceremony still marks the departure, it must remain discreet and must avoid emotion. Thus the family reception line for receiving condolences at the end of the funeral service has now been suppressed. The outward manifestations of mourning are repugned and are disappearing. Dark clothes are no longer worn; one no longer dresses differently than on any other day.

[73]   Too evident sorrow does not inspire pity but repugnance, it is the sign of mental instability or of bad manners: it is *morbid*. Within the family circle one also hesitates to let himself go for fear of upsetting the children. One only has the right to cry if no one else can see or hear. Solitary and shameful mourning is the only recourse, like a sort of masturbation. (The comparison is Gorer's.)

[74]   In countries in which the death revolution has been radical, once the dead person has been evacuated, his tomb is no longer visited. In England for example, cremation has become the dominant manner of burial. When cremation occurs, sometimes with dispersal of the ashes, the cause is more than a desire to break with Christian tradition; it is a manifestation of enlightenment, of modernity. The deep motivation is that cremation is the most radical means of getting rid of the body and of forgetting it, of nullifying it, of being "too final." Despite the efforts of cemetery offices, people rarely visit the urns today, though they may still visit gravesides. Cremation excludes a pilgrimage.

[75]   We would be committing an error if we entirely attributed this flight from death to an indifference toward the dead person. In reality the contrary is true. In the old society, the panoply of mourning scarcely concealed a rapid resignation. How many widowers remarried a few short months after the death of their wives! On the contrary, today, where mourning is forbidden, it has been noted that the mortality rate of widows or widowers during the year following the spouse's death is much higher than that of the control group of the same age.

[76]   The point has even been reached at which, according to Gorer's observations, the choking back of sorrow, the forbidding of its public manifestation, the obligation to suffer alone and secretly, has aggravated the trauma stemming from the loss of a dear one. In a family in which sentiment is given an important place and in which premature death is becoming increasingly rare (save in the event of an automobile accident), the death of a near relative is always deeply felt, as it was in the Romantic era.

[77]   A single person is missing for you, and the whole world is empty. But one no longer has the right to say so aloud.

The combination of phenomena which we have just analyzed is [78] nothing other than the imposition of an interdict. What was once required is henceforth forbidden.

The merit of having been the first to define this unwritten law of [79] our civilization goes to the English sociologist, Geoffrey Gorer.[24] He has shown clearly how death has become a taboo and how in the twentieth century it has replaced sex as the principal forbidden subject. Formerly children were told that they were brought by the stork, but they were admitted to the great farewell scene about the bed of the dying person. Today they are initiated in their early years to the physiology of love; but when they no longer see their grandfather and express astonishment, they are told that he is resting in a beautiful garden among the flowers. Such is "The Pornography of Death"— the title of a pioneering article by Gorer, published in 1955—and the more society was liberated from the Victorian constraints concerning sex, the more it rejected things having to do with death. Along with the interdict appears the transgression: the mixture of eroticism and death so sought after from the sixteenth to the eighteenth century reappears in our sadistic literature and in violent death in our daily life.

This establishment of an interdict has profound meaning. It is [80] already difficult to isolate the meaning of the interdict on sex which was precipitated by the Christian confusion between sin and sexuality (though, as in the nineteenth century, this interdict was never imposed). But the interdict on death suddenly follows upon the heels of a very long period—several centuries—in which death was a public spectacle from which no one would have thought of hiding and which was even sought after at times.

The cause of the interdict is at once apparent: the need for hap- [81] piness—the moral duty and the social obligation to contribute to the collective happiness by avoiding any cause for sadness or boredom, by appearing to be always happy, even if in the depths of despair. By showing the least sign of sadness, one sins against happiness, threatens it, and society then risks losing its *raison d'être*. . . .

CONCLUSION

Now let us try, as a sort of conclusion, to understand the general [82] meaning of the changes which we have discerned and analyzed.

First of all, we encountered a very old, very durable, very massive [83] sentiment of familiarity with death, with neither fear nor despair, half-way between passive resignation and mystical trust.

Even more than during the other vigorous periods of existence, [84] Destiny was revealed through death, and in those days the dying person accepted it in a public ceremony whose ritual was fixed by custom. The ceremony of death was then at least as important as the ceremony of the funeral and mourning. Death was the awareness by each person of a *Destiny* in which his own personality was not annihilated but *put to sleep—requies, dormitio.* This *requies* presupposed a survival, though a deadened and weakened one, the grey survival of the shades or *larvae* of paganism, of the ghosts of old and popular Christianity. This belief did not make as great a distinction as we today make between the time before and the time after, the life and the afterlife. The living and the dead in both medieval literature and in popular folk tales show the same simple and vague, yet rather racy natures. On both sides of death, one is still very near the deep wellsprings of sentiment.

[85]   This way of dying signified a surrender of the self to Destiny and an indifference to the too-individual and diverse forms of the personality. It lasted as long as familiarity with death and with the dead lasted, at least until the Romantic era.

[86]   But from the Middle Ages on, among the literati, in the upper classes, it was subtly modified, while retaining its traditional characteristics.

[87]   Death ceased being the forgetting of a self which was vigorous but without ambition; it ceased being the acceptance of an overwhelming Destiny, but one which concealed no novelty. Instead it became a place where the individual traits of each life, of each biography, appeared in the bright light of the clear conscience, a place where everything was weighed, counted, written down, where everything could be changed, lost, or saved. In this second Middle Ages, from the thirteenth to the fifteenth century, in which were laid the bases of what was to become modern civilization, a more personal, more inner feeling about death, about the death of the self, betrayed the violent attachment to the things of life but likewise—and this is the meaning of the macabre iconography of the fourteenth century—it betrayed the bitter feeling of failure, mingled with mortality: *a passion for being, an anxiety at not sufficiently being.*

[88]   In the modern period, death, despite the apparent continuity of themes and ritual, became challenged and was furtively pushed out of the world of familiar things. In the realm of the imagination it became allied with eroticism in order to express the break with the established order. In religion it signified, more than it had in the Middle Ages—which, however, gave birth to this way of thinking—a scorn for the world and an image of the void. In the family—even when they believed in the afterlife, and in a more realistic afterlife, a transposition of life into eternity—death became the unaccepted sep-

aration, the death of the other, "thy death," the death of the loved one.

Thus death gradually assumed another form, both more distant [89] and more dramatic, more full of tension. Death was sometimes exalted (the beautiful death in Lamartine) and soon was impugned (the ugly death of Madame Bovary).

In the nineteenth century death appeared omnipresent: funeral [90] processions, mourning clothes, the spread of cemeteries and of their surface area, visits and pilgrimages to tombs, the cult of memory. But did this pomp not hide the weakening of old familiarities, which alone were really deeply rooted? In any case, this eloquent decor of death toppled in our day, and death has become *unnamable.* Everything henceforth goes on as if neither I nor those who are dear to me are any longer mortal. Technically, we admit that we might die; we take out insurance on our lives to protect our families from poverty. But really, at heart we feel we are nonmortals. And surprise! Our life is not as a result gladdened!

Is there a permanent relationship between one's idea of death and [91] one's idea of oneself? If this is the case, must we take for granted, on the one hand, contemporary man's recoil from the desire to exist, the inverse of what occurred during the second Middle Ages, the thirteenth to fifteenth centuries? And, on the other hand, must we take for granted that it is impossible for our technological cultures ever to regain the naive confidence in Destiny which had for so long been shown by simple men when dying?

NOTES

1. "La mort d'Artus," *Les romans de la Table ronde,* ed. J. Boulenger (abridged ed.; Paris, 1941), p. 443. *Translator's note:* These details are generally not found in Sir Thomas Malory's *Morte d'Arthur;* the author's references to the older French versions of these romances have therefore been used.

2. "Les enfances de Lancelot du Lac," *ibid.,* p. 124.

3. Quoted by G. Duby, *L'an Mil* (Paris, 1967), p. 89.

4. Quoted by A. Tenenti, *Il senso della morte e l'amore della vita nel Rinascimento* (Turin, 1957), p. 170, n. 18.

5. Cervantes, *Don Quixote* (Baltimore: Penguin Books, 1950), Part II, chap. LXXIV, pp. 934–40.

6. Saint-Simon, *Mémoires,* ed. A. de Boislisle (Paris, 1901), Vol. XV, p. 96.

7. A. M. Bach, *The Little Chronicle,* trans. Esther Meynell (London, 1925).

8. L. Tolstoi, "Three Deaths," from "The Death of Ivan Ilyitch, and Other Stories," *Works of Leo N. Tolstoi* (New York, 1899), Vol. XI, p. 81.

9. "La quête du Saint Graal," *La Table ronde,* p. 347.

10. *La chanson de Roland,* chap. CLXVI; Durand de Mende, "Du cimetière . . . ," chap. XXXVIII, XXXIV, *Rationale divinorum officiorum,* ed. C. Barthelemy, Paris, 1854, Vol. IV, chap. 5.

11. "Dès que quelqu'un tombe malade, on ferme la maison, on allume les chandelles et tout le monde s'assemble autour du malade." Enquête médicale organisée par Vicq

d'Azyr, 1774–94. J. P. Peter, "Malades et maladies au 18c siècle," *Annales. Économies, sociétés, civilisations*, 1967, p. 712.

12. P. Craven, *Récit d'une soeur* (Paris, 1867), Vol. II, p. 197. There are numerous portrayals of this scene in the academic paintings of the second half of the nineteenth century.

13. A. Solzhenitsyn, *Cancer Ward* (New York, 1969), pp. 96–97.

14. J. Hubert, *Les cryptes de Jouarre* (IVe Congrès de l'art du haut moyen-âge) (Melun: Imprimerie de la préfecture de Seine-et-Marne, 1952).

15. Tympana of Beaulieu, Conques, Autun.

16. Tympana of the cathedrals of Paris, Bourges, Bordeaux, Amiens, etc.

17. At the rear of the apse.

18. Texts and woodcuts of an *Ars moriendi* reproduced in A. Tenenti, *La vie et la mort à travers le XVe siècle* (Paris, 1952), pp. 97–120.

19. "O charoigne, qui n'es mais hon,/Qui te tenra lors compaignée?/Ce qui istra [sortira] de ta liqueur,/Vers engendrés de la pueur/De ta vile chair encharoignée." Pierre de Nesson, "Vigiles des morts: Paraphrase sur Job," quoted in *Anthologie poétique française, Moyen-Âge*, ed. Garnier (Paris, 1967), Vol. II, p. 184.

20. M. Pacault, "De l'aberration à la logique: essai sur les mutations de quelques structures ecclésiastiques," *Revue historique*, Vol. CCXXXXII (1972), p. 313.

21. G. Bataille, *L'érotisme* (Paris, 1957).

22. P. Ariès, "La mort inversée," *Archives européennes de sociologie*, Vol. VIII (1967), pp. 169–95.

23. B. G. Glasser and A. L. Strauss, *Awareness of Dying* (Chicago, 1965).

24. G. Gorer, *Death, Grief, and Mourning in Contemporary Britain* (New York, 1965), a key work.

QUESTIONS

1. According to Ariès, what is the major difference between medieval and modern attitudes toward death?

2. What are the steps in the process of evolution that Ariès traces from medieval to modern attitudes toward death?

3. What differences does Ariès find from the twelfth century to the seventeenth century, to the nineteenth century, and to the twentieth century in the degree of control the individual has over his or her own way of dying?

4. What difference does Ariès find from the twelfth century, etc., to the twentieth century in the relation between the dying person and his or her family, community, and society?

5. What is the evidence that the cultural historian uses to make a case? Give examples of evidence from painting, literature, sculpture, and architecture?

6. Why is it useful for us to know what the cultural historian has to tell us? What are some other ways we might use Ariès's ideas? For example, can we use them in doing research on the family? or on the relation of the individual to his or her community before and

after the industrial revolution? Can we use Ariès's ideas in any practical way to modify our own attitudes toward death or toward the dying?

7. Do you believe that your own attitudes toward your own death, the death of people you love, or death in general are shaped by your culture? To what extent? Try to determine whether a twentieth-century American's attitudes toward death are most influenced by (a) society's attitudes, (b) the attitudes of his or her ethnic group, (c) the attitudes fostered by the individual's religion or lack of a religion, (d) the attitudes and values of his or her immediate family.

8. What indications do you have that Ariès is particularly sensitive to language? How does he use linguistic evidence and word origins as evidence? How skillfully does he use language as an instrument of expression?

EXERCISES

1. Collect five advertisements from funeral directors (if possible from different religious denominations). Examine the wording of the advertisement, the pictures that accompany it, if any, and the printing type in which it is written. Write a paper in which you use all this information in the way that Ariès uses his evidence to describe current American attitudes toward death.

2. Interview two people from each of three different age groups, (a) children, (b) middle aged, and (c) elderly, in your immediate community or in your extended family. Ask only two questions: (a) Are you afraid of death? and (b) How do you picture the scene of your own death? Record the interviews in your journal. On the basis of the evidence you gather, do a "profile," using the approach of a cultural historian, of how death is conceived in your community.

3. Go to a museum or to the art history section of your college library and try to find paintings, drawings, or woodcuts of dying people in the Victorian period (the latter half of the nineteenth century in England or America). Try to determine from them how much control Victorian people imagined they had over themselves and their immediate environments while they were dying. Write a paper comparing Victorian conceptions of control with current American conceptions.

4. Return to the journal entry that you started in response to Congdon, for further reflection on "My Thoughts about Death." This time

concentrate especially on books, music, art, and/or current events that have added to your understanding of the phenomenon of death. Try writing your journal entry in the style of Ariès by giving attention to particulars gleaned from the sources mentioned. Remember that your "paper" on death is in process. You are writing reflections, not a finished essay.

CHAPTER SEVENTEEN

KÜBLER-ROSS: WHAT IS IT LIKE TO BE DYING?

Psychiatry

We have learned from Philippe Ariès that human beings in all ages have been concerned with death and have pictured their attitudes toward it in various ways. Psychiatry too is concerned with attitudes toward death but from the inside out, so to speak. The psychiatrist must deal in very practical terms with our attitudes toward dying. She or he must "help us die" and must also help those, like the nurses to whom this article is addressed, to deal with the dying in ways that are helpful to them and us.

Some claim that psychiatry is not a science but an art. As you read this paper try to determine why. Elisabeth Kübler-Ross is herself a physician; moreover, the "students" she mentions are medical interns or physicians who are specializing in "thanotherapy," or care of the dying. You will be reading, in the next selections, two views toward death by medical specialists. Try to anticipate these readings by asking yourself how the psychiatric view might differ from the medical.

You will notice that Kübler-Ross approaches her study of dying through interviews with the patients themselves. Before she can help the dying, she must obviously know what feelings they experience in the actual process they are undergoing. The psychiatrist is concerned with human behavior and with the deep-seated emotions that underlie that behavior. You will discover in this account how a psychiatrist approaches the complex and difficult subject of understanding the feelings of the terminally ill toward the process of dying and how, in turn, she uses that understanding toward alleviating the patients' plight.

GLOSSARY

malignant [3]	frustrated [17]
catastrophic [3]	remission [20]
epidemics [4]	ventilate [32]
illusion [7]	impotence [34]
mausoleum [8]	prolongation [35]
euphemisms [11]	decathect [43]
dehumanized [11]	leukemia [47]
verify [12]	comatose [49]
detrimental [13]	dialysis [56]
naive [14]	psychotic [59]

——— WHAT IS IT LIKE TO BE DYING? ———

Elisabeth Kübler-Ross

[1]   What is it like to be dying? Not from the nurse's point of view, nor from the doctor's, nor the family's, but from the patient's point of view: what is it like? Because, if we have some idea of what the answer might be, then we're going to be in a better position to help.

[2]   At the University of Chicago Billings Hospital, some of us have made it our business to find out a little more about what it is like to be dying. Before sharing this information with you, though, let me first raise another question: why—at this time, in this society—must we have so many books on death and dying, so many lectures and seminars on the subject? After all, we should be experts on dying. It is the one thing that has been with mankind as long as man himself. So why has it suddenly become such a big issue?

SOURCE: From the *American Journal of Nursing*, January 1971, pp. 99–111. Copyright © 1971 by the American Journal of Nursing Company. Reprinted by permission of the *American Journal of Nursing*.

Death has always been a fearful thing to men. We have a hard   [3]
time conceiving of our own death. We believe with the psalmist who
says, "A thousand shall fall at thy side, and ten thousand at thy right
hand; *but* it shall not come nigh thee." Deep down, we believe, or
would like to believe, that we are immortal. We cannot conceive of
dying a natural death at the end of our lives, just falling asleep one
night and not waking up. Instead, when we have to conceive death,
we see it as something malignant and catastrophic: a destructive intervention from the outside that hits us suddenly and finds us unprepared.

Death in the old days came in the form of epidemics: produced by   [4]
nature, not by man. Man tried to master epidemics, he mastered
illness, he developed antibiotics and vaccinations, he learned to prolong
life, he was able to master many, many causes of death. But in his
fear of death and his need to master things, he has also developed
weapons. If he has the choice to kill or be killed, he chooses to kill.

In the old days, an enemy in the battlefield could be seen. You had   [5]
a chance to defend your family, your tribe, or your honor; you could
choose a good weapon or a good hill. You had a chance to survive.

But today, out of man's need to be stronger, to defy death, he has   [6]
developed bigger and more horrible weapons. One reason for our
present death-denying society, I believe, is that man has now created
weapons of mass destruction—man-made, mind you, not like nature's
epidemics. He has developed weapons which, in a very concrete way,
represent our fear of death, the catastrophic death that hits us from
the outside when we are not prepared. You can't see, you can't smell,
and you can't hear this enemy, whether it be chemical or bacteriological
warfare, atom bombs, or even pollution.

What do we do when we have created such weapons of mass   [7]
destruction? We cannot defend ourselves physically against them, we
have to defend ourselves psychologically. We can pretend that nobody
will push the wrong button. We can build ourselves bomb shelters
in the garden, or we can build anti-missiles and have the illusion that
we are safe.

But none of these defenses really works. What works partially is   [8]
that we can deny that we are finite. That it shall happen to thee and
thee but not come nigh to me. We can pretend that we are not finite
by developing "deep freeze societies," where we freeze those who
die and put them into some sort of mausoleum and promise the next
of kin to defrost them in 50 or 100 years from now. These societies
really exist; they serve the need to deny that people actually die.

We see this same need and tendency in the hospital. When we are   [9]
assigned to dying patients, we feel very, very uncomfortable. In fact,
even when we know that a patient is dying, we have a hard time

facing that fact and acknowledging it—not in the head but in the gut. And our patients very often die with more difficulty than they used to.

[10]   In the old days, people were more likely to die at home rather than in the hospital. When a person is at home, he's in his own familiar environment, with his family and his children around him. Dying, under these circumstances, is not only easier and more comfortable for the patient, but it also does something for his family—especially the children, who can share in the preparatory grief for a person who is dying in the house. Such a child will grow up and know that death is part of life.

[11]   But if the sick person is shipped off to the hospital, with visits limited to perhaps five minutes every hour in the intensive treatment unit, it is not the same experience. And children are not allowed to see those patients, those parents. In Europe, even now, there is no embalming, no make-believe sleep, no slumber rooms, no euphemisms. All this, I think, helps us to face death as part of life. But today, in the United States, we have a long way to go before we can accept death as part of life. Dying, as many patients have expressed to us, has become not only more lonely and more isolated, but very often more impersonalized, dehumanized, and mechanized.

[12]   Some five years ago, four theology students asked me if I couldn't help them in a project. They had to write a paper on crisis in human life, and they had chosen dying. That's the biggest crisis people have to face, they said, and they asked, "How do you go about it? How do you do research on dying? You can't experience it. You can't experiment with it, you can't verify it, you can't do all the things that one ought to do with a good research project."

[13]   So I suggested to them that it would be very simple to ask dying patients, "What is it like? How does it feel? What fears, needs, fantasies do you have? What kind of things are we doing that are helpful? What kind of things do we do that are detrimental?" The students agreed, and I volunteered to work with them and to find a seriously ill patient for our first interview.

[14]   How naive I was: I discovered that there was not a single dying patient in a 600-bed hospital! I went from ward to ward and told the nurses and the doctors that I would like to talk to a terminally ill patient.

"What about?"

"About dying."

"Oh, we have nobody dying."

[15]   If I pushed, they said, "He's too weak" or "too sick" or "too tired" or "he doesn't feel like talking." A lot of not only denial and rationalization but also hostility and some very aggressive behavior emerged. One nurse asked me, "Do you enjoy playing God?" and another:

"Do you get a kick out of telling a 20-year-old that he has one week to live?" And, of course, there was much well-meant protectiveness for the patients.

I had had the same experience a few years earlier in another hospital. There, the only way I was able to find a dying patient was to go through the wards and look at the patients and guess that somebody was very sick. That way I saw an old man who looked very sick and who was reading a paper with a headline, "Old Soldiers Never Die." I asked him if he wasn't afraid to read that, and he said, "Are you one of those doctors who can't talk about it when you can't help us no more?" So I gave him a pat on the back and said, "You're the right kind of man and I want to talk with you." [16]

Eventually, though, we started to receive an ever-increasing number of referrals. Our first patient was perhaps the most troubling one— to me, anyway. I went to see this old man the day before I was to see him with the students. He put his arms out and with pleading eyes said, "Please sit down *now*." With the emphasis on *now*. But I did what we always do. I could only hear my own needs, I was frustrated and tired of running around, and tomorrow was the day I was supposed to see him with the students. So I told him "No, I can't stay now, I'll be back tomorrow," and I left. [17]

When I came back with the students the next day, it was too late. He was in oxygen, he could hardly breathe, and the only thing he was able to say was, "Thank you for trying, anyway." And he died a short time later. He helped us a lot, however, although not in any verbal way. What he told us was that when a terminally ill patient says, "Sit down *now*," you have to sit down *now*. Because somehow these patients sense that *now* is the time that they can talk about it. There may not be such a time again, so even if you can sit down only two or three minutes, you will feel better, and so will the patient. [18]

The students and I had so many feelings when we left that man's room that we did something that we have continued to do for almost five years now: we went to my office and shared our gut reactions. Not nice things. Not the kinds of things that one ought to say and feel: those come from your head. But how does it feel in the gut? That's what we talk about. We try to get to know each other's feelings— to understand them, not to judge them. We try to help each other express them so that we can learn to listen to our gut reaction and to differentiate between the patient's needs and our own. [19]

So far, we have interviewed over 400 terminally ill patients. By "terminally ill," I mean patients with a serious illness which may end fatally. They don't necessarily die the next day or the next week. Many of them have gone home or have had a remission. Some have lived only 12 hours, and others have lived for a year or two. [20]

[21]   What have we learned from them? We have learned that our patients all know when they are dying, and I think that's consoling for us to know. Half of them have never been told that they have a serious illness. We are often asked what or whether a patient should be told. Actually, I don't think any patient should be told that he is dying. He will tell *you* that when you dare to listen, when you are able to hear it.

[22]   But patients should, I think, with very few exceptions, be told when they have a serious illness. Our patients say that they would like to be told this under two conditions: one is that the person telling them allows for some hope, and the second is that "you are going to stick it out with me—not desert me—not leave me alone." If we can, indeed, "stick it out" with them, then I think that we can help them the most.

[23]   We have learned, too, that dying patients generally go through a series of stages. The stages don't always follow one another; they overlap sometimes and sometimes they go back and forth.

[24]   Most patients, when told they have a serious illness, react with shock and denial. "No, it can't be me. It's not possible." Only three of our 400, however, maintained this denial to the very end, although many have maintained denial in the presence of other people—usually family or staff members—who need denial themselves. If a family needs denial, the patient will not talk to them about the seriousness of his illness or how he feels. But if they, or we, can tell him that we are ready to talk about it, that we are willing to listen, he will drop the denial quite quickly and will talk about his situation.

[25]   Our patients usually drop part of their denial when they have to take care of unfinished business or financial matters, especially when they begin to worry about their children. But they also drop their denial if they know that the person with them will help them to express the multitude of feelings that emerge when they face the given reality.

[26]   Perhaps the second most important and common response is anger. When a person can no longer say, "No, not me," the next question is usually "Why me?" The patient should be allowed to express this, and you don't have to have an answer because none of us will ever have an answer to that question. Just listen.

[27]   At this stage these patients will be very difficult: not only with the family (they visit too early or too late or with too many people or not enough people), but also with the nurses. You come in and shake a pillow and the patient complains, "Why are you bothering me now? I just want to take a nap." When you leave him alone, he protests that you don't straighten out his bed. The physician doesn't have the right prescriptions or the right diet or the right tests. In short, these are extremely "difficult and ungrateful" patients.

What do you do when you have a patient like that? What is your [28]
gut reaction? Remember, the harder you try, the harder the time he
gives you. What do you do? You withdraw, you get angry at him,
maybe you wait twice as long until you answer his light.

In one study, they measured the time it took nurses to answer [29]
patients' lights. And they discovered that patients who were beyond
medical help—terminally ill patients—had to wait twice as long as
the others.

That, too, you have to try to understand and not judge. It is very [30]
hard to be around patients like this for very long, especially if you
try to do your best and all you get is criticism and abuse. What we
have found to be most helpful to the patients and ourselves is not to
get angry back at them or take their abuse personally (which we
normally do) but to try to find out what they are so angry about.

We asked our patients about this. What came out was that the [31]
peppier, the more energetic, the more functioning you are when you
come into that room, the more anger you often provoke. And the
patient says angrily to you, "*You* can walk out of here again, you
know. *You* can go home again at five and see your kids. *You* can go
to work." They're not angry at you as a person, but at what you
represent—life, functioning, pep, energy, all the things they are in
the process of losing or have already partially lost.

We tried to see if it would help if we poured fuel on the fire, if we [32]
let them <u>ventilate</u>, let them express their anger. If we can say to them,
"You know, I would be angry, too. Get it off your chest. Scream if
you feel like screaming," then they will express their rage and anger,
but it never comes out as loud and frightening as you might think.

The best example is the mother of a small child who died. She [33]
looked very numb, so I said to her. "You look as though you need
to scream." And she said, "Do you have a screaming room at the
hospital?" She was serious. I said, "No, but we have a chapel," which
was a silly answer because she immediately replied, "I need just the
opposite. I need to scream and rage and curse. I've just been sitting
in the parking lot and cursing and screaming at God. 'God, why do
you let this happen to my child? Why do you let this happen to me?' "
And I said, "Do it here. It's better to do it *with* somebody than out
in a parking lot all alone."

And that's what I mean by the stage of anger, of rage, of a sense [34]
of <u>impotence</u>, of helplessness. You can help not only the patient to
<u>express this</u> rage and anger, but the family, too, because they go
through the same stages. And, from a practical point of view, the
nursing staff will be saved many, many steps. The nurse will be called
less, the patient will be more comfortable.

Sometimes the patient gets to this point—loses his anger—without [35]
any external help, and you wonder what happened. Very often it is

because he has entered the state of bargaining. Most bargaining is done with God. "If you give me one more year to live, I will be a good Christian or I will donate my kidney or this or that." Most of the time it is a promise, in exchange for some prolongation of life.

[36]   We had one patient who depended on injections around the clock to control her terrible pain. She was one of our most difficult patients, and it became very hard to keep on visiting her. Then one day she was very friendly and she said, "You know, if you help me get out of this hospital for one single day, I will be a good patient." She wanted that one day to get up and get dressed and attend her son's wedding. This was finally possible, and she left, looking like a million dollars.

[37]   And we began to wonder, "What is it like? How must it feel to ask only for one single day? It must be terribly difficult to come back to the hospital."

[38]   When she returned, she wasn't happy to see me. Before I could ask a single question she said, "Dr. Ross, don't forget I have another son." That's the briefest, quickest example of the bargaining stage I know.

[39]   In the denial stage it's "No, not me!" In the anger, "Why me?" In the bargaining, "Yes, me, but. . . ." When the patient finally drops the "but," then it's "Yes, me." And "Yes, me" means that he has the courage to acknowledge that it has indeed "come nigh" to him, and he is naturally very depressed.

[40]   After a while, these patients become silent. It's a kind of grief which is difficult for us to accept—where they don't talk much any more, where they don't want any more visitors. How do we react to them when we come into their rooms and find them crying or silently mourning? What do we do? Can we tolerate this?

[41]   This is sometimes even more difficult to bear than the angry patients. As long as they complain about all the things they have lost, it's something we can grasp. But when they become quiet and the tears are running down—and especially if it's a man—then it's very hard. We have a tendency to say, "What a beautiful day outside. Look at those lovely flowers. Cheer up. It's not so bad."

[42]   It *is* bad. If I were to lose one beloved person, everybody would allow—even expect—me to grieve. It would be perfectly normal because I would have lost one person I loved. But the dying patient is about to lose not just one beloved person but everyone he has ever loved and everything that has been meaningful to him. That is a thousand times sadder. If the patient has the courage to face this, then he should be allowed to grieve; he has a right to it.

[43]   We call this the preparatory grief. If he can prepare himself slowly, if he is allowed to grieve and, if necessary, to cry, then he becomes able to decathect, to separate himself. He will have the courage to

ask for no more relatives to come after a while, no more children. And at the very end he will want perhaps only one loved person— someone who can sit silently and comfortably by his side, without words, but just touching his hand or perhaps stroking his hair or just being there.

That's when a patient has reached the stage of acceptance. And [44] acceptance is not resignation! Resignation is a bitter kind of giving up ("What's the use?"), almost a defeat. But acceptance is a good feeling. "I have now finished all of my unfinished business. I have said all of the words that have to be said. I am ready to go."

These patients are not happy, but they are not terribly sad. They [45] usually have very little physical pain and discomfort, and they slip into a stage which very often reminds us of the beginning of life: when a person has physical needs and needs only one person to give him some tender, loving care and compassion—who can be with him but doesn't have to talk all the time. It's the comfort of being together that counts.

"Do you have to be a psychiatrist to work with these people?" I [46] am often asked. No. Many of our patients are angry when a psychiatric consultation is called because they have dared to become depressed. What I have talked about so far is the normal behavior of a dying patient, and it doesn't take a psychiatrist to help him. It doesn't take much time, either—only a very few minutes.

Last fall, we saw a young man who was the father of three small [47] children. He had never been sick, never been in the hospital before, and now he was admitted with acute leukemia. Every day when I saw him, he was on the verge of talking. He wanted to talk but he couldn't. So he would say, "Come back tomorrow." And I would come back the next day, but he would say again, "Come back tomorrow."

Finally, I said to him, "If you don't want to talk about it, that's [48] alright." He quickly responded: "No, if I don't do it now, I'll never be able to do it. Why don't you come back tomorrow morning very early, before rounds, before anybody else comes? I have to get it out." (We never talked, by the way, about what "it" meant, but both of us knew.)

The next day I came very early and the nurses told me that this [49] patient had been dying during the night, that he had put up a physical fight for about three and a half hours, that he was really not in a condition to talk. But when I promise a patient I will see him, I keep that promise even if he is comatose or not in a position to communicate. So I went to his room and, to my surprise, he almost sat up in his bed. "Come on in," he said; "close the door and sit down." And he talked as he had never talked before.

He said, "I have to tell you what happened last night, you will [50] never believe it." (I'm using his own words because I want to show you what we mean about talking about dying. Patients do not always use the word "dying" but you can talk about dying in many languages.)

[51]   "Last night," he continued, "I put up a fight for several hours. There was a big train going rapidly down the hill towards the end, and I had a big fight with the train master. I argued and fought with him. And I ordered him to stop this train one tenth of an inch short."

[52]   Then he paused and asked me, "Do you know what I am talking about?" I said, "I guess the train that goes rapidly down toward the end is your life. And you had a big fight with the train master—for just a little bit more time." Then I smiled and added, "You made it." (That's bargaining. He bargained for one tenth of an inch.)

[53]   At that moment his mother came in and I said, "How can I help you with the tenth of an inch?" using his language since I didn't know on what level this mother and son communicated. And he said, "Try to help me convince my mother that she should go home now and bake a loaf of bread and make my favorite vegetable soup; I want to eat that once more." And the mother did go home and he did get his bread and soup—his last solid food. He died about three days later.

[54]   I think this man went through all the stages of dying in this overnight struggle. He tried to maintain his denial as long as possible— and then he dropped it in that one night. The anger, the bargaining and the depression, preceded the final stage of acceptance.

[55]   My last example is a woman whose story illustrates what hope means and how the nature of hope changes from the healthy to the sick to the dying. If we can elicit the patient's hope and support *his* hope, then we can help him the most.

[56]   This woman came to our hospital feeling very sick and weak, and her doctor said that she should go to a specialist in another hospital. So she hoped at that time that it was nothing serious, that it could be treated, that she would get well. After a while she was told that she had a serious kidney disease; then she hoped for treatment that would cure it. Next, she was told her life could be prolonged if she were accepted on a dialysis program for indigent people. This, too, was something for her to hope for—but she was rejected.

[57]   The social worker and the nurses, who were really fond of this woman, could not accept this. It was hard for them to visit her after dialysis had been denied, so they asked us to see her in our death and dying seminar.

[58]   The patient was very relieved when we were frank and told her why we wanted to see her. Many little but unfortunate things had happened to her at the hospital to which she was sent—hurriedly and unprepared—to be considered for dialysis. Confusion and misunderstanding grew until finally, when all the doctors stopped at her

bedside on rounds, she realized that this was the moment of truth.

"A big cloud came over me," she said, "and I had the idea that I [59] had a kidney operation and didn't need those doctors. When I woke up they were gone." In other words, she had a fantasy that she didn't need the doctors to save her life. Considered to be <u>psychotic</u> and hallucinating, she was rejected for dialysis.

We explored a lot of feelings about that, and then we discussed [60] with her what kinds of things we could do now to make whatever time she had left more meaningful or more bearable.

She said, "Don't be so upset. When I die, it will be just like going [61] from this garden to God's garden." But something was really bothering her, she added. She didn't know quite what it was and it was hard to talk about it.

Two days later, I said to her, "You know, there was something [62] that bothered you, and that's what we call unfinished business. What is it?" And she kept saying, "I'm bad, I'm bad, I'm bad. Because what she was really saying was that she had to confess something that she felt guilty about, but she didn't know the origin of this guilt. And we searched like two children who are looking in the dark for something they have lost.

Finally, I gave up and I said, "God only knows why you should [63] be bad," which was a genuine gut reaction on my part. And she looked up and said, "That's it: God. I called on God for help for the last few days. 'God help me. God help me.' And I heard Him say in the back of my mind, 'Why are you calling me now, why didn't you call me when things were all right?' What do you say to that, Dr. Ross?" And my gut reaction was to take off. Why couldn't a priest be here? Or a minister? Or somebody? But not me.

But you can't give a patient like this a phony answer. You have to [64] be you and you have to be honest. So I struggled, and finally I said, "Just imagine that the children are playing outside and the mother is in the house and the little boy falls and hurts his knee. What happens?" And she said, "The mother goes out and helps him back on his feet and consoles him." I said, "OK, and he is all right now. What happens next?" And she said, "The boy goes back to his play and the mother goes back in the house." "He has no use for her now?" I asked, and she said, "No," and I said, "Does the mother resent this terribly?" She looked at me almost angrily and said, "A mother? A mother wouldn't resent that." And I said, "If a mother wouldn't resent that, do you think that our Father would?"

Then the happiest, most beautiful smile came over her face, and [65] she asked me something I'll never forget: "What is your concept of death?" (I felt like saying, "How dare you ask me!" It shall not "come nigh" to me, even after seeing so many dying patients.) So I said something about liking her idea about the garden, but she just shook her head and asked again, "What is your concept of death?" Then I looked at her face and said, "Peace." That was a genuine answer. And she said, "I'm going very peacefully, now, from this garden into the next one."

[66]   This patient taught us how hope can change: from hoping it's nothing serious, then hoping for treatment, then hoping for a prolongation of life. And finally hoping that "If I'm not accepted in this garden, I hope I'll be accepted in the next garden."

[67]   It is the patient's hope that we should support. I had known this woman less than an hour, yet I learned from her. And I think I helped her.

[68]   It didn't take much time. But what it did take, and will always take, is a sense of comfort in the face of death. What all of us have to learn is to accept death as part of life. When we have learned this, then maybe we can help our patients learn it, too.

QUESTIONS

1. Kübler-Ross tells us that "dying patients generally go through a series of stages." What are these stages? Why is it useful to divide the process of dying into stages?
2. Kübler-Ross says that man's mastery of many of the causes of death was accompanied by his development of weapons and that one reason for our present death-denying society is our fear of the weapons we have created. Explain what she means. Is her equation logical? Could it be logically argued instead that it is the conquest of lethal infectious disease, such as cholera and pneumonia, that creates a death-denying society?
3. Kübler-Ross argues (and Ariès implies) that death at home in the good old days was "more comfortable for the patient" and better for the family. What evidence do we have that they are right? Is the evidence Ariès provides trustworthy? Does the idealization that occurs in painting, stories, heroic accounts, and sentimental nineteenth-century songs about dying children make it possible for us to determine what dying was *actually* like in the past?
4. Does the nurse's question to Kübler-Ross—"Do you get a kick out of telling a 20-year old he has one week to live?"—express a reasonable objection to the psychiatrist's method of dealing with the dying? Could this method bring more pain than relief?
5. *Should* all patients be told when they are dying? Is there intrinsic

value in knowing one is about to die? Is the old man who has accepted his dying the same as the twenty-year-old or the child? Does Kübler-Ross advocate disclosure to patients that they are dying? Under what circumstances and why?

6. Kübler-Ross says that all of the 400 patients interviewed knew they were dying. If a very ill person *says* he is dying, is that evidence that he actually believes he is dying? Is the spoken acknowledgment that one is dying clear evidence of acceptance?

7. The case of the woman who had to die because she was not accepted into a dialysis program for indigent people raises the problem that medical ethics committees call "triage," or how to distribute medical goods and services as equitably, economically and efficiently as possible. What are some of the criteria which the director of a hospital, for example, has to take into consideration in determining who should receive treatment? Consider such questions as: Should time on a dialysis machine be given to somebody who is probably terminally ill, or should it be given to a person who has a good chance of recovery? Should ability or willingness to pay for medical services be a factor in who gets them? If funds are limited, should less money be spent on the elderly than on the young?

8. Kübler-Ross addresses these remarks to nurses. Do you think that a nurse should try to emulate Kübler-Ross in dealing with dying patients? Are there *other* attitudes toward death and dying that you would think appropriate for a nurse?

9. Why does Kübler-Ross give us the story of the young man who envisions his death as a rushing train? The equation the young man makes, My death = a rushing train, is a *metaphor*. Why might a psychiatrist be especially interested in the metaphors we use to represent horrifying or indescribable events in our lives? Can you think of other metaphors that might help describe death?

EXERCISES

1. Use Kübler-Ross's anecdotal accounts to make an argument different from, or even antithetical to, her argument. For example, using the stories of the young man who asks the train master for "one more inch," and the woman who lives long enough to attend her son's wedding, make the argument that "acceptance," which Kübler-Ross thinks is good, really undermines the will to live and no doctor or nurse should therefore urge acceptance upon a patient.

2. If you have had experience with a person who was dying, compare

your own observations of the steps toward death with those of Kübler-Ross. Did the person you knew go through the seven steps? Do you think Kübler-Ross's observations are accurate? On the basis of this comparison, write a paper in which you support Kübler-Ross's conclusions or offer a counter-conclusion of your own.

3. Choice of language is an important part of our definitions of, and response to death. Kübler-Ross implies that *euphemisms* are used as a way of talking about death in the United States. What is a euphemism? Make a list of euphemisms commonly used in reference to death. Next to each euphemism write a neutral synonym (use phrases if you cannot find adequate single-word substitutes). After you have collected a substantial list, sort out the euphemisms according to topics related to death (e.g., words referring to funeral practices, grave sites, the process of dying, bereavement). Then write an essay developing your personal view toward the use of euphemisms. Try to answer such questions as the following: (a) Can language aid in denying the reality of death? (b) Is that good or bad? (c) Are there some situations in which the use of euphemisms is more justified than in others (e.g., on bereavement cards as opposed to discussions by hospital staffs)?

_____ CHAPTER EIGHTEEN _____

AD HOC COMMITTEE, HARVARD MEDICAL SCHOOL: A DEFINITION OF IRREVERSIBLE COMA AND VEATCH: DEFINING DEATH ANEW: TECHNICAL AND ETHICAL PROBLEMS

Medical Law and Ethics

In this chapter, we will study the Harvard Medical School's definition of irreversible coma as "a new criterion for death" and a response to that statement by Robert M. Veatch, senior associate at the Institute of Society, Ethics, and the Life Sciences. While the approaches you have thus far considered may be of interest to you intellectually, your understanding of the Harvard Medical School's definition and the public policy issues that grow out of it are quite literally a matter of life and death. You may or may not choose to consider death from a philosophical point of view, but with advances in medical technology being made as rapidly as they are, there is a good chance that you will have to make a decision about medical intervention procedures— such as the use of artificial life-support systems—for yourself or for members of your family. Moreover, as a citizen you inevitably will have to make decisions that will affect the public policy growing out of medical and medical-ethical definitions of death.

To give you an example of how crucial such a decision might be, let us call to your attention Veatch's definition of what is "essentially significant" for determining whether a person is truly alive; i.e., truly human: "a capacity for integrating one's self, including one's body, with the social environment through consciousness which permits interaction with other persons." For example, an incapacity to integrate within the social environment is the criterion which the government of the Soviet Union uses to justify confining political dissidents in mental hospitals. A too narrow definition of what is "truly human" permitted the government of Nazi Germany to destroy "inferior races."

As you read the Harvard Medical School definition keep the selection from Ariès in mind and try to determine what the definition tells us about current American attitudes toward death.

As you read the Veatch article, keep the Congdon discussion in mind and closely examine the philosophical and ethical assumptions that underlie Veatch's argument. Consider also what public policy decisions could grow out of his definitions.

GLOSSARY

HARVARD MEDICAL SCHOOL

ad hoc committee

irreversible [1]

resuscitative [1]

obsolete [1]

central nervous system [2]

soluble [2]

cerebral function [5]

reflexes [8]

elicitable [8]

dilated [8]

ocular movement [8]

decerebrate [8]

abeyance [8]

amplitude [11]

ascertain [15]

credulity [20]

statutory [22]

VEATCH

craniotomy [2]	ambiguous [12]
tracheostomy [2]	operational [12]
intravenously [2]	conceptual [15]
prognosis [2]	relic [17]
fibrillation [3]	dichotomized [17]
cortical activity [5]	plausible [17]
subsequent [8]	pragmatic [18]
exonerated [10]	crude [20]

A DEFINITION OF
—— IRREVERSIBLE COMA ——

*Report of the <u>Ad Hoc Committee</u> of the Harvard Medical
School to <u>Examine the Definition</u> of Brain Death*

Our primary purpose is to define <u>irreversible</u> coma as a new criterion [1]
for death. There are two reasons why there is need for a definition:
(1) Improvements in <u>resuscitative</u> and supportive measures have led
to increased efforts to save those who are desperately injured. Sometimes these efforts have only partial success so that the result is an
individual whose heart continues to beat but whose brain is irreversibly
damaged. The burden is great on patients who suffer permanent loss
of intellect, on their families, on the hospitals, and on those in need
of hospital beds already occupied by these comatose patients. (2)
<u>Obsolete</u> criteria for the definition of death can lead to controversy
in obtaining organs for transplantation.

Irreversible coma has many causes, but *we are concerned here only* [2]
with those comatose individuals who have no discernible central nervous

SOURCE: From the *Journal of the American Medical Association*, Aug. 5, 1968, vol. 205, no.
6, pp. 337-340. Copyright 1968, American Medical Association. Reprinted by permission
of the publisher.

system activity. If the characteristics can be defined in satisfactory terms, translatable into action—and we believe this is possible—then several problems will either disappear or will become more readily soluble.

[3]   More than medical problems are present. There are moral, ethical, religious, and legal issues. Adequate definition here will prepare the way for better insight into all of these matters as well as for better law than is currently applicable.

CHARACTERISTICS OF IRREVERSIBLE COMA

[4] An organ, brain or other, that no longer functions and has no possibility of functioning again is for all practical purposes dead. Our first problem is to determine the characteristics of a *permanently* nonfunctioning brain.

[5]   A patient in this state appears to be in deep coma. The condition can be satisfactorily diagnosed by points 1, 2, and 3 to follow. The electroencephalogram (point 4) provides confirmatory data, and when available it should be utilized. In situations where for one reason or another electroencephalographic monitoring is not available, the absence of cerebral function has to be determined by purely clinical signs, to be described, or by absence of circulation as judged by standstill of blood in the retinal vessels, or by absence of cardiac activity.

[6]   1. *Unreceptivity and Unresponsitivity.*—There is a total unawareness to externally applied stimuli and inner need and complete unresponsiveness—our definition of irreversible coma. Even the most intensely painful stimuli evoke no vocal or other response, not even a groan, withdrawal of a limb, or quickening of respiration.

[7]   2. *No Movements or Breathing.*—Observations covering a period of at least one hour by physicians is adequate to satisfy the criteria of no spontaneous muscular movements or spontaneous respiration or response to stimuli such as pain, touch, sound, or light. After the patient is on a mechanical respirator, the total absence of spontaneous breathing may be established by turning off the respirator for three minutes and observing whether there is any effort on the part of the subject to breathe spontaneously. (The respirator may be turned off for this time provided that at the start of the trial period the patient's carbon dioxide tension is within the normal range, and provided also that the patient had been breathing room air for at least 10 minutes prior to the trial.)

[8]   3. *No reflexes.*—Irreversible coma with abolition of central nervous system activity is evidenced in part by the absence of elicitable reflexes. The pupil will be fixed and dilated and will not respond to a direct source of bright light. Since the establishment of a fixed, dilated pupil is clear-cut in clinical practice, there should be no uncertainty as to

its presence. Ocular movement (to head turning and to irrigation of the ears with ice water) and blinking are absent. There is no evidence of postural activity (decerebrate or other). Swallowing, yawning, vocalization are in abeyance. Corneal and pharyngeal reflexes are absent.

As a rule the stretch of tendon reflexes cannot be elicited; ie, tapping [9] the tendons of the biceps, triceps, and pronator muscles, quadriceps and gastrocnemius muscles with the reflex hammer elicits no contraction of the respective muscles. Plantar or noxious stimulation gives no response.

4. *Flat Electroencephalogram.*—Of great confirmatory value is the flat [10] or isoelectric EEG. We must assume that the electrodes have been properly applied, that the apparatus is functioning normally, and that the personnel in charge is competent. We consider it prudent to have one channel of the apparatus used for an electrocardiogram. This channel will monitor the ECG so that, if it appears in the electroencephalographic leads because of high resistance, it can be readily identified. It also establishes the presence of the active heart in the absence of the EEG. We recommend that another channel be used for a noncephalic lead. This will pick up space-borne or vibration-borne artifacts and identify them. The simplest form of such a monitoring noncephalic electrode has two leads over the dorsum of the hand, preferably the right hand, so the ECG will be minimal or absent. Since one of the requirements of this state is that there be no muscle activity, these two dorsal hand electrodes will not be bothered by muscle artifact. The apparatus should be run at standard gains 10μv/mm, 50μv/5 mm. Also it should be isoelectric at double this standard gain which is 5μv/mm or 25μv/5 mm. At least ten full minutes of recording are desirable, but twice that would be better.

It is also suggested that the gains at some point be opened to their [11] full amplitude for a brief period (5 to 100 seconds) to see what is going on. Usually in an intensive care unit artifacts will dominate the picture, but these are readily identifiable. There shall be no electroencephalographic response to noise or to pinch.

All of the above tests shall be repeated at least 24 hours later with [12] no change.

The validity of such data as indications of irreversible cerebral damage [13] depends on the exclusion of two conditions: hypothermia (temperature below 90 F [32.2 C]) or central nervous system depressants, such as barbiturates.

OTHER PROCEDURES

The patient's condition can be determined only by a physician. When [14] the patient is hopelessly damaged as defined above, the family and all colleagues who have participated in major decisions concerning the patient, and all nurses involved, should be so informed. Death is to be declared and *then* the respirator turned off. The decision to do this and the responsibility for it are to be taken by the physician-in-charge, in consultation with one or more physicians who have been directly involved in the case. It is unsound and undesirable to force the family to make the decision.

LEGAL COMMENTARY

[15]   The legal system of the United States is greatly in need of the kind of analysis and recommendations for medical procedures in cases of irreversible brain damage as described. At present, the law of the United States, in all 50 states and in the federal courts, treats the question of human death as a question of fact to be decided in every case. When any doubt exists, the courts seek medical expert testimony concerning the time of death of the particular individual involved. However, the law makes the assumption that the medical criteria for determining death are settled and not in doubt among physicians. Furthermore, the law assumes that the traditional method among physicians for determination of death is to ascertain the absence of all vital signs. To this extent, *Black's Law Dictionary* (fourth edition, 1951) defines death as

> The cessation of life; the ceasing to exist; *defined by physicians* as a total stoppage of the circulation of the blood, and a cessation of the animal and vital functions consequent thereupon, such as respiration, pulsation, etc. [italics added]

[16]   In the few modern court decisions involving a definition of death, the courts have used the concept of the total cessation of all vital signs. Two cases are worthy of examination. Both involved the issue of which one of two persons died first.

[17]   In *Thomas vs Anderson* (96 Cal App 2d 371, 211 P 2d 478) a California District Court of Appeal in 1950 said, "In the instant case the question as to which of the two men died first was a question of fact for the determination of the trial court . . ."

[18]   The appellate court cited and quoted in full the definition of death from *Black's Law Dictionary* and concluded, ". . . death occurs precisely when life ceases and does not occur until the heart stops beating and respiration ends. Death is not a continuous event and is an event that takes place at a precise time."

[19]   The other case is *Smith vs Smith* (229 Ark, 579, 317 SW 2d 275) decided in 1958 by the Supreme Court of Arkansas. In this case the

two people were husband and wife involved in an auto accident. The husband was found dead at the scene of the accident. The wife was taken to the hospital unconscious. It is alleged that she "remained in coma due to brain injury" and died at the hospital 17 days later. The petitioner in court tried to argue that the two people died simultaneously. The judge writing the opinion said the petition contained a "quite unusual and unique allegation." It was quoted as follows:

> That the said Hugh Smith and his wife, Lucy Coleman Smith, were in an automobile accident on the 19th day of April, 1957, said accident being instantly fatal to each of them at the same time, although the doctors maintained a vain hope of survival and made every effort to revive and resuscitate said Lucy Coleman Smith until May 6th, 1957, when it was finally determined by the attending physicians that their hope of resuscitation and possible restoration of human life to the said Lucy Coleman Smith was entirely vain, and

> That as a matter of modern medical science, your petitioner alleges and states, and will offer the Court competent proof that the said Hugh Smith, deceased, and said Lucy Coleman Smith, deceased, lost their power to will at the same instant, and that their demise as earthly human beings occurred at the same time in said automobile accident, neither of them ever regaining any consciousness whatsoever.

The court dismissed the petition as a *matter of law*. The court quoted [20] *Black's* definition of death and concluded,

> Admittedly, this condition did not exist, and as a matter of fact, it would be too much of a strain of credulity for us to believe any evidence offered to the effect that Mrs. Smith was dead, scientifically or otherwise, unless the conditions set out in the definition existed.

Later in the opinion the court said, "Likewise, we take judicial notice that one breathing, though unconscious, is not dead."

"Judicial notice" of this definition of death means that the court [21] did not consider that definition open to serious controversy; it considered the question as settled in responsible scientific and medical circles. The judge thus makes proof of uncontroverted facts unnecessary so as to prevent prolonging the trial with unnecessary proof and also to prevent fraud being committed upon the court by quasi "scientists" being called into court to controvert settled scientific principles at a price. Here, the Arkansas Supreme Court considered the definition of death to be a settled, scientific, biological fact. It refused to consider the plaintiff's offer of evidence that "modern medical science" might say otherwise. In simplified form, the above is the state of the law in the United States concerning the definition of death.

[22]   In this report, however, we suggest that responsible medical opinion is ready to adopt new criteria for pronouncing death to have occurred in an individual sustaining irreversible coma as a result of permanent brain damage. If this position is adopted by the medical community, it can form the basis for change in the current legal concept of death. No statutory change in the law should be necessary since the law treats this question essentially as one of fact to be determined by physicians. The only circumstance in which it would be necessary that legislation be offered in the various states to define "death" by law would be in the event that great controversy were engendered surrounding the subject and physicians were unable to agree on the new medical criteria.

[23]   It is recommended as a part of these procedures that judgment of the existence of these criteria is solely a medical issue. It is suggested that the physician in charge of the patient consult with one or more other physicians directly involved in the case before the patient is declared dead on the basis of these criteria. In this way, the responsibility is shared over a wider range of medical opinion, thus providing an important degree of protection against later questions which might be raised about the particular case. It is further suggested that the decision to declare the person dead, and then to turn off the respirator, be made by physicians not involved in any later effort to transplant organs or tissue from the deceased individual. This is advisable in order to avoid any appearance of self-interest by the physicians involved.

[24]   It should be emphasized that we recommend the patient be declared dead before any effort is made to take him off a respirator, if he is then on a respirator. This declaration should not be delayed until he has been taken off the respirator and all artificially stimulated signs have ceased. The reason for this recommendation is that in our judgment it will provide a greater degree of legal protection to those involved. Otherwise, the physicians would be turning off the respirator on a person who is, under the present strict, technical application of law, still alive.

COMMENT

[25]   Irreversible coma can have various causes: cardiac arrest; asphyxia with respiratory arrest; massive brain damage; intracranial lesions, neoplastic or vascular. It can be produced by other encephalopathic states such as the metabolic derangements associated, for example, with uremia. Respiratory failure and impaired circulation underlie all of these conditions. They result in hypoxia and ischemia of the brain.

From ancient times down to the recent past it was clear that, when [26]
the respiration and heart stopped, the brain would die in a few minutes;
so the obvious criterion of no heart beat as synonymous with death
was sufficiently accurate. In those times the heart was considered to
be the central organ of the body; it is not surprising that its failure
marked the onset of death. This is no longer valid when modern
resuscitative and supportive measures are used. These improved activities can now restore "life" as judged by the ancient standards of
persistent respiration and continuing heart beat. This can be the case
even when there is not the remotest possibility of an individual recovering consciousness following massive brain damage. In other
situations "life" can be maintained only by means of artificial respiration
and electrical stimulation of the heart beat, or in temporarily by-
passing the heart, or, in conjunction with these things, reducing with
cold the body's oxygen requirement.

In an address, "The Prolongation of Life," (1957),[1] Pope Pius XII [27]
raised many questions; some conclusions stand out: (1) In a deeply
unconscious individual vital functions may be maintained over a prolonged period only by extraordinary means. Verification of the moment
of death can be determined, if at all, only by a physician. Some have
suggested that the moment of death is the moment when irreparable
and overwhelming brain damage occurs. Pius XII acknowledged that
it is not "within the competence of the Church" to determine this.
(2) It is incumbent on the physician to take all reasonable, ordinary
means of restoring the spontaneous vital functions and consciousness,
and to employ such extraordinary means as are available to him to
this end. It is not obligatory, however, to continue to use extraordinary
means indefinitely in hopeless cases. "But normally one is held to
use only ordinary means—according to circumstances of persons,
places, times, and cultures—that is to say, means that do not involve
any grave burden for oneself or another." It is the church's view that
a time comes when resuscitative efforts should stop and death be
unopposed.

SUMMARY

The neurological impairment to which the terms "brain death syn- [28]
drome" and "irreversible coma" have become attached indicates diffuse
disease. Function is abolished at cerebral, brain-stem, and often spinal
levels. This should be evident in all cases from clinical examination
alone. Cerebral, cortical, and thalamic involvement are indicated by
a complete absence of receptivity of all forms of sensory stimulation
and a lack of response to stimuli and to inner need. The term "coma"
is used to designate this state of unreceptivity and unresponsitivity.

But there is always coincident paralysis of brain-stem and basal gan-glionic mechanisms as manifested by an abolition of all postural reflexes, including induced decerebrate postures; a complete paralysis of res-piration; widely dilated, fixed pupils; paralysis of ocular movements; swallowing; phonation; face and tongue muscles. Involvement of spinal cord, which is less constant, is reflected usually in loss of tendon reflex and all flexor withdrawal or nocifensive reflexes. Of the brain-stem-spinal mechanisms which are conserved for a time, the vasomotor reflexes are the most persistent, and they are responsible in part for the paradoxical state of retained cardiovascular function, which is to some extent independent of nervous control, in the face of widespread disorder of cerebrum, brain stem, and spinal cord.

[29]   Neurological assessment gains in reliability if the aforementioned neurological signs persist over a period of time, with the additional safeguards that there is no accompanying hypothermia or evidence of drug intoxication. If either of the latter two conditions exist, inter-pretation of the neurological state should await the return of body temperature to normal level and elimination of the intoxicating agent. Under any other circumstances, repeated examinations over a period of 24 hours or longer should be required in order to obtain evidence of the irreversibility of the condition.

DEFINING DEATH ANEW: TECHNICAL AND ETHICAL ──── PROBLEMS ────

Robert Veatch

[1]   It seems strange to ask what death means. Throughout history men have had a good enough idea to transact the business of society—to cover the corpse, bury the dead, transmit authority. But now that technology permits us to treat the body organ by organ, cell by cell, we are forced to develop a more precise understanding of what it means to call a person dead. There is a complex interaction between the technical aspects of deciding a person is dead—all the business involving stethoscopes, electroencephalograms, and intricately de-termined medical diagnoses and prognoses—and the more fundamental

SOURCE: From Robert Veatch, *Death, Dying and the Biological Revolution*, Yale University Press, New Haven, 1976. Copyright © 1976. Reprinted by permission of the publisher.

philosophical considerations which underlie the judgment that a person in a particular condition should be called dead.

On May 24, 1968, a black laborer named Bruce Tucker fell and [2] suffered a massive head injury. He was rushed by ambulance to the emergency room of the Medical College of Virginia Hospital where he was found to have a skull fracture, a subdural hematoma, and a brain stem contusion. At eleven o'clock that evening an operation was performed (described as "a right temporoparietal craniotomy and right parietal bur hole" in a later court record of the case), opening the skull to relieve the strain on the brain. A tracheostomy was also done to help his labored breathing. By the next morning Tucker was being fed intravenously, had been given medication, and was attached to a respirator. According to the court record, he was "mechanically alive"; the treating physician noted, his "prognosis for recovery is nil and death imminent."

In cases like Tucker's, the patient has frequently stopped breathing [3] by the time he arrives at the hospital, and his heart may have gone into fibrillation. However, the rapid application of an electrical shock can cajole the heart back into a normal rhythm, while a respirator forces the breath of life from the tube of the machine into the tube of the patient's trachea. Thus technology can arrest the process of dying.

The Medical College of Virginia, where Tucker was taken, is the [4] hospital of David M. Hume who, until his own recent accidental death, headed one of the eminent heart transplant teams of the world. At the time Tucker was brought in, there was a patient on the ward named Joseph Klett who was an ideal recipient. Bruce Tucker, with irreversible loss of brain function from a period of oxygen starvation in the brain and an otherwise healthy body, was an ideal heart donor.

Early in the afternoon a neurologist obtained an electroencepha- [5] logram (EEG) to determine the state of Tucker's brain activity. He saw that the electrical tracing was a flat line "with occasional artifact." Assuming the artifacts were the kind normally found from extraneous causes, this meant there was no evidence of cortical activity at that time. If the flat line on the EEG is not caused by drug overdose or low body temperature and is found again in repeated tests over several hours, most neurologists would take it to mean that consciousness would never return. Nevertheless, the respirator continued pumping oxygen into Tucker's lungs and, according to the judge's later summary, "his body temperature, pulse, and blood pressure were all normal for a patient in his condition."

In August of the same year a prestigious committee from the Harvard [6] Medical School published more rigorous criteria for irreversible coma. Drafts of the report were circulating among professionals early in the year, but there is no evidence that the physicians in Virginia had access to it. Their use of their own judgment about criteria for diagnosing irreversible coma is still the subject of controversy.

[7]   At 2:45 that afternoon Tucker was taken back into the operating room to be prepared for the removal of his heart and both kidneys. Oxygen was given to preserve the viability of these organs. According to the court record, "he maintained, for the most part, normal body temperature, normal blood pressure and normal rate of respiration," but, in spite of the presence of these vital signs, at 3:30 the respirator was cut off. Five minutes later the patient was pronounced dead and the mechanical support was resumed to preserve the organs, and his heart was removed and transplanted to Joseph Klett. According to the record, Tucker's vital signs continued to be normal until 4:30, soon before the heart was removed.

[8]   The heart was removed although it had continued functioning while the respirator continued to pump. It was removed without any attempt to get the permission of relatives although Tucker's wallet contained his brother's business card with a phone number and an address only fifteen blocks away. The brother was in his place of business that day and a close friend had made unsuccessful inquiries at three information desks in the hospital. The heart was removed although Virginia law, according to the interpretation of the judge in the subsequent trial, defines death as total cessation of all body functions.

[9]   William Tucker, the "donor's" brother, brought suit against the surgical team for wrongfully ending Bruce Tucker's life. During the trial, physicians testified that Tucker was "neurologically dead" several hours before the transplant and that his heart and respiratory system were being kept viable by mechanical means. To this William Tucker responded, "There's nothing they can say to make me believe they didn't kill him."[1] Commenting on the decision in favor of the surgeons, Dr. Hume said, "This simply brings the law in line with medical opinion."

[10]   The New York Times headlines read, "Virginia Jury Rules That Death Occurs When Brain Dies." Victor Cohn's Washington Post story announced, " 'Brain Death' Upheld in Heart Transplant." The medical news services were equally quick to treat this unquestioningly as a brain death case. The Internal Medicine News claimed, " 'Brain Death' Held Proof of Demise in Va. Jury Decision." Even a law review article considered the judgment to affirm that cessation of brain activity can be used in determining the time of death.[2] There has been some outcry, especially in the black community, over the hasty removal of a man's heart without permission from the next of kin, but the general public seemed undisturbed by the decision. The medical community felt that one of their outstanding members had been exonerated.

Although the press, public, and some legal opinion treat this case [11] as crucial in establishing the legitimacy of the use of brain criteria for death (thus bringing the law in line with "medical opinion"), more issues than that are at stake. The case raises basic questions about the definition of death.

The debate has become increasingly heated in the past decade, [12] because fundamental moral and religious issues are at stake. The very meaning of the word *definition* is ambiguous. Some of the issues are indeed matters of neurobiological fact and as such are appropriate for interpretation by medical opinion. But judgments about facts made by scientists with expertise in a particular and relevant field can be called *definitions* only in an operational sense. The debate over the definition of death also takes place at philosophical, religious, and ethical levels, probing into the meaning of life and its ending. The more practical, empirical problems are an important part of the debate, but they must be separated from the philosophical issues. The philosophical question is, What is lost at the point of death that is essential to human nature? We can avoid the serious philosophical errors committed in the Virginia trial only by carefully separating the levels of the debate.

Four separate levels in the definition of death debate must be dis- [13] tinguished. First, there is the purely formal analysis of the term *death*, an analysis that gives the structure and specifies the framework that must be filled in with content. Second, the *concept* of death is considered, attempting to fill the content of the formal definition. At this level the question is, What is so essentially significant about life that its loss is termed *death*? Third, there is the question of the locus of death: where in the organism ought one to look to determine whether death has occurred? Fourth, one must ask the question of the criteria of death: what technical tests must be applied at the locus to determine if an individual is living or dead?

Serious mistakes have been made in slipping from one level of the [14] debate to another and in presuming that expertise on one level necessarily implies expertise on another. For instance, the Report of the Ad Hoc Committee of the Harvard Medical School to Examine the Definition of Brain Death is titled "A Definition of Irreversible Coma."[3] The report makes clear that the committee members are simply reporting empirical measures which are criteria for predicting an irreversible coma. (I shall explore later the possibility that they made an important mistake even at this level.) Yet the name of the committee seems to point more to the question of locus, where to look for measurement of death. The committee was established to examine the death of the brain. The implication is that the empirical indications of irreversible coma are also indications of "brain death." But by the first sentence of the report the committee claims that "Our primary purpose is to define irreversible coma as a new criterion for death." They have now shifted so that they are interested in "death." They must be presuming a philosophical concept of death—that a person in irreversible coma should be considered dead—but they nowhere argue this or even state it as a presumption.

[15]   Even the composition of the Harvard committee membership signals some uncertainty of purpose. If empirical criteria were their concern, the inclusion of nonscientists on the panel was strange. If the philosophical concept of death was their concern, medically trained people were overrepresented. As it happened, the committee did not deal at all with conceptual matters. The committee and its interpreters have confused the questions at different levels. . . .

THE FORMAL DEFINITION OF DEATH

[16] A strictly formal definition of death might be the following:

> Death means a complete change in the status of a living entity characterized by the irreversible loss of those characteristics that are essentially significant to it.
>
>   . . .

[17]   [Early] concepts of death—the irreversible loss of the soul and the irreversible stopping of the flow of vital body fluids—strike me as quite implausible. The soul as an independent nonphysical entity that is necessary and sufficient for a person to be considered alive is a relic from the era of dichotomized anthropologies. Animalistic fluid flow is simply too base a function to be the human essence. The capacity for bodily integration is more plausible, but I suspect it is attractive primarily because it includes those higher functions that we normally take to be central—consciousness, the ability to think and feel and relate to others. When the reflex networks that regulate such things as blood pressure and respiration are separated from the higher functions, I am led to conclude that it is the higher functions which are so essential that their loss ought to be taken as the death of the person. While consciousness is certainly important, man's social nature and embodiment seem to me to be the truly essential characteristics. I therefore believe that death is most appropriately thought of as the irreversible loss of the embodied capacity for social interaction. . . .

COMPLEXITIES IN MATCHING CONCEPTS
WITH LOCI AND CRITERIA

[18] It has been our method throughout this chapter to identify four major concepts of death and then to determine, primarily by examining the

empirical evidence, what the corresponding loci and criteria might be. But there are good reasons why the holders of a particular concept of death might not want to adopt the corresponding criteria as the means of determining the status of a given patient. These considerations are primarily pragmatic and empirical. In the first place, as a matter of policy we would not want to have to apply the Harvard criteria before pronouncing death while standing before every clearly dead body. It is not usually necessary to use such technical measures as an EEG, whether one holds the fluid-flow concept, the loss of bodily integration concept, or the loss of social interaction concept.

Reliance on the old circulatory and respiratory criteria in cases [19] where the individual is obviously dead may be justified in either of two ways. First, there is the option implied in the new Kansas statute of maintaining two operating concepts of death, either of which will be satisfactory. This appears, however, to be philosophically unsound, since it means that a patient could be simultaneously dead and alive. If the philosophical arguments for either of the neurological concepts are convincing, and I think they are, we should not have to fall back on the fluid-flow concept for pronouncing death in the ordinary case.

A second way to account for the use of the heart- and lung-oriented [20] criteria is that they do indeed correlate empirically with the neurological concepts. When there is no circulatory or respiratory activity for a sufficient time, there is invariably a loss of capacity for bodily integration or capacity for consciousness or social interaction. Using circulatory and respiratory activity as tests is crude and in some cases the presence of such activity will lead to a false positive diagnosis of life; but the prolonged absence of circulation and respiration is a definitive diagnosis of death even according to the neurologically-oriented concepts. Their use is thus an initial shortcut; if these criteria are met, one need not go on to the other criteria for the purpose of pronouncing death. This would appear to be a sound rationale for continuing the use of the old criteria of respiratory and circulatory activity.

A second practical difficulty is inherent in correlating concept and [21] criteria. Let us examine this by asking why one might not wish at this time to adopt the EEG alone as a definitive criterion for pronouncing death. There are two possible reasons. First, quite obviously, there will be those who do not accept the correlated concept of death. They reject the irreversible loss of the capacity for consciousness or social interaction in favor of the irreversible loss of capacity for bodily integration or for fluid flow. Second, there are those who accept the concept of irreversible loss of consciousness or social interaction, but still are not convinced that the EEG unfailingly predicts this. If and when they can be convinced that the EEG alone accurately predicts irreversible loss of consciousness or social interaction without any false diagnosis of death, they will adopt it as the criterion. In the

Table 1 Levels of the Definition of Death

Formal Definition: Death means a complete change in the status of a living entity characterized by the irreversible loss of those characteristics that are essentially significant to it.

Concept of death:	Locus of death:	Criteria of death:
Philosophical or theological judgment of the essentially significant change at death.	Place to look to determine if a person has died.	Measurements physicians or other officials use to determine whether a person is dead—to be determined by scientific empirical study.
1. The irreversible stopping of the flow of "vital" body fluids, i.e., the blood and breath	Heart and lungs	1. Visual observation of respiration, perhaps with the use of a mirror 2. Feeling of the pulse, possibly supported by electrocardiogram
2. The irreversible loss of the soul from the body	The pineal body? (according to Descartes) The respiratory tract?	Observation of breath?

meantime they would logically continue to advocate the concept while adhering to the more conservative Harvard criteria, which appear to measure the loss of whole brain function. Since the distinction is a new one and the empirical evidence may not yet be convincing, it is to be expected that many holders of this concept will, for the time being and as a matter of policy, prefer the Harvard committee's older and more conservative criteria for determining death. The entire analysis of the four levels of definition presented thus far is summarized in Table 1.

NOTE

1. Pius XII: The Prolongation of Life, *Pope Speaks* 4:393-398 (No. 4) 1958.

NOTES

1. "Clear MD's in 'Living' Donor Case," *New York Post*, May 26, 1972, p. 2.
2. Richmond Stanfield Frederick, "Medical Jurisprudence—Determining the Time of Death of the Heart Transplant Donor," *North Carolina Law Review* 51 (1972), pp. 172–

Table 1 (*continued*)

Concept of death:	Locus of death:	Criteria of death:
3. The irreversible loss of the capacity for bodily integration and social interaction	The brain	1. Unreceptivity and unresponsivity 2. No movements or breathing 3. No reflexes (except spinal reflexes) 4. Flat electroencephalogram (to be used as confirmatory evidence)—All tests to be repeated 24 hours later (excluded conditions: hypothermia and central nervous system drug depression)
4. Irreversible loss of consciousness or the capacity for social interaction	Probably the neocortex	Electroencephalogram

NOTE: The possible concepts, loci, and criteria of death are much more complex than the ones given here. These are meant to be simplified models of types of positions being taken in the current debate. It is obvious that those who believe that death means the irreversible loss of the capacity for bodily integration (3) or the irreversible loss of consciousness (4) have no reservations about pronouncing death when the heart and lungs have ceased to function. This is because they are willing to use loss of heart and lung activity as shortcut criteria for death, believing that once heart and lungs have stopped, the brain or neocortex will necessarily stop as well.

84. For another review of the case see Ronald Converse, "But *When* Did He Die?: *Tucker v. Lower* and the Brain-Death Concept," *San Diego Law Review* 12 (1975), pp. 424-35.

3. Ad Hoc Committee of the Harvard Medical School to Examine the Definition of Brain Death, "A Definition of Irreversible Coma," *Journal of the American Medical Association* 205 (1968), pp. 337-40.

QUESTIONS

1. In your opinion, does the Harvard Medical School definition give the physician more power than he or she deserves?
2. Why should the declaration of death be made before the patient is detached from the respirator?

3. Using what you have learned from Ariès and Congdon as well as from the Harvard Medical School, do you think that brain death should be the complete and total definition of death? Would adopting such a definition make us modify our idea of what life is? Would it make us change our attitudes toward what in a human life is most valuable?

4. Veatch says there are four levels at which the debate about defining death can take place. Among them are: (1) "the purely formal analysis of the term death"—this is the level at which the philosopher approached death, and (2) "the question of the locus of death": where in an organism we should look to determine whether death has occurred—this is the level at which the Harvard Medical School approached death. First, put yourself in the place of the physician who declared Bruce Tucker dead and argue for his death at these two levels. Then put yourself in the position of Bruce Tucker's brother and argue against his death at these two levels.

5. Compare Veatch's "formal definition of death" with the definition that Congdon gives us, i.e., "the permanent absence of consciousness in a physical body." Which definition is better? Which is more inclusive? What does the difference between the two definitions tell us about the two points of view—the philosophical and the medical-ethical—from which they come?

6. In a part of his essay not reproduced here, Veatch says, "We use the term *death* to mean the loss of what is essentially significant to an entity—in the case of man the loss of his humanness." If it is the case—as in the Harvard Medical School definition—that our brain determines our essential humanness, or—as in the Veatch definition—that our neocortical activity, our conscious interaction with others, determines our essential humanness, what dangers can arise in the attitudes of physicians, nurses, and public policy officials toward (a) people who are severely brain-damaged and (b) people who are severely mentally retarded?

7. The Harvard Medical School Committee assumes that comatose patients are a "burden" to themselves, their families, and the medical facility that sustains them. What questions might you raise about these assumptions if you took the approach of a philosopher? Here is a clue: Can we know whether a comatose person is a burden to him or herself? Here is another: Does a physician have the moral right to determine whether or not a comatose patient is a burden to his or her family?

8. According to accepted medical practice, natural death (or death in which no medical intervention like a respirator was used) occurs when our hearts stop functioning. After reading the Harvard definition and Veatch's article, do you agree that death can occur even

though the heart is still functioning? Do you think that the medical development of heart transplantation has anything to do with the need for a new definition of death?

9. Look the following terms up in a dictionary: hematoma, contusion, cortical activity, fibrillation, cranestomy. Do you think it is absolutely necessary for the writers to use these technical terms rather than simple, everyday words? For example, what is the difference between using *hematoma* and using *blood clot*? What are some of the reasons that physicians use technical terms that may be difficult for the layman? Here is a clue: What do you think the difference in reaction would be between a doctor's saying "you have cancer" and his saying "this is a carcinoma"?

EXERCISES

1. The term triage is one that has been taken into the fields of medicine and hospital administration from the military. Originally it meant strategies for the most efficient deployment of weapons and military personnel in conducting a battle. In hospital administration, it means strategies for the most efficient deployment of technologies, materials, and personnel in the battle against death. Imagine that you are a hospital administrator who must decide upon the most useful deployment of an expensive medical instrument, the kidney dialysis machine. You must decide among the following patients for first-priority use of the machine:

   a. A fifty-year-old woman, mother of five, who has already had a mastectomy for breast cancer and whose case has been complicated by a temporary kidney disorder that would be corrected by use of kidney dialysis.
   b. A thirty-year-old man, a violin virtuoso, who won the Tchaikovsky Prize, suffering from congenital kidney disease, who will die without regular dialysis treatment.
   c. A five-year-old girl suffering from complex genetic birth disorders—among which is kidney malfunction—who will be mentally retarded all her life.
   d. A seventy-year-old medical scientist, who is a trustee of the hospital and whose early research contributed to the invention of the dialysis machine.

After you have chosen the best candidate for treatment (i.e. first to use the machine, which will then not be available for use by the other three), write a two-page justification of your decision to the hospital's board of trustees.

2. Imagine that you are on a jury in the Bruce Tucker case. To gain a clearer idea of what you consider to be the issues, write out, in rough draft, the reasons for your support or lack of support of Bruce Tucker's brother's case. In your argument, try to consider the medical, philosophical, and personal issues that guide your response.

3. Return to your journal entry, "My Thoughts about Death," and consider the medical-ethical implications of the Ad Hoc Committee decision and Veatch's commentary upon it. You might find it useful to compare the rigor with which Congdon approaches a definition of death with the looser method employed by Veatch. Are there new issues to consider in your thoughts about death? To what extent has your overall definition of death been changed by these selections?

CHAPTER NINETEEN

CLARK: WHOSE LIFE IS IT ANYWAY?

Drama

Whose Life Is It Anyway? is an important play for our time because it deals with the issue of the maintenance of life by artificial, medical intervention. Since it is not possible for us to reprint the whole script of the play, we will give you a synopsis of the play and present only its last scene, in which a judge renders his decision upon whether or not the patient has the right to refuse medical sustenance of life—his life as a vegetable—and to withdraw from the hospital to die.

SYNOPSIS

Ken Harrison, the patient, is a highly intelligent, very funny man who was the victim of an auto accident that severed his spinal cord and left him with no feeling, sensation, or ability to control any part of his body but his head. The play allows us to see both the excellence of his mind and the total immobility of his body. He is a sculptor, and therefore, could never do any work that was meaningful to him in his present condition. He is an extremely sexual man, but of course, his body experiences no sexual sensation. His mind, alas, does. He has decided that life as a totally immobilized human being is unacceptable to him. His doctors, who are rightly dedicated to the cause of keeping him alive, have decided to declare him a psychiatric depressive, whose decision to refuse all treatment and to die, is merely a symptom of clinical depression.

Under the guise of seeking insurance compensation, he gets to see his lawyer, and he convinces his lawyer that he has the right to refuse treatment even though the refusal means sure death for him. His lawyer decides to plead his cause under the writ of *habeas corpus*, which in Latin means "who has the body." The writ of habeas corpus determines that no citizen can be detained by any person or organization without criminal cause unless he is mentally incompetent. The hospital uses its right to confine him, by arguing that he is a patient whom it does not believe to be mentally capable of making his own decisions. Two psychiatrists examine Ken Harrison and decide that though the decision he has made is unconventional, he is legally sane and his decision to be released from the hospital is a rational decision. We are dealing in this play with the collision of two moral rights: the doctors have the right, and the obligation, to sustain life; the patient has the right to decide what constitutes "life" for him. The scene opens upon the final judgment.

_____ WHOSE LIFE IS IT ANYWAY? _____
Brian Clark

DR. EMERSON: Good morning, Mr. Harrison.

KEN: Morning, Doctor.

DR. EMERSON: There's still time.

KEN: No, I want to go on with it . . . unless you'll discharge me.

DR. EMERSON: I'm afraid I can't do that. The Judge and lawyers are conferring. I thought I'd just pop along and see if you were all right. We've made arrangements for the witnesses to wait in the Sister's office. I am one, so I should be grateful if you would remain here, with Mr. Harrison.

DR. SCOTT: Of course.

DR. EMERSON: Well, I don't want to meet the Judge before I have to. I wish you the best of luck, Mr. Harrison, so that we'll be able to carry on treating you.

KEN (*Smiling*): Thank you for your good wishes.

(DR. EMERSON *nods and goes out.*)

DR. SCOTT: If I didn't know *you* I'd say *he* was the most obstinate man I've ever met.

(As DR. EMERSON *makes for his office,* MR. HILL *comes down the corridor.*)

HILL: Good morning.

. . .

SOURCE: From *Whose Life Is It Anyway?* by Brian Clark, pp. 124–146.

DR. EMERSON: Morning.

(MR. HILL *stops and calls after* DR. EMERSON.)

HILL: Oh, Dr. Emerson . . .

DR. EMERSON: Yes?

HILL: I don't know . . . I just want to say how sorry I am that you have been forced into such a . . . distasteful situation.

DR. EMERSON: It's not over yet, Mr. Hill. I have every confidence that the law is not such an ass that it will force me to watch a patient of mine die unnecessarily.

HILL: We are just as confident that the law is not such an ass that it will allow anyone arbitrary power.

DR. EMERSON: My power isn't arbitrary; I've earned it with knowledge and skill and it's also subject to the laws of nature.

HILL: And to the laws of the state.

DR. EMERSON: If the state is so foolish as to believe it is competent to judge a purely professional issue.

HILL: It's always doing that. Half the civil cases in the calendar arise because someone is challenging a professional's opinion.

DR. EMERSON: I don't know about other professions but I do know this one, medicine, is being seriously threatened because of the intervention of law. Patients are becoming so litigious that doctors will soon be afraid to offer any opinion or take any action at all.

HILL: Then they will be sued for negligence.

DR. EMERSON: We can't win.

HILL: Everybody wins. You wouldn't like to find yourself powerless in the hands of, say, a lawyer or a . . . bureaucrat. I wouldn't like to find myself powerless in the hands of a doctor.

DR. EMERSON: You make me sound as if I were some sort of Dracula . . .

HILL: No! . . . I for one certainly don't doubt your good faith but in spite of that I wouldn't like to place *anyone* above the law.

DR. EMERSON: I don't want to be above the law; I just want to be under laws that take full account of professional opinion.

HILL: I'm sure it will do that, Dr. Emerson. The question is, whose professional opinion?

DR. EMERSON: We shall see.

(MR. ANDREW EDEN, *the hospital's barrister, and* MR. HILL *and* MR. KERSHAW *come into* KEN's *room.*)

HILL: Morning, Mr. Harrison. This is Mr. Eden who will be representing the hospital.

KEN: Hello.

(*They settle themselves into the chairs. The* SISTER *enters with the* JUDGE.)

SISTER: Mr. Justice Millhouse.

JUDGE: Mr. Kenneth Harrison?

KEN: Yes, my Lord.

JUDGE: This is an informal hearing which I want to keep as brief as possible. You are, I take it, Dr. Scott?

DR. SCOTT: Yes, my Lord.

JUDGE: I should be grateful, Doctor, if you would interrupt the proceedings at any time you think it necessary.

DR. SCOTT: Yes, my Lord.

JUDGE: I have decided in consultation with Mr. Kershaw and Mr. Hill that we shall proceed thus. I will hear a statement from Dr. Michael Emerson as to why he believes Mr. Harrison is legally detained, and then a statement from Dr. Richard Barr, who will support the application. We have decided not to subject Mr. Harrison to examination and cross-examination.

KEN: But I . . .

JUDGE (*Sharply*): Just a moment, Mr. Harrison. If, as appears likely, there remains genuine doubt as to the main issue, I shall question Mr. Harrison myself. Dr. Scott, I wonder if you would ask Dr. Emerson to come in.

DR. SCOTT: Yes, my Lord. (*She goes out.*) Would you come in now, sir?

(SISTER *and* DR. EMERSON *come into* KEN's *room.*)

JUDGE: Dr. Emerson, I would like you to take the oath.

(*The* JUDGE *hands* DR. EMERSON *a card with the oath written on it.*)

DR. EMERSON: I swear the evidence that I give shall be the truth, the whole truth and nothing but the truth.

JUDGE: Stand over there, please.

(*The* JUDGE *nods to* MR. EDEN.)

EDEN: You are Dr. Michael Emerson?

DR. EMERSON: I am.

EDEN: And what is your position here?

DR. EMERSON: I am a consultant physician and in charge of the intensive care unit.

EDEN: Dr. Emerson, would you please give a brief account of your treatment of this patient.

DR. EMERSON (*Referring to notes*): Mr. Harrison was admitted here on the afternoon of October 9th, as an emergency following a road accident. He was suffering from a fractured left tibia and right tibia and fibia, a fractured pelvis, four fractured ribs, one of which had punctured the lung, and a dislocated fourth vertebra, which had ruptured the spinal cord. He was extensively bruised and had minor lacerations. He was deeply unconscious and remained so for thirty hours. As a result of treatment all the broken bones and ruptured tissue have healed with the exception of a severed spinal cord and this, together with a mental trauma, is now all that remains of the initial injury.

EDEN: Precisely, Doctor. Let us deal with those last two points. The spinal cord. Will there be any further improvement in that?

DR. EMERSON: In the present state of medical knowledge, I would think not.

EDEN: And the mental trauma you spoke of?

DR. EMERSON: It's impossible to injure the body to the extent that Mr. Harrison did and not affect the mind. It is common in these cases that depression and the tendency to make wrong decisions goes on for months, even years.

EDEN: And in your view Mr. Harrison is suffering from such a depression?

DR. EMERSON: Yes.

EDEN: Thank you, Doctor.

JUDGE: Mr. Kershaw?

KERSHAW: Doctor. Is there any objective way you could demonstrate this trauma? Are there, for example, the results of any tests, or any measurements you can take to show it to us?

DR. EMERSON: No.

KERSHAW: Then how do you distinguish between a medical syndrome and a sane, even justified, depression?

DR. EMERSON: By using my thirty years' experience as a physician, dealing with both types.

KERSHAW: No more questions, my Lord.

JUDGE: Mr. Eden, do you wish to re-examine?

EDEN: No, my Lord.

JUDGE: Thank you, Doctor. Would you ask Dr. Barr if he would step in please?

(DR. EMERSON *goes out.*)

DR. EMERSON: It's you now, Barr.

(SISTER *brings* DR. BARR *into* KEN's *room.*)

SISTER: Dr. Barr.

JUDGE: Dr. Barr, will you take the oath please. (*He does so.*) Mr. Kershaw.

KERSHAW: You are Dr. Richard Barr?

DR. BARR: I am.

KERSHAW: And what position do you hold?

DR. BARR: I am a consultant psychiatrist at Norwood Park Hospital.

KERSHAW: That is primarily a mental hospital is it not?

DR. BARR: It is.

KERSHAW: Then you must see a large number of patients suffering from depressive illness.

DR. BARR: I do, yes.

KERSHAW: You have examined Mr. Harrison?

DR. BARR: I have, yes.

KERSHAW: Would you say that he was suffering from such an illness?

DR. BARR: No, I would not.

KERSHAW: Are you quite sure, Doctor?

DR. BARR: Yes, I am.

KERSHAW: The court has heard evidence that Mr. Harrison is depressed. Would you dispute that?

DR. BARR: No, but depression is not necessarily an illness. I would say that Mr. Harrison's depression is reactive rather than endogenous. That is to say, he is reacting in a perfectly rational way to a very bad situation.

KERSHAW: Thank you, Dr. Barr.

JUDGE: Mr. Eden?

EDEN: Dr. Barr. Are there any objective results that you could produce to prove Mr. Harrison is capable?

DR. BARR: There are clinical symptoms of endogenous depression, of course, disturbed sleep patterns, loss of appetite, lassitude, but, even if they were present, they would be masked by the physical condition.

EDEN: So how can you be sure this *is* in fact just a reactive depression?

DR. BARR: Just by experience, that's all, and by discovering when I talk to him that he has a remarkably incisive mind and is perfectly capable of understanding his position and of deciding what to do about it.

EDEN: One last thing, Doctor, do you think Mr. Harrison has made the right decision?

KERSHAW (*Quickly*): Is that really relevant, my Lord? After all . . .

JUDGE: Not really . . .

DR. BARR: I should like to answer it though.

JUDGE: Very well.

DR. BARR: No, I thought he made the wrong decision. (*To* KEN:) Sorry.

EDEN: No more questions, my Lord.

JUDGE: Do you wish to re-examine, Mr. Kershaw?

KERSHAW: No, thank you, my Lord.

JUDGE: That will be all, Dr. Barr.

(DR. BARR *goes out. The* JUDGE *stands.*)

JUDGE: Do you feel like answering some questions?

KEN: Of course.

JUDGE: Thank you.

KEN: You are too kind.

JUDGE: Not at all.

KEN: I mean it. I'd prefer it if you were a hanging judge.

JUDGE: There aren't any any more.

KEN: Society is now much more sensitive and humane?

JUDGE: You could put it that way.

KEN: I'll settle for that.

JUDGE: I would like you to take the oath. Dr. Scott, his right hand, please. (KEN *takes the oath*.) The consultant physician here has given evidence that you are not capable of making a rational decision.

KEN: He's wrong.

JUDGE: When then do you think he came to that opinion?

KEN: He's a good doctor and won't let a patient die if he can help it.

JUDGE: He found that you were suffering from acute depression.

KEN: Is that surprising? I am almost totally paralyzed. I'd be insane if I *weren't* depressed.

JUDGE: But there is a difference between being unhappy and being depressed in the medical sense.

KEN: I would have thought that my psychiatrist answered that point.

JUDGE: But, surely, wishing to die must be strong evidence that the depression has moved beyond a mere unhappiness into a medical realm?

KEN: I don't wish to die.

JUDGE: Then what is this case all about?

KEN: Nor do I wish to live at any price. Of course I want to live, but as far as I am concerned I'm dead already. I merely require the doctors to recognize the fact. I cannot accept this condition constitutes life in any real sense at all.

JUDGE: Certainly, you're alive legally.

KEN: I think I could challenge even that.

JUDGE: How?

KEN: Any reasonable definition of life must include the idea of its being self-supporting. I seem to remember something in the papers—when all the heart transplant controversy was on—about it being all right to take someone's heart if they require constant attention from respirators and so on to keep them alive.

JUDGE: There also has to be absolutely no brain activity at all. Yours is certainly working.

KEN: It is and sanely.

JUDGE: That is the question to be decided.

KEN: My Lord, I am not asking anyone to kill me. I am only asking to be discharged from this hospital.

JUDGE: It comes to the same thing.

KEN: Then that proves my point; not just the fact that I will spend the rest of my life in hospital, but that whilst I am here, everything is geared just to keeping my brain active, with no real possibility of it ever being able to direct anything. As far as I can see, that is an act of deliberate cruelty.

JUDGE: Surely, it would be more cruel if society let people die, when it could, with some effort, keep them alive.

KEN: No, not *more* cruel, *just* as cruel.

JUDGE: Then why should the hospital let you die—if it is just as cruel?

KEN: The cruelty doesn't reside in saving someone or allowing them to die. It resides in the fact that the choice is removed from the man concerned.

JUDGE: But a man who is very desperately depressed is not capable of making a reasonable choice.

KEN: As you said, my Lord, that is the question to be decided.

JUDGE: All right. You tell me why it is a reasonable choice that you decided to die.

KEN: It is a question of dignity. Look at me here. I can do nothing, not even the basic primitive functions. I cannot even urinate, I have a permanent catheter attached to me. Every few days my bowels are washed out. Every few hours two nurses have to turn me over or I would rot away from bedsores. Only my brain functions unimpaired but even that is futile because I can't act on any conclusions it comes to. This hearing proves that. Will you please listen.

JUDGE: I am listening.

KEN: I choose to acknowledge the fact that I am in fact dead and I find the hospital's persistent effort to maintain this shadow of life an indignity and it's inhumane.

JUDGE: But wouldn't you agree that many people with appalling physical handicaps have overcome them and lived essentially creative, dignified lives?

KEN: Yes, I would, but the dignity starts with their choice. If I choose to live, it would be appalling if society killed me. If I choose to die, it is equally appalling if society keeps me alive.

JUDGE: I cannot accept that it is undignified for society to devote resources to keeping someone alive. Surely it enhances that society.

KEN: It is not undignified if the man wants to stay alive, but I must restate that the dignity starts with his choice. Without it, it is degrading because technology has taken over from human will. My Lord, if I cannot be a man, I do not wish to be a medical achievement. I'm fine . . . I am fine.

JUDGE: It's all right. I have no more questions.

(*The* JUDGE *stands up and walks to the window. He thinks a moment.*)

JUDGE: This is a most unusual case. Before I make a judgment, I want to state that I believe all the parties have acted in good faith. I propose to consider this for a moment. The law on this is fairly clear. A deliberate decision to embark on a course of action that will lead inevitably to death is not *ipso facto* evidence of insanity. If it were, society would have to reward many men with a dishonorable burial rather than a posthumous medal for gallantry. On the other hand, we do have to bear in mind that Mr. Harrison has suffered massive physical injuries and it is possible that his mind is affected. Any judge in his career will have met men who are without doubt insane in the meaning of the Act and yet appear in the witness box to be rational. We must, in this case, be most careful not to allow Mr. Harrison's obvious wit and intelligence to blind us to the fact that he could be suffering from a depressive illness . . . and so we have to face the disturbing fact of the divided evidence . . . and bear in mind that, however much we may sympathize with Mr. Harrison in his cogently argued case to be allowed to die, the law instructs us to ignore it if it is the product of a disturbed or clinically depressed mind . . . However, I am satisfied that Mr. Harrison is a brave and cool man who is in complete control of his mental faculties and I shall therefore make an order for him to be set free. (*A pause. The* JUDGE *walks over to* KEN.) Well, you got your hanging judge!

KEN: I think not, my Lord. Thank you.

(*The* JUDGE *nods and smiles.*)

JUDGE: Goodbye. (*He turns and goes. He meets* DR. EMERSON *in the* SISTER's *room. While he talks to him, everyone else, except* DR. SCOTT, *comes out.*) Ah, Dr. Emerson.

DR. EMERSON: My Lord?

JUDGE: I'm afraid you'll have to release your patient.

DR. EMERSON: I see.

JUDGE: I'm sorry. I understand how you must feel.

DR. EMERSON: Thank you.

JUDGE: If ever I have to have a road accident, I hope it's in this town and I finish up here.

DR. EMERSON: Thank you again.

JUDGE: Goodbye.

(*He walks down the corridor.* DR. EMERSON *stands a moment, then slowly goes back to the room.* KEN *is looking out of the window.* DR. SCOTT *is sitting by the bed.*)

DR. EMERSON: Where will you go?

KEN: I'll get a room somewhere.

DR. EMERSON: There's no need.

KEN: Don't let's . . .

DR. EMERSON: We'll stop treatment, remove the drips. Stop feeding you if you like. You'll be unconscious in three days, dead in six at most.

KEN: There'll be no last minute resuscitation?

DR. EMERSON: Only with your express permission.

KEN: That's very kind; why are you doing it?

DR. EMERSON: Simple! You might change your mind.

(KEN *smiles and shakes his head.*)

KEN: Thanks. I won't change my mind, but I'd like to stay.

(DR. EMERSON *nods and goes.* DR. SCOTT *stands and moves to the door. She turns and moves to* KEN *as if to kiss him.*)

KEN: Oh, don't, but thank you.

(DR. SCOTT *smiles weakly and goes out.*)

(*The lights are held for a long moment and then snap out.*)

QUESTIONS

1. Dr. Emerson, the head of the hospital, who wants to prolong Ken Harrison's life against his will, says, "Medicine . . . is being seriously threatened because of the intervention of law. Patients are becoming so litigious [i.e. ready to go to court] that doctors will soon be afraid to offer any opinion or take any action at all." In what way do the Harvard Medical School Committee report and the article by Veatch support Dr. Emerson's opinion? Do you think that he is right? Is the threat of medical malpractice suits, or of government intervention (as in Baby Doe cases where government can countermand the wishes of parents or doctors regarding severely damaged newborns), hampering the freedom of doctors to make sound professional judgment?

2. Mr. Hill, Ken's lawyer, says that citizens must be protected from finding themselves "powerless in the hands of [a doctor,] a lawyer or a . . . bureaucrat," i.e. any "professional." He is arguing that legal and ethical questions cannot be answered by the rules of any profession; they must be tested, tried. Is he right? Should a

doctor, lawyer, philosopher decide who shall live, for how long, under what circumstances? Or is this a question that can only be answered by the person whose life is at stake?

3. Is Dr. Emerson lying when he tells the lawyer, Mr. Eden, that he believes Ken Harrison is suffering from a "mental trauma," a depression that is forcing him to want to end his life? Why might a doctor, who is personally in good health, have the tendency to think that a patient's desire to end his or her life is a form of mental illness or aberration?

4. Is Dr. Barr, the psychiatrist, right or wrong in thinking that Ken's reaction is not a form of mental illness, but "a perfectly rational way [to react] to a very bad situation"? Is it significant that Dr. Barr, a psychiatrist, thinks Ken is not being irrational, while Dr. Emerson, who heads an intensive care unit, thinks *any* decision to die is irrational? Might the difference between their fields of medicine cause the difference in their opinions?

5. Is it important that both Dr. Barr and Dr. Emerson come to their opposite judgments on the basis of "experience"? How important is subjective experience to a doctor when he or she is making a medical judgment? How important is it in a court of law?

6. The judge asks Dr. Barr, who has testified that Ken is sane—and therefore that the hospital cannot hold him against his will—whether he thinks that Ken has made the right decision (to refuse treatment and die). Dr. Barr says he thinks Ken has made the wrong decision. Why does he think that? What in Dr. Barr's field, psychiatry, might make him consider that there are better alternatives to Ken's decision? What might a psychiatrist think that those alternatives should be?

7. What do you think Dr. Elisabeth Kübler-Ross would decide about Ken Robinson? Do you think she would advise the hospital that a patient has the *right* to die? Do you think she would urge Ken to an "acceptance" of life as she helps her dying patients to the "acceptance" of death stage?

8. Ken tells the judge that he does not want to die but also that he does not wish to live at any price. His argument is that he is already dead. Do you agree with him? Think back to Veatch's discussion. Is Ken really *alive* by Veatch's definition of life and death?

9. Ken argues that "everything [in the hospital] is geared just to keeping [his] brain active, with no possibility of it ever being able to direct anything." This he says is "an act of deliberate cruelty." Do you think he is right? If we take Ken's position, how must we modify the Harvard Medical School's definition of death as "brain death"? Can there be "death" without brain death?

10. Why is the right to exercise some degree of control over one's life and death "a question of dignity"? How would the people of the Middle Ages, as described by Ariès, view Ken's conception of human dignity in dying? Would they agree or disagree with Ken?

EXERCISES

1. Carefully reread the Judge's summation and decision on p. 333. The judge says he believes that "all the parties have acted in good faith." This suggests that he *might* have decided in favor of the hospital and against Ken. Pretend that you are judging the case. List three reasons for making the opposite—pro-hospital—decision. Write a passage of dialogue of two pages between the Judge and Ken in which the Judge renders a pro-hospital decision.
2. Imagine that there is an epilogue to the play. Two days after the hospital removes the support systems, Ken changes his mind. Write a one-page dialogue of this scene between Ken and Dr. Emerson.
3. Imagine that you are a court reporter and that you were present at the hearing covered by the scene represented in the play. Write a report of that scene. Be as objective as you can on the premise that you are reporting, not editorializing. Then pretend that your editor is taken with your report and with the incident. He wants you to write an editorial in which you express the opinion of the newspaper. The editor has agreed that whatever opinion you adopt he will print as the opinion of the paper. Write that editorial.

CHAPTER TWENTY

AUDEN: IN MEMORY OF
W. B. YEATS

Poetry

This selection is not only written by a famous twentieth-century poet, W. H. Auden, but is also about the death of a famous poet, William Butler Yeats, perhaps the greatest poet who wrote in the English language in the twentieth century. Poetry is a quite different form of expression from prose. A poem expresses itself with the tight economy of a mathematical formula. A poem does not use words the way an article or a story does; it does not "tell us about . . ." Instead it gives us sharp verbal "pictures of . . ." The poet uses words the way a painter uses colors or a musician uses notes: not to "tell us about" but to make an image or a design "with." These images call forth a sharp emotional response from us. For instance, ask yourself whether these images—"But for him it was his last afternoon as himself / An afternoon of nurses and rumours; / the provinces of his body revolted"— create in your mind the atmosphere of the hospital where Kübler-Ross works? Or to take another example, ask whether these lines, "Far from his illness / The wolves ran on through the evergreen forests / The peasant river was untempted by the fashionable quays," shape the conflict between *nature*, its rhythms unbroken by a single human death, and *society* (the "fashionable quays," or docks), the cities where we live in a man-made environment.

Like Shakespeare and many other great poets, Auden sets up a comparison between the frail human being and the immortal poetry he makes. Shakespeare said it like this:

Not marble nor the gilded monuments of princes
Shall outlive this powerful rhyme.

IN MEMORY OF
_____ W. B. YEATS (*d. Jan. 1939*) _____
W. H. Auden

1

He disappeared in the dead of winter:
The brooks were frozen, the airports almost deserted,
And snow disfigured the public statues;

The mercury sank in the mouth of the dying day.
O all the instruments agree
The day of his death was a dark cold day.

Far from his illness
The wolves ran on through the evergreen forests,
The peasant river was untempted by the fashionable quays;
By mourning tongues
The death of the poet was kept from his poems.

But for him it was his last afternoon as himself,
An afternoon of nurses and rumours;
The provinces of his body revolted,
The squares of his mind were empty,
Silence invaded the suburbs,
The current of his feeling failed: he became his admirers.

Now he is scattered among a hundred cities
And wholly given over to unfamiliar affections;
To find his happiness in another kind of wood
And be punished under a foreign code of conscience.
The words of a dead man
Are modified in the guts of the living.

But in the importance and noise of tomorrow
When the brokers are roaring like beasts on the floor of the
    Bourse,
And the poor have the sufferings to which they are fairly
    accustomed,
And each in the cell of himself is almost convinced of his
    freedom;

SOURCE: From W. H. Auden, *The Collected Poetry*, Random House, N.Y., 1945.

A few thousand will think of this day
As one thinks of a day when one did something slightly unusual.
O all the instruments agree
The day of his death was a dark cold day.

2

You were silly like us: your gift survived it all;
The parish of rich women, physical decay,
Yourself; mad Ireland hurt you into poetry.
Now Ireland has her madness and her weather still,
For poetry makes nothing happen: it survives
In the valley of its saying where executives
Would never want to tamper; it flows south
From ranches of isolation and the busy griefs,
Raw towns that we believe and die in; it survives,
A way of happening, a mouth.

3

Earth, receive an honoured guest;
William Yeats is laid to rest:
Let the Irish vessel lie
Emptied of its poetry.

Time that is intolerant
Of the brave and innocent,
And indifferent in a week
To a beautiful physique,

Worships language and forgives
Everyone by whom it lives;
Pardons cowardice, conceit,
Lays its honours at their feet.

Time that with this strange excuse
Pardoned Kipling and his views,
And will pardon Paul Claudel,
Pardons him for writing well.

In the nightmare of the dark
All the dogs of Europe bark,
And the living nations wait,
Each sequestered in its hate;

Intellectual disgrace
Stares from every human face,
And the seas of pity lie
Locked and frozen in each eye.

Follow, poet, follow right
To the bottom of the night,
With your unconstraining voice
Still persuade us to rejoice;

With the farming of a verse
Make a vineyard of the curse,
Sing of human unsuccess
In a rapture of distress;

In the deserts of the heart
Let the healing fountain start,
In the prison of his days
Teach the free man how to praise.

QUESTIONS

Thinking about poetry is somewhat different from thinking about
other verbal forms of communication. Until you get used to it, reading
poetry can be difficult. The following questions are designed to help
you reread the poem closely and think about it.

1. Why does Auden use the word "disappeared" instead of "died"
   in the first line?
2. Why does Auden say that all the "instruments" measure the day
   as dark and cold?
3. In the second stanza, Auden sets up a dichotomy (an opposition)
   between *nature* (wolves running in forests of trees that never die,
   peasant rivers) and *human nature* (the span of life of a human
   being, which unlike nature's "evergreen" life, is limited). Why
   does he end this stanza with the line "The death of the poet was
   kept from his poems"? What is the difference between the life
   span of a poet and the life span of his poems?
4. Auden uses the image of the human body as a city in describing
   the actual process of dying: "The provinces of his body revolted
   / The squares of his mind were empty / Silence invaded the suburbs."
   Why is this metaphor (human body = city) a good way of explaining
   that "it was his last afternoon as himself"?
5. What does "he became his admirers" mean? Why does a poet,
   when he dies, *become* his readers?
6. What does Auden mean when he says, "The words of a dead
   man / Are modified in the guts of the living"? How do you think
   that Auden's words were modified in your guts? This takes us
   back to the philosopher's approach; remember *phenomenology*?
   How does the whole history of my experience modify, or change,
   what words mean to me? Does any phrase from this poem mean
   exactly the same thing to you as it does to me, or to the person

sitting next to you? How can it, since we all carry around a different emotional history?

7. What point is Auden making when, in stanza 6, he introduces the brokers of the Bourse (the stock exchange in Paris) and the suffering poor?

8. In Part 2, Auden makes the contrast even sharper. Here he contrasts Yeats the human being, "who was silly like us," and Yeats the poet, whose gift survives his silly, frail humanness. Having thought in Questions 6 and 7 about where poetry happens and how it means, speculate about the meaning of the equation that closes Part 2: Poetry = "a way of happening, a mouth." Why does Auden change his verse form in Part 3? What does this change of tone to a musical, almost hymn-like incantation, do to the meaning of the poem? How does the *invocation* ("calling") to Earth ("Earth, receive an honoured guest") and the invocation to the spirit of Yeats ("Follow, poet, follow right") change the direction of our response?

9. What is Auden saying about time in Part 3? What point is he making about Yeats and about poetry in general with the several allusions to time?

10. The line "Sing of human unsuccess / In a rapture of distress" is a *paradox*, a self-contradiction. It makes us wonder, "How can a human being be successful in talking about unsuccess?" How can a *rapture*, a moment of transcendent joy, arise out of distress, terrible sorrow?

11. How is poetry's approach to death different from all the other approaches in this unit? Does poetry help us to understand death, or does it give us a better sense of our condition in being creatures who must die? What is the *use* of poetry?

EXERCISES

1. Read Shakespeare's sonnet "Not marble nor the gilded monuments / of Princes (Sonnet 55), Emily Dickenson's "Because I Could Not Stop for Death," and Louis Simpson's "My Father in the Night Commanding No." What attitudes do these poems express about the mortality of the imagination? Write a paper on one of these poets' attitudes toward death.

2. W. B. Yeats was an old man when he died. Thus, the man W. H. Auden can acknowledge that though Yeats's death is a loss to the world, the poet/man's death is not a loss to nature. Therefore

Auden can concentrate his attention on what survived the man
and yet survived in the society, or culture. Read Randall Jarrell's
"The Death of the Ball-Turret Gunner," which is about the death
of a young man in war. To what does Jarrell's poem call our emotional
response? How does our emotional response to this poem differ
from the response evoked from Auden's poem? In your journal,
make a list of your responses to both poems.

3. Write a short stanza-by-stanza paraphrase of Auden's poem. A
paraphrase is a prose statement of the content of a piece of writing.
The value of a paraphrase is that it sets forth the reader's understanding of a poem's meaning. However, a paraphrase is never
an equivalent of the original that it restates. When you have written
what you consider a successful paraphrase of Auden's poem (you
can allow the preceding questions to guide you in this exercise),
consider what essential differences there are in the original and its
prose restatement. What, for example, does the original contain
in the way of sound patterns that are not repeated in the paraphrase?
Which of Auden's images cannot be easily reproduced in the prose
version? On the basis of this examination, write out your thoughts
on how poetry differs from prose.

_____ CHAPTER TWENTY-ONE _____

SCHONGAUER AND WOLGEMUT: THREE FIFTEENTH-CENTURY WOODCUTS

Art

One of the central topics of Western art over the centuries has been the death of Jesus. The artist's rendering of the Crucifixion is basically a subjective interpretation since there is no historical or documentary evidence that can authenticate any facts concerning the life of Jesus. The closest we can come to what might be considered a record of his life are the four gospel accounts of Mark, Matthew, Luke, and John, but even these, written years after the events they chronicle, give us few narrative details. What a picture does, that no written account can do, is to give us the *instant* imaginative response of an artist as he *thinks* about an important human event. The author thinks the event whole and asks us, with his picture, to visualize a whole from the vantage point, or perspective, from which he asks us to look. Consider the following account of the Crucifixion from the Gospel of St. Mark, the earliest of the four:

> And they brought him unto the place Golgotha, which is, being interpreted, "the place of a skull." (which the word means in Hebrew).
> And they gave him to drink wine mingled with myrrh, but he received *it* not.

343

> And when they had crucified him, they parted his garments, casting lots upon them, what every man should take.
>
> And it was the third hour, and they crucified him.
>
> And the superscription of his accusation was written over, THE KING OF THE JEWS.
>
> And with him they crucify two thieves; the one on his right hand, and the other on his left.
>
> [15:22–27]

Later, Mark adds a few other narrative details, including the following: His enemies (left unspecified) passed by and railed at him; the scribes and the Pharisees mocked him and taunted him to use his "kingly" powers to descend from the cross; there was darkness from the sixth until the ninth hour; at the ninth hour Jesus cried out to God, "Why hast thou forsaken me?"; one man filled a sponge full of vinegar, put it on a reed, and gave it to Jesus to drink from; several women witnessed his death from afar, including his mother Mary, Mary Magdalene, and Mary, the mother of James and John.

We have given this summary of Mark as background for examining three woodcuts of the Crucifixion, presented on pages 345–347. You might read all four of the Gospel accounts to see just how many of the details in the pictures are warranted by the earliest and nearest testimony we have of the death of Jesus. You will see that the artist supplied many specific details, including, of course, such highly subjective images as the expression of Jesus' face at the time of his death. What inspired these images? Surely, they came in part from the artists' own perceptions of what that highly dramatic moment must have been like, and probably also they were indebted to the way in which scholars, other painters, and writers of narratives that he knew conceived of that moment. The point is that the moment of Jesus' death is a subject open for the artist's interpretation.

The woodcuts we have chosen are from the late Middle Ages. Woodcuts were the earliest form of printmaking, and their wide circulation coincided closely with the invention and the use of the printing press. A woodcut was made through the transfer of an image from a raised surface on a block of wood (much like a modern rubber stamp) onto paper or vellum. Woodcuts were often used in early printed books as illustrations, and pictures of the Crucifixion appeared particularly in missals (the official texts of the liturgy). The study of woodcuts, together with works of art from other media, is conducted by art historians, who specialize in dating and localizing works of art as well as in studying the style and meaning of individual works, schools, and periods of art.

As you are looking at the pictures, keep in mind Ariès's account of the ways in which death was experienced in the Middle Ages.

Figure 1. Woodcut by Martin Schongauer, ca. 1470.

Figure 2. Woodcut by Martin Schongauer, ca. 1480.

Figure 3. Woodcut by Michael Wolgemut, ca. 1490.

QUESTIONS

1. The death of Christ can be seen from two antithetical perspectives: either as the moment of great joy when mankind, through the death of the incarnated God, is redeemed; or as the moment of great sorrow when man tortures and kills his own God. Which of the three versions gives us the most intense representation of Christ as "The Man of Sorrows"? Look for as many details as you can to support your choice.

2. The critical study of works of art can sharpen our capacity to *see* details—it can improve what might be called our "visual literacy." The woodcuts you have examined differ in many particulars. Focus, for some minutes, on the background, and list as many details as you can, noting especially how the three woodcuts differ. Choose one of the landscapes and interpret its significance for the overall meaning of the picture. What, for example, does the artist gain by placing the Crucifixion into the unhistorical setting of a Northern landscape (his own city)? Does this use of setting say anything to us about the timelessness of Jesus' death?

3. Figures 1 and 2 are by the same artist, though several years apart. Examine the two pictures closely and describe how the artist's representation of the death of Christ changes from one to the other.

4. Review the details of the Crucifixion scene in the Gospel of Mark. Does Mark emphasize the joy or the sorrow of Jesus' death? Which of the woodcuts in your mind comes closest to the mood projected by Mark?

5. Examine the expression on the faces of the soldiers in Figure 2. Note their preoccupation with the dice game, the prize of which, according to legend, is Christ's garment, which presumably has the magical property of protecting its wearer from death. The soldiers' attitude is quite different from that depicted in Figure 3. What impression do you take away from each? Which, in your mind, is the more cruel response? Explain.

6. Study the wounds of Christ in the three pictures. How for example does Figure 1 differ from Figure 3 in its depiction of bleeding? What special purpose is served by the four angels in Figure 1? Can you think of any reasons why they are holding cups to Christ's wounds? Does this depiction add to the artist's interpretation of Christ's death? (Remember: Christ's blood is thought to have divine properties.)

7. Which of the three woodcuts do you consider to be the most realistic? What qualities in the depictions create the illusion of realism? Would

you say that Jesus is not treated realistically in any of the woodcuts? Explain.

EXERCISES

1. Visit a local museum or art gallery, or if you prefer, browse through the art history section of the library at your college/school. Look for medieval pictures of the Crucifixion. Choose one—preferably from the fifteenth century but any picture of the Crucifixion, medieval or modern, will do—and carefully note in your journal everything of importance that you see in the picture. Then write a description of what you perceive to be the artist's conception of the death of Christ. Focus on any details you wish. You might, for example, look at the attitudes, expression, and placement of the mourners or the torturers or Christ himself (or perhaps all of these).

2. A close comparative examination of Figures 1 and 3 will show a distinct difference in the representation of Jesus' death. The great cultural historian J. Huizinga, in his book *The Waning of the Middle Ages*, observes that in the fifteenth century (the time of our woodcuts) "the conception of death took a spectral and fantastic shape. A new and vivid shudder was added to the great primitive horror of death." Do any of the woodcuts reflect this attitude toward the death of Jesus? Do you think that the representation of the torture or the suffering of Christ strengthens or weakens the concept that he is immortal? Write a critical paper in which you reflect upon one or both of these questions.

3. Return to your journal entry entitled "My Thoughts about Death." Using the foregoing woodcuts as your stimulus, think about the relationship of death and immortality. Most religions are, of course, concerned with the immortal and with the presence of divine figures that exist outside the temporal limits experienced by humankind. To what extent did your thoughts about death incorporate ideas of the immortal? If not at all, was this omission an oversight or does it reflect your general outlook? Make any necessary revisions or additions provoked by the discussion of these woodcuts and the questions we have raised to your journal entry.

UNIT IV

THE FUTURE

We have been exploring issues and questions that are either exclusively or centrally human. This unit continues that exploration, for the capacity to envision the future is a distinctively human endeavor. In order to function at all in the present, we must project images or programs of future events. Sometimes predicting the future is purely personal, or even trivial (e.g., "I will wear my red dress tomorrow rather than my purple jeans"); at other times future projection can have national significance ("The Federal Reserve chairman says that inflation will increase during the next fiscal year"); or global significance ("The likelihood of nuclear war before the end of this century has increased by 50 percent"); or even cosmic significance ("The Battle of Armageddon will begin in the year 1997 and the second coming of Christ will occur in the year 2000").

The foregoing examples are not, of course, real predictions; we have just invented them. What is true, however, is that we humans do predict the future all the time. We are compelled to do so by our very nature: as the selection by Alvin Toffler tells us, we suffer psychological, physical, and emotional shock when we *cannot* predict the future. In fact, we prize a future orientation so highly that we usually pay very large salaries to people who reliably predict the future, as, for example, political pollsters, TV forecasters, or stock-market analysts.

Or take the popular American preoccupation with weather forecasts. Has it ever occurred to you that since very few Americans are farmers, whose activities depend upon the weather, and since there is nothing whatever that we can do about the weather, we seem strangely obsessed with weather forecasts? We are also strangely attracted to astrological predictions, and even though we *know* that the indexes on which such predictions are based are completely false, we still seem to want to believe them. There are probably very, very few people in America who believe that the sun revolves around the earth. Astrology, and any kind of astrological prediction of the future, depends entirely upon the utterly false notion that the sun revolves around the earth—an idea that was disproved over 500 years ago. And yet millions of Americans know their astrological signs intimately. Have you caught your-self—well educated as you are—reading the astrologer's column in the news-paper to find out what your life is going to be like today, tomorrow, or next month? We probably all have at one time or another.

There is a deep, almost mysterious need to know the future; not knowing, or not having some images of what is likely to happen, fills us with fear. The seventeenth-century poet John Dryden put it this way:

> Distrust and darkness of a future state
> Make poor mankind so fearful of their fate.
> Death in itself is nothing, but we fear
> To be we know not what, we know not where.
>   *Aureng-Zebe*

Moreover we *hope* in the future, usually against what our most basic com-monsense tells us:

> None would live past years again
> Yet all hope pleasure in what yet remain;
> And from the dregs of life think to receive
> What the first sprightly running could not
> give.
>   *Aureng-Zebe*

What *is* this strange gift, or curse, we humans have, and how important is it? We will begin this unit with an interview with the Stanford University psychologist Philip Zimbardo, who believes that the ways we envision the future determine the very shape of our consciousness and of our lives. Zimbardo provides us with a fundamental outlook upon which our work and our vision are based. Science-fiction writing, of the kind we encounter in Ursula le Guin's frightening story "The New Atlantis," is a fictional projection into future time; it offers us a view of what the future can be if human beings are not more sensitive to the effects of their present social behavior upon generations to come. Martin Luther King's sociopolitical "dream" is an alternative vision of the future, one that we can work toward each time we *choose* brotherhood. The relation of John Cage's prophecies forty years ago about the future of music to Brian Eno's experiments with "ambient" and "discreet" music in the present day illustrates one of the ways that history grows into present and future, while Quentin Fiore's exploration and demonstration of the possible book of the future links the book you are reading to its own possible progeny.

We have deliberately collected disparate visions of the future to demonstrate in what different modalities experts in various disciplines think about the future and with what hopes and apprehensions they scan their horizons. The future that allows some to envision utopia and others apocalypse is always uncertain.

_____ CHAPTER TWENTY-TWO _____

ZIMBARDO: FUTURE ORIENTATION

Psychology

Philip G. Zimbardo, a professor at Stanford University, is a very well-known psychologist. The most salient characteristics of Philip Zimbardo's work are its versatility, its careful design, and its cultural scope. Professor Zimbardo has been as adept at taking pressing social problems into the laboratory as he has been at bringing laboratory findings to bear in considering social phenomena. For example, in his now classic "prison experiment," he simulated the social interactions of prisons in a carefully designed laboratory experiment at Stanford. The experiment showed that "guard" mentality and behavior and "prisoner" mentality and behavior, as they actually exist in American prisons, are elicited by the social role which a human being plays. These behaviors were actually induced in a randomly chosen population of normal, well-balanced, college-student subjects. In other experiments, Zimbardo has brought his findings on the effects of anonymity to bear on such social problems as vandalism, alienation, and shyness.

In Zimbardo's view, the first requirement for a student specializing in social psychology is to learn to be a "people watcher." We are offering you the opportunity in this interview to watch a people watcher, to "hear" a scientist thinking on his feet about the various perspectives he takes—cultural, phenomenal, clinical—as he zeroes in on an issue upon which he is planning to conduct research—the effects of time orientation on social behavior.

Because this selection is an interview and not a published piece of writing, we have not added the usual questions and exercises at its conclusion. What you will be reading is a spontaneous report by an expert who is speaking extemporaneously. We have included it for three reasons:

1. We want you to have some firsthand experience with what has been called "the kitchen of the intellect." Listening to Zimbardo as he *thinks* about a problem allows you to see the kind of intellectual activity that goes on *before* an experiment is conducted, *before* a paper is written. You are getting a tour of the kitchen before the banquet is spread on the table.
2. We want you to see the value of the kind of cross-disciplinary approach that we have offered you in this book. Philip Zimbardo shows you in this interview that his expertise is strengthened because he is able to assume a variety of perspectives upon a problem he is considering.
3. An interview corresponds more nearly to the kind of intellectual stimulation and provocation you will experience in the personal encounter of the classroom than a written paper does. In addition to being a first-rate research psychologist, Professor Zimbardo is a distinguished teacher, who has won Chancellors Awards for distinguished teaching in two different states. You meet him here not only as an expert but also as a teacher.

The interview was conducted by Rose Zimbardo, who is also a member of the Zimbardo family.

FUTURE ORIENTATION

An Interview with Philip Zimbardo

RZ: What would you say are the particular strengths of psychology in approaching the timeless issues of death, love, work, and the future? That is, what unique insights, methods, or techniques has psychology to offer?

PZ: The psychologist differs from the novelist, dramatist or philosopher—in many cases even other social scientists—in going beyond his or her own feelings or ideas about these topics to try to discover what other people think and feel and how they act. The psychologist

SOURCE: Interview conducted at Stanford University, June 30, 1983.

tries to collect special kinds of information from a representative sample of people rather than to obtain one person's interpretation of ways to view the world. So, what a psychologist's approach adds to the approaches of other disciplines is to give insights into how the average person or selected kinds of people think about or are affected by these issues.

RZ: So that you would say, in effect, psychology on the one hand is more subjective than, say, philosophy, because it is getting at the feelings of people, and on the other hand the psychologist is more objective than the novelist or the poet, who can only deal with his own, personal responses. In a sense it's a median between absolute objectivity and absolute subjectivity.

PZ: Yes, you could say that. If, for example, you want to know about dying, psychologists would interview people who are in the process of dying or people who had recently lost someone who died. That approach gets at the subjective experience of dying, and after many such interviews or after observing the behavior of people who are going through the experience of dying, the psychologist as theorist would classify these behavioral events, place them into a meaningful conceptual framework, and come up with a psychological interpretation of the human process of dying or the cycle of dying.

RZ: Are you yourself interested in doing research on any of the issues I mentioned?

PZ: Yes. I am interested in a number of the topics you mentioned, but I have been working particularly on a problem related to what you call "the future"—that is, on understanding the impact of time perspectives on the way people think, feel, and act. What I am referring to is the tendency of individuals to segment time into categories of past, present, and future—that is, to create a balanced time perspective where for many adults the world is parcelled into those three categories. Now we take for granted those categories of representing experience, but in fact the only empirical reality is the present. The past and the future are actually psychological constructs—they are your memory, your sense of history, your expectations, your anticipations. These are learned phenomena. The child learns how to remember accurately what was or to anticipate future events, predicting what will be.

RZ: Would you say then that since people can't remember everything that happened to them in the past, they explain who they are in the present by what they select to remember of their past?

PZ: Yes, that is the approach I am taking: each of us is indeed the architect of this time construction, this arbitrary structure that we impose on our own life experiences. The extent to which that structure is heavily weighted in the foundation of a past, has more room devoted to the present, or is filled with skylights pointed up to the future is individually determined by personal experiences, but also collectively influenced by cultural background, by social class considerations, by religious ties as well as by the language in the culture. What I want to say is that individual differences result from the overuse of one of these categories: people can be future-oriented, present-oriented, or past-oriented. They will tend to overuse references or language tenses in one of the three categories and think and act less in response to the other two time modes. For example, if you are present-oriented, you tend to think in terms of the here and now. Like the Apostle Thomas, you believe only what you can see or feel. You believe in concrete reality, and your thinking is likely to be more concrete than abstract. Your behavior will be less directly controlled by deterrents, by incentives, or expectations of future rewards. You would more than likely not be good at or even engage in planning, in organizing behavior, or in setting goals and having objectives set forth in means-ends relations. On the other hand, you would be more likely to behave spontaneously or impulsively, be more emotional and able to enjoy more fully the transient things of the present moment—the proverbial "wine, woman, and song."

RZ: Then what about future-oriented people? Would they be likely to fall into two different categories—that is, those who anticipate the future and plan for it, and those who are frightened of the future, expecting a catastrophe or the Second Coming or nuclear devastation?

PZ: That's right. In each of these categories you can see a normal and a pathological version. For instance, the pathology of present-oriented persons is failure to plan ahead, missing appointments, never being on time. They live for the here and now and do things which result in short-term pleasure but perhaps long-term destruction. Drug addicts are persons who lack a future orientation and who are focused too much on the present. On the other hand, a normal, healthy present-orientation is the capacity to enjoy relationships and events that are consumable, like a good meal, companionship, or reading a book for pleasure. It's to experience these events without concern for what one ought to get out of them. Persons with a healthy present orientation experience each event as if it happened for the first time; they don't see things in terms of blinders set from the past. In turn, people with a healthy future orientation will be good at planning or organizing. They are likely to be successes in a technological society like ours, where value is placed upon achieving.

RZ: That would apply really to all the major institutions in our society.

PZ: Exactly. You couldn't have a technologically sophisticated society without the qualities that we associate with a future orientation—like saving for a rainy day, putting money into insurance, planning retirements. You wouldn't have banks and insurance companies if you didn't have future-oriented people. The pathological side of a future orientation is the failure to take joy in the present. It is characterized by the person who is always working toward some future goal, the person who says, "I will do such and such next year as soon as the budget allows." The workaholic suffers from this pathology—his sole pleasure comes from planning the future. This focus can also lead him to think too much of what can go wrong in the future and to develop dread or anxiety.

RZ: What about people with a past orientation?

PZ: People with a past orientation are essentially nostalgia buffs—people who focus on how good things used to be. The healthy side of that orientation is to have a sense of roots, a sense of continuity in your life, and some historical perspective. People with a healthy past orientation tend to be stable, conservative, and they traditionally see themselves as part of a lineage. The pathological side of that orientation is that the behavior of such people tends to be overly controlled by guilt—by contracts they made with their mother or with God, or contracts they imagined they made. The whole Freudian notion of personality development and psychopathology is one in which the adult's behavior at any time is influenced by symbolic events in the past. If you are a past-oriented person, you make yourself vulnerable to reliving all these traumatic experiences and conflicts. If you are a present- or future-oriented person, Freudian notions are irrelevant; they don't exist; they have no impact on you. Without a past perspective, the concept of guilt can exert no influence on behavior. What I am saying is that a person's temporal perspective exerts a powerful influence on his or her chances of success, pleasure, and even cast of mind.

RZ: E. P. Thompson, the British historian, makes a very interesting point about the working class. He says that in the post eighteenth-century world, workers were shifted from being task-oriented to being time-oriented—to believe that time is money, that time must be used and planned. Do you think that in our technological age societal changes can be made in what our temporal orientation should be?

PZ: I think it's not possible to go back. In a sense, the flower children, the hippie subculture of the sixties and early seventies thought precisely in the terms that you just outlined. They were looking around, seeing a military-industrial establishment whose values they rejected because those values included not being concerned for the joy of living in the present but rather to kill people for the future goal of peace, and so they turned on, tuned in, and dropped out. Dropping out of a future-oriented society by taking drugs, tuning into the reality of the here and now, as in the play *Hair*, or in rock concerts, and setting up communes are all ways of getting into the mental state that I call the "expanded present." But this response creates a paradox: you can't sustain a drug high forever (or the ecstasy of a new love), and sooner or later you will begin talking either about how good it was (and you are talking about the past) or you plan on how to get your next fix (and you are talking about the future).

RZ: But to what extent, then, can the individual control his or her own time perspective?

PZ: I think the most satisfying orientation in our current society would be one in which individuals learn to choose which of the three time perspectives they want to govern their lives at any given period of their life. All too often as things are we are slaves of one or another time zone. Take the future-oriented person who is a successful businessman and who can never enjoy his family or friends or all the gifts that his accomplishments have gained for him. It's this locked-in time perspective that is probably responsible for what we call "middle age crisis." The crisis occurs when he is suddenly faced with the thought that in ten years he will die and that he has not really enjoyed what he has worked for. Or on the other hand, the present-oriented person who has enjoyed life fully even without sufficient money and he comes to the point of realizing that he hasn't really accomplished anything. Accomplishments take work, and work takes planning. What is needed is some balanced perspective. From the point of view of a student, for example, when a paper is due, you delay gratification— you don't go to the movies or go out for a pizza—because for the moment nothing is more important than to get that paper done. But you also don't allow that to become a life style the way that Type A people do, who live under such time urgency that they are always delaying gratification. When you don't have some demand to fulfill, you can drop into the present totally and get lost in a novel or a good movie, listen to music, talk to friends or make love.

RZ: Do you think that this way of responding to time perspectives is a peculiar trait of our society or is it universal?

PZ: That's an interesting question. I'd like to answer it by saying something about the relationships among language, thought, and perception. There are cultures, for example, that do not have a future tense and others that don't have a past tense. Still others are focused entirely on the past and everything is interpreted in terms of ancestors. And some societies, of course, do not have a written language at all. So the question becomes, can a society without a written language be future-oriented? I don't think so. Societies that depend on oral transmission are likely to be past-oriented. So I guess I would say that the way we think about and respond to time perspectives is in many respects a function of our language. We have a future tense, so we can be future-oriented, and we develop such a perspective by socializing children to think and talk about what they *will* be when they grow up and so forth.

RZ: Would you say then that it's possible for people to change their time orientation by changing their language?

PZ: Definitely. You ought to be able to help reorient a future-minded person by getting him to use fewer future tense verbs and to increase the number of present tense or past tense verbs. Another thing is relevant here. Like language, class is an index of time orientation. For example, as you move up the socioeconomic hierarchy, you tend to be more future-oriented. Upper-class people tend to think about the more distant future, projecting their line—their great-grandchildren. Middle-class people, in turn, think about a more narrow future—their own careers, their children. As you move down, you get less focus on the future, more living for the present, so that time perspective is both a cause and a consequence of socioeconomic class. In our society, it's unlikely that you will become affluent if you are not future-oriented, and if you are not future-oriented it's likely you are going to be in one of the lower classes.

RZ: That's an interesting thing. I was trying to think how one would break out of the lower classes, and it seems that to obtain a college education is one possible way. Isn't a college education in itself structured to make people future-oriented? For instance, you have to plan your curriculum, declare a major, take prerequisites, and so on.

PZ: Exactly. But I would argue even more extremely and say that the single most important contribution that education makes is to take children who are naturally present-oriented and make them future-oriented. What education teaches is the delay of gratification, the importance of planning and setting goals, the need to keep commitments. Isn't a future-time perspective the foundation for being declared "disciplined," "responsible," "prudent," and other qualities that we like to see mentioned in our letters of recommendation? I think that time orientation is the primary category of relating to the world, of experiencing things. An argument can be made that you learn a time perspective from cultural, social, and economic experiences. You cannot have a sense of the future unless you have grown up in a stable environment where you have learned to have faith in the future—faith that things will be there tomorrow, faith that the banks won't fail, faith that when your father promises you a bicycle if you have been a good boy he will deliver. In an environment where there isn't that predictability, the only thing that you can have faith in is your own ability to produce something right now and to consume it, or you can put your faith in "Lady Luck." Hard-core gamblers are likely to be quite present-oriented. It's a circular thing; you cannot develop this future orientation unless you live in a stable environment, and if you do live in a stable environment it is more likely that you will develop a future orientation which in turn will put stability into your life and that of your children.

RZ: Do you think it's ever possible for someone who is future-oriented to lose his time perspective and become present-oriented?

PZ: Yes. In fact, we know that future-oriented people who are suddenly put into an unstable environment—where the banks are failing, where there is political upheaval—become present-oriented. They live for the moment. You put someone into a concentration camp, regardless of whether he was a college professor, a workaholic Type A who lived all his life in the future, and he begins to parcel his life in ten-minute segments—to get to the food line "on time," not too early so that he won't have to work a longer time after eating and not too late so that he doesn't get beaten up or have no solid food left in the bottom of the soup pot.

We have done research in which we have taken future-oriented students at Stanford and Berkeley (students who wouldn't get into those universities unless they were future-oriented) and under hypnosis gave them the posthypnotic suggestion that the past and future were distant and insignificant and that all that mattered was the present. In a matter of minutes we saw the most dramatic changes in their personalities that I have ever seen in adults. They went from being analytical and reflective to being impulsive, emotional, acting-out; they didn't follow orders where the consequences were some payoff or punishment in the future. In other, related experiments, people who were in the expanded present turned out to be much more creative. These people, on the other hand, did more poorly when given a maze to solve because apparently they had more fun getting lost in the maze. We also concluded that a profound difference between the present and future-oriented person is that the future-oriented person judges him or herself and the worth of an experience in the form of *products* or some tangible outcome, and the present-oriented person judges things in terms of *process*, who enjoys the trip, enjoys going, likes being and becoming part of the experiences.

RZ: Would you say that this generation of students on the one hand becomes paralyzed in the face of nuclear annihilation and on the other becomes more future-oriented when they think about economic matters? They seem to say, "Everybody else is going to suffer economically, but I'm going to make it."

PZ: Yes, I think we are seeing a generation of students who are extremely future-oriented but with a narrow focus. They think they have to accomplish as much as they can in a short time because they think they might not have a distant future or allow themselves even to think of one.

RZ: Do you think there are other reasons besides fear of a nuclear holocaust that cause this difference in the expectation of present-day college students?

PZ: Yes, decidedly. One important factor is the breakdown in fundamental social structures, most clearly the family. There are more single-parent families, fewer extended families with the result that young people don't have a sense of a significant past, one filled with rituals and old tales and intimate associations. Also there are the inroads of the electronic media which encourage a present orientation, the passive consuming of the here and now, as in video games, and so what you are getting is a bifurcation in the society. There are those we can identify as without roots, with no real past, loss of the past and an increased emphasis on living in the present. Another group of young people is focused on the short-term future; they somehow will make it but they may not enjoy what they make. The down side of people who live more and more in the present is the tremendous increase in unwanted teenage pregnancies. Practically all the campaigns to give information about birth control have proven futile. It's not information that's needed but an altered time perspective. Because if you don't have a sense of the future, then an abstract negative consequence—like having a baby you don't want—will have no impact on current pleasure-centered behavior.

RZ: I have observed in working with very poor runaway girls that they really do want the baby but not a child. It's not that they want the sexual gratification as much as having something of their own.

PZ: That's true. Among the teenage girls who get pregnant and who in fact want the baby, there is a second tier of this present orientation where they want a child to establish their own ability to produce something but even here there is no sense of obligation, of consequence or liability, of having to have money to take care of the child. So that even if the cause of the pregnancy is not the expanded present being swept away by the passion of the moment, of not wanting to go through with buying a diaphragm which interferes with the romance of making love, there is also the willed pregnancy with no thought of how the girl is dooming herself to poverty by having children as a teenager without means of support—financial and social.

RZ: Let me move to another area for a moment. As a psychologist, do you think that comparative study of critical thinking and critical writing among the various disciplines is a more useful introduction to college than intensive study in one of the disciplines or in English usage?

PZ: I think it's absolutely essential to have both. American psychologists as compared with European can be characterized as vertical rather than horizontal thinkers. Vertical thinkers tend to work intensively from an idea either up or down and ask, "What does it lead to?" And the objective of psychology as a science is that ideas should lead to testable experiments—hypotheses that fit into a theoretical framework that tell you something about human nature. We do not generally think about the idea in its broadest context; that is, we are not used to the horizontal thinking more characteristic of European psychology—which seeks to link across ideas—as well as of humanistic and scholarly thinking generally. American psychologists tend rather to be noncultural and ahistorical. But in fact you need both—vertical and horizontal thinking. Let me show you what I mean by going back to our discussion of time. The psychologist would say: "How do you define past, present, and future orientation?" "What creates these individual differences in time perspective?" "How could you demonstrate that people are different in this way?" "What behaviors does it lead to?" For instance, she might show that intelligent people who do not fare well in college tend to be present-oriented. But the horizontal or comparative thinker would look at time as it operates in different cultures or possibly from the point of view of the physicist, or from an historical perspective—for example, how concepts of time were changed by the industrial revolution or how time was different in Hebrew and Greek thought. The advantage that psychology has over some of the other disciplines is that we usually go beyond talking about things. Philosophers and novelists talk about phenomena, whereas the psychologist tries to demonstrate in experiments or in therapy that ideas are behaviorally valid—that they make a difference in people's lives. On the negative side, many psychologists tend to follow guideposts and not large-scale road maps.

RZ: My final question, then, is to ask, what would you like your students who major in psychology to read when they are not reading psychology?

PZ: I guess there are two ways I would answer your question. The first thing that students in psychology should do, besides reading what wise and smart psychologists have written—like old William James and young Amos Tversky—is to become people watchers—to spend more time in observing themselves and other people, to learn how to observe and to make sense of what they see. Second, they should read broadly authors who themselves were very good observers of human nature—writers like Dostoyevsky or Shakespeare or every kind of autobiographical writing where people try to reconstruct the time lines of their existence. It's also important for students in psychology to be widely read in cultural anthropology in order to see cultural differences—things that make life different in one place from another. Probably the most important thing is for students in psychology to be more well-read and more excited by the history of ideas. One of the worst things that happens in a college education is that important ideas are segmented and parceled to different areas, different disciplines, and different time periods, so that students, and even faculty, don't have a real appreciation of the confluence of events and ideas that occurred at a given time. What for instance happened politically, scientifically in Europe in 1865 when the Civil War was happening here? They should try to understand the *Zeitgeist* of periods like the Renaissance when in one century there were hundreds of great painters, sculptors, and artisans of every type working in Florence, Italy. How could that be? What social, political, and cultural forces created this crucible of creative genius? Students tend not to think in this broad a framework. So, the single most important change that I would like to see in all of education is the use of a comparative approach to see how different disciplines approach a common theme and how a given idea emerges or develops at different times in history and is treated differently. This might imply, for example, that a student would get excited by investigating the concept of the self as it exists in drama, history, philosophy, and in people with different temporal perspectives.

RZ: I want to thank you very much for taking the time to answer these questions.

CHAPTER TWENTY-THREE

LE GUIN: "THE NEW ATLANTIS"

Fiction

Ursula le Guin is one of the most popular writers of science fiction in America. She is also one of the most intelligent and talented. Her novels, *The Lathe of Heaven*, which was brilliantly televised on the PBS network, and *The Left Hand of Darkness*, winner of the Hugo and Nebula awards in 1969, and her *Earthsea Trilogy* helped to elevate science fiction writing to the status of serious literature.

Le Guin tells wonderful tales, and for that alone we should value her, but she is also scientifically knowledgeable, and her stories inform us, and help us to think more clearly, in many diverse fields, including anthropology, history, sociology, and politics. She is herself very well-educated and comes from a family of intellectuals: her father, Alfred Kroeber, was a distinguished anthropologist; her mother, Theodora Kroeber, wrote the well-known *Ishi in Two Worlds*; and her husband, Charles le Guin, is a historian. In addition to giving us wonderful stories to read, le Guin, simply by being herself, gives us a model of the joys and the rewards of being widely educated, and shows us how creative we can be when we cultivate and treasure learning.

As you are reading, consider:

1. What is the central comparison le Guin is making in this story?
2. What is the relation between the future le Guin envisions for us and the lives we live now?

——— THE NEW ATLANTIS ———
Ursula le Guin

Coming back from my Wilderness Week I sat by an odd sort of man
in the bus. For a long time we didn't talk; I was mending stockings,
and he was reading. Then the bus broke down a few miles outside
Gresham. Boiler trouble, the way it generally is when the driver insists
on trying to go over thirty. It was a Supersonic Superscenic Deluxe
Long Distance coalburner, with Home Comfort, that means a toilet,
and the seats were pretty comfortable, at least those that hadn't yet
worked loose on their bolts, so everybody waited inside the bus;
besides, it was raining. We began talking, the way people do when
there's a breakdown and a wait. He held up his pamphlet and tapped
it—he was a dry-looking man with a school-teacherish way of using
his hands—and said, "This is interesting. I've been reading that a
new continent is rising from the depths of the sea."

The blue stockings were hopeless. You have to have something
besides holes to darn onto. "Which sea?"

"They're not sure yet. Most specialists think the Atlantic. But there's
evidence it may be happening in the Pacific too."

"Won't the oceans get a little crowded?" I said, not taking it seriously.
I was a bit snappish, because of the breakdown, and because those
blue stockings had been good warm ones.

He tapped the pamphlet again and shook his head, quite serious.
"No," he said. "The old continents are sinking, to make room for the
new. You can see that that is happening."

You certainly can. Manhattan Island is now under eleven feet of
water at low tide, and there are oyster beds in Ghirardelli Square.

"I thought that was because the oceans are rising from polar melt."

He shook his head again. "That is a factor. Due to the greenhouse
effect of pollution, indeed Antarctica may become inhabitable. But
climatic factors will not explain the emergence of the new—or, possibly,
very old—continents in the Atlantic and Pacific." He went on explaining
about continental drift, but I liked the idea of inhabiting Antarctica,
and daydreamed about it for a while. I thought of it as very empty,
very quiet, all white and blue, with a faint golden glow northward
from the unrising sun behind the long peak of Mount Erebus. There
were a few people there; they were very quiet, too, and wore white
tie and tails. Some of them carried oboes and violas. Southward the
white land went up in a long silence towards the pole.

SOURCE: Ursula Le Guin, *The Compass Rose*, Bantam Books, Toronto, N.Y., London,
Sydney, 1982, Harper & Row Publishers, 10 E. 53rd St., N.Y. 10022.

Just the opposite, in fact, of the Mount Hood Wilderness Area. It had been a tiresome vacation. The other women in the dormitory were all right, but it was macaroni for breakfast, and there were so many organized sports. I had looked forward to the hike up to the National Forest Preserve, the largest forest left in the United States, but the trees didn't look at all the way they do in the postcards and brochures and Federal Beautification Bureau advertisements. They were spindly, and they all had little signs on, saying which union they had been planted by. There were actually a lot more green picnic tables and cement Men's and Women's than there were trees. There was an electrified fence all around the forest to keep out unauthorized persons. The Forest Ranger talked about mountain jays, "bold little robbers," he said, "who will come and snatch the sandwich from your very hand," but I didn't see any. Perhaps because it was the weekly Watch Those Surplus Calories! Day for all the women, and so we didn't have any sandwiches. If I'd seen a mountain jay I might have snatched the sandwich from his very hand, who knows. Anyhow it was an exhausting week, and I wished I'd stayed home and practiced, even though I'd have lost a week's pay because staying home and practising the viola doesn't count as planned implementation of recreational leisure as defined by the Federal Union of Unions.

When I came back from my Antarctic expedition the man was reading again, and I got a look at his pamphlet; and that was the odd part of it. The pamphlet was called "Increasing Efficiency in Public Accountant Training Schools," and I could see from the one paragraph I got a glance at that there was nothing about new continents emerging from the ocean depths in it—nothing at all.

Then we had to get out and walk on into Gresham, because they had decided that the best thing for us all to do was get onto the Greater Portland Area Rapid Public Transit Lines, since there had been so many breakdowns that the charter bus company didn't have any more busses to send out to pick us up. The walk was wet, and rather dull, except when we passed the Cold Mountain Commune. They have a wall around it to keep out unauthorized persons, and a big neon sign out front saying "Cold Mountain Commune," and there were some people in authentic jeans and ponchos by the highway selling macrame belts and sand-cast candles and soybean bread to the tourists. In Gresham, I took the 4:40 GPARTL Superjet Flyer train to Burnside and East 230th, and then walked to 217th and got the bus to the Goldschmidt Overpass, and transferred to the shuttlebus, but it had boiler trouble too, so I didn't reach the downtown transfer point until 8:10, and the busses go on a once-an-hour schedule at eight, so I got a meatless hamburger at the Longhorn Inch-Thick Steak House Dinerette and caught the nine o'clock bus and got home about ten. When I let myself into the apartment I turned on the lights, but there still weren't any. There had been a power outage in West Portland for three weeks. So I went feeling about for the candles in the dark, and it was a minute or so before I noticed that somebody was lying on my bed.

I panicked, and tried again to turn the lights on.

It was a man, lying there in a long thin heap. I thought a burglar had got in somehow while I was away, and died. I opened the door so I could get out quick or at least my yells could be heard, and then I managed not to shake long enough to strike a match, and lighted the candle, and came a little closer to the bed.

The light disturbed him. He made a sort of snoring in his throat, and turned his head. I saw it was a stranger, but I knew his eyebrows, then the breadth of his closed eyelids, then I saw my husband.

He woke up while I was standing there over him with the candle in my hand. He laughed and said still half asleep, "Ah, Psyche! from the regions which are holy land."

Neither of us made much fuss. It was unexpected, but it did seem so natural for him to be there, after all, much more natural than for him not to be there; and he was too tired to be very emotional. We lay there together in the dark, and he explained that they had released him from the Rehabilitation Camp early because he had injured his back in an accident in the gravel quarry, and they were afraid it might get worse. If he died there it wouldn't be good publicity abroad, since there have been some nasty rumors about deaths from illness in the Rehabilitation Camps and the Federal Medical Association Hospitals; and there are scientists abroad who have heard of Simon, since somebody published his proof of Goldbach's Hypothesis in Peking. So they let him out early, with eight dollars in his pocket, which is what he had in his pocket when they arrested him, which made it, of course, fair. He had walked and hitched home from Coeur d'Alene, Idaho, with a couple of days in jail in Walla Walla for being caught hitchhiking. He almost fell asleep telling me this, and when he had told me, he did fall asleep. He needed a change of clothes and a bath but I didn't want to wake him. Besides, I was tired too. We lay side by side and his head was on my arm. I don't suppose that I have ever been so happy. No; was it happiness? Something wider and darker, more like knowledge, more like the night: joy.

It was dark for so long, so very long. We were all blind. And there was the cold, a vast, unmoving, heavy cold. We could not move at all. We did not move. We did not speak. Our mouths were closed, pressed shut by the cold and by the weight. Our eyes were pressed shut. Our limbs were held still. Our minds were held still. For how long? There was no length of time; how long is death? And is one dead only after living, or before life as well? Certainly we thought, if we thought anything, that we were dead; but if we had ever been alive, we had forgotten it.

There was a change. It must have been the pressure that changed first, although we did not know it. The eyelids are sensitive to touch. They must have been weary of being shut. When the pressure upon them weakened a little, they opened. But there was no way for us to know that. It was too cold for us to feel anything. There was nothing to be seen. There was black.

But then—"then," for the event created time, created before and after, near and far, now and then—"then" there was the light. One light. One small, strange light that passed slowly, at what distance we could not tell. A small, greenish-white, slightly blurred point of radiance, passing.

Our eyes were certainly open, "then," for we saw it. We saw the moment. The moment is a point of light. Whether in darkness or in the field of all light, the moment is small, and moves, but not quickly. And "then" it is gone.

It did not occur to us that there might be another moment. There was no reason to assume that there might be more than one. One was marvel enough: that in all the field of the dark, in the cold, heavy, dense, moveless, timeless, placeless, boundless black, there should have occurred, once, a small, slightly blurred, moving light! Time need be created only once, we thought.

But we were mistaken! The difference between one and more-than-one is all the difference in the world. Indeed, that difference is the world.

The light returned.

The same light, or another one? There was no telling.

But, "this time," we wondered about the light: was it small and near to us, or large and far away? Again there was no telling; but there was something about the way it moved, a trace of hesitation, a tentative quality, that did not seem proper to anything large and remote. The stars, for instance. We began to remember the stars.

The stars had never hesitated.

Perhaps the noble certainty of their gait had been a mere effect of distance. Perhaps in fact they had hurtled wildly, enormous furnace fragments of a primal bomb thrown through the cosmic dark; but time and distance soften all agony. If the universe, as seems likely, began with an act of destruction, the stars we had used to see told no tales of it. They had been implacably serene.

The planets, however. . . . We began to remember the planets. They had suffered certain changes of appearance and course. At certain times of the year Mars would reverse its direction and go backwards through the stars. Venus had been brighter and less bright as she went through her phases of crescent, full, and wane. Mercury had shuddered like a skidding drop of rain on the sky flushed with daybreak. The light we now watched had that erratic, trembling quality. We saw it, unmistakably, change direction and go backwards. It then grew smaller and fainter; blinked—an eclipse?—and slowly disappeared.

Slowly, but not slowly enough for a planet.

Then—the third "then"!—arrived the indubitable and positive Wonder of the World, the Magic Trick, watch now, watch, you will not believe your eyes, mama, mama, look what I can do—

Seven lights in a row, proceeding fairly rapidly, with a darting movement, from left to right. Proceeding less rapidly from right to left, two dimmer, greenish lights. Two-lights halt, blink, reverse course, proceed hastily and in a wavering manner from left to right. Seven-lights increase speed, and catch up. Two-lights flash desperately, flicker, and are gone.

Seven-lights hang still for some while, then merge gradually into one streak, veering away, and little by little vanish into the immensity of the dark.

But in the dark now are growing other lights, many of them: lamps, dots, rows, scintillations: some near at hand, some far. Like the stars, yes, but not stars. It is not the great Existences we are seeing, but only the little lives.

In the morning Simon told me something about the Camp, but not until after he had had me check the apartment for bugs. I thought at first he had been given behavior mod and gone paranoid. We never had been infested. And I'd been living alone for a year and a half; surely they didn't want to hear me talking to myself? But he said, "They may have been expecting me to come here."

"But they let you go free!"

He just lay there and laughed at me. So I checked everywhere we could think of. I didn't find any bugs, but it did look as if somebody had gone through the bureau drawers while I was away in the Wilderness. Simon's papers were all at Max's, so that didn't matter. I made tea on the Primus, and washed and shaved Simon with the extra hot water in the kettle—he had a thick beard and wanted to get rid of it because of the lice he had brought from Camp—and while we were doing that he told me about the Camp. In fact he told me very little, but not much was necessary.

He had lost about twenty pounds. As he only weighed 140 to start with, this left little to go on with. His knees and wrist bones stuck out like rocks under the skin. His feet were all swollen and chewed-looking from the Camp boots; he hadn't dared take the boots off, the last three days of walking, because he was afraid he wouldn't be able to get them back on. When he had to move or sit up so I could wash him, he shut his eyes.

"Am I really here?" he asked. "Am I here?"

"Yes," I said. "You are here. What I don't understand is how you got here."

"Oh, it wasn't bad so long as I kept moving. All you need is to know where you're going—to have some place to go. You know, some of the people in Camp, if they'd let them go, they wouldn't have had that. They couldn't have gone anywhere. Keeping moving was the main thing. It's just that my back's seized up, now."

When he had to get up to go to the bathroom he moved like a ninety-year-old. He couldn't stand straight, but was all bent out of shape, and shuffled. I helped him put on clean clothes. When he lay down on the bed again a sound of pain came out of him, like tearing thick paper. I went around the room putting things away. He asked me to come sit by him, and said I was going to drown him if I went on crying. "You'll submerge the entire North American continent," he said. I can't remember what else he said, but he made me laugh finally. It is hard to remember things Simon says, and hard not to laugh when he says them. This is not merely the partiality of affection: he makes everybody laugh. I doubt that he intends to. It is just that a mathematician's mind works differently from other people's. Then when they laugh, that pleases him.

It was strange, and it is strange, to be thinking about "him," the man I have known for ten years, the same man, while "he" lay there changed out of recognition, a different man. It is enough to make you understand why most languages have a word like "soul." There are various degrees of death, and time spares us none of them. Yet something endures, for which a word is needed.

I said what I had not been able to say for a year and a half: "I was afraid they'd brainwash you."

He said, "Behavior mod is expensive. Even just with drugs. They save it mostly for the V.I.P.s. But I'm afraid they got a notion I might be important after all. I got questioned a lot the last couple of months. About my 'foreign contacts.' " He snorted. "The stuff that got published abroad, I suppose. So I want to be careful and make sure it's just a Camp again next time, and not a Federal Hospital."

"Simon, were they . . . are they cruel, or just righteous?"

He did not answer for a while. He did not want to answer. He knew what I was asking. He knew what thread hangs hope, the sword, above our heads.

"Some of them . . ." he said at last, mumbling.

Some of them had been cruel. Some of them had enjoyed their work. You cannot blame everything on society.

"Prisoners, as well as guards," he said.

You cannot blame everything on the enemy.

"Some of them, Belle," he said with energy, touching my hand— "some of them, there were men like gold there—"

The thread is tough; you cannot cut it with one stroke.

"What have you been playing?" he asked.

"Forrest, Schubert."

"With the quartet?"

"Trio, now. Janet went to Oakland with a new lover."

"Ah, poor Max."

"It's just as well, really. She isn't a good pianist."

I make Simon laugh, too, though I don't intend to. We talked until it was past time for me to go to work. My shift since the Full Employment Act last year is ten to two. I am an inspector in a recycled paper bag factory. I have never rejected a bag yet; the electronic inspector catches all the defective ones first. It is a rather depressing job. But it's only four hours a day, and it takes more time than that to go through all the lines and physical and mental examinations, and fill out all the forms, and talk to all the welfare counselors and inspectors every week in order to qualify as Unemployed, and then line up every day for the ration stamps and the dole. Simon thought I ought to go to work as usual. I tried to, but I couldn't. He had felt very hot to the touch when I kissed him goodbye. I went instead and got a black-market doctor. A girl at the factory had recommended her, for an abortion, if I ever wanted one without going through the regulation two years of sex-depressant drugs the fed-meds make you take after they give you an abortion. She was a jeweler's assistant in a shop on Alder Street, and the girl said she was convenient because if you didn't have enough cash you could leave something in pawn at the jeweler's as payment. Nobody ever does have enough cash, and of course credit cards aren't worth much on the black market.

The doctor was willing to come at once, so we rode home on the bus together. She gathered very soon that Simon and I were married, and it was funny to see her look at us and smile like a cat. Some people love illegality for its own sake. Men, more often than women. It's men who make laws, and enforce them, and break them, and think the whole performance is wonderful. Most women would rather just ignore them. You could see that this woman, like a man, actually enjoyed breaking them. That may have been what put her into an illegal business in the first place, a preference for the shady side. But there was more to it than that. No doubt she'd wanted to be a doctor, too; and the Federal Medical Association doesn't admit women into the medical schools. She probably got her training as some other doctor's private pupil, under the counter. Very much as Simon learned mathematics, since the universities don't teach much but Business Administration and Advertising and Media Skills any more. However she learned it, she seemed to know her stuff. She fixed up a kind of homemade traction device for Simon very handily, and informed him that if he did much more walking for two months he'd be crippled the rest of his life, but if he behaved himself he'd just be more or less lame. It isn't the kind of thing you'd expect to be grateful for being told, but we both were. Leaving, she gave me a bottle of about two hundred plain white pills, unlabelled. "Aspirin," she said. "He'll be in a good deal of pain off and on for weeks."

I looked at the bottle. I had never seen aspirin before, only the Super-Buffered Pane-Gon and the Triple Power N-L-G-Zic and the Extra Strength Apansprin with the miracle ingredient more doctors recommend, which the fed-meds always give you prescriptions for, to be filled at your FMA-approved private-enterprise friendly drugstore at the low, low prices established by the Pure Food and Drug Administration in order to inspire competitive research.

"Aspirin," the doctor repeated. "The miracle ingredient more doctors recommend." She cat-grinned again. I think she liked us because we were living in sin. That bottle of black-market aspirin was probably worth more than the old Navajo bracelet I pawned for her fee.

I went out again to register Simon as temporarily domiciled at my address, and to apply for Temporary Unemployment Compensation ration stamps for him. They only give them to you for two weeks and you have to come every day; but to register him as Temporarily Disabled meant getting the signatures of two fed-meds, and I thought I'd rather put that off for a while. It took three hours to go through the lines and get the forms he would have to fill out, and to answer the crats' questions about why he wasn't there in person. They smelled something fishy. Of course it's hard for them to prove that two people are married, if you move now and then, and your friends help out by sometimes registering one of you as living at their address; but they had all the back files on both of us and it was obvious that we had been around each other for a suspiciously long time. The State really does make things awfully hard for itself. It must have been simpler to enforce the laws, back when marriage was legal and adultery was what got you into trouble. They only had to catch you once. But I'll bet people broke the law just as often then as they do now.

> The lantern creatures came close enough at last that we could see not only their light, but their bodies in the illumination of the light. They were not pretty. They were dark-colored, most

often a dark red, and they were all mouth. They ate one another whole. Light swallowed light all swallowed together in the vaster mouth of the darkness. They moved slowly, for nothing, however small and hungry, could move fast under that weight, in that cold. Their eyes, round with fear, were never closed. Their bodies were tiny and bony, behind the gaping jaws. They wore queer, ugly decorations on their lips and skulls: fringes, serrated wattles, featherlike fronds, gauds, bangles, lures. Poor little sheep of the deep pastures! Poor ragged, hunch-jawed dwarfs squeezed to the bone by the weight of the darkness, chilled to the bone by the cold of the darkness, tiny monsters burning with bright hunger, who brought us back to life!

Occasionally, in the wan, sparse illumination of one of the lantern creatures, we caught a momentary glimpse of other large, unmoving shapes: the barest suggestion, off in the distance, not of a wall, nothing so solid and certain as a wall, but of a surface, an angle. . . . Was it there?

Or something would glitter, faint, far off, far down. There was no use trying to make out what it might be. Probably it was only a fleck of sediment, mud or mica, disturbed by a struggle between the lantern creatures, flickering like a bit of diamond dust as it rose and settled slowly. In any case, we could not move to go see what it was. We had not even the cold, narrow freedom of the lantern creatures. We were immobilized, borne down, still shadows among the half-guessed shadow walls. Were we there?

The lantern creatures showed no awareness of us. They passed before us, among us, perhaps even through us—it was impossible to be sure. They were not afraid, or curious.

Once something a little larger than a hand came crawling near, and for a moment we saw quite distinctly the clean angle where the foot of a wall rose from the pavement, in the glow cast by the crawling creature, which was covered with a foliage of plumes, each plume dotted with many tiny, bluish points of light. We saw the pavement beneath the creature and the wall beside it, heartbreaking in its exact, clear linearity, its opposition to all that was fluid, random, vast, and void. We saw the creature's claws, slowly reaching out and retracting like small stiff fingers, touch the wall. Its plumage of light quivering, it dragged itself along and vanished behind the corner.

So we knew that the wall was there; and that it was an outer wall, a housefront, perhaps, or the side of one of the towers of the city.

We remembered the towers. We remembered the city. We had forgotten it. We had forgotten who we were; but we remembered the city, now.

When I got home, the FBI had already been there. The computer at the police precinct where I registered Simon's address must have flashed it right over to the computer at the FBI building. They had questioned Simon for about an hour, mostly about what he had been doing during the twelve days it took him to get from the Camp to Portland. I suppose they thought he had flown to Peking or something. Having a police record in Walla Walla for hitchhiking helped him establish his story. He told me that one of them had gone to the bathroom. Sure enough I found a bug stuck on the top of the bathroom doorframe. I left it, as we figured it's really better to leave it when you know you have one, than to take it off and then never be sure they haven't planted another one you don't know about. As Simon said, if we felt we had to say something unpatriotic we could always flush the toilet at the same time.

I had a battery radio—there are so many stoppages because of power failures, and days the water has to be boiled, and so on, that you really have to have a radio to save wasting time and dying of typhoid—and he turned it on while I was making supper on the Primus. The six-o'clock All-American Broadcasting Company news announcer announced that peace was at hand in Uruguay, the President's confidential aide having been seen to smile at a passing blonde as he left the 613th day of the secret negotiations in a villa outside Katmandu. The war in Liberia was going well; the enemy said they had shot down 17 American planes but the Pentagon said we had shot down 22 enemy planes, and the capital city—I forget its name, but it hasn't been inhabitable for seven years anyway—was on the verge of being recaptured by the forces of freedom. The police action in Arizona was also successful. The Neo-Birch insurgents in Phoenix could not hold out much longer against the massed might of the American Army and Air Force, since their underground supply of small tactical nukes from the Weatherpeople in Los Angeles had been cut off. Then there was an advertisement for Fed-Cred cards, and a commercial for the Supreme Court—"Take your legal troubles to the Nine Wise Men!" Then there was something about why tariffs had gone up, and a report from the stock market which had just closed at over 2000, and a commercial for U.S. Government canned water, with a catchy little tune: "Don't be sorry when you drink—It's not as healthy as you think—Don't you think you really ought to—Drink coo-ool, puu-uure U.S.G. Water?"—with three sopranos in close harmony on the last line. Then, just as the battery began to give out and his voice was dying away into a faraway tiny whisper, the announcer seemed to be saying something about a new continent emerging.

"What was that?"

"I didn't hear," Simon said, lying with his eyes shut and his face pale and sweaty. I gave him two aspirins before we ate. He ate little, and fell asleep while I was washing dishes in the bathroom. I had been going to practice, but a viola is fairly wakeful in a one-room apartment. I read for a while instead. It was a bestseller Janet had given me when she left. She thought it was very good, but then she likes Franz Liszt too. I don't read much since the libraries were closed down, it's too hard to get books; all you can buy is bestsellers. I don't remember the title of this one, the cover just said Ninety Million Copies in Print!!! It was about small-town sex life in the last century, the dear old 1970s when there weren't any problems and life was so simple and nostalgic. The author squeezed all the naughty thrills he could out of the fact that all the main characters were married. I looked at the end and saw that all the married couples shot each other after all their children became schizophrenic hookers, except for one brave pair that divorced and then leapt into bed together with a clear-eyed pair of Government-employed lovers for eight pages of healthy group sex as a brighter future dawned. I went to bed then, too. Simon was hot, but sleeping quietly. His breathing was like the sound of soft waves far away, and I went out to the dark sea on the sound of them.

I used to go out to the dark sea, often, as a child, falling asleep. I had almost forgotten it with my waking mind. As a child all I had to do was stretch out and think, "the dark sea . . . the dark sea . . ." and soon enough I'd be there, in the great depths, rocking. But after I grew up it only happened rarely, as a great gift. To know the abyss of the darkness and not to fear it, to entrust oneself to it and whatever may arise from it—what greater gift?

We watched the tiny lights come and go around us, and doing so, we gained a sense of space and of direction—near and far, at least, and higher and lower. It was that sense of space that allowed us to become aware of the currents. Space was no longer entirely still around us, suppressed by the enormous pressure of its own weight. Very dimly we were aware that the cold darkness moved, slowly, softly, pressing against us a little for a long time, then ceasing, in a vast oscillation. The empty darkness flowed slowly along our unmoving unseen bodies; along them, past them; perhaps through them; we could not tell.

Where did they come from, those dim, slow, vast tides? What pressure or attraction stirred the deeps to these slow drifting movements? We could not understand that; we could only feel their touch against us, but in straining our sense to guess their origin or end, we became aware of something else: something out there in the darkness of the great currents: sounds. We listened. We heard.

So our sense of space sharpened and localized to a sense of place. For sound is local, as sight is not. Sound is delimited by silence; and it does not rise out of the silence unless it is fairly close, both in space and in time. Though we stand where once the singer stood we cannot hear the voice singing; the years have carried it off on their tides, submerged it. Sound is a fragile thing, a tremor, as delicate as life itself. We may see the stars, but we cannot hear them. Even were the hollowness of outer space an atmosphere, an ether that transmitted the waves of sound, we could not hear the stars; they are too far away. At most if we listened we might hear our own sun, all the mighty roiling, exploding storm of its burning, as a whisper at the edge of hearing.

A sea wave laps one's feet: it is the shock wave of a volcanic eruption on the far side of the world. But one hears nothing.

A red light flickers on the horizon: it is the reflection in smoke of a city on the distant mainland, burning. But one hears nothing.

Only on the slopes of the volcano, in the suburbs of the city, does one begin to hear the deep thunder, and the high voices crying.

Thus, when we became aware that we were hearing, we were sure that the sounds we heard were fairly close to us. And yet we may have been quite wrong. For we were in a strange place, a deep place. Sound travels fast and far in the deep places, and the silence there is perfect, letting the least noise be heard for hundreds of miles.

And these were not small noises. The lights were tiny, but the sounds were vast: not loud, but very large. Often they were below the range of hearing, long slow vibrations rather than sounds. The first we heard seemed to us to rise up through the currents from beneath us: immense groans, sighs felt along the bone, a rumbling, a deep uneasy whispering.

Later, certain sounds came down to us from above, or borne along the endless levels of the darkness, and these were stranger yet, for they were music. A huge, calling, yearning music from far away in the darkness, calling not to us. *Where are you? I am here.*

Not to us.

They were the voices of the great souls, the great lives, the lonely ones, the voyagers. Calling. Not often answered. *Where are you? Where have you gone?*

But the bones, the keels and girders of white bones on icy isles of the South, the shores of bones did not reply.

Nor could we reply. But we listened, and the tears rose in our eyes, salt, not so salt as the oceans, the world-girdling deep bereaved currents, the abandoned roadways of the great lives; not so salt, but warmer.

I am here. Where have you gone?

No answer.

Only the whispering thunder from below.

But we knew now, though we could not answer, we knew because we heard, because we felt, because we wept, we knew that we were; and we remembered other voices.

Max came the next night. I sat on the toilet lid to practise, with the bathroom door shut. The FBI men on the other end of the bug got a solid half hour of scales and double stops, and then a quite good performance of the Hindemith unaccompanied viola sonata. The bathroom being very small and all hard surfaces, the noise I made was really tremendous. Not a good sound, far too much echo, but the sheer volume was contagious, and I played louder as I went on. The man up above knocked on the floor once; but if I have to listen to the weekly All-American Olympic Games at full blast every Sunday morning from his TV set, then he has to accept Paul Hindemith coming up out of his toilet now and then.

When I got tired I put a big wad of cotton over the bug, and came out of the bathroom half deaf, Simon and Max were on fire. Burning, unconsumed. Simon was scribbling formulae in traction, and Max was pumping his elbows up and down the way he does, like a boxer, and saying, "The e-lec-tron emission . . ." through his nose, with his eyes narrowed, and his mind evidently going light-years per second faster than his tongue, because he kept beginning over and saying, "The e-lec-tron emis-sion . . ." and pumping his elbows.

Intellectuals at work are very strange to look at. As strange as artists. I never could understand how an audience can sit there and *look* at a fiddler rolling his eyes and biting his tongue, or a horn player collecting spit, or a pianist like a black cat strapped to an electrified bench, as if what they *saw* had anything to do with the music.

I damped the fires with a quart of black-market beer—the legal kind is better, but I never have enough ration stamps for beer, I'm not thirsty enough to go without eating—and gradually Max and Simon cooled down. Max would have stayed talking all night, but I drove him out, because Simon was looking tired.

I put a new battery in the radio and left it playing in the bathroom, and blew out the candle and lay and talked with Simon; he was too excited to sleep. He said that Max had solved the problems that were bothering them before Simon was sent to Camp, and had fitted Simon's equations to (as Simon put it) the bare facts: which means they have achieved "direct energy conversion." Ten or twelve people have worked on it at different times since Simon published the theoretical part of it when he was twenty-two. The physicist Ann Jones had pointed out right away that the simplest practical application of the theory would be to build a "sun-tap," a device for collecting and storing solar energy, only much cheaper and better than the U.S.G. Sola-Heetas that some rich people have on their houses. And it would have been simple only they kept hitting the same snag. Now Max has got around the snag.

I said that Simon published the theory, but that is inaccurate. Of course he's never been able to publish any of his papers, in print; he's not a Federal employee and doesn't have a Government clearance. But it did get circulated in what the scientists and poets call Sammy's-dot, that is, just handwritten or hectographed. It's an old joke that the FBI arrests everybody with purple fingers, because they have either been hectographing Sammy's-dots, or they have impetigo.

Anyhow, Simon was on top of the mountain that night. His true joy is in the pure math; but he had been working with Clara and Max and the others in this effort to materialise the theory for ten years, and a taste of material victory is a good thing, once in a lifetime.

I asked him to explain what the sun tap would mean to the masses, with me as a representative mass. He explained that it means we can tap solar energy for power, using a device that's easier to build than a jar battery. The efficiency and storage capacity are such that about ten minutes of sunlight will power an apartment complex like ours, heat and lights and elevators and all, for twenty-four hours; and no pollution, particulate or thermal or radioactive. "There isn't any danger of using up the sun?" I asked. He took it soberly—it was a stupid question, but after all not so long ago people thought there wasn't any danger of using up the earth—and said no, because we wouldn't be pulling out energy, as we did when we mined and forested and split atoms, but just using the energy that comes to us anyhow: as the plants, the trees and grass and rosebushes, always have done. "You could call it Flower Power," he said. He was high, high up on the mountain, ski jumping in the sunlight.

"The State owns us," he said, "because the corporative State has a monopoly on power sources, and there's not enough power to go round. But now, anybody could build a generator on their roof that would furnish enough power to light a city."

I looked out the window at the dark city.

"We could completely decentralise industry and agriculture. Technology could serve life instead of serving capital. We could each run our own life. Power is power! . . . The State is a machine. We could unplug the machine, now. Power corrupts; absolute power corrupts absolutely. But that's true only when there's a price on power. When

groups can keep the power to themselves; when they can use physical
power-to in order to exert spiritual power-over; when might makes
right. But if power is free? If everybody is equally mighty? Then
everybody's got to find a better way of showing that he's right. . . ."

"That's what Mr. Nobel thought when he invented dynamite," I
said. "Peace on earth."

He slid down the sunlit slope a couple of thousand feet and stopped
beside me in a spray of snow, smiling. "Skull at the banquet," he
said, "finger writing on the wall. Be still! Look, don't you see the sun
shining on the Pentagon, all the roofs are off, the sun shines at last
into the corridors of power. . . . And they shrivel up, they wither
away. The green grass grows through the carpets of the Oval Room,
the Hotline is disconnected for nonpayment of the bill. The first thing
we'll do is build an electrified fence outside the electrified fence around
the White House. The inner one prevents unauthorized persons from
getting in. The outer one will prevent authorized persons from getting
out. . . ."

Of course he was bitter. Not many people come out of prison sweet.

But it was cruel, to be shown this great hope, and to know that
there was no hope for it. He did know that. He knew it right along.
He knew that there was no mountain, that he was skiing on the wind.

The tiny lights of the lantern creatures died out one by one,
sank away. The distant lonely voices were silent. The cold, slow
currents flowed, vacant, only shaken from time to time by a
shifting in the abyss.

It was dark again, and no voice spoke. All dark, dumb, cold.

Then the sun rose.

It was not like the dawns we had begun to remember: the
change, manifold and subtle, in the smell and touch of the air;
the hush that, instead of sleeping, wakes, holds still, and waits;
the appearance of objects, looking grey, vague, and new, as if
just created—distant mountains against the eastern sky, one's
own hands, the hoary grass full of dew and shadow, the fold in
the edge of a curtain hanging by the window—and then, before
one is quite sure that one is indeed seeing again, that the light
has returned, that day is breaking, the first abrupt, sweet stammer
of a waking bird. And after that the chorus, voice by voice: This
is my nest, this is my tree, this is my egg, this is my day, this is
my life, here I am, here I am, hurray for me! I'm here!—No, it
wasn't like that at all, this dawn. It was completely silent, and
it was blue.

In the dawns that we had begun to remember, one did not
become aware of the light itself, but of the separate objects touched

by the light, the things, the world. They were there, visible again, as if visibility were their own property, not a gift from the rising sun.

In this dawn, there was nothing but the light itself. Indeed there was not even light, we would have said, but only color: blue.

There was no compass bearing to it. It was not brighter in the east. There was no east or west. There was only up and down, below and above. Below was dark. The blue light came from above. Brightness fell. Beneath, where the shaking thunder had stilled, the brightness died away through violet into blindness.

We, arising, watched light fall.

In a way it was more like an ethereal snowfall than like a sunrise. The light seemed to be in discrete particles, infinitesimal flecks, slowly descending, faint, fainter than flakes of fine snow on a dark night, and tinier; but blue. A soft, penetrating blue tending to the violet, the color of the shadows in an iceberg, the color of a streak of sky between grey clouds on a winter afternoon before snow: faint in intensity but vivid in hue: the color of the remote, the color of the cold, the color farthest from the sun.

On Saturday night they held a scientific congress in our room. Clara and Max came, of course, and the engineer Phil Drum, and three others who had worked on the sun tap. Phil Drum was very pleased with himself because he had actually built one of the things, a solar cell, and brought it along. I don't think it had occurred to either Max or Simon to build one. Once they knew it could be done, they were satisfied and wanted to get on with something else. But Phil unwrapped his baby with a lot of flourish, and people made remarks like, "Mr. Watson, will you come here a minute," and "Hey, Wilbur, you're off the ground!" and "I say, nasty mould you've got there, Alec, why don't you throw it out?" and "Ugh, ugh, burns, burns, wow, ow," the latter from Max, who does look a little Pre-Mousterian. Phil explained that he had exposed the cell for one minute at four in the afternoon up in Washington Park during a light rain. The lights were back on on the West Side since Thursday, so we could test it without being conspicuous.

We turned off the lights, after Phil had wired the tablelamp cord to the cell. He turned on the lamp switch. The bulb came on, about twice as bright as before, at its full 40 watts—city power of course was never full strength. We all looked at it. It was a dime-store table lamp with a metallized gold base and a white plasticloth shade.

"Brighter than a thousand suns," Simon murmured from the bed.

"Could it be," said Clara Edmonds, "that we physicists have known sin—and have come out the other side?"

"It really wouldn't be any good at all for making bombs with," Max said dreamily.

"Bombs," Phil Drum said with scorn. "Bombs are obsolete. Don't you realize that we could move a mountain with this kind of power? I mean pick up Mount Hood, move it, and set it down. We could thaw Antarctica, we could freeze the Congo. We could sink a continent. 'Give me a fulcrum and I'll move the world.' Well, Archimedes, you've got your fulcrum. The sun."

"Christ," Simon said, "the radio, Belle!"

The bathroom door was shut and I had put cotton over the bug, but he was right; if they were going to go ahead at this rate there had better be some added static. And though I liked watching their faces in the clear light of the lamp—they all had good, interesting faces, well worn, like the handles of wooden tools or the rocks in a running stream—I did not much want to listen to them talk tonight. Not because I wasn't a scientist; that made no difference. And not because I disagreed or disapproved or disbelieved anything they said. Only because it grieved me terribly, their talking. Because they couldn't rejoice aloud over a job done and a discovery made, but had to hide there and whisper about it. Because they couldn't go out into the sun.

I went into the bathroom with my viola and sat on the toilet lid and did a long set of sautillé exercises. Then I tried to work at the Forrest trio, but it was too assertive. I played the solo part from *Harold in Italy*, which is beautiful, but wasn't quite the right mood either. They were still going strong in the other room. I began to improvise.

After a few minutes in E minor the light over the shaving mirror began to flicker and dim; then it died. Another outage. The table lamp in the other room did not go out, being connected with the sun, not with the twenty-three atomic fission plants that power the Greater Portland Area. Within two seconds somebody had switched it off too, so that we shouldn't be the only window in the West Hills left alight; and I could hear them rooting for candles and rattling matches. I went on improvising in the dark. Without light, when you couldn't see all the hard shiny surfaces of things, the sound seemed softer and less muddled. I went on, and it began to shape up. All the laws of harmonics sang together when the bow came down. The strings of the viola were the cords of my own voice, tightened by sorrow, tuned to the pitch of joy. The melody created itself out of air and energy; it raised up the valleys, and the mountains and hills were made low, and the crooked straight, and the rough places plain. And the music went out to the dark sea and sang in the darkness, over the abyss.

When I came out they were all sitting there and none of them was talking. Max had been crying. I could see little candle flames in the tears around his eyes. Simon lay flat on the bed in the shadows, his eyes closed. Phil Drum sat hunched over, holding the solar cell in his hands.

I loosened the pegs, and put the bow and the viola in the case, and cleared my throat. It was embarrassing. I finally said, "I'm sorry."

One of the women spoke: Rose Abramski, a private student of Simon's, a big shy woman who could hardly speak at all unless it was in mathematical symbols. "I saw it," she said. "I saw it. I saw the white towers, and the water streaming down their sides, and running back down to the sea. And the sunlight shining in the streets, after ten thousand years of darkness."

"I heard them," Simon said, very low, from the shadow. "I heard their voices."

"Oh, Christ! Stop it!" Max cried out, and got up and went blundering out into the unlit hall, without his coat. We heard him running down the stairs.

"Phil," said Simon, lying there, "could we raise up the white towers, with our lever and our fulcrum?"

After a long silence Phil Drum answered, "We have the power to do it."

"What else do we need?" Simon said. "What else do we need, besides power?"

Nobody answered him.

The blue changed. It became brighter, lighter, and at the same time thicker: impure. The ethereal luminosity of blue-violet turned to turquoise, intense and opaque. Still we could not have said that everything was now turquoise-colored, for there were still no things. There was nothing, except the color of turquoise.

The change continued. The opacity became veined and thinned. The dense, solid color began to appear translucent, transparent. Then it seemed as if we were in the heart of a sacred jade, or the brilliant crystal of a sapphire or an emerald.

As at the inner structure of a crystal, there was no motion. But there was something, now, to see. It was as if we saw the motionless, elegant inward structure of the molecules of a precious stone. Planes and angles appeared about us, shadowless and clear in that even, glowing, blue-green light.

These were the walls and towers of the city, the streets, the windows, the gates.

We knew them, but we did not recognize them. We did not dare to recognize them. It had been so long. And it was so strange.

We had used to dream, when we lived in this city. We had lain down, nights, in the rooms behind the windows, and slept, and dreamed. We had all dreamed of the ocean, of the deep sea. Were we not dreaming now?

Sometimes the thunder and tremor deep below us rolled again, but it was faint now, far away; as far away as our memory of the thunder and the tremor and the fire and the towers falling, long ago. Neither the sound nor the memory frightened us. We knew them.

The sapphire light brightened overhead to green, almost green-gold. We looked up. The tops of the highest towers were hard to see, glowing in the radiance of light. The streets and doorways were darker, more clearly defined.

In one of those long, jewel-dark streets something was moving: something not composed of planes and angles, but of curves and arcs. We all turned to look at it, slowly, wondering as we did so at the slow ease of our own motion, our freedom. Sinuous, with a beautiful flowing, gathering, rolling movement, now rapid and now tentative, the thing drifted across the street from a blank garden wall to the recess of a door. There, in the dark blue shadow, it was hard to see for a while. We watched. A pale blue curve appeared at the top of the doorway. A second followed, and a third. The moving thing clung or hovered there, above the door, like a swaying knot of silvery cords or a boneless hand, one arched finger pointing carelessly to something above the lintel of the door, something like itself, but motionless—a carving. A carving in jade light. A carving in stone.

Delicately and easily the long curving tentacle followed the curves of the carved figure, the eight petal limbs, the round eyes. Did it recognize its image?

The living one swung suddenly, gathered its curves in a loose knot, and darted away down the street, swift and sinuous. Behind it a faint cloud of darker blue hung for a minute and dispersed, revealing again the carved figure above the door: the sea flower, the cuttlefish, quick, great-eyed, graceful, evasive, the cherished sign, carved on a thousand walls, worked into the design of cornices, pavements, handles, lids of jewel boxes, canopies, tapestries, tabletops, gateways.

Down another street, at about the level of the first-floor windows, came a flickering drift of hundreds of motes of silver. With a single motion all turned towards the cross street, and glittered off into the dark blue shadows.

There were shadows, now.

We looked up, up from the flight of silver fish, up from the streets where the jade-green currents flowed and the blue shadows fell. We moved and looked up, yearning, to the high towers of our city. They stood, the fallen towers. They glowed in the ever-brightening radiance, not blue or blue-green, up there, but gold. Far above them lay a vast, circular, trembling brightness: the sun's light on the surface of the sea.

We are here. When we break through the bright circle into life, the water will break and stream white down the white sides of the towers, and run down the steep streets back into the sea. The water will glitter in dark hair, on the eyelids of dark eyes, and dry to a thin white film of salt.

We are here.

Whose voice? Who called to us?

He was with me for twelve days. On January 28th the crats came from the Bureau of Health Education and Welfare and said that since he was receiving unemployment compensation while suffering from an untreated illness, the Government must look after him and restore him to health, because health is the inalienable right of the citizens of a democracy. He refused to sign the consent forms, so the chief Health Officer signed them. He refused to get up, so two of the policemen pulled him up off the bed. He started to try to fight them. The chief Health Officer pulled his gun and said that if he continued to struggle he would shoot him for resisting welfare, and arrest me for conspiracy to defraud the Government. The man who was holding my arms behind my back said they could always arrest me for un-reported pregnancy with intent to form a nuclear family. At that Simon stopped trying to get free. It was really all he was trying to do, not to fight them, just to get his arms free. He looked at me, and they took him out.

He is in the Federal Hospital in Salem. I have not been able to find out whether he is in the regular hospital or the mental wards.

It was on the radio again yesterday, about the rising land masses in the South Atlantic and the Western Pacific. At Max's the other night I saw a TV special explaining about geophysical stresses, and subsidence, and faults. The U.S. Geodetic Service is doing a lot of advertising around town; the commonest one is a big billboard that says "It's Not Our Fault!" with a picture of a beaver pointing to a schematic map that shows how even if Oregon has a major earthquake and subsidence as California did last month, it will not affect Portland, or only the western suburbs perhaps. The news also said that they plan to halt the tidal waves in Florida by dropping nuclear bombs where Miami was. Then they will re-attach Florida to the mainland with landfill. They are already advertising real estate for housing developments on the landfill. The President is staying at the Mile High White House in Aspen, Colorado. I don't think it will do him much good. Houseboats down on the Willamette are selling for $500,000. There are no trains or busses running south from Portland, because all the highways were badly damaged by the tremors and landslides last week, so I will have to see if I can get to Salem on foot. I still have the rucksack I bought for the Mount Hood Wilderness Week. I got some dry lima beans and raisins with my Federal Fair Share Super Value Green Stamp minimal ration book for February—it took the whole book—and Phil Drum made me a tiny camp stove powered with the solar cell. I didn't want to take the Primus, it's too bulky, and I did want to be able to carry the viola. Max gave me a half pint of brandy. When the brandy is gone I expect I will stuff this notebook into the bottle and put the cap on tight and leave it on a hillside somewhere between here and Salem. I like to think of it being lifted up little by little by the water, and rocking, and going out to the dark sea.

Where are you?
We are here. Where have you gone?

QUESTIONS

1. Consider the following paragraph: "Our eyes were certainly open, 'then,' for we saw it [the small, greenish-white light]. We saw the moment. The moment is a point of light. . . . the moment is small, and moves, but not quickly. And 'then' it is gone." What does this have to tell us about how we measure time into past, present, and future? How does time measurement begin for the characters who are ascending from beneath the sea as the New Atlantis emerges? How does time on the newly emerging continent differ from time, or, more precisely, Belle's sense of time, in the future police state of the story?
2. Consider the following paragraph: "The stars had never hesitated. . . . They had been implacably serene." How does the fiction writer's image of the universe differ from the scientist's or the science writer's? Can a fiction writer take liberties with our scientific understanding of the universe? Is the operation of the universe central in le Guin's story? How is the rising of Atlantis used within

the story as a whole? Is the rising of Atlantis even a remote possibility in *fact*?

3. When le Guin is envisioning the future horror of the thought-controlling, life-denying state, she makes an interesting distinction. Belle asks Simon whether the people who run the camp in which he has been imprisoned for being a brilliant mathematician are "cruel, or just righteous?" What distinction is le Guin making here? What is the difference in a prison guard between being cruel and being righteous? Remember Belle's next observation is, "You cannot blame everything on society. . . . You cannot blame everything on the enemy." What is le Guin saying about the society of the future? What is she saying about American society of the present? Are we morally responsible for our actions in a society which exercises thought control upon us?

4. How is marriage looked upon in the future society? Why? In what ways does an intimate human relationship which is stable and long-lasting threaten a society that is bent on controlling the thoughts and actions of all people?

5. How is work thought of in the future society? Why must Belle go through the trouble of inspecting paper bags that do not need inspection for four hours a day? Why is she not allowed to work as a musician since that is what she's best at? How does creative work and individual talent threaten a society that is bent on controlling the thoughts and actions of all people?

6. How does education change in the society of the future? Why did the doctor have to study illegally as another doctor's private pupil and Simon have to study mathematics that way? What point is le Guin making when she says the universities are teaching only business administration, advertising, and media skills? Is le Guin criticizing American education in the present and warning of where current educational policies will lead us in the future? What is the difference between a "fed-med" and a doctor?

7. What comparison is le Guin making between, on the one hand, the inhabitants of Atlantis rising from the sea and remembering their city, their former lives, who they were and, on the other, Belle and Simon in their mechanistic, federally controlled, starving city of the future?

8. What do the numerous, incomprehensible wars that are being waged in the future America tell us about the society? Why must a society that wants to control the thoughts and actions of its citizens maintain continuous small wars and crises all around the world? How does a government benefit in its ability to control people during states of war? How does warfare confer the delusion of personal and national identity?

9. When Belle goes "out to the dark sea" in imagination, what is she seeking? Do the newly emerging inhabitants of Atlantis have what Belle wants? What is their state of mind and soul? What is the state of Belle and Simon?
10. The emerging citizens hear "the voices of great souls, the great lives, the lonely ones, the voyagers. Calling. . . . *Where are you? Where have you gone?"* Who *are* the great souls? To whom do the great souls, the voyagers—the thinkers, artists, scientists—call? And why do they call? Is Belle one of the great souls? What is the significance of her performing Hindemith in the bathroom? Whom is she shutting out of her world and whom is she calling in?
11. Why does the state *not* want Simon to find a way to make limitless cheap energy? Do you think that our government now and big business interests now would like to see a very cheap way to produce energy for the whole world? If so, why? If not, why not?
12. Is the ending of the story consistent with the story as whole? What is the relation between America sinking and Atlantis rising?

EXERCISES

1. Pick out and list the reasons for the decline of our civilization that le Guin gives—e.g., the pervasive power of government, the suppression of individual talent, the destruction of the natural environment. Consider each one separately and decide whether or not you agree with le Guin about its potential danger. Write a short paragraph for each that expresses your agreement with le Guin or the grounds for disagreement with her. For instance, if you disagree about the virtues or vices of government control, show where le Guin's reasoning is faulty or her assumptions are wrong.
2. Read Isaiah, Chapter 13 (the destruction of Babylon) and Chapter 29 (the redemption); *or* read Revelation, Chapters 18, 19 and 21. How is le Guin's story related to the great prophets of our tradition in its way of envisioning the decline of the old civilization—and the reasons for its decline—and the new world to come? Write a short account of what *you* believe our civilization will be like in a hundred years.

CHAPTER TWENTY-FOUR

CAGE: THE FUTURE OF MUSIC: CREDO, EXPERIMENTAL MUSIC AND ENO: AMBIENT MUSIC, DISCREET MUSIC

Musicology

John Cage is a famous experimental composer and theoretician. As a pioneer in the music of the twentieth century, he has led us to explore a whole new frontier. He is largely responsible for causing us to think of music not as a structured composition of *notes*, but as an amalgamation, or gestalt, of *sounds*.

Cage first delivered "The Future of Music: Credo" as an address to the Seattle Arts Society almost fifty years ago. Later it was published as a paper to accompany the twenty-five-year retrospective concert of his works performed at Town Hall in New York in 1958. Astonishing in his foresight, Cage here anticipates the electronic, technological revolution that was to transform music. At the time Cage first gave the address, the synthesizer, which he calls the Theremin machine, had just been invented, and tape recording was in its infancy. The synthesizer was being used only to simulate sounds made by conventional musical instruments, and even Cage did not envision the conditions of the present-day world where musicians routinely use portable synthesizers in on-stage performance and when synthesizers are sold in music stores for about four hundred dollars.

The well-known minimalist composer, Philip Glass, whose operas *Einstein on the Beach* and *The Photographer* have been enthusiastically received, has said that although the great classics have certainly influenced his work, he has been even more influenced by popular New Wave groups such as the Talking Heads. The electronic revolution in music has had some very interesting consequences. First of all, it has erased, or at least dimmed, the line of demarcation between "classical," or "serious," music and popular music. In many cases young and daring performers, with little training in musicology have taken advantage of technological advances and moved music into its new age. Second, it has released the enjoyment of music from class and generational stratification—young New Wave musicians are as enthusiatic about the learned, formidable Philip Glass as he is about them. And finally, it has made theoreticians think more deeply about what music is, and why human beings create and need it. It has even created new academic fields, such as the physics of sound.

As you read, consider these ideas:

1. How does the way that John Cage expresses himself in language resemble the way that he expresses himself in music? If you have never heard any of Cage's music, think about his verbal expression in terms of what he is saying about musical expression.
2. What effects have John Cage's "credo" had upon (a) what we hear, (b) what our expectations from a piece of music are, and (c) what the relation of tone to note has become in popular music.
3. Does Cage's conception of the dichotomy between new ideas and old formulas for thinking bear any resemblance to the dominant contrasts in le Guin?

Brian Eno is one of the most interesting young composers of our day. Whether we should think of him as a composer of "classical" or "popular" music is uncertain because, just as Cage predicted, that distinction is irrelevant in our time. We have included this selection so that you can judge for yourself how accurately John Cage predicted the future of music.

As you read these two short descriptions by Eno, use them to test the ideas of Cage. Ask some of these questions:

1. How accurate was Cage in predicting that the new technologies would influence the ways composers think about music?
2. How accurate was Cage's prediction about "environmental" music that would correspond to conceptions in art and architecture?
3. Does Eno think of music as "the organization of sound"?

4. What is the relation of composer to musical piece? What is the relation of listener to musical piece? What is the relation between composer and listener, and how is it established?
5. John Cage's writing style bears some resemblance to what he attempts in music. Does Brian Eno's?

GLOSSARY

CAGE

amplitude [2]	improvisations [17]
frequency [2]	fugue [19]
Novachord [6]	sonata [19]
Solovox [6]	ardor [23]
vibrato [6]	beatific [23]
tones [7]	anechoic [27]
duration [7]	juxtaposition [29]
synthetic [8]	timbre [29]
audible [9]	morphology [29]
dissonance [10]	determinants [29]
consonance [10]	counterpoint [30]
twelve-tone system [13]	harmony [30]
analogous [14]	

_____ THE FUTURE OF MUSIC: CREDO _____

John Cage

[1] I BELIEVE THAT THE USE OF NOISE

[2]   Wherever we are, what we hear is
mostly noise. When we ignore it, it disturbs us. When we listen to
it, we find it fascinating. The sound of a truck at fifty miles per hour.
Static between the stations. Rain. We want to capture and control
these sounds, to use them not as sound effects but as musical instruments. Every film studio has a library of "sound effects" recorded on
film. With a film phonograph it is now possible to control the amplitude
and frequency of any one of these sounds and to give to it rhythms
within or beyond the reach of the imagination. Given four film phonographs, we can compose and perform a quartet for explosive motor,
wind, heartbeat, and landslide.

[3]   TO MAKE MUSIC

[4]   If this word "music"
is sacred and reserved for eighteenth- and nineteenth-century instruments, we can substitute a more meaningful term: organization of
sound.

[5]   WILL CONTINUE AND
INCREASE UNTIL WE REACH A MUSIC PRODUCED THROUGH THE AID OF
ELECTRICAL INSTRUMENTS

[6]   Most inventors of electrical musical instruments
have attempted to imitate eighteenth- and nineteenth-century instruments, just as early automobile designers copied the carriage. The
Novachord and the Solovox are examples of this desire to imitate the
past rather than construct the future. When Theremin provided an
instrument with genuinely new possibilities, Thereministes did their
utmost to make the instrument sound like some old instrument, giving
it a sickeningly sweet vibrato, and performing upon it, with difficulty,
masterpieces from the past. Although the instrument is capable of a
wide variety of sound qualities, obtained by the turning of a dial,
Thereministes act as censors, giving the public those sounds they
think the public will like. We are shielded from new sound experiences.

[7]   The special function of electrical instruments
will be to provide complete control of the overtone structure of tones

SOURCE: From John Cage, *Silence*, MIT Press, Cambridge, 1966.

(as opposed to noises) and to make these tones available in any frequency, amplitude, and <u>duration</u>.

WHICH WILL MAKE AVAILABLE FOR MUSICAL [8]
PURPOSES ANY AND ALL SOUNDS THAT CAN BE HEARD. PHOTOELECTRIC,
FILM, AND MECHANICAL MEDIUMS FOR THE <u>SYNTHETIC</u> PRODUCTION OF MUSIC

It is now possible for composers to make music [9]
directly, without the assistance of intermediary performers. Any design
repeated often enough on a sound track is <u>audible</u>. Two hundred and
eighty circles per second on a sound track will produce one sound,
whereas a portrait of Beethoven repeated fifty times per second on a
sound track will have not only a different pitch but a different sound
quality.

WILL BE EXPLORED. WHEREAS, IN THE PAST, THE POINT [10]
OF DISAGREEMENT HAS BEEN BETWEEN <u>DISSONANCE</u> AND <u>CONSONANCE</u>,
IT WILL BE, IN THE IMMEDIATE FUTURE, BETWEEN NOISE AND SO-CALLED
MUSICAL SOUNDS.

THE PRESENT METHODS OF WRITING MUSIC, PRINCIPALLY [11]
THOSE WHICH EMPLOY HARMONY AND ITS REFERENCE TO PARTICULAR
STEPS IN THE FIELD OF SOUND, WILL BE INADEQUATE FOR THE COMPOSER,
WHO WILL BE FACED WITH THE ENTIRE FIELD OF SOUND.

The composer (organizer of sound) will be faced not only with the [12]
entire field of sound but also with the entire field of time. The "frame"
or fraction of a second, following established film technique, will
probably be the basic unit in the measurement of time. No rhythm
will be beyond the composer's reach.

NEW METHODS WILL BE DISCOVERED, BEARING A DEFINITE RELATION TO [13]
SCHOENBERG'S <u>TWELVE-TONE SYSTEM</u>

Schoenberg's method assigns to [14]
each material, in a group of equal materials, its function with respect
to the group. (Harmony assigned to each material, in a group of
unequal materials, its function with respect to the fundamental or
most important material in the group.) Schoenberg's method is <u>analogous</u> to a society in which the emphasis is on the group and the
integration of the individual in the group.

AND PRESENT METHODS OF WRITING [15]
PERCUSSION MUSIC

Percussion music is a contemporary transition from [16]
keyboard-influenced music to the all-sound music of the future. Any
sound is acceptable to the composer of percussion music; he explores

the academically forbidden "non-musical" field of sound insofar as is manually possible.

[17]   Methods of writing percussion music have as their goal the rhythmic structure of a composition. As soon as these methods are crystallized into one or several widely accepted methods, the means will exist for group improvisations of unwritten but culturally important music. This has already taken place in Oriental cultures and in hot jazz.

[18]   AND ANY OTHER METHODS WHICH ARE FREE FROM THE CONCEPT OF A FUNDAMENTAL TONE.

[19]   THE PRINCIPLE OF FORM WILL BE OUR ONLY CONSTANT CONNECTION WITH THE PAST. ALTHOUGH THE GREAT FORM OF THE FUTURE WILL NOT BE AS IT WAS IN THE PAST, AT ONE TIME THE FUGUE AND AT ANOTHER THE SONATA, IT WILL BE RELATED TO THESE AS THEY ARE TO EACH OTHER:

[20]   Before this happens, centers of experimental music must be established. In these centers, the new materials, oscillators, turntables, generators, means for amplifying small sounds, film phonographs, etc., available for use. Composers at work using twentieth-century means for making music. Performances of results. Organization of sound for extra-musical purposes (theatre, dance, radio, film).

[21]   THROUGH THE PRINCIPLE OF ORGANIZATION OR MAN'S COMMON ABILITY TO THINK.

------

[22]   It was a Wednesday. I was in the sixth grade. I overheard Dad saying to Mother, "Get ready: we're going to New Zealand Saturday." I got ready. I read everything I could find in the school library about New Zealand. Saturday came. Nothing happened. The project was not even mentioned, that day or any succeeding day.

[23]   M. C. Richards went to see the Bolshoi Ballet. She was delighted with the dancing. She said, "It's not what they do; it's the ardor with which they do it." I said, "Yes: composition, performance, and audition or observation are really different things. They have next to nothing to do with one another." Once, I told her, I was at a house on Riverside Drive where people were invited to be present at a Zen service conducted by a Japanese Roshi. He did the ritual, rose petals and all. Afterwards tea was served with rice cookies. And then the hostess and her husband, employing an out-of-tune piano and a cracked voice, gave a wretched performance of an excerpt from a third-rate Italian opera. I was em-

barrassed and glanced towards the Roshi to see how he was taking it. The expression on his face was absolutely <u>beatific</u>.

A young man in Japan arranged his circumstances so that he was [24] able to travel to a distant island to study Zen with a certain Master for a three-year period. At the end of the three years, feeling no sense of accomplishment, he presented himself to the Master and announced his departure. The Master said, "You've been here three years. Why don't you stay three months more?" The student agreed, but at the end of the three months he still felt that he had made no advance. When he told the Master again that he was leaving, the Master said, "Look now, you've been here three years and three months. Stay three weeks longer." The student did, but with no success. When he told the Master that absolutely nothing had happened, the Master said, "You've been here three years, three months, and three weeks. Stay three more days, and if, at the end of that time, you have not attained enlightenment, commit suicide." Towards the end of the second day, the student was enlightened.

——— EXPERIMENTAL MUSIC ———

Formerly, whenever anyone said the music I presented was experi- [25] mental, I objected. It seemed to me that composers knew what they were doing, and that the experiments that had been made had taken place prior to the finished works, just as sketches are made before paintings and rehearsals precede performances. But, giving the matter further thought, I realized that there is ordinarily an essential difference between making a piece of music and hearing one. A composer knows his work as a woodsman knows a path he has traced and retraced, while a listener is confronted by the same work as one is in the woods by a plant he has never seen before.

Now, on the other hand, times have changed; music has changed; [26] and I no longer object to the word "experimental." I use it in fact to describe all the music that especially interests me and to which I am devoted, whether someone else wrote it or I myself did. What has happened is that I have become a listener and the music has become something to hear. Many people, of course, have given up saying "experimental" about this new music. Instead, they either move to a halfway point and say "controversial" or depart to a greater distance and question whether this "music" is music at all.

For in this new music nothing takes place but sounds: those that [27] are notated and those that are not. Those that are not notated appear in the written music as silences, opening the doors of the music to the sounds that happen to be in the environment. This openness exists in the fields of modern sculpture and architecture. The glass houses of Mies van der Rohe reflect their environment, presenting to the eye images of clouds, trees, or grass, according to the situation. And while looking at the constructions in wire of the sculptor Richard Lippold, it is inevitable that one will see other things, and people too, if they happen to be there at the same time, through the network of wires. There is no such thing as an empty space or an empty time. There is always something to see, something to hear. In fact, try as we may to make a silence, we cannot. For certain engineering purposes, it is desirable to have as silent a situation as possible. Such a room is called an anechoic chamber, its six walls made of special material, a room without echoes. I entered one at Harvard University several years ago and heard two sounds, one high and one low. When I described them to the engineer in charge, he informed me that the high one was my nervous system in operation, the low one my blood in circulation. Until I die there will be sounds. And they will continue following my death. One need not fear about the future of music.

[28]   But this fearlessness only follows if, at the parting of the ways, where it is realized that sounds occur whether intended or not, one turns in the direction of those he does not intend. This turning is psychological and seems at first to be a giving up of everything that belongs to humanity—for a musician, the giving up of music. This psychological turning leads to the world of nature, where, gradually or suddenly, one sees that humanity and nature, not separate, are in this world together; that nothing was lost when everything was given away. In fact, everything is gained. In musical terms, any sounds may occur in any combination and in any continuity.

[29]   And it is a striking coincidence that just now the technical means to produce such a free-ranging music are available. When the Allies entered Germany towards the end of World War II, it was discovered that improvements had been made in recording sounds magnetically such that tape had become suitable for the high-fidelity recording of music. First in France with the work of Pierre Schaeffer, later here, in Germany, in Italy, in Japan, and perhaps, without my knowing it, in other places, magnetic tape was used not simply to record per-formances of music but to make a new music that was possible only because of it. Given a minimum of two tape recorders and a disk recorder, the following processes are possible: 1) a single recording of any sound may be made; 2) a rerecording may be made, in the course of which, by means of filters and circuits, any or all of the physical characteristics of a given recorded sound may be altered; 3) electronic mixing (combining on a third machine sounds issuing from two others) permits the presentation of any number of sounds in

combination; 4) ordinary splicing permits the juxtaposition of any sounds, and when it includes unconventional cuts, it, like rerecording, brings about alterations of any or all of the original physical characteristics. The situation made available by these means is essentially a total sound-space, the limits of which are ear-determined only, the position of a particular sound in this space being the result of five determinants: frequency or pitch, amplitude or loudness, overtone structure or timbre, duration, and morphology (how the sound begins, goes on, and dies away). By the alteration of any one of these determinants, the position of the sound in sound-space changes. Any sound at any point in this total sound-space can move to become a sound at any other point. But advantage can be taken of these possibilities only if one is willing to change one's musical habits radically. That is, one may take advantage of the appearance of images without visible transition in distant places, which is a way of saying "television," if one is willing to stay at home instead of going to a theatre. Or one may fly if one is willing to give up walking.

Musical habits include scales, modes, theories of counterpoint and [30] harmony, and the study of the timbres, singly and in combination of a limited number of sound-producing mechanisms. In mathematical terms these all concern discrete steps. They resemble walking—in the case of pitches, on steppingstones twelve in number. This cautious stepping is not characteristic of the possibilities of magnetic tape, which is revealing to us that musical action or existence can occur at any point or along any line or curve or what have you in total sound-space; that we are, in fact, technically equipped to transform our contemporary awareness of nature's manner of operation into art.

Again there is a parting of the ways. One has a choice. If he does [31] not wish to give up his attempts to control sound, he may complicate his musical technique towards an approximation of the new possibilities and awareness. (I use the word "approximation" because a measuring mind can never finally measure nature.) Or, as before, one may give up the desire to control sound, clear his mind of music, and set about discovering means to let sounds be themselves rather than vehicles for man-made theories or expressions of human sentiments.

This project will seem fearsome to many, but on examination it [32] gives no cause for alarm. Hearing sounds which are just sounds immediately sets the theorizing mind to theorizing, and the emotions of human beings are continually aroused by encounters with nature. Does not a mountain unintentionally evoke in us a sense of wonder? otters along a stream a sense of mirth? night in the woods a sense of fear? Do not rain falling and mists rising up suggest the love binding heaven and earth? Is not decaying flesh loathsome? Does not the death of someone we love bring sorrow? And is there a greater hero than the least plant that grows? What is more angry than the flash of lightning and the sound of thunder? These responses to nature are mine and will not necessarily correspond with another's. Emotion takes place in the person who has it. And sounds, when allowed to be themselves, do not require that those who hear them do so unfeelingly. The opposite is what is meant by response ability.

[33]   New music: new listening. Not an attempt to understand something that is being said, for, if something were being said, the sounds would be given the shapes of words. Just an attention to the activity of sounds.

[34]   Those involved with the composition of experimental music find ways and means to remove themselves from the activities of the sounds they make. Some employ chance operations, derived from sources as ancient as the Chinese *Book of Changes*, or as modern as the tables of random numbers used also by physicists in research. Or, analogous to the Rorschach tests of psychology, the interpretation of imperfections in the paper upon which one is writing may provide a music free from one's memory and imagination. Geometrical means employing spatial superimpositions at variance with the ultimate performance in time may be used. The total field of possibilities may be roughly divided and the actual sounds within these divisions may be indicated as to number but left to the performer or to the splicer to choose. In this latter case, the composer resembles the maker of a camera who allows someone else to take the picture.

[35]   Whether one uses tape or writes for conventional instruments, the present musical situation has changed from what it was before tape came into being. This also need not arouse alarm, for the coming into being of something new does not by that fact deprive what was of its proper place. Each thing has its own place, never takes the place of something else; and the more things there are, as is said, the merrier.

[36]   But several effects of tape on experimental music may be mentioned. Since so many inches of tape equal so many seconds of time, it has become more and more usual that notation is in space rather than in symbols of quarter, half, and sixteenth notes and so on. Thus where on a page a note appears will correspond to when in a time it is to occur. A stop watch is used to facilitate a performance; and a rhythm results which is a far cry from horse's hoofs and other regular beats.

[37]   Also it has been impossible with the playing of several separate tapes at once to achieve perfect synchronization. This fact has led some towards the manufacture of multiple-tracked tapes and machines with a corresponding number of heads; while others—those who have accepted the sounds they do not intend—now realize that the score, the requiring that many parts be played in a particular togeth-

erness, is not an accurate representation of how things are. These now compose parts but not scores, and the parts may be combined in any unthought ways. This means that each performance of such a piece of music is unique, as interesting to its composer as to others listening. It is easy to see again the parallel with nature, for even with leaves of the same tree, no two are exactly alike. The parallel in art is the sculpture with moving parts, the mobile.

It goes without saying that dissonances and noises are welcome in this new music. But so is the dominant seventh chord if it happens to put in an appearance. [38]

Rehearsals have shown that this new music, whether for tape or for instruments, is more clearly heard when the several loud-speakers or performers are separated in space rather than grouped closely together. For this music is not concerned with harmoniousness as generally understood, where the quality of harmony results from a blending of several elements. Here we are concerned with the co-existence of dissimilars, and the central points where fusion occurs are many: the ears of the listeners wherever they are. This disharmony, to paraphrase Bergson's statement about disorder, is simply a harmony to which many are unaccustomed. [39]

Where do we go from here? Towards theatre. That art more than music resembles nature. We have eyes as well as ears, and it is our business while we are alive to use them. [40]

And what is the purpose of writing music? One is, of course, not dealing with purposes but dealing with sounds. Or the answer must take the form of paradox: a purposeful purposelessness or a purposeless play. This play, however, is an affirmation of life—not an attempt to bring order out of chaos nor to suggest improvements in creation, but simply a way of waking up to the very life we're living, which is so excellent once one gets one's mind and one's desires out of its way and lets it act of its own accord. [41]

When Xenia and I came to New York from Chicago, we arrived in the bus station with about twenty-five cents. We were expecting to stay for a while with Peggy Guggenheim and Max Ernst. Max Ernst had met us in Chicago and had said, "Whenever you come to New York, come and stay with us. We have a big house on the East River." I went to the phone booth in the bus station, put in a nickel, and dialed. Max Ernst answered. He didn't recognize my voice. Finally he said, "Are you thirsty?" I said, "Yes." He said, "Well, come over tomorrow for cocktails." I went back to Xenia and told her what had happened. She said, "Call him back. We have everything to gain and [42] nothing to lose." I did. He said, "Oh! It's you. We've been waiting for you for weeks. Your room's ready. Come right over."

[43]   Dad is an inventor. In 1912 his submarine had the world's record for staying under water. Running as it did by means of a gasoline engine, it left bubbles on the surface, so it was not employed during World War I. Dad says he does his best work when he is sound asleep. I was explaining at the New School that the way to get ideas is to do something boring. For instance, composing in such a way that the process of composing is boring induces ideas. They fly into one's head like birds. Is that what Dad meant?

————— AMBIENT MUSIC —————

Brian Eno

The concept of music designed specifically as a background feature in the environment was pioneered by Muzak Inc. in the fifties, and has since come to be known generically by the term Muzak. The connotations that this term carries are those particularly associated with the kind of material that Muzak Inc. produces—familiar tunes arranged and orchestrated in a lightweight and derivative manner. Understandably, this has led most discerning listeners (and most composers) to dismiss entirely the concept of environmental music as an idea worthy of attention.

Over the past three years, I have become interested in the use of music as ambience, and have come to believe that it is possible to produce material that can be used thus without being in any way compromised. To create a distinction between my own experiments in this area and the products of the various purveyors of canned music, I have begun using the term Ambient Music.

An ambience is defined as an atmosphere, or a surrounding influence: a tint. My intention is to produce original pieces ostensibly (but not exclusively) for particular times and situations with a view to building up a small but versatile catalogue of environmental music suited to a wide variety of moods and atmospheres.

Whereas the extant canned music companies proceed from the basis of regularizing environments by blanketing their acoustic and atmospheric idiosyncracies, Ambient Music is intended to enhance these. Whereas conventional background music is produced by stripping away all sense of doubt and uncertainty (and thus all genuine interest)

SOURCE: Album notes from "Ambient I: Music for Airports," 1978.

from the music, Ambient Music retains these qualities. And whereas their intention is to 'brighten' the environment by adding stimulus to it (thus supposedly alleviating the tedium of routine tasks and levelling out the natural ups and downs of the body rhythms) Ambient Music is intended to induce calm and a space to think.

Ambient Music must be able to accommodate many levels of listening attention without enforcing one in particular; it must be as ignorable as it is interesting.

_____ DISCREET MUSIC _____

Since I have always preferred making plans to executing them, I have gravitated towards situations and systems that, once set into operation, could create music with little or no intervention on my part.

That is to say, I tend towards the roles of planner and programmer, and then become an audience to the results.

Two ways of satisfying this interest are exemplified on this album. "Discreet Music" is a technological approach to the problem. If there is any score for the piece, it must be the operational diagram of the particular apparatus I used for its production. The key configuration here is the long delay echo system with which I have experimented since I became aware of the musical possibilities of tape recorders in 1964. Having set up this apparatus, my degree of participation in what it subsequently did was limited to (a) providing an input (in this case, two simple and mutually compatible melodic lines of different duration stored on a digital recall system) and (b) occasionally altering the timbre of the synthesizer's output by means of a graphic equalizer.

It is a point of discipline to accept this passive role, and, for once, to ignore the tendency to play the artist by dabbling and interfering. In this case, I was aided by the idea that what I was making was simply a background for my friend Robert Fripp to play over in a series of concerts we had planned. This notion of its future utility, coupled with my own pleasure in "gradual processes" prevented me from attempting to create surprises and less than predictable changes in the piece. I was trying to make a piece that could be listened to and yet could be ignored . . . perhaps in the spirit of Satie who wanted to make music that could "mingle with the sound of the knives and forks at dinner."

SOURCE: Album notes from Brian Eno's "Discreet Music," 1975.

In January this year I had an accident. I was not seriously hurt, but I was confined to bed in a stiff and static position. My friend Judy Nylon visited me and brought me a record of 18th century harp music. After she had gone, and with some considerable difficulty, I put on the record. Having laid down, I realized that the amplifier was set at an extremely low level, and that one channel of the stereo had failed completely. Since I hadn't the energy to get up and improve matters, the record played on almost inaudibly. This presented what was for me a new way of hearing music—as part of the ambience of the environment just as the colour of the light and the sound of the rain were parts of that ambience. It is for this reason that I suggest listening to the piece at comparatively low levels, even to the extent that it frequently falls below the threshold of audibility.

Another way of satisfying the interest in self-regulating and self-generating systems is exemplified in the 3 variations on the Pachelbel Canon. These take their titles from the charmingly inaccurate translation of the French cover notes for the "Erato" recording of the piece made by the orchestra of Jean François Paillard. That particular recording inspired these pieces by its unashamedly romantic rendition of a very systematic Renaissance canon.

In this case the "system" is a group of performers with a set of instructions—and the "input" is the fragment of Pachelbel. Each variation takes a small section of the score (two or four bars) as its starting point, and permutates the players' parts such that they overlay each other in ways not suggested by the original score. In "Fullness of Wind" each player's tempo is decreased, the rate of decrease governed by the pitch of his instrument (bass = slow). "French Catalogues" groups together sets of notes and melodies with time directions gathered from other parts of the score. In "Brutal Ardour" each player has a sequence of notes related to those of the other players, but the sequences are of different lengths so that the original relationships quickly break down.

QUESTIONS

1. What is important in the initial distinction Cage makes between "music" and "organization of sound"? Is the distinction theoretically important?
2. In discussing Schoenberg's method, Cage says that while nine-teenth-century harmony assigned to each material, in a group of unequal materials, a relation to the strongest, or most important

material in the group, the new music assigns the function of *each* material to the equal group of materials, as a whole. We seldom think of musicology as being in any way related to politics, but if we remember that this talk was given in 1937, during the Hitler era, can we make the supposition that the old harmonics might have been thought of as a fascistic, or ultraconservative, mode and the new harmonics as reflecting democratic principles? Speculate about whether artists, even those as removed in their work from mundane affairs as musicologists are, might be influenced by political or social conditions. Take Belle in Ursula le Guin's story into account. Is she using music as a form of political protest?

3. Cage says, "The principle of form will be our only constant connection with the past. Although the great form of the future will not be as it was in the past. . . ." How accurate a forecast was this? Is the form of present music, popular or classical, connected to the past? How is it connected? How is it different from the music of the past?

4. Cage says that the organization of sound in the future will rest upon "man's common ability to think." What does that mean? Is he saying that anything we can conceive of musically will be the principle on which musical composition rests? How is musical thinking different from scientific thinking? How is musical thinking the same? Remember that for centuries in our Western tradition we thought that thinking musically was the most accurate way of thinking about the cosmos.

5. What do the anecdotal interludes—accounts of Dad the inventor, of M. C. Richards' response to the Bolshoi Ballet, of the Zen master—have to do with the argument Cage is making for experimental music? What do they *mean*? How do they relate to the main argument? Are they "asides"? Are they illustrations? *What* are they?

6. Cage relates his experimental music to the architecture of Mies van der Rohe and the sculpture of Richard Lippold. How are they related? Why would an experimental music "let in" the external environment? What is Cage saying about the relation between the forms which the human mind makes and the forms and sounds that external nature makes? Would it be good or bad for an experimental scientist to adopt Cage's philosophy?

7. Cage describes the old habits in music in mathematical terms as concerned with "discrete steps." They resemble "cautious stepping" in walking, he says. Quantum theory, as you are probably aware from your high school physics course, was a revolutionary theory in physics in this century. It posits that the motion of electrons, the smallest units of which everything in the universe is made,

is *random*, i.e. does not occur in predictable "cautious stepping." Do you think that great artists and musicians in a particular age are likely to think about the universe in the same ways as great scientists do?

8. Cage says that liberating music so that what we hear in it are "sounds" will liberate our emotions in relation to music—"Hearing sounds which are just sounds immediately sets the theorizing mind to theorizing, and the emotions of human beings are continually aroused by encounters with nature." Do you think this is true? Does this mean that the "composer" of music comes to be the person listening to it and not the man who *writes* the music? Under this system would there be as many *meanings* of a John Cage work as there are listeners to it?

9. If listening to music is "not an attempt to understand" but "an attention to the activity of sounds," does that make music less interesting? Less valuable to us? What is the difference, given Cage's system, between listening to Beethoven and listening to the garbage truck collecting the garbage at 6:00 A.M.? Would Cage think the difference was important?

10. Cage ends his talk on experimental music by asking, "And what is the purpose of writing music?" Do you think the answer he gives is satisfying? Do *you* think that his purpose in writing resembles your purpose in listening?

EXERCISES

1. Listen very closely to your favorite contemporary piece of music. Answer the following in your journal;

   a. Does the piece use what Cage calls the *old* principle of harmonics (scales) or the *new*, atonal principle?

   b. If there are words to the music, what is the relation between the two?

   c. What instrumentation do the musicians use that they could not have used fifty years ago—i.e., electronic instruments, the use of tapes in recording, stereophonic sound, overdubbing.

   d. How great an effect does instrumentation have upon the meaning of the piece of music?

   e. *How* does the music *mean*? Is its primary appeal to the listener's immediate response to sound? to structure? to lyric?

    f.   What, if any, is the relation between the music and the title of the piece?

Write a three-page assessment of John Cage as a prophet of the future of music.

2. Write a three-page, completely speculative essay on this topic: The invention of LSD and the popularization of marijuana usage could not have been foretold by John Cage. How has the use of psychotropic drugs influenced the evolution of modern music?

3. The first Cage essay is experimental in style as well as in its observations about "the future of music." Examine closely the interrelationship of the several parts and try to determine by what principles they fit together. Note, for example, that the sections written in capitals (they look almost like headings) hook together and make one continuous paragraph. Why do you suppose Cage used this curious typographic arrangement to get his thoughts across? How is the reader meant to read the two juxtaposed passages? You are aware that Cage delivered this essay as a talk. How do you suppose he would have read the selection out loud? Do you think that the piece has greater continuity when it is read out loud? Try it, perhaps by "casting" several friends and having them read parts. After experimenting in this fashion write some notes about Cage's prose style and your reactions to it in your journal. Consider whether there are appropriate occasions when you might experiment with form the way Cage did (e.g. in personal letters?).

CHAPTER TWENTY-FIVE

McDERMOTT: DO NOT BEQUEATH A SHAMBLE

Educational Philosophy

John McDermott, distinguished professor of philosophy and head of the department of Humanities in Medicine at Texas A&M University, is a philosopher in the truest sense. *Philo-Sophy* means "the love of wisdom." A person who truly loves wisdom does not keep learning in a separate compartment of his or her life. He or she not only studies wisdom, but also lives it.

In our time, philosophy came to be a very abstract discipline. Often philosophers thought of their discipline as solid, or worthy, only if it was related as closely as possible to mathematics and the "pure," theoretical sciences. Therefore, in many universities epistemology, thinking about thinking, was the darling child of philosophy departments, while ethics, how we *live* in the light of wisdom, was a Cinderella stepsister, barely tolerated in the curriculum and, at best, given a backseat in importance.

Because he is a brilliant teacher, McDermott trained a whole generation of philosophers who began to right the balance and to remember that the fathers of Western philosophy—Socrates, Plato, and Aristotle—thought of themselves primarily as students and as teachers. McDermott reminds us that the great work of philosophy is not only to seek and preserve wisdom, but to bequeath it from generation to generation. In this endeavor, he has indirectly reminded us of the importance that continuity holds in the building of a future and how crucial it is for us not to succumb to the provincial thinking of the specialist. While this issue is only indirectly linked to the next essay, it is clear that McDermott's own road to what he calls a "global consciousness" was the attempt to look for universals in the culture that we have inherited and to use those universals in reinterpreting the crises of our world, especially the short supply of food and the imminent growth of populations. He is, as his essay proclaims, an admirer of the Italian educator Maria Montessori, who in the early part of this century, gave up her professorship at the University of Rome, to found and implement a whole new method of educating children, the Montessori method, which stresses two principles in teaching: first, that children, with proper guidance, teach themselves (we do not beat or bully them into learning; we evoke from them the creativity and eagerness to know that is already within them); and second, that learning is not an abstract process that occurs in their minds only; it is rather a growing organism's *whole* response to its surrounding environment. In the United States, while we have eagerly adopted the Montessori system for preschool and kindergarten teaching, we have not considered it useful after the child begins "serious" education. Among other methods, McDermott advocates in this essay a Montessori method for educating *ourselves* to the terrible realities of twentieth-century life as well as bequeathing this method of dealing with reality to our children.

As you read consider these points:

1. Does McDermott have a political stance in this essay? Is he addressing one or another political party, one or another country, one or the other side—East or West?
2. Is his assessment of the three major problems facing mankind— i.e. the food-population ratio, the energy crises, the destruction of ecological balance—valid? Compare McDermott's vision of the problems that will face us in the twenty-first century with that of Ursula le Guin. What are the similarities and what are the differences in their conceptions of the future?
3. What would McDermott consider to be the cause of war?
4. What are the alternatives in thinking that we adopt to escape confronting these problems? Do you find yourself in one or another group of escapists?
5. Does McDermott's philosophy of education for the future seem to you to be an effective, useful way of dealing with global problems?

GLOSSARY

poignant [1]	ecosystem [9]
gaunt [1]	haplessness [11]
penultimate [2]	trivialized [11]
millennium [2]	amelioration [11]
connoted [2]	nostrums [11]
vulgar [2]	*seriatim* [12]
gainsay [2]	pedagogy [12]
penchant [3]	auto-didactic [13]
gawked [3]	optimum [15]
deracinated [3]	nuclear family [15]
geopolitics [4]	panacea [16]
pluralism [4]	irrevocable [16]
salutary [5]	simplistic [17]
ecology [5]	purview [17]
bourgeois [6]	ethos [17]
impervious [6]	recalcitrant [17]
triage [6]	didactic [18]
irresolute [8]	internecine [18]
aleatory [8]	caveat [19]
episodic [8]	tactile [19]
noxious [9]	seminal [19]

sensorial [20]

nascent [20]

conflagration [23]

pollyanna [23]

aggrandizement [23]

_____ DO NOT BEQUEATH A SHAMBLE _____

*The Child in the Twenty-First Century: Innocent Hostage
to Mindless Oppression or Children as Messengers to the World*

John J. McDermott

What the best and wisest parent wants for his [her] own child,
that must the community want for all of its children.

John Dewey[1]

[We] will not be the victim of events, but will have the clarity of
vision to direct and shape the future of human society.

Maria Montessori[2]

I

What could be more poignant and disturbing than the photographs [1]
of the faces of victimized children over the past fifty years. Beginning
with the children of the holocaust and on through the devastation of
the second world war, Biafra, Vietnam, Laos, until our own time in
Cambodia, their blank, bewildered stares flare out from their gaunt,
malnutritioned bodies. The ravages of global violence are especially
addressed to the children. Their innocence in these conflicts [is a]
stark reminder of the systematic madness that plagues all societies,
which one by one, become self-righteous and oblivious to the nature
of their victims as one cause or another is pursued. I would be more
confident in the possibility of the praiseworthy movement for care of
the unborn generations, if I were to see equal care for those who have
just been born, the children of the world.

As we begin its penultimate decade, the twentieth century has [2]
been a tumultuous and inordinately complex century. We should

SOURCE: Article by John McDermott, "Do Not Bequeath A Shamble," from *The American
Montessori Bulletin*, 1980, vol. 18.

remind ourselves that we not only approach the end of a century,
but of a millennium as well. In that regard, the twentieth century
brings to a head, hundreds of years of yearning and cultural experiences,
which yield a legacy that we avoid at deep peril. Some decades ago,
we viewed the coming of the twenty-first century with considerable
romantic optimism. The year 2001 connoted the marvels of space
technology and liberation from the burdens of the industrial world.
Recent events have rendered that version of our future unrealistic
and, dare we say it, experientially shallow. I say shallow, because the
vision of the next century left out the gnawing problems of the planet
earth, as though they could be transcended and thereby, forgotten.
This attitude, it now turns out, was vulgar naiveté. No, the legacy of
the twentieth century is more sobering, although I do not gainsay the
potential significance of its spiritual bequest. Let us examine this
legacy in some detail.

[3]   As the inheritors of Western culture, we have witnessed a dramatic
shift in our consciousness. We now think and feel in global terms.
The second world war signaled both the end of the colonialism and
the beginning of the full planetary consciousness. Those of us who
were educated in the first fifty years of this century, were introduced
to a warped cultural map of the past. We were taught one version or
another of a Euro-American provincialism, as though a majority of
the world's population and their historical achievements were obsolete.
Our strident refusal to learn the language of other lands was peculiarly
coupled with our penchant for quick tours in which we gawked at
the monuments of what we too often took to be a dead past. The
splendid Cambodian monument of Angkor Wat attests to the majesty
of a storied history but in our time, the photo-teletype sends us the
pictures of hordes of deracinated and emaciated Cambodian children,
victims of the power politics which rage around them, as indifferent
to their future as to their past.

[4]   The last four decades of geopolitics have profoundly transformed
our consciousness. Now, to be truly human, we must think in planetary,
global terms. I remember vividly when this transformation began to
take shape in my own mind. The year was 1954 and I read of the
impending Conference to be held at Bandung, Indonesia. They announced that no "white" nations would be invited, and it was at that
Conference, that the gathered nations described themselves as "the
third world." The impact of that Conference was obvious; East and
West were no longer apt planetary divisions. Subsequent to the event,
we have seen the re-emergence of Africa, China and the nations of
the Latin America as distinctive and distinguished forces on the world
stage. Human culture is now truly world culture. Our experience of
literature, religion, philosophy, dance, music, art and costume have

been immeasurably enriched. The only viable strategy for our global future is the adoption of a pluralism, in which the angles of visions, styles, and beliefs of the world's cultures, mesh in the creation of a genuinely egalitarian world society.

There is no question that this spiritual bequest of the twentieth [5] century on behalf of global consciousness is salutary. Nonetheless, there is a dark side to our newfound awareness, for no sooner do we become aware of the riches of global culture, than we realize the attendant problems which also emerge. In truth, the glaring fact of the matter is that we are now faced with a crisis of global proportions. This situation takes the form of a crisis in energy, food, ecology and population, to which is added the ambivalence of high technology. We talk now about the world in which our children's children will come to consciousness.

However difficult it may be for us to comprehend existentially, it [6] is necessary for us to project the future and to assess its viability by analysis of our present plight. Although I am not given to Cassandra-like prophecies of doom, we must face the fact, nonetheless, that we are witness to a planetary siege mentality.[3] Our most serious difficulty, despite its being hidden from most of the bourgeois world, is that of food. Despite the extraordinary advances of modern agricultural tech-nology, the geometric increase in the world's population has raised the spectre of widening human sectors in which future starvation is a high probability. It is a well-known paradox that the people who can least afford to have children, have them, whereas the birth rate among the affluent, and especially among the middle class, has dropped. As contemporary anthropologists have detailed, the reasons for this are culturally complex and perhaps impervious to a solution. Yet, the brutal fact prevails; there exists an inverse ratio between those who have the resources and those who have the need. So serious is this matter, that allegedly thoughtful people have introduced the notion of triage into the field of world hunger. Taken over from the language of the battlefield, the word triage refers to tripartite division of the wounded as found in the field hospital. The breakdown is as follows: those who will die, even if treated; those who will live, even if not treated; and those who will live, only if treated. The first category is abandoned, the second is asked to suffer through to resolution, whereas the resources are given only to the last group. The analog to world hunger does not hold, for all, if fed, could live. But food triage, depressingly, has been considered as a serious option on the ground that in time, there will be enough food for some but not for all. The question facing our children is who gets the food. Or is the question different, that is, who among the next generations will be willing to cut their consumption drastically, so that all may eat? Of course, the true doomsday prophet foresees a solution to world starvation and overpopulation, the latter estimated conservatively at seven billion people forty years from now, namely, nuclear conflagration.

[7]   To the twin problems of food and population, we now add the depletion of nonrenewable resources, known in the jargon as the energy crisis. In addition to the obvious economic hardships this crisis can generate, we should focus also on the deeply personal disadvantages which will accrue. The key word here is accessibility, namely, the denial of the possibility of visiting the distant environs which surround us and still more crucial, the denial of the possibility of visiting each other. We face a social impacting and a loss of national, let alone global consciousness. We must implore our children to search for viable alternatives so that this crisis will be averted, else they will plunge backward into the provincial limitations of centuries past.

[8]   The irony of the above difficulties is that a resolution would be forthcoming if it were not for the emergence of still another world problem, that of ecological trashing. Symbolically, this is the most unsettling of all of our problems, for it results from the fallout of some of our most successful endeavors. John Dewey long ago told us that we were in an irresolute struggle with the affairs of nature, and that nature, if abused would strike back.

> Time is brief, and this statement must stand instead of the discourse which the subject deserves. Man finds himself living in an aleatory world; his existence involves, to put it baldly, a gamble. The world is a scene of risk; it is uncertain, unstable, uncannily unstable. Its dangers are irregular, inconstant, not to be counted upon as to their times and seasons. Although persistent, they are sporadic, episodic. It is darkest just before dawn; pride goes before a fall; the moment of greatest prosperity is the moment most charged with ill-omen, most opportune for the evil eye. Plague, famine, failure of crops, disease, death, defeat in battle, are always just around the corner, and so are abundance, strength, victory, festival and song. Luck is proverbially both good and bad in its distributions. The sacred and the accursed are potentialities of the same situation; and there is no category of things which has not embodied the sacred and accursed: persons, words, places, times, directions in space, stones, winds, animals, stars.

[9]   Surely, the warning is clear, "the world is a scene of risk." The solution of those problems most bothersome to one generation, often become irresolute difficulties of a subsequent generation. Time extracts its price. We and our children are inheriting polluted oceans, rivers, lakes, streams and air. Some of us live on top of Love Canals, obviously inappropriately named as their noxious fumes and chemicals penetrate

our deepest genetic structure. We, in our generation, have committed the cardinal sin. Instead of bequeathing a "leg up," a better world, or whatever cliché comes to mind, we have passed on a time bomb. Our children's ecological future is fraught with the residue of chemical seedings, poisonous in the long run. Our present generation is trapped in a classic case of Catch-22. The energy crisis threatens our economic stability, our social patterns, and even penetrates to our long held image of ourselves as a necessarily mobile people. Yet, our potential resolutions of this problem are foreboding in their own right. If we re-open our massive coal reserves, we heighten our pollution level and expand the deadly presence of acid rain, which has already deadened hundreds of lakes and thousands of fish in upper New York State. The turn to nuclear power is even more frightening, as the events of Three Mile Island graphically attest. The genius of high technology is necessary to ameliorate the world's problems just detailed. Yet, it is that same high technology which has so threatened the delicate balance of the world's ecosystem, especially in its bio-chemical arrangements.

The rights and needs of the present generations must be set over [10] against the rights and needs of unborn generations, world-wide. Our children will have to be the generation which effects the transition from the present-mindedness which has dominated the recent centuries to a forward looking care for future generations by assuring a perpetuity of resources and by a resisting of the short-run exploitation of nature. Further, although not sufficient for a resolution of these perplexing and abiding problems, it would be symbolically significant if the present generation would begin a concerted effort to stop trashing our environment. And, on this behalf, the messages of ecologists should be built into every curriculum, from the teaching of pre-school children on to university life and adult education. As we know, there is considerable religious fervor loose in the world. I, for one, am not very impressed by its ideological self-righteousness and its abandonment of the problems most pressing to most of us. Better if that energy were addressed to what is truly sacred in our lives, our land, our things, and living space and above all, our ability to provide for a creative future for our children.

What we must avoid, is the increasing sense of our haplessness in [11] the face of these difficulties. Many of us feel dwarfed or even trivialized by the events of this century. Too often, then, our tendency is to abandon our best instincts for amelioration and to dilute our energies in favor of either a laissez-faire attitude or some form of extra-terrestrial resolution. This will not do, for the forces of exploitation and manipulation do not so sleep or become seduced by nostrums of another worldly cast. Rather, we must begin and where begun, intensify, a re-education of our attitudes toward the future and especially toward our use of the planet earth.

II

[12]   Obviously, it is beyond the scope of this paper and, more tellingly, beyond my competence, to offer technical and specific resolutions of these difficulties. Fortunately, we have a different task at hand, namely, our educational bequest, such that our children and their children will be better prepared for the next century than we seem to be. And, in this context, the backdrop of our consideration is the work of Maria Montessori. Her explicit contributions to our discussion are threefold. First, she is the first and, in fact, the only truly global educator. Second, however unwitting it may have been, she has anticipated the decline of the nuclear family as the primary source of pre-school education. In this regard, she has been especially acute in helping us to cut between the twin pitfalls of sentimentality and indifference in our relationship to children. Third, we can learn from her notion of the prepared environment and her structuring of the attitudes of care for that environment on the part of participating children. Her work in this area could become an important strand in rebuilding our care for the earth. Let us examine these contributions, *seriatim*, in an effort to forge a pedagogy more sensitive to our actual situation than is the haphazard methodology of most of our peers.

[13]   Initially, the most striking feature of Montessori's work is that her method, her teachers and her learning children in her programs are to be found throughout the world. No other educator has such global influence, for although Pestalozzi, Rousseau, Herbart, and Piaget have each made their contributions, they are restricted for the most part to western culture. John Dewey, it is true, has had enormous influence in the Orient but not in Western Europe, nor the third world. Montessori, to the contrary, has struck a universal chord in the lives of children, wherever they are found. I trace this important fact to three sources. First, she wisely believed that children of very early age had abilities to learn, independent of their peer group cultures, which were rarely tapped in any formal way. Second, it was not necessary to import teachers who had a secret message to deliver. Indeed, teachers in the usual sense were not part of the Montessori picture. Rather, the presence of Montessori directresses and later directors, could be either imported or homegrown, so long as they honored the auto-didactic activities of the children. It was the children, after all, who taught themselves, so long as the environment was prepared, the materials utilized and the goals or directions made clear. In very young children this could and has taken place in a wide variety of cultures

throughout the world. Third, the Montessori children were not class structured. From the first days of the Casa dei Bambini, Montessori was convinced that children of all backgrounds and all cultural limitations were capable of self-learning.[4] Indeed, it is often characteristic of a Montessori program that the children are representative of a far wider range of cultural and economic advantages than the more traditional programs.

The global influence of Montessori was not an accident of history. [14] Long before our own awareness of the inextricability of our lives on this planet, she saw the need for the recognition and development of the abilities of children throughout the world. As early as 1910, she resigned her lectureship at the University of Rome and struck her name from the list of practicing physicians, and committed herself to "all the children in the world, born and as yet unborn."[5] She then began a life-long journey on behalf of children's rights and of their liberation from the darkness of unknowing. Her work was to take her beyond Italy to the United States, Latin America, India, Ceylon, France, Germany, Holland, Ireland, Spain, Austria, and Pakistan. Unesco had its spritual if unsung founder and the global consciousness of our time can look back now on its remarkable anticipation by this remarkable woman educator.

I turn now to Montessori's second contribution to our time and its [15] significance for the future, namely her contributions to the potential independence of young children from parental structures for the purpose of learning. Allow me to be front-out at this point. I do not believe that pre-school programs or day-care centers are the optimum environment for young children. In that regard, I am an unabashed believer, only so far as children are concerned, in the structure of the nuclear family. Increasingly, for a wide variety of reasons, this belief is out of step with the social realities of our present situation in America, to say nothing of cultures distant from us. Speaking only of our own American culture, the signs are telling, for the growing irrelevance of my point of view. Soaring divorce rates, single parents, homosexual marriages and most of all, the tremendous increase of women's participation in the public economic sector, all point to the need for an extraordinary increase in the care of preschool children. And, these developments, of course, are in addition to the always shocking displacement of children in various countries due to war, famine or one or another lethal political dispute.

I do not see Montessori's approach to the education of young [16] children as a panacea, any more than could that of any single perspective. Yet, in these troubled times, which point to still more vast difficulties, her philosophy of the child takes on increased meaning. Of special importance is her insistence that we have both a deep and abiding care for the child and a firm commitment to the independence and irrevocable liberty of the child. It is the persistent transaction of these two attitudes, situation by situation, which gives the wisdom to Montessori's educational practice. As parents and teachers, we are often vulnerable to the children in our care, such that out of a sense of our own inadequacy, or frustration at their inadequacy, we either indulge them or lose confidence in their ability and thereby shut them down.

[17]   Montessori teaches us that young children are more capable than we assume, but she also stresses that they need more shepherding than we are often willing to give. For those who came to consciousness under the influence of Freud, there seems to be something irreducibly simplistic about Montessori's version of the child, to say nothing of her ineptitude on the crucial problem of sexual development. Yet, as we develop global consciousness and take into our purview, the lives of children around the world, the high bourgeois ethos of Freud and other practitioners of our assorted neuroses, despite its intrinsic fascination, seems to fade in the order of relevance. So too with the much ballyhooed electronic revolution that we were told was imminent. An occasional child may have an "R2D2" as a companion, but the more likely future will be characterized by the struggle for physical sustenance and for a place rather than a room of one's own. If we truly believe in the future of our children, we shall teach them to care about the world in which they are going to find themselves, a world notably more recalcitrant than the one in which we live. And this leads us to Montessori's third contribution to life in the twenty-first century, that of her notion of a prepared environment and her doctrine of things.[6]

[18]   In speaking of the prepared environment and the didactic materials, I have no intention of returning to the earlier internecine struggles among Montessorians as to whether the environment and the materials were either impervious to innovation or in desperate need of innovation. Fifteen years ago I wrote on this issue as follows:[7] The notion of structure, so central to Montessori's thought, does not of itself preclude the variety of experiences that is indispensable for learning. The entire criticism of her approach is rendered ineffectual by Montessori's explicit remarks in *Spontaneous Activity in Education*, relative to novelty. She writes, "as a fact, every object may have infinite attributes; and if, as often happens in object-lessons, the origins and ultimate ends of the object itself are included among these attributes, the mind has literally to range throughout the universe."[8] It is not simply a question of quantity that is at stake here; rather the relationship between the potentialities of the child and the *kind* of experiences offered. It is not the number of options that constitutes novelty, for as Montessori

states, "it is the qualities of the objects, not the objects themselves which are important."[9]

With this important caveat of Montessori in mind, and in the light [19] of our present discussion, let us consider the significance of the prepared environment and of the didactic materials. The Montessori environment is prepared in that certain material are to be used, and used in an orderly way. It is, however, just as much a preparing environment, for the child must come to grips with its structure, its advantages and its limitations. The Montessori child is not a robot who is slotted into a tight, rigid and programmed environment. Rather, the key to Montessori's philosophy of education is that the child is a potentially explosive organism, who will respond to the proper tactile stimuli. The prepared environment is an open-ended nest, in which feeding, growth and finally maturation beyond its bounds, takes place. The most creative and seminal characteristic of the prepared environment is that the children take responsibility for it and for their relationship to it. In a word, they care. Further, they care about each other, for each is dependent on the rest, if the environment is to be truly seminal for the awakening of each child's ability. The entire endeavor is shared, although each child has his or her distinct personal process underway, as is symbolized in the periodic experience of silence undergone by the children.[10] Even more significant, for our present discussion, is that the children, when finished with the materials, return them to their proper resting place where they can be used by another child. This use of the materials is analogous to our deep need in the next generations to arrive at a state wherein we do not plunder, that is, do not go beyond the fixed limits of the nonrenewable resource. How different would be our situation if the present generation were taught as children, the existential reality that others follow us and must subsequently use the things that we use.

We have still one more dimension of Montessori's use of materials. [20] She has a superb sense of their tactility and the way in which children are profoundly informed and conceptually transformed by the activities of their bodies, especially their hands. The intimacy of the child to the world is thereby not limited to the affairs of nature. Indeed, things, artifacts, are neither neutral, nor inert, but carry with them the capacity to stir and provoke the sensorial foundations for learning, which each of us carries deep within our nascent person. To learn to read with the hands as well as with the eyes, is a marvelous melding of mind and body, concept and percept, in a pedagogical strategy that is worthy of the fact that such dualisms are not experientially separate in the first place. For Montessori, to touch is to be touched. She places herself in that long tradition of thought which holds that the world and all of its doings, speak to us out of the very depth of being and meaning.

[21]   Montessori has offered us a first step in understanding the power of our things. Her materials, sparse in number and comparatively simple are but an opening wedge into the vast range of possibilities upon which we can call to educate our children. Modern technology has made available an endless range of materials, each different in shape, composition, surface and function. Children throughout the world should place their hands on samples of all of them and so learn of their viability, their use, their fragility and above all, of their danger. In the context of classical Montessori education, allow me to introduce just three new ways of dealing with the environment, all of which are essential to education in the twenty-first century. In addition to the classical materials, I would introduce materials that are highly desirable, but not enough of them to go around, rather just enough to be frustrating. This situation would introduce the children to a structural sense of scarcity. Other materials would be introduced, but when used, would be consumed and non-renewable. The question here, is who gets to use them. Finally, I would introduce materials which not only corrode themselves, but corrode the other materials as well. And here, we have the experience of pollution. Unpleasant pedagogy? Yes, decidedly so, but a necessary pedagogy, nonetheless.

[22]   I, for one, take the message of the ecologists at dead reckoning. In my judgment, the classroom should be structured as a miniature ecosystem. What better than a Montessori approach as suitable for this pedagogical move to the twenty-first century? Combined with the best implications of the revolution in the arts, and the revolution in design, we could encourage our children to begin, from their beginning, to participate in and slowly develop on their own terms, an environment which is aesthetically alive, pedagogically responsive and ecologically responsible. I offer that it is our responsibility on behalf of succeeding generations, that we forge this new creative and fail-safe pedagogy.

[23]   Finally, what after all are our options, our alternatives? One is the voice of the doomsday squad, who divide over two equally reprehensible and unacceptable alternatives; nuclear conflagration and world-wide starvation. At the opposite pole, we have the pollyanna optimists, combined with science fiction, who see half of the world re-locating to outer space by the twenty-second century. If the first alternative is unacceptable, the second is unlikely. Do we have a third alternative? I believe that we do, although it is neither as foreboding nor as dramatic as the first two options. Let us own up to our situation, honestly and without illusion. We must remake the earth in the image of our best qualities. We must dilute and even topple the forces of aggrandizement and exploitation. Nothing will rescue us except ourselves. Neither the gods nor the forces of nature are on our side. We must reconstitute

the awe and the reverence of the earliest people in our quest for a new relationship with the world in which we find ourselves. We are the enemy and we are the saviors. The planet awaits our decision. Which shall it be? This is the message I tell my children and I suggest that it is the message you tell your children and that they should tell their children. Shall our children be innocent hostages to mindless oppression and ecological disaster, or shall they be in fact and in deed, and in imagination, messengers to the building of a truly human world?

NOTES

1. John Dewey, *The School and Society* (Chicago: The University of Chicago Press, 1915), p. 7.

2. Maria Montessori, *Education for a New World* (Adyar: Kalakshetra Publications, 1959), p. 3.

3. Apocalyptic literature, which portends our impending disaster, is not pleasant to read. Still, if only half of the predictions are correct, our children and their children, face an enormously hazardous future. cf; e.g., Gordon Rattray Taylor, *The Doomsday Book* (Greenwich: Fawcett Publications, 1970); *Blueprint for Survival* (New York: New American Library, 1972); Donella H. Meadows, et al., *The Limits of Growth* (New York: Universe Books, 1972); Raymond F. Dasmann, *Planet in Peril* (New York: Meridian Books, 1972); Lester Brown, *The Twenty Ninth Day* (New York: W. W. Norton, 1978); Paul Colinvaux, *Why Big Fierce Animals are Rare and Other Essays* (Princeton: Princeton University Press, 1979); Wendell Berry, *The Unsettling of America, Culture and Agriculture* (New York: Avon Books, 1977).

4. cf. Rita Kramer, *Maria Montessori, A Biography* (New York: G. P. Putnam's Sons, 1976), pp. 107–157.

5. cf. E. M. Standing, *Maria Montessori, Her Life and Work* (New York: New American Library, 1962), p. 61. cf. also, Kramer, *op. cit.*, pp. 155–157.

6. cf. John J. McDermott, "Introduction," Maria Montessori, *Spontaneous Activity in Education* (New York: Schocken Books, 1965) (1977), pp. xvi-xxiv, for a discussion of the prepared environment in the light of the culturally disadvantaged child.

7. The following passage, with editorial changes, is taken from McDermott, *op. cit.*, p. xii.

8. Maria Montessori, *Spontantous Activity in Education*, p. 207.

9. Montessori, *op. cit.*, p. 203.

10. Maria Montessori, *The Montessori Method* (New York: Schocken Books, 1964) (1912), p. 212–214.

QUESTIONS

1. Consider the alternatives McDermott presents to us in his subtitle— the child as "innocent hostage to mindless oppression or children as messengers to the world." Are these the only possibilities? To what extent does the way we teach our children determine the future of the world?

2. Has the position we took some decades ago, of thinking of the new millennium with romantic optimism, altogether faded? Why can new technologies not cure the wounds that technology has inflicted on the earth? Does the "fall-out" from present technology obviate the creation of a supertechnology that would correct the effects of fall-out? What would McDermott think of this kind of solution?

3. In 1983 *The New York Times* did a survey of the attitudes of women toward work. They discovered that whereas in 1970, 52 percent of the American women surveyed cited motherhood as one of the best parts of being a woman, in 1983 only 26 percent thought so. If this finding indicates an irreversible trend, how does that influence the role of educational philosophers in determining methods of education at the preschool level? In your judgment, is the nuclear family a better or worse environment for educating children in preparation for the twenty-first century? Take into account what you have learned from le Guin's story about a future in which families are illegal.

4. McDermott says, "Our children will have to be the generation which effects transition from the present-mindedness that has dominated the recent centuries to a forward-looking care for future generations by assuming a perpetuity of resources and by a resisting of the short-run exploitation of nature." You are probably one of "our children" of whom McDermott is talking. (a) Do you ever feel the burden of being asked to make this transition? and (b) Since ours is called the "age of narcissism," do you think there is a good chance, or any chance, that you will be able to give up the "present-mindedness" that we have fostered in you, to do so?

5. One of the assumptions of the Montessori method is that "children are profoundly informed and conceptually transformed by the activities of their bodies, especially their hands." Looking back upon your own experience and that of your friends, do you believe that this assumption is valid? A current expression talks about "hands-on" experience. Do you think that sufficient "hands-on" experience is provided by your college curriculum? Do you think that such experience would add to, or distract from, what you are learning?

6. McDermott says that he would introduce into the preschool environment "materials that are desirable, but not enough of them to go around, rather just enough to be frustrating" as a method of acquainting children early with the realities of global economics. Do you think the method would work? Is there a possibility that the method would have effects opposite to those intended—i.e., to teach children to scramble competitively for desirable materials

rather than to share them? Is induced frustration consistent with Montessori methods as you understand them from this article?

7. McDermott says that a classroom should be constructed as a "miniature ecosystem." Does he offer practical suggestions for how this could be done? If you were asked to construct a classroom that was a miniature ecosystem, what environmental elements would you include? Would you say that the present-day classroom is a miniature *social* system? What is right, and what is wrong with it?

8. McDermott says that he would introduce into preschool education an "unpleasant pedagogy" that would teach children the realities of "unrenewable" goods and "corrosive" materials. How *effective* do you think such a procedure would be? How consistent is this procedure with the Montessori principle that learning is pleasurable? Do you think that lessons we learn as children about personal deprivation are extended in our adulthood to give us a better sense of global deprivation? What counterproductive side effects could such procedures have?

9. McDermott says that alternative arguments to his own position are the voices of "the doomsday squad" or those of "the pollyanna optimists." On a scale stretching from doomsdayers to pollyannas, where would you put McDermott? Does the proposal he makes stand midway between the two positions? Does it vacillate—now one way, now the other—between them? What position on the scale do you yourself hold?

EXERCISES

1. Think of yourself as a parent or a preschool teacher. Having read McDermott's article, write a three-page proposal to the local school board explaining what you would like to see included in the kindergarten curriculum of your local school. The proposal might take the form of a letter to the school board from a local, concerned citizen.

2. A college student we know recently said that he would like to return to kindergarten to experience the irresponsible fun in learning that he had there. Write a recollection of your kindergarten experience. Make it a free association exercise of the experiences, sights, and sounds that you had there. Then write an assessment

of that experience. What would you like to see retained, and what changed, and why?

3. List in your journal the five most important ways in which childhood education (at home or at school) influences adult ethical outlook. Take a day or two to speculate upon why you included these five as the central ways in which your own ethical outlook was influenced. Then write a five-page paper on the topic: Childhood education is an important determinant in ethics.

CHAPTER TWENTY-SIX

TOFFLER: FUTURE SHOCK: THE PSYCHOLOGICAL DIMENSION

Social Criticism

Alvin Toffler is a world-renowned scholar and social critic. His book *Future Shock*, from which this selection is taken, met with an enthusiastic reception throughout the world, and received the prestigious *Prix du Meilleur Livre Etranger* award in France. It describes a serious ailment from which we suffer in the twentieth century:

> . . . future shock is no longer a distantly potential danger, but a real sickness from which increasingly large numbers already suffer. This psycho-biological condition can be described in medical and psychiatric terms. It is the disease of change. (*Future Shock*, p. 2)

In the interview with Philip Zimbardo that heads this unit, we learned something about how pervasively our temporal orientation—i.e. whether we are past-, present-, or future-directed people—influences our behavior and the very ways in which we structure our lives. In this article Toffler talks about the deep psychological distress that results from an excessive future orientation. The world is changing so rapidly, and the demands that this rapid pace of life make upon us are so great, that those of us who try to be future-oriented, and to keep pace, are often battered by our effort into a state of physical and psychological shock. It can almost be said that we endure the future as we would a cataclysm. Toffler compares this condition to battle shock and the psychological response to natural disasters such as earthquakes.

As you read consider these ideas:

1. What has happened to our time sense in the postindustrial period that makes us envision the future as an onslaught? You might find it useful to refer back to Unit II, "Work in the 80s" to consider the implications of super-technology in the workplace upon our conceptions of the future and our ability to keep pace with technological advances.
2. Is dropping out, or paralysis, a reasonable response to future shock? Is this the momentary response of the generation caught in the transition? Will the next generations adapt to the new demanding pace, or will the pace have to be controlled to make psychological health possible? The book was first published in 1970; are there signs that the generation who were children in the 1970s are adapting to a new, faster rhythm of life?
3. Toffler believes that one of the major causes of future shock is "information overload." We learned in "The Computer Age" that the amount of information is bound to increase with the further and further development of the electronic revolution. Since it is not possible to reverse the tide of this proliferation of information, how are future generations likely to respond to information overload?

GLOSSARY

nihilism [2]

nostalgia [2]

apathy [2]

lassitude [7]

lethargy [7]

irascible [8]

acutely [18]

bizarre [20]

anti-adaptive behavior [20]

cognitive [21]

chaotic [22]

arsenal [22]

kaleidoscopy [22]

mantras [23]

neural [25]

plummets [29]

array [37]

blithering [37]

ineptitude [37]

incessant [39]

schizophrenia [41]

metabolic [44]

transcience [46]

stultifying [50]

sacrosanct [53]

alien [55]

crescendo [59]

paroxysms [61]

bucolic [65]

deification [65]

veneration [65]

knee-jerk answers [66]

obsolescence [70]

topple [72]

tinged [76]

narcotize [79]

lotus-eaters [79]

troglodytes [80]

FUTURE SHOCK: THE PSYCHOLOGICAL
——— DIMENSION ———
Alvin Toffler

If future shock were a matter of physical illness alone, it might be   [1]
easier to prevent and to treat. But future shock attacks the psyche as
well. Just as the body cracks under the strain of environmental
overstimulation, the "mind" and its decision processes behave erratically
when overloaded. By indiscriminately racing the engines of change,
we may be undermining not merely the health of those least able to
adapt, but their very ability to act rationally on their own behalf.

The striking signs of confusional breakdown we see around us—   [2]
the spreading use of drugs, the rise of mysticism, the recurrent outbreaks
of vandalism and undirected violence, the politics of <u>nihilism</u> and
nostalgia, the sick <u>apathy</u> of millions—can all be understood better
by recognizing their relationship to future shock. These forms of social

SOURCE: From Alvin Toffler, *Future Shock*, Random House, New York, 1981, pp. 343–367.

irrationality may well reflect the deterioration of individual decision-making under conditions of environmental overstimulation.

[3]   Psychophysiologists studying the impact of change on various organisms have shown that successful adaptation can occur only when the level of stimulation—the amount of change and novelty in the environment—is neither too low nor too high. "The central nervous system of a higher animal," says Professor D. E. Berlyne of the University of Toronto, "is designed to cope with environments that produce a certain rate of . . . stimulation . . . It will naturally not perform at its best in an environment that overstresses or overloads it." He makes the same point about environments that understimulate it. Indeed, experiments with deer, dogs, mice and men all point unequivocally to the existence of what might be called an "adaptive range" below which and above which the individual's ability to cope simply falls apart.

[4]   Future shock is the response to overstimulation. It occurs when the individual is forced to operate above his adaptive range. Considerable research has been devoted to studying the impact of inadequate change and novelty on human performance. Studies of men in isolated Antarctic outposts, experiments in sensory deprivation, investigations into on-the-job performance in factories, all show a falling off of mental and physical abilities in response to understimulation. We have less direct data on the impact of overstimulation, but such evidence as does exist is dramatic and unsettling.

THE OVERSTIMULATED INDIVIDUAL

[5]   Soldiers in battle often find themselves trapped in environments that are rapidly changing, unfamiliar, and unpredictable. The soldier is torn this way and that. Shells burst on every side. Bullets whiz past erratically. Flares light the sky. Shouts, groans and explosions fill his ears. Circumstances change from instant to instant. To survive in such overstimulating environments, the soldier is driven to operate in the upper reaches of his adaptive range. Sometimes, he is pushed beyond his limits.

[6]   During World War II, a bearded Chindit soldier, fighting with General Wingate's forces behind the Japanese lines in Burma, actually fell asleep while a storm of machine gun bullets splattered around him. Subsequent investigation revealed that this soldier was not merely reacting to physical fatigue or lack of sleep, but surrendering to a sense of overpowering apathy.

[7]   Death-inviting lassitude was so common, in fact, among guerrilla troops who had penetrated behind enemy lines that British military physicians gave it a name. They termed it Long Range Penetration

Strain. A soldier who suffered from it became, in their words, "incapable of doing the simplest thing for himself and seemed to have the mind of a child." This deadly lethargy, moreover, was not confined to guerrilla troops. One year after the Chindit incident, similar symptoms cropped up en masse among the allied troops who invaded Normandy, and British researchers, after studying 5000 American and English combat casualties, concluded that this strange apathy was merely the final stage in a complex process of psychological collapse.

Mental deterioration often began with fatigue. This was followed [8] by confusion and nervous irritability. The man became hypersensitive to the slightest stimuli around him. He would "hit the dirt" at the least provocation. He showed signs of bewilderment. He seemed unable to distinguish the sound of enemy fire from other, less threatening sounds. He became tense, anxious, and heatedly irascible. His comrades never knew when he would flail out in anger, even violence, in response to minor inconvenience.

Then the final stage of emotional exhaustion set in. The soldier [9] seemed to lose the very will to live. He gave up the struggle to save himself, to guide himself rationally through the battle. He became, in the words of R. L. Swank, who headed the British investigation, "dull and listless . . . mentally and physically retarded, preoccupied." Even his face became dull and apathetic. The fight to adapt had ended in defeat. The stage of total withdrawal was reached.

That men behave irrationally, acting against their own clear interest, [10] when thrown into conditions of high change and novelty is also borne out by studies of human behavior in times of fire, flood, earthquake and other crises. Even the most stable and "normal" people, unhurt physically, can be hurled into anti-adaptive states. Often reduced to total confusion and mindlessness, they seem incapable of the most elementary rational decision-making.

Thus in a study of the responses to tornadoes in Texas, H. E. Moore [11] writes that "the first reaction . . . may be one of dazed bewilderment, sometimes one of disbelief, or at least of refusal to accept the fact. This, it seems to us, is the essential explanation of the behavior of persons and groups in Waco when it was devastated in 1953 . . . On the personal level, it explains why a girl climbed into a music store through a broken display window, calmly purchased a record, and walked out again, even though the plate glass front of the building had blown out and articles were flying through the air inside the building."

A study of a tornado in Udall, Kansas, quotes a housewife as [12] saying: "After it was over, my husband and I just got up and jumped out the window and ran. I don't know where we were running to but . . . I didn't care. I just wanted to run." The classic disaster photograph shows a mother holding a dead or wounded baby in her arms, her face blank and numb as though she could no longer comprehend the reality around her. Sometimes she sits rocking gently on her porch with a doll, instead of a baby, in her arms.

In disaster, therefore, exactly as in certain combat situations, individuals can be psychologically overwhelmed. Once again the source may be traced to a high level of environmental stimulation. The disaster victim finds himself suddenly caught in a situation in which familiar objects and relationships are transformed. Where once his house stood, there may be nothing more than smoking rubble. He may encounter a cabin floating on the flood tide or a rowboat sailing through the air. The environment is filled with change and novelty. And once again the response is marked by confusion, anxiety, irritability and withdrawal into apathy.

[14]   Culture shock, the profound disorientation suffered by the traveler who has plunged without adequate preparation into an alien culture, provides a third example of adaptive breakdown. Here we find none of the obvious elements of war or disaster. The scene may be totally peaceful and riskless. Yet the situation demands repeated adaptation to novel conditions. Culture shock, according to psychologist Sven Lundstedt, is a "form of personality maladjustment which is a reaction to a temporarily unsuccessful attempt to adjust to new surroundings and people."

[15]   The culture shocked person, like the soldier and disaster victim, is forced to grapple with unfamiliar and unpredictable events, relationships and objects. His habitual ways of accomplishing things—even simple tasks like placing a telephone call—are no longer appropriate. The strange society may itself be changing only very slowly, yet for him it is all new. Signs, sounds and other psychological cues rush past him before he can grasp their meaning. The entire experience takes on a surrealistic air. Every word, every action is shot through with uncertainty.

[16]   In this setting, fatigue arrives more quickly than usual. Along with it, the cross-cultural traveler often experiences what Lundstedt describes as "a subjective feeling of loss, and a sense of isolation and loneliness."

[17]   The unpredictability arising from novelty undermines his sense of reality. Thus he longs, as Professor Lundstedt puts it, "for an environment in which the gratification of important psychological and physical needs is predictable and less uncertain." He becomes "anxious, confused and often appears apathetic." In fact, Lundstedt concludes, "culture shock can be viewed as a response to stress by emotional and intellectual withdrawal."

[18]   It is hard to read these (and many other) accounts of behavior breakdown under a variety of stresses without becoming acutely aware

of their similarities. While there are differences, to be sure, between a soldier in combat, a disaster victim, and a culturally dislocated traveler, all three face rapid change, high novelty, or both. All three are required to adapt rapidly and repeatedly to unpredictable stimuli. And there are striking parallels in the way all three respond to this overstimulation.

First, we find the same evidences of confusion, disorientation, or [19] distortion of reality. Second, there are the same signs of fatigue, anxiety, tenseness, or extreme irritability. Third, in all cases there appears to be a point of no return—a point at which apathy and emotional withdrawal set in.

In short, the available evidence strongly suggests that overstimulation [20] may lead to bizarre and anti-adaptive behavior.

BOMBARDMENT OF THE SENSES

We still know too little about this phenomenon to explain authoritatively [21] why overstimulation seems to produce maladaptive behavior. Yet we pick up important clues if we recognize that overstimulation can occur on at least three different levels: the sensory, the cognitive and the decisional.*

The easiest to understand is the sensory level. Experiments in [22] sensory deprivation, during which volunteers are cut off from normal stimulation of their senses, have shown that the absence of novel sensory stimuli can lead to bewilderment and impaired mental functioning. By the same token, the input of too much disorganized, patternless or chaotic sensory stimuli can have similar effects. It is for this reason that practitioners of political or religious brainwashing make use not only of sensory deprivation (solitary confinement, for example) but of sensory bombardment involving flashing lights, rapidly shifting patterns of color, chaotic sound effects—the whole arsenal of psychedelic kaleidoscopy.

The religious fervor and bizarre behavior of certain hippie cultists [23] may arise not merely from drug abuse, but from group experimentation with both sensory deprivation and bombardment. The chanting of monotonous mantras, the attempt to focus the individual's attention on interior, bodily sensation to the exclusion of outside stimuli, are efforts to induce the weird and sometimes hallucinatory effects of understimulation.

At the other end of the scale, we note the glazed stares and numb, [24] expressionless faces of youthful dancers at the great rock music au-

* The line between each of these is not completely clear, even to psychologists, but if we simply, in commonsense fashion, equate the sensory level with perceiving, the cognitive with thinking, and the decisional with deciding, we will not go too far astray.

ditoriums where light shows, split-screen movies, high decibel screams, shouts and moans, grotesque costumes and writhing, painted bodies create a sensory environment characterized by high input and extreme unpredictability and novelty.

[25]   An organism's ability to cope with sensory input is dependent upon its physiological structure. The nature of its sense organs and the speed with which impulses flow through its neural system set biological bounds on the quantity of sensory data it can accept. If we examine the speed of signal transmission within various organisms, we find that the lower the evolutionary level, the slower the movement. Thus, for example, in a sea urchin egg, lacking a nervous system as such, a signal moves along a membrane at a rate of about a centimeter an hour. Clearly, at such a rate, the organism can respond to only a very limited part of its environment. By the time we move up the ladder to a jellyfish, which already has a primitive nervous system, the signal travels 36,000 times faster: ten centimeters per second. In a worm, the rate leaps to 100 cps. Among insects and crustaceans, neural pulses race along at 1000 cps. Among anthropoids the rate reaches 10,000 cps. Crude as these figures no doubt are, they help explain why man is unquestionably among the most adaptable of creatures.

[26]   Yet even in man, with a neural transmission rate of about 30,000 cps, the boundaries of the system are imposing. (Electrical signals in a computer, by contrast, travel billions of times faster.) The limitations of the sense organs and nervous system mean that many environmental events occur at rates too fast for us to follow, and we are reduced to sampling experience at best. When the signals reaching us are regular and repetitive, this sampling process can yield a fairly good mental representation of reality. But when it is highly disorganized, when it is novel and unpredictable, the accuracy of our imagery is necessarily reduced. Our image of reality is distorted. This may explain why, when we experience sensory overstimulation, we suffer confusion, a blurring of the line between illusion and reality.

INFORMATION OVERLOAD

[27]   If overstimulation at the sensory level increases the distortion with which we perceive reality, cognitive overstimulation interferes with our ability to "think." While some human responses to novelty are involuntary, others are preceded by conscious thought, and this depends upon our ability to absorb, manipulate, evaluate and retain information.

[28]   Rational behavior, in particular, depends upon a ceaseless flow of data from the environment. It depends upon the power of the individual to predict, with at least fair success, the outcome of his own actions.

To do this, he must be able to predict how the environment will respond to his acts. Sanity, itself, thus hinges on man's ability to predict his immediate, personal future on the basis of information fed him by the environment.

When the individual is plunged into a fast and irregularly changing [29] situation, or a novelty-loaded context, however, his predictive accuracy plummets. He can no longer make the reasonably correct assessments on which rational behavior is dependent.

To compensate for this, to bring his accuracy up to the normal [30] level again, he must scoop up and process far more information than before. And he must do this at extremely high rates of speed. In short, the more rapidly changing and novel the environment, the more information the individual needs to process in order to make effective, rational decisions.

Yet just as there are limits on how much sensory input we can [31] accept, there are in-built constraints on our ability to process information. In the words of psychologist George A. Miller of Rockefeller University, there are "severe limitations on the amount of information that we are able to receive, process, and remember." By classifying information, by abstracting and "coding" it in various ways, we manage to stretch these limits, yet ample evidence demonstrates that our capabilities are finite.

To discover these outer limits, psychologists and communications [32] theorists have set about testing what they call the "channel capacity" of the human organism. For the purpose of these experiments, they regard man as a "channel." Information enters from the outside. It is processed. It exits in the form of actions based on decisions. The speed and accuracy of human information processing can be measured by comparing the speed of information input with the speed and accuracy of output.

Information has been defined technically and measured in terms [33] of units called "bits."† By now, experiments have established rates for the processing involved in a wide variety of tasks from reading, typing, and playing the piano to manipulating dials or doing mental arithmetic. And while researchers differ as to the exact figure, they strongly agree on two basic principles: first, that man has limited capacity; and second, that overloading the system leads to serious breakdown of performance.

Imagine, for example, an assembly line worker in a factory making [34] children's blocks. His job is to press a button each time a red block passes in front of him on the conveyor belt. So long as the belt moves

---

† A bit is the amount of information needed to make a decision between two equally likely alternatives. The number of bits needed increases by one as the number of such alternatives doubles.

at a reasonable speed, he will have little difficulty. His performance will approach 100 percent accuracy. We know that if the pace is too slow, his mind will wander, and his performance will deteriorate. We also know that if the belt moves too fast, he will falter, miss, grow confused and uncoordinated. He is likely to become tense and irritable. He may even take a swat at the machine out of pure frustration. Ultimately, he will give up trying to keep pace.

[35]   Here the information demands are simple, but picture a more complex task. Now the blocks streaming down the line are of many different colors. His instructions are to press the button only when a certain color pattern appears—a yellow block, say, followed by two reds and a green. In this task, he must take in and process far more information before he can decide whether or not to hit the button. All other things being equal, he will have even greater difficulty keeping up as the pace of the line accelerates.

[36]   In a still more demanding task, we not only force the worker to process a lot of data before deciding *whether* to hit the button, but we then force him to decide *which* of several buttons to press. We can also vary the number of times each button must be pressed. Now his instructions might read: For color pattern yellow-red-red-green, hit button number two once; for pattern green-blue-yellow-green, hit button number six three times; and so forth. Such tasks require the worker to process a large amount of data in order to carry out his task. Speeding up the conveyor now will destroy his accuracy even more rapidly.

[37]   Experiments like these have been built up to dismaying degrees of complexity. Tests have involved flashing lights, musical tones, letters, symbols, spoken words, and a wide array of other stimuli. And subjects, asked to drum fingertips, speak phrases, solve puzzles, and perform an assortment of other tasks, have been reduced to blithering ineptitude.

[38]   The results unequivocally show that no matter what the task, there is a speed above which it cannot be performed—and not simply because of inadequate muscular dexterity. The top speed is often imposed by mental rather than muscular limitations. These experiments also reveal that the greater the number of alternative courses of action open to the subject, the longer it takes him to reach a decision and carry it out.

[39]   Clearly, these findings can help us understand certain forms of psychological upset. Managers plagued by demands for rapid, incessant and complex decisions; pupils deluged with facts and hit with repeated tests; housewives confronted with squalling children, jangling telephones, broken washing machines, the wail of rock and roll from the teenager's living room and the whine of the television set in the parlor—may well find their ability to think and act clearly impaired

by the waves of information crashing into their senses. It is more than possible that some of the symptoms noted among battle-stressed soldiers, disaster victims, and culture shocked travelers are related to this kind of information overload.

One of the men who has pioneered in information studies, Dr. [40] James G. Miller, director of the Mental Health Research Institute at the University of Michigan, states flatly that "Glutting a person with more information than he can process may . . . lead to disturbance." He suggests, in fact, that information overload may be related to various forms of mental illness.

One of the striking featurs of schizophrenia, for example, is "incorrect [41] associative response." Ideas and words that ought to be linked in the subject's mind are not, and vice versa. The schizophrenic tends to think in arbitrary or highly personalized categories. Confronted with a set of blocks of various kinds—triangles, cubes, cones, etc.—the normal person is likely to categorize them in terms of geometric shape. The schizophrenic asked to classify them is just as likely to say "They are all soldiers" or "They all make me feel sad."

In the volume *Disorders of Communication*, Miller describes experiments [42] using word association tests to compare normals and schizophrenics. Normal subjects were divided into two groups, and asked to associate various words with other words or concepts. One group worked at its own pace. The other worked under time pressure—i.e., under conditions of rapid information input. The time-pressed subjects came up with responses more like those of schizophrenics than of self-paced normals.

Similar experiments conducted by psychologists G. Usdansky and [43] L. J. Chapman made possible a more refined analysis of the types of errors made by subjects working under forced-pace, high information-input rates. They, too, concluded that increasing the speed of response brought out a pattern of errors among normals that is peculiarly characteristic of schizophrenics.

"One might speculate," Miller suggests, ". . . that schizophrenia [44] (by some as-yet-unknown process, perhaps a metabolic fault which increases neural 'noise') lowers the capacities of channels involved in cognitive information processing. Schizophrenics consequently . . . have difficulties in coping with information inputs at standard rates like the difficulties experienced by normals at rapid rates. As a result, schizophrenics make errors at standard rates like those made by normals under fast, forced-input rates."

In short, Miller argues, the breakdown of human performance [45] under heavy information loads may be related to psychopathology in ways we have not yet begun to explore. Yet, even without under-standing its potential impact, we are accelerating the generalized rate of change in society. We are forcing people to adapt to a new life pace, to confront novel situations and master them in ever shorter intervals. We are forcing them to choose among fast-multiplying options. We are, in other words, forcing them to process information at a far more rapid pace than was necessary in slowly evolving societies. There can be little doubt that we are subjecting at least some of them to cognitive overstimualtion. What consequences this may have for mental health in the techno-societies has yet to be determined.

DECISION STRESS

[46]   Whether we are submitting masses of men to information overload or not, we are affecting their behavior negatively by imposing on them still a third form of overstimulation—decision stress. Many individuals trapped in dull or slowly changing environments yearn to break out into new jobs or roles that require them to make faster and more complex decisions. But among the people of the future, the problem is reversed. "Decisions, decisions . . ." they mutter as they race anxiously from task to task. The reason they feel harried and upset is that transience, novelty and diversity pose contradictory demands and thus place them in an excruciating double bind.

[47]   The accelerative thrust and its psychological counterpart, transience, force us to quicken the tempo of private and public decision-making. New needs, novel emergencies and crises demand rapid response.

Yet the very newness of the circumstances brings about a revolutionary change in the nature of the decisions they are called upon to make. The rapid injection of novelty into the environment upsets the delicate balance of "programmed" and "non-programmed" decisions in our organizations and our private lives.

[48]   A programmed decision is one that is routine, repetitive and easy to make. The commuter stands at the edge of the platform as the 8:05 rattles to a stop. He climbs aboard, as he has done every day for months or years. Having long ago decided that the 8:05 is the most convenient run on the schedule, the actual decision to board the train is programmed. It seems more like a reflex than a decision at all. The immediate criteria on which the decision is based are relatively simple and clear-cut, and because all the circumstances are familiar, he scarcely has to think about it. He is not required to process very much information. In this sense, programmed decisions are low in psychic cost.

[49]   Contrast this with the kind of decisions that same commuter thinks about on his way to the city. Should he take the new job Corporation X has just offered him? Should he buy a new house? Should he have an affair with his secretary? How can he get the Management Committee to accept his proposals about the new ad campaign? Such questions

demand non-routine answers. They force him to make one-time or first-time decisions that will establish new habits and behavioral procedures. Many factors must be studied and weighed. A vast amount of information must be processed. These decisions are non-programmed. They are high in psychic cost.

For each of us, life is a blend of the two. If this blend is too high [50] in programmed decisions, we are not challenged; we find life boring and stultifying. We search for ways, even unconsciously, to introduce novelty into our lives, thereby altering the decision "mix." But if this mix is too high in non-programmed decisions, if we are hit by so many novel situations that programming becomes impossible, life becomes painfully disorganized, exhausting and anxiety-filled. Pushed to its extreme, the end-point is psychosis.

"Rational behavior . . . ," writes organization theorist Bertram M. [51] Gross, "always includes an intricate combination of routinization and creativity. Routine is essential . . . [because it] frees creative energies for dealing with the more baffling array of new problems for which routinization is an irrational approach."

When we are unable to program much of our lives, we suffer. [52] "There is no more miserable person," wrote William James, "than one . . . for whom the lighting of every cigar, the drinking of every cup . . . the beginning of every bit of work, are subjects of deliberation." For unless we can extensively program our behavior, we waste tremendous amounts of information-processing capacity on trivia.

This is why we form habits. Watch a committee break for lunch [53] and then return to the same room: almost invariably its members seek out the same seats they occupied earlier. Some anthropologists drag in the theory of "territoriality" to explain this behavior—the notion that man is forever trying to carve out for himself a sacrosanct "turf." A simpler explanation lies in the fact that programming conserves information-processing capacity. Choosing the same seat spares us the need to survey and evaluate other possibilities.

In a familiar context, we are able to handle many of our life problems [54] with low-cost programmed decisions. Change and novelty boost the psychic price of decision-making. When we move to a new neighborhood, for example, we are forced to alter old relationships and establish new routines or habits. This cannot be done without first discarding thousands of formerly programmed decisions and making a whole series of costly new first-time, non-programmed decisions. In effect, we are asked to re-program ourselves.

Precisely the same is true of the unprepared visitor to an alien [55] culture, and it is equally true of the man who, still in his own society, is rocketed into the future without advance warning. The arrival of the future in the form of novelty and change makes all his painfully pieced-together behavioral routines obsolete. He suddenly discovers to his horror that these old routines, rather than solving his problems, merely intensify them. New and as yet unprogrammable decisions are demanded. In short, novelty disturbs the decision mix, tipping the balance toward the most difficult, most costly form of decision-making.

[56]   It is true that some people can tolerate more novelty than others. The optimum mix is different for each of us. Yet the number and type of decisions demanded of us are not under our autonomous control. It is the society that basically determines the mix of decisions we must make and the pace at which we must make them. Today there is a hidden conflict in our lives between the pressures of acceleration and those of novelty. One forces us to make faster decisions while the other compels us to make the hardest, most time-consuming type of decisions.

[57]   The anxiety generated by this head-on collision is sharply intensified by expanding diversity. Incontrovertible evidence shows that increasing the number of choices open to an individual also increases the amount of information he needs to process if he is to deal with them. Laboratory tests on men and animals alike prove that the more the choices, the slower the reaction time.

[58]   It is the frontal collision of these three incompatible demands that is now producing a decision-making crisis in the techno-societies. Taken together these pressures justify the term "decisional overstimulation," and they help explain why masses of men in these societies already feel themselves harried, futile, incapable of working out their private futures. The conviction that the rat-race is too tough, that things are out of control, is the inevitable consequence of these clashing forces. For the uncontrolled acceleration of scientific, technological and social change subverts the power of the individual to make sensible, competent decisions about his own destiny.

VICTIMS OF FUTURE SHOCK

[59]   When we combine the effects of decisional stress with sensory and cognitive overload, we produce several common forms of individual maladaptation. For example, one widespread response to high-speed change is outright denial. The Denier's strategy is to "block out" unwelcome reality. When the demand for decisions reaches crescendo, he flatly refuses to take in new information. Like the disaster victim whose face registers total disbelief, The Denier, too, cannot accept the evidence of his senses. Thus he concludes that things really are the same, and that all evidences of change are merely superficial. He finds comfort in such cliches as "young people were always rebellious"

or "there's nothing new on the face of the earth," or "the more things change, the more they stay the same."

An unknowing victim of future shock, The Denier sets himself up [60] for personal catastrophe. His strategy for coping increases the likelihood that when he finally is forced to adapt, his encounter with change will come in the form of a single massive life crisis, rather than a sequence of manageable problems.

A second strategy of the future shock victim is specialism. The [61] Specialist doesn't block out *all* novel ideas or information. Instead, he energetically attempts to keep pace with change—but only in a specific narrow sector of life. Thus we witness the spectacle of the physician or financier who makes use of all the latest innovations in his profession, but remains rigidly closed to any suggestion for social, political, or economic innovation. The more universities undergo pa- roxysms of protest, the more ghettos go up in flames, the less he wants to know about them, and the more closely he narrows the slit through which he sees the world.

Superficially, he copes well. But he, too, is running the odds against [62] himself. He may awake one morning to find his specialty obsolete or else transformed beyond recognition by events exploding outside his field of vision.

A third common response to future shock is obsessive reversion [63] to previously successful adaptive routines that are now irrelevant and inappropriate. The Reversionist sticks to his previously programmed decisions and habits with dogmatic desperation. The more change threatens from without, the more meticulously he repeats past modes of action. His social outlook is regressive. Shocked by the arrival of the future, he offers hysterical support for the not-so-status quo, or he demands, in one masked form or another, a return to the glories of yesteryear.

The Barry Goldwaters and George Wallaces of the world appeal to [64] his quivering gut through the politics of nostalgia. Police maintained order in the past; hence, to maintain order, we need only supply more police. Authoritarian treatment of children worked in the past; hence, the troubles of the present spring from permissiveness. The middle-aged, right-wing reversionist yearns for the simple, ordered society of the small town—the slow-paced social environment in which his old routines were appropriate. Instead of adapting to the new, he continues automatically to apply the old solutions, growing more and more divorced from reality as he does so.

If the older reversionist dreams of reinstating a small-town past, [65] the youthful, left-wing reversionist dreams of reviving an even older social system. This accounts for some of the fascination with rural communes, the bucolic romanticism that fills the posters and poetry of the hippie and post-hippie subcultures, the deification of Ché Guevara (identified with mountains and jungles, not with urban or post-urban environments), the exaggerated veneration of pre-technological societies and the exaggerated contempt for science and technology. For all their fiery demands for change, at least some sectors of the left share with the Wallacites and Goldwaterites a secret passion for the past.

[66]   Just as their Indian headbands, their Edwardian capes, their Deerslayer boots and gold-rimmed glasses mimic various eras of the past, so, too, their ideas. Turn-of-the-century terrorism and quaint Black Flag anarchy are suddenly back in vogue. The Rousseauian cult of the noble savage flourishes anew. Antique Marxist ideas, applicable at best to yesterday's industrialism, are hauled out as knee-jerk answers for the problems of tomorrow's super-industrialism. Reversionism masquerades as revolution.

[67]   Finally, we have the Super-Simplifier. With old heroes and institutions toppling, with strikes, riots, and demonstrations stabbing at his consciousness, he seeks a single neat equation that will explain all the complex novelties threatening to engulf him. Grasping erratically at this idea or that, he becomes a temporary true believer.

[68]   This helps account for the rampant intellectual faddism that already threatens to outpace the rate of turnover in fashion. McLuhan? Prophet of the electric age? Levi-Strauss? Wow! Marcuse? Now I see it all! The Maharishi of Whatchmacallit? Fantastic! Astrology? Insight of the ages!

[69]   The Super-Simplifier, groping desperately, invests every idea he comes across with universal relevance—often to the embarrassment of its author. Alas, no idea, not even mine or thine, is omni-insightful. But for the Super-Simplifier nothing less than total relevance suffices. Maximization of profits explains America. The Communist conspiracy explains race riots. Participatory democracy is the answer. Permissiveness (or Dr. Spock) are the root of all evil.

[70]   This search for a unitary solution at the intellectual level has its parallels in action. Thus the bewildered, anxious student, pressured by parents, uncertain of his draft status, nagged at by an educational system whose obsolescence is more strikingly revealed every day, forced to decide on a career, a set of values, and a worthwhile life style, searches wildly for a way to simplify his existence. By turning on to LSD, Methedrine or heroin, he performs an illegal act that has, at least, the virtue of consolidating his miseries. He trades a host of painful and seemingly insoluble troubles for one big problem, thus radically, if temporarily, simplifying existence.

[71]   The teen-age girl who cannot cope with the daily mounting tangle of stresses may choose another dramatic act of super-simplification: pregnancy. Like drug abuse, pregnancy may vastly complicate her life later, but it immediately plunges all her other problems into relative insignificance.

Violence, too, offers a "simple" way out of burgeoning complexity   [72]
of choice and general overstimulation. For the older generation and
the political establishment, police truncheons and military bayonets
loom as attractive remedies, a way to end dissent once and for all.
Black extremists and white vigilantes both employ violence to narrow
their choices and clarify their lives. For those who lack an intelligent,
comprehensive program, who cannot cope with the novelties and
complexities of blinding change, terrorism substitutes for thought.
Terrorism may not topple regimes, but it removes doubts.

Most of us can quickly spot these patterns of behavior in others—   [73]
even in ourselves—without, at the same time, understanding their
causes. Yet information scientists will instantly recognize denial, spe-
cialization, reversion and super-simplification as classical techniques
for coping with overload.

All of them dangerously evade the rich complexity of reality. They   [74]
generate distorted images of reality. The more the individual denies,
the more he specializes at the expense of wider interests, the more
mechanically he reverts to past habits and policies, the more desperately
he super-simplifies, the more inept his responses to the novelty and
choices flooding into his life. The more he relies on these strategies,
the more his behavior exhibits wild and erratic swings and general
instability.

Every information scientist recognizes that some of these strategies   [75]
may, indeed, be necessary in overload situations. Yet, unless the
individual begins with a clear grasp of relevant reality, and unless he
begins with cleanly defined values and priorities, his reliance on such
techniques will only deepen his adaptive difficulties.

These preconditions, however, are increasingly difficult to meet.   [76]
Thus the future shock victim who does employ these strategies experiences a deepening sense of confusion and uncertainty. Caught in
the turbulent flow of change, called upon to make significant, rapid-
fire life decisions, he feels not simply intellectual bewilderment, but
disorientation at the level of personal values. As the pace of change
quickens, this confusion is tinged with self-doubt, anxiety and fear.
He grows tense, tires easily. He may fall ill. As the pressures relentlessly
mount, tension shades into irritability, anger, and sometimes, senseless
violence. Little events trigger enormous responses; large events bring
inadequate responses.

Pavlov many years ago referred to this phenomenon as the "par-   [77]
adoxical phase" in the breakdown of the dogs on whom he conducted
his conditioning experiments. Subsequent research has shown that
humans, too, pass through this stage under the impact of overstimulation, and it may explain why riots sometimes occur even in the
absence of serious provocation, why, as though for no reason, thousands
of teenagers at a resort will suddenly go on the rampage, smashing

windows, heaving rocks and bottles, wrecking cars. It may explain why pointless vandalism is a problem in all of the techno-societies, to the degree that an editorialist in the *Japan Times* reports in cracked, but passionate English: "We have never before seen anything like the extensive scope that these psychopathic acts are indulged in today."

[78]   And finally, the confusion and uncertainty wrought by transience, novelty and diversity may explain the profound apathy that de-socializes millions, old and young alike. This is not the studied, temporary withdrawal of the sensible person who needs to unwind or slow down before coping anew with his problems. It is total surrender before the strain of decision-making in conditions of uncertainty and overchoice.

[79]   Affluence makes it possible, for the first time in history, for large numbers of people to make their withdrawal a full-time proposition. The family man who retreats into his evening with the help of a few martinis and allows televised fantasy to narcotize him, at least works during the day, performing a social function upon which others are dependent. His is a part-time withdrawal. But for some (not all) hippie dropouts, for many of the surfers and lotus-eaters, withdrawal is full-time and total. A check from an indulgent parent may be the only remaining link with the larger society.

[80]   On the beach at Matala, a tiny sun-drenched village in Crete, are forty or fifty caves occupied by runaway American troglodytes, young men and women who, for the most part, have given up any further effort to cope with the exploding high-speed complexities of life. Here decisions are few and time plentiful. Here the choices are narrowed. No problem of overstimualtion. No need to comprehend or even to feel. A reporter visiting them in 1968 brought them news of the assassination of Robert F. Kennedy. Their response: silence. "No shock, no rage, no tears. Is this the new phenomenon? Running away from America *and* running away from emotion? I understand uninvolvement, disenchantment, even noncommitment. But where has all the feeling gone?"

[81]   The reporter might understand where all the feeling has gone if he understood the impact of overstimulation, the apathy of the Chindit guerrilla, the blank face of the disaster victim, the intellectual and emotional withdrawal of the culture shock victim. For these young people, and millions of others—the confused, the violent, and the apathetic—already evince the symptoms of future shock. They are its earliest victims.

THE FUTURE-SHOCKED SOCIETY

[82]   It is impossible to produce future shock in large numbers of individuals without affecting the rationality of the society as a whole. Today,

according to Daniel P. Moynihan, the chief White House advisor on urban affairs, the United States "exhibits the qualities of an individual going through a nervous breakdown." For the cumulative impact of sensory, cognitive or decisional overstimulation, not to mention the physical effects of neural or endocrine overload, creates sickness in our midst.

This sickness is increasingly mirrored in our culture, our philosophy, [83] our attitude toward reality. It is no accident that so many ordinary people refer to the world as a "madhouse" or that the theme of insanity has recently become a staple in literature, art, drama and film. Peter Weiss in his play *Marat/Sade* portrays a turbulent world as seen through the eyes of the inmates of the Charenton asylum. In movies like *Morgan*, life within a mental institution is depicted as superior to that in the outside world. In *Blow-Up*, the climax comes when the hero joins in a tennis game in which players hit a non-existent ball back and forth over the net. It is his symbolic acceptance of the unreal and irrational—recognition that he can no longer distinguish between illusion and reality. Millions of viewers identified with the hero in that moment.

The assertion that the world has "gone crazy," the graffiti slogan [84] that "reality is a crutch," the interest in hallucinogenic drugs, the enthusiasm for astrology and the occult, the search for truth in sensation, ecstasy and "peak experience," the swing toward extreme subjectivism, the attacks on science, the snowballing belief that reason has failed man, reflect the everyday experience of masses of ordinary people who find they can no longer cope rationally with change.

Millions sense the pathology that pervades the air, but fail to un- [85] derstand its roots. These roots lie not in this or that political doctrine, still less in some mystical core of despair or isolation presumed to inhere in the "human condition." Nor do they lie in science, technology, or legitimate demands for social change. They are traceable, instead, to the uncontrolled, non-selective nature of our lunge into the future. They lie in our failure to direct, consciously and imaginatively, the advance toward super-industrialism.

Thus, despite its extraordinary achievements in art, science, intel- [86] lectual, moral and political life, the United States is a nation in which tens of thousands of young people flee reality by opting for drug-induced lassitude; a nation in which millions of their parents retreat into video-induced stupor or alcoholic haze; a nation in which legions of elderly folk vegetate and die in loneliness; in which the flight from family and occupational responsibility has become an exodus; in which masses tame their raging anxieties with Miltown, or Librium, or Equanil, or a score of other tranquilizers and psychic pacifiers. Such a nation, whether it knows it or not, is suffering from future shock.

[87]   "I'm not going back to America," says Ronald Bierl, a young expatriate
in Turkey. "If you can establish your own sanity, you don't have to
worry about other people's sanity. And so many Americans are going
stone insane." Multitudes share this unflattering view of American
reality. Lest Europeans or Japanese or Russians rest smugly on their
presumed sanity, however, it is well to ask whether similar symptoms
are not already present in their midst as well. Are Americans unique
in this respect, or are they simply suffering the initial brunt of an
assault on the psyche that soon will stagger other nations as well?

[88]   Social rationality presupposes individual rationality, and this, in
turn, depends not only on certain biological equipment, but on continuity, order and regularity in the environment. It is premised on
some correlation between the pace and complexity of change and
man's decisional capacities. By blindly stepping up the rate of change,
the level of novelty, and the extent of choice, we are thoughtlessly
tampering with these environmental preconditions of rationality. We
are condemning countless millions to future shock.

QUESTIONS

1. Toffler says that recent research, using animals as well as humans,
   points to an "adaptive range" below or above which the individual's
   ability to cope with his or her environment collapses. Having read
   the article by McDermott, do you think that it is possible to widen
   our adaptive range by means of education? For example, would
   it be possible to train children at an early age to respond to high
   stimulation in the environment in a way that would prevent them
   from feeling threatened?

2. Toffler describes overstimulation in terms of battle shock. Can we
   find an alternative explanation from some of our readings in Unit
   II, "Work," and Unit III, "Death"? For example, can we compare
   the soldier in battle to the factory worker (cf. Terkel) who has no
   control over, or participation in, the work he is required to do?
   Can we compare him to the person in the grip of terminal illness,
   who has no control over the changes occurring in her body? Is
   the condition of future shock related to the human desire for
   mastery of our environment?

3. Toffler describes the three steps that are the future-shock victim's
   response to the need "to adapt rapidly and repeatedly to unpredictable stimuli" as follows:

> First we find . . . evidences of confusion, disorientation, or dis-
> tortion of reality. Second there are . . . signs of fatigue, anxiety,
> tenseness, or extreme irritability. Third . . . there appears to be
> a point of no return—a point at which apathy and emotional
> withdrawal set in.

He calls this "anti-adaptive behavior." Is that an accurate description
of the behavior? Could we not argue that fatigue and apathy are
highly efficient ways for the mind and body to adapt to stress?
Does our cultural conditioning lead us to think that action is the
best response to stress? Could it be argued that withdrawal is
sometimes an appropriate response?

4. Toffler provides convincing evidence that an organism's ability
   to cope with sensory input is biologically limited. He then compares
   the imposing transmission rate of the human organism with the
   even more imposing, indeed staggering, rate of transmission rate
   of electrical signals on a computer. If the age to come, as we have
   been convincingly led to believe, is the age of the computer, what
   changes will have to occur in human adaptability if the race is to
   survive?

5. Does our "channel capacity" increase or decrease with age? If we
   compare the rate with which infants or children are required to
   respond to "novelty-loaded" contexts, or environments, with the
   rate at which adults, who have to some degree developed the
   ability to predict their immediate, personal future, which age
   group exhibits the greater "channel capacity"? Is there any validity
   in the suggestion that it may be necessary for us to respond to
   the future in the way that small children respond to stimuli?

6. Dr. James G. Miller says that "glutting a person with more information than he can process may . . . lead to disturbance." Do
   you think that the college curriculum sometimes gluts you with
   more information than you can process? Do you think that college
   curricula might be designed to take fuller account of such ideas
   as the "channel capacity" of human beings and the effects of
   "information overload?" Have you had any personal experience
   of "future shock" as Toffler describes it as the consequence of
   coming to college?

7. Toffler describes four maladaptive responses to future shock: denial,
   or "blocking out unwelcome reality"; specialism, or keeping pace
   with change only in a narrow sector of life; obsessive reversion
   to previously successful routines that are now irrelevant and inappropriate; and oversimplification. Are these strategies *always*
   maladaptive? Would it be possible to employ different ones at
   different times in short-run situations? Why will they not work

well in long-range terms? Are there efficient ways of dealing with the immediate future and inefficient ways of dealing with the long-range future? Are they useful for individuals but bad or destructive when they are expanded into social policies?

8. Toffler links full-scale withdrawal with affluence. Is that a valid connection? What kinds of withdrawal might be employed by a low-income factory worker, by a homemaker, by the indigent poor?

9. Toffler says "Social rationality presupposes individual rationality, and this, in turn, depends . . . on continuity, order and regularity in the environment." Considering what he has told us about the pace of life in industrial society, is it likely that "continuity, order, and regularity" will occur in the future? If the environment will probably not become stable, ordered, and regular, what changes will have to occur in the human psyche?

10. Is future shock a sign of the human desire to impose stable order upon, and to acquire mastery of, the world and the unknowable, and therefore frightening, future?

EXERCISES

1. Write a short biographical account of your own experience or that of someone you know with a condition of "overstimulation," disaster shock, culture shock, or "information overload." Test the validity of Toffler's three stages of response against your own experience. Did you behave as the people Toffler describes did? Did you experience the stages he describes? How did you recover from the condition? Were your strategies of response adaptive or maladaptive? Do a psychological analysis of your own experience.

2. Do you think that society in the 1980s is a "future-shocked" society? Closely examine the evidence Toffler offers to support his assertion that American society in 1970 was future-shocked. Do these conditions still exist? Write a three-page response to Toffler's section "The Future-Shocked Society" in which you argue *either* that "society in the America of the 1980s is experiencing future shock" or that "society in America of the 1980s has recovered from the future shock of the 1970s."

3. In the section "Victims of Future Shock," Toffler identifies four personifications of individual maladaptation whom he gives the names of (1) the Denier (pars. 59–60), (2) the Specialist (pars. 61–

62), (3) the Reversionist (pars. 63–66), and the Super-Simplifier (pars. 67–72). For the next week, take notes in your journal in an attempt to define these terms with real examples, either of people and incidents you remember, or of people whom you have a chance to observe, or of people about whom you have read or are reading. As the examples amass, choose one of the four personifications and concentrate on preparing a full definition. Your instructor may ask you to write a paper on that subject.

CHAPTER TWENTY-SEVEN

MARTIN LUTHER KING, JR.: I HAVE A DREAM

Speech and Oratory

As this introduction is being written, the United States Congress has just declared Martin Luther King, Jr.'s birthday a national holiday. It would be as presumptuous for this book to introduce Martin Luther King as it would be to tell you who George Washington or Abraham Lincoln was. Therefore, this introduction will differ somewhat from the others in the book. Rather than presenting an impersonal, third-person discussion, we have based this introduction on our own recollection of the day in 1963 when we heard Martin Luther King deliver the address at the Lincoln Memorial in Washington, D.C.

Thankfully, the condition of black people when the Civil Rights Movement of the 1960s began is probably not within your living memory. The scenes of children being struck with cattle prods for their desire to go to segregated schools, or of the bodies of civil rights workers being dredged from a dam where they had been thrown for their desire to register voters in Mississippi, or of a church that was bombed because it was a meeting place of the Southern Christian Leadership Conference, are not events that you have actually witnessed. But for that very reason, it is necessary for those of us who did see them either in person or on the nightly news to bear witness and to remind ourselves and you that they did take place.

The March on Washington took place on a sweltering day in August. Those of us who had been involved in the Civil Rights Movement were tired and discouraged. We felt that our efforts were having very little affect in actually changing the conditions of blacks, or even in raising the moral consciousness of the public. We were even a little scared, because of recent attacks against people taking part in civil rights demonstrations. And there were the usual thugs at the rally; and there were the ubiquitous FBI men (in those days one could spot them in a minute because for some unaccountable reason they all wore grey hats—even in summer). And the Nazi Party was marching up and down across from the mall.

And then this unassuming, rather ordinary-looking man, got up and delivered an electrifying speech. He was inspired, and he inspired us and gave us courage and a certain degree of fearlessness. Sometimes now, at moments of discouragement when we see the unemployment figures for black Americans as compared with white Americans, or when we consider that ten human beings die of starvation every minute somewhere in the world, we still feel that nothing we did made much of a difference. But then we see a bunch of ordinary children coming home from school, jostling and shouting and fooling around—easy with each other—and some of them are black and some are white and nobody seems to notice that particular difference, and we realize that Martin Luther King's dream, maybe like all great dreams, has been fulfilled in some of the small ways in which our cultural consciousness has changed.

King's words are impressive even now as we read them, but hearing him speak was a case in which the "medium" really was "the message." He was the medium and his voice was the voice of a Biblical prophet. Listen to him.

I HAVE A DREAM

Martin Luther King, Jr.

I am happy to join with you today in what will go down in history as the greatest demonstration for freedom in the history of our nation.

Five score years ago, a great American, in whose symbolic shadow we stand today, signed the Emancipation Proclamation. This momentous decree came as a great beacon light of hope to millions of Negro slaves who had been seared in the flames of withering injustice. It came as a joyous daybreak to end the long night of their captivity.

SOURCE: Delivered at the Lincoln Memorial, Washington, D.C., August 28, 1963. Copyright © 1963 by Martin Luther King, Jr. (Southern Christian Leadership Conference). Reprinted by permission of Joan Daves.

But one hundred years later, the Negro still is not free; one hundred years later, the life of the Negro is still sadly crippled by the manacles of segregation and the chains of discrimination; one hundred years later, the Negro lives on a lonely island of poverty in the midst of a vast ocean of material prosperity; one hundred years later, the Negro is still languished in the corners of American society and finds himself in exile in his own land.

So we've come here today to dramatize a shameful condition. In a sense we've come to our nation's capital to cash a check. When the architects of our Republic wrote the magnificent words of the Constitution and the Declaration of Independence, they were signing a promissory note to which every American was to fall heir. This note was the promise that all men, yes, black men as well as white men, would be guaranteed the unalienable rights of life, liberty, and the pursuit of happiness.

It is obvious today that America has defaulted on this promissory note in so far as her citizens of color are concerned. Instead of honoring this sacred obligation, America has given the Negro people a bad check; a check which has come back marked "insufficient funds." We refuse to believe that the bank of justice is bankrupt. We refuse to believe that there are insufficient funds in the great vaults of opportunity of this nation. And so we've come to cash this check, a check that will give us upon demand the riches of freedom and the security of justice.

We have also come to this hallowed spot to remind America of the fierce urgency of now. This is no time to engage in the luxury of cooling off or to take the tranquilizing drug of gradualism. Now is the time to rise from the dark and desolate valley of segregation to the sunlit path of racial justice; now is the time to lift our nation from the quicksands of racial injustice to the solid rock of brotherhood; now is the time to make justice a reality for all God's children. It would be fatal for the nation to overlook the urgency of the moment. This sweltering summer of the Negro's legitimate discontent will not pass until there is an invigorating autumn of freedom and equality.

Nineteen sixty-three is not an end, but a beginning. And those who hope that the Negro needed to blow off steam and will now be content, will have a rude awakening if the nation returns to business as usual. There will be neither rest nor tranquility in America until the Negro is granted his citizenship rights. The whirlwinds of revolt will continue to shake the foundations of our nation until the bright day of justice emerges.

But there is something that I must say to my people, who stand on the warm threshold which leads into the palace of justice. In the process of gaining our rightful place, we must not be guilty of wrongful deeds. Let us not seek to satisfy our thirst for freedom by drinking from the cup of bitterness and hatred. We must forever conduct our struggle on the high plain of dignity and discipline. We must not allow our creative protest to degenerate into physical violence. Again and again we must rise to the majestic heights of meeting physical force with soul force; and the marvelous new militancy, which has engulfed the Negro community, must not lead us to a distrust of all white people. For many of our white brothers, as evidenced by their presence here today, have come to realize that their destiny is tied up with our destiny. And they have come to realize that their freedom is inextricably bound to our freedom. We cannot walk alone. And as we walk, we must make the pledge that we shall always march ahead. We cannot turn back.

There are those who are asking the devotees of civil rights, "when will you be satisfied?" We can never be satisfied as long as the Negro is the victim of the unspeakable horrors of police brutality; we can never be satisfied as long as our bodies, heavy with the fatigue of travel cannot gain lodging in the motels of the highways and the hotels of the cities; we cannot be satisfied as long as the Negro's basic mobility is from a smaller ghetto to a larger one; we cannot be satisfied as long as our children are stripped of their selfhood and robbed of their dignity by signs stating "for whites only"; we cannot be satisfied as long as the Negro in Mississippi cannot vote and a Negro in New York believes he has nothing for which to vote. No! No, we are not satisfied, and we will not be satisfied until "justice rolls down like waters and righteousness like a mighty stream."

I am not unmindful that some of you have come here out of great trials and tribulations. Some of you have come fresh from narrow jail cells. Some of you have come from areas where your quest for freedom left you battered by the storms of persecution and staggered by the winds of police brutality. You have been the veterans of creative suffering. Continue to work with the faith that unearned suffering is redemptive. Go back to Mississippi. Go back to Alabama. Go back to South Carolina. Go back to Georgia. Go back to Louisiana. Go back to the slums and ghettos of our northern cities, knowing that somehow this situation can and will be changed. Let us not wallow in the valley of despair.

I say to you today, my friends, even though we face the difficulties of today and tomorrow, I still have a dream. It is a dream deeply rooted in the American dream. I have a dream that one day this nation will rise up and live out the true meaning of its creed. "We hold these truths to be self-evident, that all men are created equal." I have a dream that one day on the red hills of Georgia, sons of former slaves and the sons of former slave owners will be able to sit down together at the table of a state sweltering with the heat of injustice, sweltering with the heat of oppression, will be transformed into an oasis of freedom and justice. I have a dream that my four little children will one day live in a nation where they will not be judged by the color of their skin, but by the content of their character.

I have a dream today!

I have a dream that one day down in Alabama—with its vicious racists, with its governor having his lips dripping with the words of interposition and nullification—one day right there in Alabama, little black boys and black girls will be able to join hands with little white boys and white girls as sisters and brothers.

I have a dream today!

I have a dream that one day "every valley shall be exalted and every hill and mountain shall be made low. The rough places will be made plain and the crooked places will be made straight, and the glory of the Lord shall be revealed, and all flesh shall see it together."

This is our hope. This is the faith that I go back to the South with. With this faith we will be able to hew out of the mountain of despair, jangling discords of our nation into a beautiful symphony of brotherhood. With this faith we will be able to work together, to pray together, to struggle together, to go to jail together, to stand up for freedom together. Knowing that we will be free one day. And this will be the day. This will be the day when all of God's children will be able to sing with new meaning, "My country tis of thee, sweet land of liberty, of thee I sing. Land where my fathers died, land of the pilgrims' pride, from every mountain side, let freedom ring." And if America is to be a great nation, this must become true.

So let freedom ring from the prodigious hilltops of New Hampshire; let freedom ring from the mighty mountains of New York; let freedom ring from the heightening Alleghenies of Pennsylvania; let freedom ring from the snow-capped Rockies of Colorado; let freedom ring from the curvaceous slopes of California. But not only that. Let freedom ring from Stone Mountain of Georgia; let freedom ring from Lookout Mountain of Tennessee; let freedom ring from every hill and mole hill of Mississippi. From every mountainside, let freedom ring.

QUESTIONS

1. Why does King begin the second paragraph with the phrase "five score years ago"? How does the phrase function as allusion, and why does he want to make that allusion?

2. Why does he repeat the phrase "one hundred years later" three times in the next paragraph? What does the burden of repetition do to underline the sense of what he says?

3. Why does he use the phrase "in exile in his own land"? It is a subtle allusion to Jesus' observation that "no prophet is honored in his own land." Why does King want to associate the Negro of 1963 with Jesus as the Suffering Servant? What effect do you think that unspoken association might have had upon those who did not find any incongruity in thinking of themselves as Christians and still hating black people?

4. Why does King switch over from Biblical tones and phrases to the metaphor of commerce—"defaulted on a promissory note," "bad check," check "marked 'insufficient funds,' " etc.? What association does the jump from sacred time to ordinary, banal present time force us to make? What point does the association make that is relevant to Christian ethics?

5. How does the verbal echo in "this hallowed spot" (Remember the *Gettysburg Address*, "We cannot dedicate; we cannot consecrate, we cannot hallow this ground . . ." etc.) relate to "the urgency of now"? How does it relate the present moment to the American tradition?

6. Why does King use the term "all God's children"? Why is that an effective argument for the concept of brotherhood?

7. Why does King move from the rhetoric of American historical tradition back to the rhetoric of a Biblical prophet in warning his people not to satisfy their thirst for freedom by drinking "from the cup of bitterness and hatred"? Why is it effective to revert to the terminology of a Biblical prophet in giving this warning? Consider what the prophets of the Old Testament usually warned the children of Israel about and why.

8. Why, after acknowledging that many of his people had come to the rally after great suffering, does he urge them to "go back"? And why does he repeat the phrase "go back"? What effect do you think that the tone had upon people who were very discouraged?

9. He gives them his "dream" to "go back" with. What does calling it a "dream" do? How do the words operate upon our visual imagination? What is the style and tone that King assumes in telling his dream? Why does he conclude his telling of the dream with a direct quotation from the Bible? Who is speaking at this point in the address: Martin Luther King the patriot? Martin Luther King the hero? Martin Luther King the leader of a moral revolution? Or the Reverend Martin Luther King, Jr.?

10. Why does he conclude the speech with nine repetitions of the sentence "Let freedom ring"? And why does he end the whole speech with that sentence? How do you imagine that the last paragraph *sounded*?

EXERCISES

1. Our treatment of this selection and of the March on Washington is obviously and intentionally biased. Get *The New York Times* for August 28, 1963, from your college library's back-newspaper file. Also read any other eyewitness reports you can locate, for example, the coverage in *Time, Newsweek,* or *Life.* If your local newspaper keeps archives, try to obtain a copy of that paper's report. Then compare the coverage of the event. Try to assess how personal and political bias affects the style of a news report. Write a three-page summary of your findings in the manner of a social science report.
2. Write a three-page entry for the *Dictionary of American Biography* on Martin Luther King, Jr.
3. Imagine that you have been asked to contribute a piece on Martin Luther King, Jr., to a book that deals with American oratory. You are directed to base your remarks specifically on the "I Have a Dream" speech. If you can listen to a recording of the speech—your library probably has one—you will have an idea of how eloquently it was delivered. With that background and the facts you obtain from an analysis of the text of the speech, make notes on the following categories by which orations are usually judged: style, organization (or arrangement of ideas), invention (or the sources of the ideas expressed), and delivery. Then write your piece for the book. (If you cannot find a recording of the speech, omit the remarks on delivery.)

CHAPTER TWENTY-EIGHT

FIORE: THE FUTURES OF THE BOOK

Information Sciences

Quentin Fiore coauthored with Marshall McLuhan the very influential book *The Medium is the Message*. Like McLuhan's first book, *The Gutenberg Galaxy*, it argues that human perception is in a constant state of change and that the environmental stimuli to which we respond are themselves the cause of that change. In *The Gutenberg Galaxy* McLuhan tried to establish that the ways in which we understand, and, indeed, the ways in which we actually *see*, were changed by the invention of printing. The Gutenberg Bible, the first printed book in the Western world, made the scriptures available to anybody who could read. We must remember that before the invention of printing, manuscripts of the scriptures —as beautiful and gorgeously illustrated as they were— were handwritten on parchment, and were, therefore, available only to the very rich. Printing on paper made the great truths available to every person who could read. The invention of the printing press was thus one of the great events in human history. If it is the case that "the truth shall make you free," then imagine how liberating it was for the truth to "make free" everybody who had mastered the talent of reading. Since knowledge is power, the availability of the truth on the basis of *intellectual* mastery, rather than *riches* or feudal inheritance rights, made power accessible to people who had never, over centuries, had any power at all. It changed the whole Western power system.

Now, McLuhan and Fiore argued, we are at another crossroads. If the ability to read opened new horizons of experience for fifteenth-century man, how much wider will those horizons be opened by the invention of new communication media in the twentieth century—television, the computer, radio, all media of instant information-transmittal? And how will that widening of what Toffler calls "channel capacity" influence what we see and hear, and consequently, *how* we perceive and the ways in which we think?

We have chosen this selection to end our book because we believe that, to some extent, information-transmittal techniques of the twenty-first century may make *our* book, (and all traditionally written books), as well as the critical reading and writing strategies that we have been trying to teach you, obsolete. You already perceive—in subtle ways—differently from the ways in which we perceive. It is probably the case that because you grew up with a television set readily available, whereas we grew up when television was a luxury available only to the affluent, you have a different perception of the written word from ours. Do you *hear*, as we do, an internal voice sounding in your head when you read? Do you see images first and hear words second, or do you, as we do, find the images only an accompaniment to the words? Our perceptual set is fixed by the boundaries of the printed page; we doubt that yours are.

That these questions can arise in the latter decades of the twentieth century is what Quentin Fiore's article is all about. As you read consider:

1. Is the placement of graphics and text merely eccentric showing off, or is Fiore making a legitimate statement in his arrangement?
2. Is the random bombardment of stimuli upon our senses (each stimulus evoking a *separate* response) comparable to the arrangement of stimuli in an electronic communication?
3. Is the fragmented way in which the discrete stimuli offered by the article comparable to the ways in which we consciously or unconsciously perceive our surrounding environment in the twentieth century?
4. How does what we might call "the organization of *sights*" resemble what Cage calls the organization of sound in experimental music? How does it resemble what Brian Eno calls "ambient music"?

_____ THE FUTURES OF THE BOOK _____

Quentin Fiore

SOURCE: Quentin Fiore, "The Futures of the Book," from *The Future of Time*, Doubleday (New York: 1971).

Quentin Fiore

People say
that life is the thing,
but I prefer reading.

high-probability future

low-probability future

Logan Pearsall Smith
"Afterthoughts"

the
future
of
the
book

near future

foreseeable future

distant future

alternative futures

in the future

000,000 years from now

But **so many** books thou readest,
But **so many** schemes thou breedest,
But **so many** wishes feedest,
    That thy poor head almost turns.

—Matthew Arnold (1822-88)
The Second Best

ALL HAIL THE WITCH DOCTORS

DAR-ES-SALAAM, Tanzania, Feb. 22, 1968 (AP).—Seven witch doctors who became angry with villagers refusing to pay their annual fee for controlling the weather have been arrested for creating hailstorms which destroyed crops.

The incident occurred in the Kibondo district of Western Tanzania. Soon after the villagers refused to pay their usual fees, a heavy hailstorm swept over the region.

The shocked villagers appealed to the regional administration for help, and the witch doctors admitted they were responsible.

Area Commissioner M. A. Msengkazila ordered their immediate arrest. It is intended to prosecute them but the exact charge has not yet been worked out.

. . . such are the hazards of prediction.

It's comforting to think of the future in the singular, and as some sort of reward. No term exists to express "plural possibilities" — many futures living side by side, contradicting and often canceling each other out. We assume that the business of living is a relatively static and orderly affair, and to get some notion of the future, we need only make simple straight-line projections of present trends. The future of THE BOOK?— simple: ". . . it will always be, come hell, high water or McLuhan." (*Good Housekeeping* ad, N.Y. Times, Sept. 17, 1968.)

The FUTURE to most of us means new *things* — "inventions." We rarely think of the new *people* new technologies will shape—people with totally new responses and attitudes.

Even the most common realities admit of wholly new perceptions in today's atmosphere of innovation—and often the untrained *naive* eyes see clearest. *What is new is new not because it has never been there before, but because it has changed in quality.*

456

A witty observer once remarked that life could only be understood backward, but must be lived forward.

—THAT WAS ONCE UPON A TIME.

We can't understand backward anymore. Few of the guide lines of the past relate to our time. Looking for an O.K. from the past just won't do. Indeed, one of the first victims of the vast changes new communication media have brought about was the change in our "sense of history."

". . . How come nothing's like it was until it's gone?"

"History," says Norman O. Brown, "is a nightmare from which we have awakened." That nightmare has been replaced by our waking night mare of accelerated change and information overload. In an environment of rapid information flow, ideas and institutions swiftly become obsolete. As we fix a situation in order to think about it, it changes. No wonder so many of our new attitudes lack a sense of wholeness and grace.

"INSIDE I WAS CRYING, UNTIL I LOST 105 POUNDS."

A. N. Whitehead: *"The rate of progress is such that an individual human being of ordinary length of life, will be called upon to face novel situations which find no parallel in his past. The fixed person for fixed duties, who in older societies was such a godsend, in the future will be a public danger."*

The prospect of change brought about by the swift flow of information has now become so great that we cannot find a point to rest—we're not given a still picture to contemplate at leisure.

45

THERE'S JUST TOO MUCH!
Spy Output Too Much For Chief.

WASHINGTON, July 9 (UPI)—. . . A House sub-committee reported today that spies for the United States were collecting in-formation so fast that their chiefs did not have time to read it. The backlog, the panel said, may have contributed to recent in-telligence failures such as the capture of the intelli-gence ship Pueblo off North Korea.

*   *   *

The Defense Appropria-tions subcommittee said unprocessed reports on Southeast Asia alone re-cently filled 517 linear feet of file drawer space at the headquarters of the Defense Intelligence Agenc⁻ . . .

Making sense of this overload is becoming our major industry. The New Publisher will have a major role to play—but he will have to learn to play a new game with a new deck. ". . . But this is nothing we've had any experience with." He said, "The rules aren't very detailed or formal. It all has to be very theoretical."

"Next summer is too close for comfort."
—Airtemp ad.

Practical men who claim they're only interested in "facts"—here-and-now facts—really mean they're interested in the future. They're *obsessed* with the future. As self-admitted realists, they gather "facts"—data (varied and often contradictory), and must somehow predict a future that will directly concern them—a future whose benefits and consequences they must know in advance if they are to act with a minimum of risk.

"Millions of Ducks To Migrate Soon, F.A.A. Tells Pilots."

Milliseconds

Nanoseconds

Picoseconds

Disbelief? Astonishment! The first new punctuation mark since the introduction of the question mark in 1671. An epigram for our times ????? !!!!!

"By the time they're in, they're out."
—Eastern Airlines ad

"It takes all the running you can do, to keep in the same place."

LEWIS CARROLL,
Through the Looking Glass

Computer technologists are reported to be very unhappy about present computer speeds. They claim that 16,000,000 moves a second is simply not fast enough

459

to do the jobs that need to be done, and are pressing their search for faster machines. Evidence suggests that the only way to prod these slow-pokes is to reduce their size; then, of course, it takes less time for the electrical signal to travel within the computer. The current logic circuits using miniaturized components receive, process and send electric signals to the next circuit in four to five billionths of a second. This "delay time," hope the physicists, will someday be reduced to five hundred trillionths of a second, or ten times faster than current circuits.

To-day, To-morrow, Yesterday
With thee are one, and instant aye.
—ROBERT HERRICK

"Every radical adjustment is a crisis of self-esteem."

AND
AND
AND

is forbidden without written permission
of the publisher.

But, almost in spite of itself, publishing (whose history George Haven Putnam called one of erroneous conclusions), is doomed to succeed.

Those who regard publishing as the last bastion of traditional values do it a mammoth disservice. It is historically the one institution that thrives on change. Whereas in the past, the book was adequate to the task of making available information public, in today's mass society it cannot hope to compete with mass media—film, TV, or other means of moving information, "now known or hereafter invented." A mass-ive commitment is now required, and the first dramatic steps are being taken.

In the past decade corporate research in "information technology" has been so intensive that both institutional and individual investors have been almost promiscuous in their eagerness to forego immediate returns on their investments in favor of "growth potential." *Glamor* afforded sufficient lead-time in the investor's quest for megabucks. But this lead time has shrunk drastically. Only a few years ago, new companies with breakthrough products could enter uninhabited markets and could enjoy several years of very high growth in earnings. But today, companies are finding that there is less and less time to exploit their discoveries. INFORMATION theory and expertise has now become a commodity—an article of commerce. Aggressive sales and service programs, sudden and strange mergers have replaced R&D. Just as the early utilities could not monopolize the utilities field, which mushroomed because of the demand for new appliances, so the giant telecommunications companies will in turn create any number of smaller independent manufacturers of appliances—a trickle-down process. The larger the animal, the wider the interstices between its toes.

Publishing, that industry of "erroneous conclusions," has leaped into today's world of megabusiness. Recent mergers or joint ventures between electronic giants and long-established publishers —such as the RCA-Random House merger—are more than straws in the wind.

THE LITANY OF CHANGE

From *Forbes*—Impending changes lie behind some of the strange moves made by major American companies in the past year. They help explain why CBS paid a staggering $280 million to buy Holt, Rinehart and Winston, with earnings of only $6.6 million. They help explain ABC's eagerness to merge with ITT. They are a major reason why RCA is working on new methods of printing and typesetting.

Xerox spent $120 million acquiring Ginn & Co. because it felt that this take-over would provide an entry in the "basal" market of coursebooks. They stated, *"We are just beginning to define what we want to do."* In 1966 RCA spent $37.7 million to acquire Random House. IBM purchased Science Research Associates in 1964 for $62 million. General Learning Corporation (1967 sales of $28 million) is owned jointly by Time, Inc. and General Electric.

"We're calming down now. We have a better idea of where we're going."

—FRANCIS KEPPEL, head of
General Learning

The secret of being a bore is to tell everything.

VOLTAIRE

Very high electronic speeds have
made predictive techniques of amazing
accuracy possible. Sophisticated
probing tools such as correlation,
sampling, and simulation now permit
us to learn from <u>projected</u> experience
without having to suffer the possible
bitter consequences of these experiences.
The rapid information movement of
computer technology transforms the
future into the present, and, in an
environment envisaged by some physicists,
TIME may have little meaning – there
may very well be no such thing as
"before" and "after."

It is in this very disturbing and
highly perplexing environment of
accelerated change that a wholly new
psychic situation of "future-presents,"
of time mixes, is beginning to emerge.
It is a wholly new environment, which
is forcing us to entertain some very
new notions about ourselves and about
most of our institutions.

Our appetite for information has become
so voracious that even our present, high-
speed printing techniques are incapable
of satisfying the need. In a decade,
information will have become so
abundant that it will have to be
transmitted by methods other than print,
or remain in a state of perpetual
suspension. The priority given to timely
books alone (assassinations, presidential
commission reports, political biographies,
etc.) is already playing havoc with the
production schedules of a number of
publishing houses. One can imagine the
staggering amount of information that will
be available in ten years, much of which
will become obsolete even before it
reaches the composing room! The National
Library of Medicine in Bethesda indexed
almost a quarter of a million technical
articles, books and monographs last year;
the nation's space program yearly adds
more than a million pages of technical data
to the pile. Scientists and engineers
turn out more than a million reports,
articles and publications annually. These
huge amounts of published material are
expected to double in only five years—
discounting rebuttals!

Various responses to this lust for more
and more information are now, or will
soon be, available.

Some of these methods, developed to
transmit words and pictures faster and
more economically, have already begun to
wipe out the present clutter of operations
and apparatus between copy and printed
page. Some communications technologies
that will be available in the foreseeable
"high-probability" future:

—Computer-driven cathode ray tube printers capable of composing text of graphic arts quality at speeds up to 6,000 characters a second.

—Microprinter—a xerographic device that previews microfilm images on a screen and enlarges them onto ordinary paper.

—Advanced typesetting methods that can set composition for an entire encyclopaedia in only a couple of days—and with as many different type faces, weights, etc., as are needed.

—Computer light-pen techniques that can be "printed" on paper.

—"Data Tablets" (Sylvania) : Draw a picture, and this device will take it from there. As your ball-point stylus writes on the tablet, it creates an electrical field that the tablet converts into the language of numbers computers understand.

—Picturephones: Eyeball-to-eyeball conversations.

—Nation wide facsimile transmission services, capable of transmitting or receiving any printed or written material (photographs and drawings too) . Stations to be located in airports, train and bus stations, hotels, banks, libraries, etc.

—Computers that chatter away directly to warehouses, distributors, customers.

—2,400-pound communications satellites, synchronously orbiting over the U.S., serving as relay stations for cross-country TV broadcasting, phone service, data transmission, or any other kind of wireless signals.

—Inexpensive home/office xerox machines.

—"Telepapers" which can broadcast the equivalent of a page of printed material into the home every 10 seconds.

—Talking typewriters: The computer will talk back to you, offering new facts, etc., and print out the words you spoke into it.

—Systems for the dissemination of technical information from a national data center, with accesses by companies and libraries via electronic input-output devices. This device is expected also to be available to individuals by means of home/office consoles.

—Low-cost, 3-D color communications services, reducing need for business travel. No longer "take her a-long!"

—Coherent-light telephone communications sevices.

LDX (LONG DISTANCE XEROGRAPHY): This new, high quality, high-speed device (Xerox) enables you to transmit any printed, written, or drawn document to anyone, anywhere in the country—all in a matter of seconds. A young lady in New York (above) feeds a document into an LDX Printer—the document is then transmitted over long-distance telephone wires, and is received by her boss in Los Angeles (below), on an LDX Scanner. Broadband transmission links join the two units.

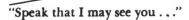

"Speak that I may see you . . ."

A specially trained computer can now
speak a designer's highly subjective
language with dizzying speed and precision. It can evaluate and manipulate in
a matter of seconds complex free-form
designs which used to be laboriously
plotted over days and weeks. The designer can also control every step and
every aspect of his sketch as it evolves,
"erasing" as the need arises—all without
first having to translate his ideas into
a highly complex computer language.

The miracle of microelectronics—18
diodes, 4 transistors and 8 resistors
packed into an integrated unit—here
shown balanced on the eye of a 2½"
sewing needle. The techniques of microelectronics indicate the possibility of
someday reducing an entire computer
to the size of a postage stamp.

". . . . The delicious melodies of Purcell
or Cimarosa might be disjointed stam-
merings to a hearer whose partition of
time should be a thousand times subtler
than ours, just as the edge of a razor
would become a saw to a finer visual
sense."

—COLERIDGE

This tiny two-inch square of plastic contains all 1,245 pages of the Bible—a 48,000 to 1 reduction.

It's now possible to publish a shelf of book on 24 two-inch square plastic cards. Costing less than a dollar a set, the subscriber can gaily toss out his old microset as he periodically receives updated "volumes." Every home may someday have microlibraries that contain the entire written record of humanity.

And now back to the commericals

"Taut, tense drama filmed on location in Munich. East versus West. Worth watching. Presented by Pepto-Bismol Tablets."

Sophisticated practioners of this totally new art form are in rebellion against the purely visual and "meaningful." Often delightful, often irritating, these short self-sufficient ideograms are truly creative responses to television's challenge.

Selective inattention has always been a popular strategy to avoid thinking about the future.

A nineteenth-century German optician once made spectacles to "correct" El Greco's elongated figures, thereby adjusting the master's "astigmatism."

"Find a classic that wasn't first regarded as light entertainment."

—*Marshall McLuhan*

Alice was beginning to get very tired of sitting by her sister on the bank and of having nothing to do; once or twice she had peeped into the book her sister was reading, but it had no pictures or conversations in it, "And what is the use of a book," thought Alice, "without pictures or conversations?"

Alison Knowles "Bean Rolls Collection" Published by Fluxus-Something Else Press, Inc., 1962

Some thoughts about a magazine's tremendous audience of one.

In the year 2051, when the travel-weary passenger on the moon-shuttle has had his fill of: dinner on the anti-gravity magnetic tray, three-dimensional TV, inter-galactic weather reports and conversational banter with the stewardess, as she floats by—he'll then settle back in his contour couch, and return to that important, private activity each of us does alone. *Reading*. (It will be, we trust, a magazine.)

The act of reading is essentially a process of thinking. It has scan and scope beyond any camera—as you have just demonstrated on the cosmic screen of your own mind. It is a concentratively individual act. An involvement. The reader makes the printed communication happen... releases the magic that causes words on a page to leap into living thoughts, ideas, emotions.

And no matter how many millions may be on the receiving end of the message, it is addressed to, and received by *individuals*, one at a time—each in the splendid solitude of his or her own mind. There, the silent language of print can whisper, rage, implore, accuse, burst into song, explode into revelation, stab the conscience. Or work a healing faith. And so it will always be, come hell, high water or McLuhan.

Aeschylus knew this when he called written words "physicians". And so did Hitler when he burned them. Because mobs roar, but individuals think. They think. They read. And they ask questions that alter the course of the world.

What prompts these reflections is a special occasion taking place today. It is sponsored by an industry devoted to the annual output of billions—no, trillions of words and pictures. It provides: information, instruction, inspiration, religion, science, psychology, philosophy, art, poetry, eugenics, cookery, fashion—along with whimsy and diversion. The occasion is Magazine Day in New York. It celebrates more than the excellence, the vivid beauty and the impact of modern graphics. It pays tribute to the American audience, seemingly boundless in its mental appetite for the best that magazines can offer.

But we would carry the thought and the tribute to that ultimate audience of one. And for good reason.

Never before in our history has the identity of the individual been so obscured by so many collective labels and tags. Take political communications. They're addressed far less to voters than to blocs: southern and northern, urban and farm, blue collar and white collar, left and right, hawk and dove. Almost forgotten is the idea that on a given Tuesday in November the green curtain of Democracy envelops one individual citizen at a time.

On a larger scale, the headlines that chronicle a day on our planet, betray the same collective reflex. "USSR rejects..." and "U.S. replies..." and even "U.N. declines..."

All of which suggests to us, as magazine publishers, the need for a redoubled consciousness and responsibility toward our citizens as individuals. And a heightened awareness that in our field of communications, the basic relationship is between the magazine and an individual reader.

Our particular reader, considered one at a time, is most usually a wife and mother—the central radiating influence over an American family. To her, the words and pictures we communicate are an idea-bridge; and her response is a communication about herself, back to us. This need for communication—magazine to reader and reader to magazine—is dramatized to us in the voluminous amount of mail and telephone calls received by our editors and by the Good Housekeeping Institute, day after day, month after month.

We think of our magazine as a time-bridge, too. Our faded, tattered copy of the first issue tells us much about that reader of Good Housekeeping 83 years ago. And perhaps 83 years from now, circa 2051, our successors may learn much about our readers and our times from the content, the advertisements, the varied human perspectives to be found in Good Housekeeping and the other definitive magazines of today.

Perhaps those moon-travellers will look back smugly from an era in which cancer is as antiquated as the bubonic plague, and war, as an instrument of international policy, is equally obsolete. We hope so.

On that far-distant day, however, whatever new conditions harass and plague mankind, we have no doubt that the individual will still find within the fortress of self, great comfort and guidance in the civilized, thinking act of reading. There, in the infinite treasury of print the reader will discover not only all that humankind is and does, but what it can hope to be.

Good Housekeeping

We must countenance the possibility that the study of the transmission of literature may be of only marginal significance, a passionate luxury like the preservation of the antique.

GEORGE STEINER

this butterfly is visible to my fingers. To me it is a symbol of immortal things -Faith! Beauty! Friendship! Helen Keller

1931

WILLIAM BURROUGHS: ". . . I've recently
done a lot of experiments with
scrapbooks. I'll read in the newspaper
something that reminds me of, or has
relation to, something I've written.
I'll cut out the picture or the article and
paste it in a scrapbook beside the words
from my book . . .

". . . I've been interested in precisely
how word and image get around on
very, very complex association lines."

"Writers at Work"
The Paris Review Interviews
3rd series. Viking, 1967

QUESTIONS

1. How does the map of the future that begins the article correspond to your own internal future map? Why does Fiore try to make it seem like a Rorschach inkblot? Is our conception of the future always an informationally neutral inkblot upon which we project many possible interpretions?

2. What does the quotation from Matthew Arnold, "So many books thou readest," add to the puzzle? Is Fiore suggesting the kind of confusion between information we have mastered and new information introduced into our intellectual environment that Toffler describes? How does the *way* Fiore makes his point differ from the way Toffler does?

3. Why does Fiore balance the witch doctor story against the quotation from *Good Housekeeping*, which says that "the business of living is a relatively static and orderly affair." Is the business of living orderly or static in the 1980s? Is Fiore suggesting that the degree of human control of the future is *like* the degree of control of the weather in the witch doctor story?

4. When Fiore assumes his own voice, he says, *"What is new is not new because it has never been there before, but because it has changed in quality."* What does he mean by that? How do things that have always been there change in quality? Consider this situation: Suppose that it stopped raining for a year. How would that change the quality of rain, which has always been there? Would people complain about a rainy day? Would people feel annoyed at getting wet?

5. Fiore says, "We can't understand backward anymore." How does that relate to what Toffler says about the conditions of future shock? How would Toffler categorize a person who tried to "understand backward" in the face of the rapidly changing pace of life?

6. Fiore argues, against Norman O. Brown that it is not history that is a nightmare but accelerated change. Why would rapid change make our attitudes lack "a sense of wholeness and grace"? Why is it that history—even if it is the history of a terrible time—gives us a sense of wholeness? Think of the great architect, the human imagination, and consider the ways in which it can structure what is past and visualize possible futures. Why does the architect fail in dealing with present time?

7. Suddenly, Fiore shoves an ad in front of us—"INSIDE I WAS CRYIN UNTIL I LOST 105 POUNDS." with a picture of a very distress

gargoyle accompanying it. Of course, he's having fun with us, but is there any deeper, more significant point to the fun he is making? Imagine yourself on a train, bus, or airplane. You are pondering essential questions, such as how human consciousness is aware of time. You see that ad. What is the impact of the ad on your own mental activity? Suppose you feel fat that day. Now, how does the ad shift the focus of your concentration from abstract speculation to body consciousness? Does that kind of shift in focus occur in our daily lives? What is Fiore saying in the juxtaposition between the ad and the preceding train of thought on the nature of history? What is Fiore saying about the impact of trivia upon human consciousness in the twentieth century?

8. How does what Fiore says in the quotations "Spy Output Too Much for Chief" and "The New Publisher will have a major role to play" correspond to what Toffler told us about "information overload"? Why does Fiore not explain the problem in the logical prose style of Toffler? In what ways does his style illustrate his belief that "The Medium is the Message"?

9. Why does "Every radical adjustment [come in] a crisis of self-esteem"? What happens to our sense of identity and our self-esteem when we are bombarded with information that we cannot process fast enough? Why do we find security in forms of "acquired knowledge"? What sense of ourselves does the acquisition of knowledge give us?

10. As the article progresses, the amount of text diminishes and the graphics increase. Why? What developments in our ways of acquiring information and dealing with rapidly accelerating change does Fiore *force* us to deal with even in the course of the article? How is this an instance of the medium being the message?

EXERCISES

1. Make a collage—out of pictures cut from magazines—on one of the following:

   a. The central contrast in Ursula le Guin's story.
   b. The central problem in McDermott's talk.
   c. Change in information transmittal in the twentieth century.
   How does your picture differ from what you might have said in an essay on the subject? How does interrelation among parts differ in a collage from an expository essay? Which is the easier, more

familiar medium in which you express yourself—the picture or the word?

2. Write a speculative essay on the relation of this textbook to the textbook of the past and the English textbook of the future. In what ways might this textbook be inadequate to the needs of the future generation?

3. Imagine that you are a school superintendent. Write a proposal to the State Board of Regents assessing the relative importance of teaching video games and computer skills in relation to teaching reading and writing skills in elementary education.